One Touch
of Shakespeare

Frontispiece. Joseph Crosby. Courtesy of The Folger Shakespeare Library.

One Touch of Shakespeare

Letters of Joseph Crosby to Joseph Parker Norris, 1875–1878

Edited by
John W. Velz *and* Frances N. Teague

"One touch of Shakespeare makes
the whole world kin"

Joseph Crosby to Frederick
Gard Fleay (July 1876, July 1877)

Folger Books
Washington: The Folger Shakespeare Library
London and Toronto: Associated University Presses

Associated University Presses
440 Forsgate Drive
Cranbury, NJ 08512

Associated University Presses
25 Sicilian Avenue
London WC1A 2QH, England

Associated University Presses
2133 Royal Windsor Drive
Unit 1
Mississauga, Ontario
Canada L5J 1K5

The paper used in this publication meets the
minimum requirements of the American
National Standard for Permanence of Paper
for Printed Library Materials Z39.48-1984.

Library of Congress Cataloging in Publication Data

Crosby, Joseph.
  One touch of Shakespeare.

  "Folger books."
  Includes index.
  1. Crosby, Joseph—Correspondence. 2. Shakespeare,
William, 1564–1616—Miscellanea. 3. Shakespeare,
William, 1564–1616—Criticism and interpretation—
History—19th century—Sources. 4. Norris, Joseph
Parker, 1847–1916—Correspondence. 5. Book collectors
—United States—Correspondence. I. Norris, Joseph
Parker, 1847–1916. II. Velz, John W. III. Teague,
Frances N. IV. Title.
PR2972.C76A45   1985   822.3′3   83-49506

ISBN 0-918016-74-6 (alk. paper)

Printed in the United States of America

For my father, Clarence,
my wife, Sarah,
and my daughters, Jody and Emily
J.W.V.

For my parents
Phyllis Christine Bowie Nicol
William Kennedy Nicol
F.N.T.

CONTENTS

ACKNOWLEDGMENTS

Anyone who has edited an eclectic author will understand our contention that this book is a collaboration broader than our shared efforts. We are glad to be able to thank many institutions, friends, colleagues, and correspondents for help of all kinds given over the years of our work on the Crosby letters.

Oldest in time and first in importance is our debt to Laetitia Yeandle, Curator of Manuscripts at the Folger Shakespeare Library, who first introduced one of us to Joseph Crosby in August of 1975 and has been a constant source of encouragement, information, and friendship to us ever since. The Trustees of the Folger Shakespeare Library and the Library's Director at the time, O.B. Hardison, generously granted us permission to edit and publish the Crosby correspondence, and Folger Books, under the direction of John F. Andrews, has undertaken that publication. To John Andrews we owe thanks for understanding what we mean by "the Shakespearian general reader." Our editor at Associated University Presses, Katharine Turok, has been a model of patience and good sense. Many Folger staff members, notably Jean Miller, Art Cataloguer, and Patricia Senia, Reading Room Supervisor, directed our attention to materials we would otherwise have missed and showed us how to find elusive answers; their enthusiasm for the quest is a pleasure to recall.

We have received help from many other libraries and archives as well. The curators of the Furness Shakespeare Library at the University of Pennsylvania, the Rutherford B. Hayes Library in Fremont, Ohio, and the Archives of American Art at the Smithsonian Institution have granted us access to Crosby and Norris papers in their keeping. The Department of Rare Books and Special Collections in the University of Michigan's Harlan Hatcher Graduate Library houses a significant fraction of Joseph Crosby's library and his scrapbooks—his "Collectanea." We are grateful to Harriet Jameson, the former Director, and to Margaret Berg, the former Reference Librarian, for help in a preliminary sorting-out of these Crosby materials during two visits to Ann Arbor. The "Collectanea" were later sorted out more thoroughly in a descriptive bibliography compiled by Susan P. Cerasano and a research team under her direction; we have found Susan's

9

catalogue a valuable resource, and it is a pleasure to acknowledge her personal encouragement of our work. The University of Wisconsin Library (Madison) houses another fraction of Crosby's library; Richard Knowles and Mark Eccles introduced one of us to these books in the winter of 1976.

We have also consulted materials personally or by correspondence in the following libraries and archives: the National Register of Archives (London), Cumbria County Council Archives (Kendal and Carlisle), the Parish Registers St. Michael's Church (Kirkby Thore and Temple Sowerby, Cumbria), the Shakespeare Birthplace Trust Archives, the British Library, the Birmingham (England) Public Library; Archives of the Episcopal Diocese of Cleveland, the Ohio Historical Society (Columbus), Muskingum County Ohio Probate Court (Records Division), the Public Library of Cincinnati and Hamilton County, the Cleveland Public Library, the Ohio State University Library; the Missouri Historical Society Library (St. Louis), the John M. Olin Library at Cornell University, the Historical Society of Pennsylvania (Philadelphia), the Athenaeum of Philadelphia, the Library of Congress, the libraries of Julius-Maximilians Universität Würzburg, the Shakespeare Bibliothek Universität München, the libraries of l'Université Paul Valéry Montpellier, the University of Georgia Libraries, the University of Texas Libraries. We thank the staffs of all these institutions for many courtesies.

Our knowledge of Crosby's personal history and his family lineage we owe to the generosity respectively of Norris F. Schneider of Zanesville, Ohio, and Richard Crosby of York, England. Norris Schneider opened his antiquarian files to us and shared his rich storehouse of memory. He was our guide to the Courthouse archives and the newspaper morgues of Zanesville. He supplied us with tear sheets of his articles on Crosby and with the photograph that is the frontispiece to this edition. From the beginning Richard Crosby took a generous-minded interest in our search for Crosbiana in the north of England, and to his wise and witty anecdotes we owe much of our sense of what life would have been like for Joseph Crosby growing up in the Eden River Valley, Westmorland, in the 1820s and 1830s. Richard Crosby, like Norris Schneider, has been a gracious host as well as a long-standing correspondent and a good friend.

Other members of the Crosby family have generously shared their knowledge of family history with strangers from abroad. We are grateful to Andrew Crosby for advice, and to John Crosby, Edith Margaret Crosby Horn, and Anne Crosby Lane, each for an invaluable piece of information or for access to a family document.

Friends and correspondents everywhere have enriched the annotations in this book or otherwise made our path smoother. Each of the following people will perhaps remember, as we do vividly, which brick in the edifice belongs, as it were, to him or her: David Armstrong, Peter Blayney, Ingeborg Boltz, Arthur J. Breton, Carol Chillington, Norman Colbeck, Susan

E. H. Davis, T. S. Dorsch, Karen Elmore, Kate Foster, David and Rita George, James M. Gibson, Lewis Gould, Ian Hancock, Ernst Häublein, Edgar Hinchcliffe, Janis Butler Holm, Roy Hudleston, R. W. Ingram, William Ingram, G. P. Jones, Rev. G. Michael C. Jones, Irwin C. Lieb, Charles Lower, Louis Marder, William E. Miller, Douglass Parker, Peter J. Parker, Sandra L. Powers, Norman Sanders, James L. Sanderson, Catherine Shaw, Rolf Soellner, Christopher Spencer, Marvin Spevack, William B. Todd, and George Walton Williams. Thanks to all of you.

The officers of the International Shakespeare Association and the Shakespeare Association of America took an interest in the Crosby letters almost as soon as the material came to light, giving both of us and Laetitia Yeandle an opportunity to discuss them in a special session at the I.S.A. Congress in Washington, D.C. in April 1976. We also appreciate the interest in Crosby shown by officers of the Midwest MLA (1976), of the MLA (1976), and of the Philological Association of the Carolinas (1981).

The Modern Language Association's Center for Scholarly Editions and its Director, Don L. Cook, were invaluable to us as we began our research. Frank D. Shaw, Editor of *The Cumberland and Westmorland Herald*, wrote about our research in 1976 in a way that put us in touch with great resources of information. Facts we needed came to us from National Public Radio, the Reference Division of the United States Copyright Office, and the Appleby School, Cumbria.

A grant from the University of Texas Research Institute in the winter of 1976 made possible a tour in search of Crosbiana at the University of Wisconsin, the University of Michigan, and the Ohio State University. A second substantial grant from the University Research Institute made possible the transcription of the entire Folger MS.Y.c. 1372 from microfilm and photocopy in 1976, a project capably carried out over seven months by Virginia Brown Machann, with help from Jeanne Emmons Frisch. The University of Georgia English Department contributed extensively to photocopying for the project and provided much needed clerical assistance in the person of Philip Genetti. Some of the research for the edition was carried out in France and Germany with partial funding from the Fulbright Commission (1977–78, 1981–82). Funds from the University of Georgia, the National Endowment for the Humanities, and the Folger Shakespeare Library supported one of us in the last stages of research during the summer of 1982. A National Endowment for the Humanities Grant for Travel to Special Collections made possible a final check on the text at the Folger Shakespeare Library in December–January, 1983–84.

Parts of several letters reprinted in this edition were quoted in articles that appeared in *Shakespeare Quarterly* 27 (1976), 316–28, *Shakespeare Newsletter* (May 1977) and *Papers of the Bibliographical Society of America*, 71 (1977), 279–94. We are grateful to the editors and publishers of these journals for permission to make use of these excerpts and of the annotations that derive from research for those articles.

Our deepest gratitude is for our families, who have seen this project ripen slowly and have hastened the ripening with practical assistance, sympathy, and patience.

J.W.V. F.N.T.

INTRODUCTION

When Joseph Crosby's excellent working library of Shakespeare editions and Shakespeariana was sold at auction in March 1886, the auctioneer's catalogue described the owner as, with Richard Grant White and Horace Howard Furness, one of the three Americans who could be called learned Shakespearians "in an eminent sense."[1] In the belief that this statement was accurate, we are making available in this edition excerpts from Joseph Crosby's correspondence (1875–1878) with his friend and fellow Shakespearian, Joseph Parker Norris.

Crosby's 251 surviving letters to Norris are a scholar's letters, concerned nearly entirely with such subjects as Shakespearian book collecting,[2] the history of Shakespeare scholarship, stage production and stage history of Shakespeare's plays, the state of the English language in Shakespeare's time and related philological questions, the current state of Shakespeare criticism, and, most prominently, the interpretation of the text of Shakespeare, Joseph Crosby's favorite subject. Nearly every question that might be of interest to a Shakespearian in the 1870s is thoroughly discussed somewhere in the 2,200 pages of the letters to Norris—from the Perkins Folio and the Baconian theory to the Becker deathmask and the squabbling between F. J. Furnivall and his colleagues in the New Shakspere Society.[3]

In other places, however, Crosby does not write like a man of his time: he introduces subjects and intellectual perspectives more characteristic of the mid-twentieth century than of the late nineteenth. So one can find in the letters *inter alia* consideration of the rationale of copy text and of the relation between printing-house practice and textual anomaly; advocacy of explication over emendation as an editorial method; illustration of Shakespearian usage from the works of Shakespeare's contemporaries; explanation of the meaning of Elizabethan slang and regional dialect in Shakespeare; documentation of the prominence and meaning of bawdy in the Shakespeare canon. In these and some other approaches to Shakespeare, Crosby is three-quarters of a century or more ahead of his time.[4] One finds in the Crosby letters, then, a well-informed Victorian sensibility mixed with an oddly modern intellectual orientation. The combination, we feel, justifies the attention of Shakespearians to the informal letters of a forgotten man.

For all his learning and intellectual vigor, Joseph Crosby—a shy widower, a grocer in Zanesville, Ohio—was not well known in his time outside the circle of Shakespeare scholars in England and America with whom he corresponded. He never published the Shakespeare edition he clearly envisioned, though he was instrumental in the shaping and publication of the books of others. C. M. Ingleby's revised edition of *The Still Lion: Shakespearian Hermeneutics* (1874–75), Denton J. Snider's *System of Shakespeare's Dramas* (1877), and Norris's *The Portraits of Shakespeare* (1885) all owe something to Crosby's criticism, advice, and encouragement.[5] Crosby also contributed in a small way to H. H. Furness's Variorum *Hamlet* (1877),[6] and he revised the proofs of John S. Hart's life of Shakespeare after Hart's death (see letter 246). He made an important contribution to Henry N. Hudson's second Shakespeare edition, the Harvard (1880–81), by providing explanatory notes on the text and restraining Hudson's tendency toward speculative excess.[7] Others also knew Crosby as a scholar and a collector: W. J. Rolfe, C. M. Ingleby, John Payne Collier, Frederick Gard Fleay, Hiram Corson, Samuel Timmins, and Andrew Brae, all better known than Crosby, corresponded with him, some of them fairly regularly. But it was inevitable that Crosby should be forgotten after his death. He never published a book,[8] and what is more his career ended in scandal and flight from justice. Henry Clay Folger must have had some awareness of Crosby's merits, because at the auction of Norris's library in November 1922 he bought the letters from Crosby that Norris had preserved for half a century. But in essence Crosby had been entirely forgotten when his letters were brought to light in cataloguing at the Folger Shakespeare Library in 1975. We take some satisfaction in regarding these excerpts from Folger Manuscript Y.c. 1372 as the book which Joseph Crosby's modesty prevented him from writing more formally and more publicly.

Joseph Crosby's Life

Joseph Crosby was born 25 July 1821 in the village of Kirkby Thore on the Eden River in Westmorland, what is now eastern Cumbria. His family of prosperous yeoman farmers can be traced in the region to Shakespeare's time; Crosbys, descendants of his younger brother John (1824–95), still live in Powis House outside of Kirkby Thore, working the farm that has been in the family since the 1680s.[9] Mount Pleasant Farm, in a neighboring parish, goes even further back in the family history. Joseph's parents, Jane (1794?– 1840 née Bleamire) and Samuel (1798–1878), were Methodists of the strictest sort, with all the zeal of the convert. The "Methody" in the North Country in the early nineteenth century was typically straitlaced, conservative, unbending. Whiggery and dour piety went together in the Crosby family, and it does not seem an accident that when Joseph left that world for America he became an Episcopalian and a Republican.[10] His best memories of childhood are of the festivity at Lowther Castle on Lady Day and Michaelmas when his father paid his rent to the Earl of Lonsdale.[11] There was, no doubt, little enough of this spirit to remember: an obituary eulogy of Jane Crosby remembered with approval that characteristically "Her presence threw a damper over the levities of a farmer's kitchen," and that her affection for her three children was "seldom manifested by foolish caresses or ill-judged commendations."[12]

Joseph loved the North Country; one sees this in his explications of Shakespearian locutions from the dialect he knew as a child.[13] But remote Westmorland must have been a grim world to a boy who preferred Latin composition to sheep-dipping. Sadly, Joseph's place of exile from this world was more like it than he would have wished; Zanesville, Ohio, was eminently provincial, a place "where hardly one out of one thousand has ever *read* a line of Shakespeare, & not one out of ten thousand read the Poet with any Critical care" (letter 99). Joseph's emigration to America about 1843 was no doubt precipitated by a disagreement with his unyielding and irascible father "Sammy," possibly about the relative merits of the scholar's life and the farmer's.[14]

Joseph Crosby certainly was a scholar by temperament and native gifts. He speaks with pride in a letter to Norris (135) of having committed to memory the Gospel of St. Matthew *verbatim* at the age of ten and of having memorized the six books of Cowper's *The Task* "when I was a school-boy." His retentive memory was evident much later in life: when traveling far from his library he could make close paraphrases of Shakespeare, even of lesser-known passages, and he characteristically quoted Latin authors in his letters without book, as we can tell when he alters the wording in trivial ways or assigns a passage to the wrong author. He was linguistically attuned, a perfectionist about English style, a fair Latinist with passable if rusty Greek. He was a very scholarly philologist, especially interested in etymology and grammatical usage. He had a variorum editor's eagerness to ferret out, assimilate, and appraise all opinions on a crux. He thought aesthetic criticism a will-o'-the-wisp unless founded on a firm grasp of the lexical meaning of a text. But for Joseph Crosby literature was more than its grammar: his favorite reading—Shakespeare, the Bible, Horace, Milton—is indicative of his taste.

It was probably at Appleby School, founded in 1453 and located a few miles from Kirkby Thore, that Crosby learned his classics and imbibed the scholarly cast of mind that he retained four decades later in the uncongenial environment of the American Midwest.[15] He won a prize at age fifteen for his translation of the *Ars Poetica* (35) and went on in due course in 1840 to The Queens College, Oxford, which had a standing scholarship arrangement with Appleby. An occasional reminiscence of his life at Oxford shows that he was very happy there. He remembers with pleasure, e.g., his professor's reply when he used Cicero's *Epistles* as authority for a Latin colloquialism he intruded into a composition (228). He wistfully speaks of passing through Stratford on his way to matriculate at Oxford as "Happy, Happy, Happy days, never to return!" (52). But he gives Norris few details of his college days.

He makes no allusion in the letters to the circumstances of his departure from England and few to his years in Zanesville before the Civil War. Zanesville would be a natural place for Joseph to settle in America, since his father's brother James was established there in the insurance business. Joseph and his uncle opened a wholesale and retail grocery store in 1843, possibly using as capital the patrimony which we may guess Samuel Crosby offered Joseph when he abdicated his birthright, the Powis House Farm. Within a few years the store was a Zanesville institution, and Joseph became an American citizen in 1849. The younger partner in "J. and J. Crosby" was woefully unsuited to running a grocery store; he is said to have left the day-to-day operation to his managers in later years, aggravating the effects of the severe economic depression of the mid-1870s.[16] Crosby seldom mentions the business in his letters to Norris except to grumble when his customers default. And when he wants a contemptuous metaphor for philistine behavior, he finds it in the grocery business: to write to a publisher's formulaic prescription is to "fill the order 'as per sample'" (108). From the 1850s Crosby also was in the insurance business, and in the late 1870s he was staving off bankruptcy by serving as regional supervisor for a group of American and British insurance companies. Insurance was more congenial to him than shopkeeping, though he resented the extensive traveling necessitated by the size of the territory in which he settled fire claims and collected premiums from local agents.

What Crosby disliked about traveling was being away from his library. It was a moral home to him; he often read there most of the night, making learned annotations in the margins of his favorite editions and books of explication[17] or writing long letters to Norris that drew on the resources of the collection. Crosby had begun gathering the library in the mid-1860s (64); by 1884 he owned 175 complete Shakespeare editions, which is to say every edition of any consequence published between 1709 (the first Rowe) and 1881 (the second Hudson).[18] He also had more than 300 editions of individual plays and a Shakespeariana collection that was very nearly complete for the eighteenth and nineteenth centuries. Crosby's philological orientation was reflected in his "stock" of thirty dictionaries and his fine collection of books on English usage. He owned a few unique or very rare books, including Robert Nares's annotated copy of Capell's *Notes and Various Readings* and one of the twenty copies of Halliwell's edition (1851) of Shakespeare's comedies.[19] This library was an improbable anomaly in a provincial town like Zanesville and a rarity in any milieu; Crosby must have grieved when impending financial disaster forced him to sell part of it to the Wisconsin Historical Society in the spring of 1883[20] and more of it to

Isaac Demmon, curator of the University of Michigan McMillan Shakespeare Library, later that same year.[21]

Reclusive as he was, Crosby did have some part in Zanesville community life, though he often spoke in letters of the cultural world around him "here in the West" as remote and barren. He was twice elected a city councilman and twice appointed examiner of teachers for the Zanesville Public Schools.[22] He was a Mason, a director of the Zanesville Athenaeum, and a vestryman in St. James's Episcopal Church. He sometimes attended the lectures and readings that were a staple of entertainment in a place like Zanesville in the days of the Chautauqua movement.[23] And of course he saw Shakespeare in the theater whenever a touring production played Columbus or Cincinnati while he was there on business. His descriptions of these performances are sprinkled through the letters.[24]

Some of Crosby's shy bookishness was a result of the tragedy of his family life. He married Ellen Grosvenor Fitch in 1859, but she died five years later after bearing him three sons, two of whom died in infancy. The sole survivor, Albert, a twin born in 1862, lived with his mother's parents in Cleveland where at the time of his father's letters to Norris he was preparing for the high school, as academically inclined as his father. Like his father also, "Bertie" entered the grocery business eventually (in Cleveland) and like his father he eventually failed at it. He seems not to have married by 1903, at which point we lose his traces.[25]

After thirteen years of widowerhood, Crosby married again in 1878, making a love match with a spinster nearing thirty-five. Agnes Fillmore, a relative of Millard Fillmore, was intelligent, morally self-reliant, and serious enough about Shakespeare to offer Crosby a meaningful companionship. Their close relationship began when she founded the Zanesville Shakespeare Reading Club in the spring of 1877 and induced him to assume its presidency.[26] During the year of courtship that followed, the letters to Norris offer a vivid account of what a serious reading club was like west of the Alleghenies in the 1870s, and they are also a pleasingly human account of growing love.

Agnes Fillmore inevitably became a rival to Joseph Parker Norris for Crosby's affections, as Norris was quick to perceive. His petulance about Agnes must have been a major factor in the decline of the correspondence, though Crosby (and Agnes) stoutly denied that marriage would make any difference to an old friendship. Norris, always something of a faultfinder, pushed Crosby very hard in the spring and summer of 1878.[27] The end of the run of letters Norris preserved came in August 1878, just as the couple were returning from their honeymoon. A complete rupture certainly did not occur, because in the years that followed Crosby mentioned to other correspondents that he had heard from Norris.[28] But any diminution of the relation between Crosby and Norris would have been a break in old and fond habits.

Crosby and Norris had been correspondents about Shakespearian subjects since 1872, when Norris was in his mid-twenties. In the years 1875–78 Crosby wrote to his friend on the average six times a month letters that ran as long as forty-three pages and averaged nine. From the beginning Crosby played the role of scholarly mentor and older friend, though there is nothing patronizing in his tone.[29]

Joseph Parker Norris (1847–1916) belonged to the old and wealthy Philadelphia family founded by the Quaker Isaac Norris in the late seventeenth century. He was a prosperous trial lawyer for whom Shakespeare, especially the controversial subject of Shakespearian portraiture and iconography, was an absorbing avocation. Norris did not have Crosby's discriminating scholarly intelligence, and his interest ran to collecting Shakespeariana rather than to true scholarship. We have lost little, perhaps, in the disappearance of his half of the correspondence. But Crosby loved him like a son, rejoicing at the annual growth of his family and of his library, admonishing him gently when he foolishly engaged in public controversy with adversaries more formidable than he. Norris enthusiastically took up lost causes like the opening of Shakespeare's grave and the authenticity of the Shakespeare deathmask, and Crosby tried to suggest better wisdom without giving offense. Norris was more often wrong than right—by modern standards—about the worth of contemporary scholarship, often rejecting Crosby's judicious appraisals.[30]

Norris began editing a column called "Shakespearian Gossip" in Joseph Sabin and Sons' *The American Bibliopolist* early in 1875, just as the correspondence as we have it takes up. Crosby supported his friend with regular contributions—book reviews, notes of explication, aesthetic criticism—while the journal lasted; the letters in the Folger are, then, in part a minor record of American magazine journalism in the 1870s.

The letters we have printed will cumulatively give a full picture of Norris's character and of Crosby's, so little further comment is needed here. But we might emphasize that Crosby was personally appealing as well as intellectually impressive. He was witty, sometimes at his own expense, [31] modest, gentle of spirit, tenacious of values—from the Episcopal Church and the Republican Party to the authority of the "good old Folio"—which he held important. Despite this conservative temper he was ready to learn and he was generous to ideas other than his own—or at least tactful where generosity was beyond him. He was abstemious without puritanism, aloof without autism. His photograph (see *frontispiece*) shows a man of bearded dignity with somewhat elevated head and intense gaze. If the townspeople of Zanesville thought him comically odd for carrying a volume of Shakespeare in his pocket to read while breakfast was cooking (136) or even while walking in the street,[32] we may take a more generous view of his single-mindedness.

The scholarly commitment to Shakespeare surely contributed to the bankruptcy of Crosby's grocery house in the summer of 1884. It was not that he siphoned capital out of the business in order to buy books, though Crosby obviously always spent as much on books as he could afford. The neglect of his affairs, which must have encouraged mismanagement or even pilfering, was the real reason for his failure. Crosby could not ride out the long economic depression that followed the Panic of 1873. By the summer of '84 he was said to have an indebtedness of $20,000, and he could no longer put off ruin.[33] It is possible that his health was a factor also. He had severe neuralgia, for which he may have taken opium. A letter from H. H. Furness to Henry Clay Folger written in 1897 (Folger Shakespeare Library) speaks of Crosby's opium habit, his mounting debts, and his efforts to borrow from friends in the months before his financial collapse. There is, however, no hint of addiction in the letters—unless we attach significance to his observation (146) about the private misfortune of J. O. Halliwell-Phillipps: "Did it ever strike you, that there is a skeleton in everybody's closet? We look at people, & imagine them perfectly happy. Yet who knows but God, how they feel, or where the skeleton is concealed?" At all events, as late as the spring of 1884 Crosby's handwriting was as bold and his mind as lucid as in the tranquil years of his correspondence with Norris.[34]

Whatever the full story, Crosby forged his father-in-law's name to a promissory note when hard pressed in May 1884. The creditor prosecuted in July when the fraud was discovered. Released from custody on bail (part of it posted by the Fillmore family), Crosby fled, abandoning wife, library, and respectable place in Zanesville society. The disgrace must have been awful for this quiet, dignified scholar who had so often expressed strong feelings about the plagiarisms and forgeries of Shakespeare scholarship and who had himself had the duty of prosecuting insurance agents when they were tempted into embezzlement. In a sad irony of fate, Crosby was arraigned after his arrest in the Muskingum County Courthouse for which he had devised the motto: "LG.S.J.," i.e., "Legem servare jubeo" ("I command you to observe the law").[35]

Joseph Crosby's last years were spent in Montreal, Canada, beyond the reach of prosecution; he died there 31 October 1891. But a letter to W. H. Wyman in the Folger Shakespeare Library, written in the fall of 1884, shows that he had been hearing from Agnes, of whom he speaks with deep affection, and that he had been making arrangements to pay his debts in Zanesville. He found work as a journalist and despite poor health and low spirits he attempted seriously to repair the past. The task was not easy: one sees it in the absence of his name from the membership list of the Montreal Shakespeare Club, one of the two most scholarly Shakespeare clubs in North America (founded in 1882 and very active in the late 1880s).[36] And it seems from the will Agnes Crosby made a week before her death in September 1887 that she did not know then whether her husband was still alive. No obituary appeared in *Shakespeariana* in 1891 or 1892, though the journal regularly published obituaries of Shakespearians; H. H. Furness was unaware of Crosby's death nearly six years after it occurred.[37] In his last years Crosby had made unobtrusive attempts to go on with the old life that is so vividly revealed in the letters to Norris: he still haunted book-shops; letters to W. H. Wyman about Shakespearian subjects survive in the Folger Shakespeare Library; and one article, a major philological study of Shakespeare's peculiar use of the word *though* in a causative sense, ap-peared under the pseudonym "Senior" shortly after his departure from Zanesville.[38] But well before his death Joseph Crosby had disappeared into an obscurity that was to last for nearly a century.

The Text

This edition of excerpts comprises 27 percent of the corpus of Joseph Crosby's extant letters to Joseph Parker Norris; two-thirds of the 251 letters are represented. The criterion of selection has been Shakespearian interest. We have not been able to print more than a fraction of the "Shakespearian" material in the letters—actually there is little in them, relatively speaking, that is not about Shakespeare in one way or another.[39] Nevertheless, all of Crosby's major interests in Shakespeare are represented. A reader seeking Crosby's view of a given topic should enter this book through its index, and he will not be assured of completeness unless he consults the larger *Index to the Letters of Joseph Crosby to Joseph Parker Norris in Folger Manuscript Y.c. 1372* (copies in the Folger and certain other libraries—see note 3 to this Introduction). The text of our edition is based on microfilm and photocopy of Folger MS. Y.c. 1372, checked against the manuscript. Minor anomalies in the numbering of letters and pagination in them follow the Folger catalo-guing. We print a clear reading-text, with minimal textual apparatus.

MS. Y.c. 1372 in the Folger Shakespeare Library contains 260 letters from Joseph Crosby to other Shakespearians, arranged alphabetically by recip-ient. Of these, 250 are to Norris[40] January 1875–August 1878, 2,224 pages of manuscript. The remaining ten were addressed at various dates from 1870 to 1884 to F. G. Fleay (3), C. E. Flower (2), C. M. Ingleby (1), Karl Knortz (3), and W. H. Wyman (1)—an additional total of forty-three pages. The manuscript is in excellent condition (only one letter is badly dog-eared), written in a bold, firm hand in dark ink on a variety of papers. Crosby wrote on the stationery of his residence hotel, The Mills House, on bills and advertising flyers from his grocery store, on hotel stationery from the Ohio and West Virginia towns he stayed in while engaged in insurance business, on stationery of the insurance companies he represented, and more often than not on any of a variety of plain white papers. He character-istically scribbled addenda to letters on half-sheets or even scraps of paper of any kind (to Norris's annoyance), and once in a while he put a final postscript on the envelope.

The hand is easily legible; not more than a dozen words in the manuscript have entirely defeated us, and of these only two or three are in passages transcribed here. Only capitals, paragraphing, and some punctuation are in any way troublesome in Crosby's hand. Initial capitals are indistinguishable from lower case for the letters *E*, *K*, and *V*, and sometimes uncertain for the letters *A*, *C*, *M*, *N*, *O*, *S*, *T*, and *U*. Crosby's intention in paragraphing is sometimes unclear, as is his terminal punctuation (internal? external?) in quotations. We have silently normalized *E*, *K*, and *V*, aware that this distorts somewhat Crosby's rather free use of capitals. We have silently supplied (and sometimes deleted) paragraphing on rhetorical grounds. We have followed Crosby's apparent intention in punctuating quotations, i.e., contemporary British and American style (commas and periods internal; semicolons and colons external).[41] For typographical reasons we have simplified Crosby's varying degrees of added emphasis: words single-underlined in the manuscript appear in our text in italics; words that appear in the manuscript with further emphasis—double-underlined, or (rarely) triple-underlined, or (very rarely) in a boldface hand—we have printed in boldface type. We have silently omitted verbal redundancies where manuscript pages end; omitted quotation marks at the beginning of each line of a quoted text; reduced superscript letters, regularized false ligatures and separations (*ofthe*; *any where*); and ignored the few ornamental capitals, flourishes, and other calligraphic devices in the manuscript. Though the master *Index* in the Folger is perforce keyed to letter number, sheet, and (our supplied) page number within sheet (e.g., 135 a2–3), we have omitted from our text as superfluous indications of page-beginnings in the Folger MS.

The textual notes are a record of our other interventions (except ellipsis, which is indicated in the text in the usual way). We have made emendations for clarity, sometimes supplying an antecedent that appears in a passage we deleted, sometimes supplying sentence capitals after ellipsis, occasionally opening or closing a parenthesis or a quotation, rarely making a guess at an illegible word, once or twice correcting erroneous Act-scene references to Shakespeare. Where ambiguous end-of-line hyphenation appears in the manuscript, we have taken as our guide Crosby's other uses of the questionable words; where this was not possible we have relied on the *OED*, which was begun under James A. H. Murray's direction in 1878, a date contemporary with the letters. The largest number of textual notes record Crosby's afterthoughts: deletions and interlinear insertions.

Otherwise Crosby is allowed to appear as he put himself on paper, including his added emphasis, bracketing of passages, occasional anacoluthon, British spelling, and other anomalies of spelling, wording, syntax, capitalization, and citation. (Square brackets in the text are Crosby's; brackets in the annotations and textual notes are editorial.) We have not corrected slips in foreign languages (there are a good many in Crosby's

Agency at _____ March 28/75 187

I am glad you have got for yourself a copy of the last Edn. of Webster's Unabridged
Dictionary; and you got it cheap enough. I paid $15.00 for mine. You will
find it of daily & nightly use & value. I have had one for several years; and I
keep it on a little round table, with a revolving top, at my elbow, so I can turn to it,
without the trouble of getting up & going to it, any moment. It is a multum in
magno — tho' one might still say "parvo", compared with some others, Latham's
for instance. Altho' my copy is strongly bound in full russia (red edges), yet
the wear and tear of the binding shows that it has been "Nocturnâ versata
manu, versata diurnâ". I confess, however, that the "dictionary of Noted Names
of Fiction", &c, and all the various tables of pronunciation of Scripture, Latin
and Greek, biographical & geographical proper Names, have been more used
than the great body of the Dictionary. I can always get better satisfaction, either
in Etymology or Definition, & especially in Examples quoted from various sources,
from Latham, & Richardson, than I can from Webster. By the by, you will find
some curious information about Webster's (?) Dictionary in R. G. White's book
"Words and their Uses"; if you have not read it, be sure & do so. That whole chapter (p. 365, &c) is very interesting. It is really Dr. Mahn's Dictionary, & not Webster's or Goodrich's,
at least in the Etymology. But read what White says: it will amuse you hugely.
I am very fortunate in my stock of Dictionaries. My library boasts of all the best.
Did I ever tell you how many I had? In addn. to Webster's, just mentioned, in
full russia, I have Worcester's Unabridged, in full morocco, gilt edges; Dr
Latham's grand work, in 4 Vol. 4to, Hf. russia, very strongly bound; Richardson's
2 Vols. 4to, Hf. morocco; Craig's Universal Dictionary, last Ed. by Nuttall, 2 vols,
roy 8vo., Hf. mor, uncut, gilt top; Ogilvie's Imperial Dictionary, 2 vols. 4to;
Hf Calf; Chambers' Etymological Dictionary; Johnson & Walker's Dictionary by
Worcester; Minsheu; Nares' Glossary — 2 editions, both full bound; Halliwell's Archaic Dictiony, 2 vols. 8vo. Hf. mor, uncut, gilt tops; Wright's Provincial Dictionary, 2 vols. in one, Hf. mor., uncut, gilt top; 2 Biographical Dictionaries; Brandt's Encyclopædia (last edn); Appleton's Cyclopædia,

Pages three and four of Crosby's letter dated 28 March 1875 (letter 33).
Courtesy of The Folger Shakespeare Library.

16 Vols., Hf. Cf.; Allibone's Dic. of Authors, 3 vols. Hf. morocco; Bohn's Lowndes 6 vols., large paper, Hf. roxburghe; Chambers' Cyclo. of Literature, 2 vols. full calf (Engl. Edn.); Riddle's Latin Lexicon, 1 vol. 4to. thick, Hf. morocco; Leverett's Latin Dictionary, sheep; Donnegan's Greek Lexicon, new Edn., sheep; 1 German Dictionary (Adler's); 1 French Dictionary; Brockett's Glossary of North Country words; 2 Bible Dictionaries, & "Bible Word-Book" (an admirable little production, (thick 16mo.) by Eastwood & W. Aldis Wright; and I have subscribed to the Ninth (last) Edition of the Encyclopædia Britannica. I have just received the 1st Vol., — the only one out yet. I took my copy in Hf. russia; it will consist of 22 vols., and in Hf. russia costs $11.00 a Vol. — (cloth 9ff a Vol.); and it will be issued at the rate of about 3 vols. a year. You know what a magnificent work this is, of course, and I need not describe it to you. This new Edn. is about three-fourths of it new-written, & by the very best writers & authors in the world, on each department. It is beautifully printed — good large clear type — good paper — in large quarto; and contains hundreds of the finest steel engravings — Maps &c., and thousands of wood-cuts. All the information is of course brought down to the very latest date, literary and scientific. Each article is a complete Essay on the subject treated of; so that the complete work makes simply a nearly-perfect library in itself. Fifteen years ago, I took the Eighth Edition; and about a year ago, I got an inkling that a new Edition was to be prepared & published; and was lucky enough to sell my copy here, for nearly what I gave for it, after using it freely for 13 or 14 years. So I am just ready for the new one. I cannot speak in too high terms of this magnificent work. It is just as superior to Chambers' and Appleton's, & any other that I ever saw, as you can imagine. It seems expensive; but considering the immense cost of producing the work, and the enormous amount of information on all subjects that it lays before us, it is not dear. Taking it a Vol. at a time, at long intervals, one hardly feels it; & when once acquired, one has a κτῆμα ἐς ἀεί. —

I expect I have omitted some of my Dictionaries, &c. in the above enumeration; yet from what are there, you can see how fortunate I am in so good & select a stock. I have sent for Bailey's Etymological Dict.; & also B. F. Smart's Pronouncing Dict., both useful for different reasons; & I expect them soon. — I have also Hayden's Dictionary of Dates, last Edn., one very thick 8vo volume, — Hf. mor. — a very, very useful reference book. —

French). There is flavor in the manner of expression in this manuscript as well as in the content; as Crosby puts it (58), "a grammatical error, or a dozen of them, in a warm enthusiastic friendly conversational chat . . . but show the mind is more intent on *convincing* another mind, of telling the truth, of conveying an idea or picture as it appears to one—rather than of making an impression of smartness, or eloquence." Therefore, aware that we may fall between stools, we have tried for a middle position between fidelity to our text and the freedom with it that one expects in an edition intended for the general reader.

Similarly, our annotations are intended for the "Shakespearian general reader," assuming (we hope) neither too much nor too little knowledge. So we have identified many people, but left unannotated many others who seemed to us likely to be known to the educated general reader. We translate sparingly but identify the sources of all Crosby's non-Shakespearian quotations. When Crosby alludes in passing to a Shakespearian passage (as he often does, solemnly or facetiously) we are silent, but when he explicates or discusses a passage, we locate it unless he has done so adequately.[42] An explanatory note appears only the first time it is appropriate, since through the index the reader can locate a note, if there is one, on any indexable concept, fact, or person. Those cross-references that do appear in the explanatory notes (and the Introduction) simply direct the reader to a letter if our excerpts from that letter are of moderate length; for longer letters the reader is directed to a page or to a letter and explanatory note number. Explanatory notes accompanying a letter follow it immediately and are signalled in the text by superscript numbers; textual notes for a letter follow its explanatory notes and are signalled in the text by superscript lowercase letters.

Though each letter in the manuscript has its salutation ("My dear Norris") and its valediction, the correspondence of these two men has the continuity of a conversation: one can often reconstruct a Norris letter in detail from Crosby's reply, and Crosby will sometimes resume in a letter where he left off in the preceding one. With these characteristics in mind, we have understated the breaks between letters: unless a place is given, the letter was written and posted at Zanesville, and we do not include a salutation or valediction unless our text begins or ends where the letter does. Our arrangement is, of course, by date as in the catalogued manuscript, but date and sequence are not of the essence in much of what the reader will encounter in these eclectic letters. Crosby moves from subject to subject without transition for the most part, and our editorial format imitates this feature of the letters, picking up a new subject without prologue after an ellipsis.

One can, therefore, read the excerpts in this edition *seriatim* and experience a collocation—of allusion and extended discussion, of the seriocomic and the dignified, of the immediate and the remote in Shakespeare scholarship—not unlike what Norris experienced in reading any given letter or group of letters. Or one can regard this edition as a *livre de chevet* to be dipped into at random. And of course one can consult this edition for (some of) Crosby's observations on a given passage in Shakespeare, on a book or author, an actress, bookseller, or Shakespearian character. It is our hope that the text and apparatus offered here will assist any of these styles of reading.

Joseph Crosby's Place in the Scholarly Tradition

Something has been said above about the interest and importance of Joseph Crosby's letters to Joseph Parker Norris, but something more remains to be said. We would like to point out some of the special merits of Crosby's scholarship as it is informally recorded in the letters, because we feel confident that had he published his best work he would hold a place today among the dozen best Anglo-American Shakespeare scholars of the last half of the nineteenth century.

He would certainly be remembered for his command of the history of Shakespeare scholarship and criticism. Crosby had read widely, especially on textual questions, and his retentive memory kept his reading constantly at his service. Crosby knew about and properly valued some eighteenth-century scholarship that was generally ignored or contemned in his time. For instance, Walter Whiter, whose Lockean approach to Shakespeare's imagery may be thought a distant prototype of the modern study of "image clusters," was known to Crosby as he was to few Shakespearians in the mid-Victorian era.[43] And Crosby respected Edward Capell, who was largely ignored or denigrated as an obscure pedant between the time of Samuel Johnson and George Steevens and the advent of the "new bibliography."[44] Crosby recognized Capell as the father of the rationale of copy text that he held himself—the most authentic text is a folio or quarto not yet subjected to editorial alteration.

His detailed and astute command of the tradition enabled Crosby to trace claimed discoveries to their true sources. Again and again in the letters he demonstrates that the roots of an idea appeared earlier than its flowering. And with impressive logic he shows that famous scholars like Richard Grant White and Henry Norman Hudson were flagrant plagiarists. The prevalence of fraud among editors is perhaps not surprising in a century that produced the Collier Controversy and the alleged forgeries of Peter Cunningham,[45] and in which international literary piracy was accepted practice;[46] but the extent of intellectual dishonesty among Victorian Shakespeare scholars is only just now beginning to be known as it was known to Crosby.[47]

Crosby's thorough knowledge of the tradition also made him an expert on editorial practice and editorial format. There are many judicious appraisals of competing Shakespeare editions in the letters to Norris.[48] Unlike Norris, who was contemptuous of Shakespeare editions that were aimed at the general public, Crosby understood and approved of the cultural impact which a popular edition of Shakespeare could have. Mass-produced Shakespeare editions, sold in parts by subscription as encyclopedias are sold today (and to the same kind of consumer for just the same reasons), were a nineteenth-century innovation, largely the invention of Charles Knight in the late 1830s. Crosby's account of the marketing forty years later in Zanesville of Virtue and Yorston's inexpensive reprint of a Knight edition is an excellent resource for anyone interested in the mass dissemination of culture in nineteenth-century America.[49]

The letters are equally informative about editions intended for schools and colleges and about scholarly editions, "a well-read, classical, intelligent Scholar's Shakespeare" (69). There is no question that Crosby's own preferred *métier* would have been editing, especially the informed and conservative explication of texts in light of Elizabethan English and Shakespearian usage. He had an edition in his mind's eye which, he told Norris half seriously, he would realize at a cost of some five or six thousand dollars if he inherited money from his father.[50] He describes it in detail in letter 69 and elsewhere:

> . . . The *text* shall be *my own*—based chiefly on the Folio, of course, with many returns to it in passages that now vary from it quite needlessly. But it will be neither the Cambridge, nor Dyce's, nor Collier's, nor Knight's, nor the Variorum of 1821, nor anybody's, but a Text selected just to suit myself alone. . . . [The] Notes will be textual, & critical, & explanatory; but all re-written or original; & *only* explain such difficulties as the *Most advanced* Shakespearian students want. . . . Great care should be taken about these *Notes.* There should be no *useless* reading, or display of learning by references to other authors or editors. Plain intelligible explanations of *real* difficulties, where explainable, & where not, to say so. . . .

The proposed independence of this edition would have made it special among Victorian Shakespeare texts, which borrowed extensively from their predecessors, with or without acknowledgement.[51]

Crosby's ideal edition would not have been expurgated. Unlike his contemporaries, Crosby believed in making Shakespeare speak as he wrote, even when read aloud in mixed company: "Aut Shakespeare, aut nullus." The decorum of reading from an unbowdlerized Shakespeare is unpretentiously spelled out in letter 230. Crosby was interested in Shakespearian obscenity, contrasting it with what one finds in Fletcher, considering its social roots and its dramatic import, and explicating it learnedly and convincingly.[52] He interprets many bawdy phrases in Shakespeare, in one case devoting a whole letter (55) to three of them. Sometimes the interpretation he makes had been rediscovered by Eric Partridge's time, but often it had not been.[53]

As with bawdy, so with textual cruxes generally. Crosby explicates dozens of difficult passages, nearly always making sense of the Folio text without emendation.[54] We have found the majority of his interpretations convincing; very few had been made before and some have not yet been made by editors.[55] In our judgment Crosby's best achievement is the illumination of textual obscurities in Shakespeare.

Frankness about obscenity and respect for the Folio text are only two of the ties between Crosby and modern scholarship. Crosby's extended essay on Desdemona in the form of a letter (226) to Norris might almost be taken for the interpretation of a modern feminist critic. Her tragedy, he reasons, results from a lack of independence of spirit: had she not been so morally dependent on her husband she would not have remained passive under his unjust imputation. Crosby was proud of the intellectual and moral self-sufficiency of Agnes Fillmore: "I want some self-reliance in a wife, and I could put up with considerable independence in one, so she would have some backbone. . ."; he once compared Agnes to Portia (203), whom he admired for her ability to control events in the courtroom without abdicating her feminine compassion (113). On the other hand, Crosby had no liking for the militant feminists, "the 'strong-minded' *bas-bleux* of a 'Woman's rights' meeting" (234).

Two other stances in which Crosby anticipates twentieth-century scholarship ought to be mentioned. He was very interested in dialect and other forms of nonstandard English; his comments on the survival of Elizabethan diction, usage, and pronunciation in New England dialect still have value. He distantly foreshadows the generation of the New Critics in his recognition that a single reverberating image, even a single word repeated, may dominate a play and only that play. He offers the metaphor of horsemanship in *Julius Caesar* (*to bear someone hard*) as an instance (241), reminding us of what Caroline F. E. Spurgeon was to say of "leading images" sixty years later.[56]

Sometimes in attacking the critical excesses of his time Crosby unwittingly says something to us as well. He insisted, for instance, that scholarship must be prior to aesthetic interpretation—his contemporaries, caught up in a new wave of aesthetics, were, many of them, reversing these priorities. The notes in the Rugby School Shakespeare, e.g., were almost entirely confined to aesthetic observations. For Crosby here, scholarship would be "verbal criticism," the lexical and syntactic understanding of a text. He shows that Hudson, whom Furness thought the best aesthetic critic of Shakespeare America had produced, sometimes made woeful howlers in his ignorance of the semantic meaning of the text. Several of these howlers would have found their way into the Harvard Edition (1880–

81) had it not been for Crosby.[57] Perhaps it is suggestive that in his own hypothetical Shakespeare edition aesthetic criticism was to occupy an appendix—to be encountered after the rest of the editorial apparatus had had its effect on the reader (69). One must *know* something to appreciate it as it really is.

With equal firmness Crosby defends the position that Shakespeare's characters are individuals, not moral *exempla* (238). He rejects the schematic views of Shakespeare which British and American critics in the 1870s were eagerly importing from Germany. The fallacy Crosby deplored was imposing a precontrived moral framework on the *dramatis personae* of a Shakespeare play and ignoring or warping those characters that did not fit it. For Crosby, Denton J. Snider's *System of Shakespeare's Dramas* (1877) risked this Procrustean fallacy, though Crosby respected Snider's powers of structural interpretation and actually encouraged him to publish the book (see note 5 to this Introduction). Snider was original in his application of Hegelian dialectic to Shakespeare, and he was modest in presenting his work, but he was "essentially a *mathematician*" on whom Shakespeare's poetry and his flexibility were lost (238). In Snider's book the "System" precedes and threatens to supersede the "Dramas," and Crosby rejects that hierarchy, though he admits that Snider is less rigid and programmatic than the transcendentalist Germans who shaped him.[58] After reading Crosby's indictment of schematic criticism, it is easy to infer what he would say, were he alive, about the doctrinaire readings of our time, whether Freudian, Marxist, Feminist, or Christian, that fit Shakespeare's plays and characters onto *a priori* templates, by force if necessary.

Joseph Crosby's was not a towering mind; he is not always right, and he should not be thought of as an oracle, for our time or his own. But he had a sharp intelligence, an excellent philological education, energy, and an open mind. We can be grateful to him for what he wrote out of these resources and to Joseph Parker Norris and Henry Clay Folger for having the good sense to preserve what he wrote.[59]

NOTES

1. Isaac N. Demmon, who compiled the *Catalogue* for Bangs, the auction house, was probably quoting from Henry N. Hudson's *Essay on Education, English Studies, and Shakespeare* (1881); the comment also appeared earlier in the Prefaces to Hudson's Annotated English Classics edns. of *Jn.* (1879) and *AYL* (1880). Copies of the *Catalogue* are in the Folger Shakespeare Library and the New York Public Library; copies of an abbreviated (all Shakespearian) version are in the Ohio State University Library and the University of Michigan Library.

2. Joseph Parker Norris and Joseph Crosby owned two of the three best Shakespearian libraries in private hands in America in the 1870s. (The third, and best, belonged to Horace Howard Furness.)

3. Copies of our *Index* (1978) to topics discussed in the letters are in the Folger Shakespeare Library, the University of Michigan Library, the University of Texas Library, the University of

Georgia (English Department) Library, the Library of the Ohio Historical Society, and the Library of Congress.

4. A fuller account of Crosby's place in the scholarly tradition will be found at the conclusion of this Introduction.

5. Of the three only Ingleby credited Crosby publicly for the encouragement we learn about from confidences made to Norris. (See headnote to the third edn., 1875.) Snider told Crosby in a private letter (see letter 248) that he was the "godfather" of the 900-page book that grew out of Snider's essays on moral patterns in Shakespeare's plays, but Crosby is not mentioned in the book. Norris's omission of Crosby's name from his acknowledgements is a sad one, accountable to Crosby's criminal disgrace the year before (see "Joseph Crosby's Life" below). Crosby's encouragement and his advice to Norris about the strategy of a book on the Shakespeare portraits are prominent in the letters. As late as 1882, ill and financially beleaguered, Crosby was urging W. H. Wyman to expand his bibliography of the anti-Stratfordian question into a book-length refutation of its rationale (letter of 16 July, Folger Shakespeare Library).

6. Crosby's contribution was perforce small, because he had given all his notes on *Hamlet* to H. N. Hudson, who therefore had a prior right in them (42). Crosby did some hunting up of references for Furness and some searching out of actors' interpretations (146). Furness later disparaged Crosby's work in a letter (9 Mar. 1897) to Henry Clay Folger (Folger Shakespeare Library), but it seems clear that Crosby's scholarship was worthy of his good opinion: see letter 111 for Furness's ill-informed rejection of C's plausible interpretation of the "politic worms" that feed on Polonius (108). Crosby made convincing negative criticisms of Furness's planned adoption of two readings (1.1.227; 2.4.210) from Collier's Perkins Folio in *King Lear* (letter to Furness in Furness Memorial Library, 9 Feb. 1879), though Furness did not follow his conservative advice. Furness cites Crosby's cogent explication of Fl *King Lear* 3.7.65 in the *Variorum*, but does not accept it. Earlier Furness had complimented Crosby on work he did toward the *Hamlet Variorum* (146; cf. 113).

7. Hudson devotes the last paragraph of his preface to grateful acknowledgment of Crosby's large contribution to the edition (see letter 171 n.2); Hudson's gratitude extended to obtaining for Crosby a nomination as Foreign Honorary Member of the Royal Society of Literature.

8. A two-page list of Joseph Crosby's publications (not quite complete to its date) can be found in the "Shakespeare-Bibliographie" in *Shakespeare Jahrbuch* 16 (1881). See also ibid., 18 (1883); 20 (1885).

9. John Crosby's grandson, John, of Powis House has generously supplied us with a family genealogy. Joseph's brother John inherited the farm and the role of eldest son when Joseph emigrated to America. Joseph's second brother, William (1827–48), was drowned in a flash flood while dipping sheep in the Eden River; the accident, in which a hired man also died, is still vivid in family memory. Joseph also had a much younger half-brother, Richard Winter Crosby (1844–89), child of his father's second marriage, with whom he corresponded affectionately in the 1870s.

10. On the other hand, in mid-life Joseph was following his parents in being a teetotaler, so as to set an example of temperance.

11. See the vivid account of these feasts, letter 235.

12. We are grateful to Edith Margaret Crosby Horn for a transcript of this long eulogy in her possession. After Jane's death in 1840, Samuel married (1842) Isabella Winter Atkinson, a widow. In the letters Joseph never mentions any member of his family in England except his father Samuel and (veiled in letter 203) his half-brother, Richard.

13. See "dialects: North Country" in the Index to this edition. An outstanding instance is Crosby's explication of the "rooky wood" in *Mac.* (letter 233).

14. This is the opinion of Richard Crosby of York, England, a descendant of Joseph's brother John. Much of what we know of the family history we owe to Richard Crosby's genial generosity. Another family legend has Joseph's exile the result of a love affair; the letters offer no hint of an explanation. Joseph's departure may have been precipitate; he did not take his beloved copy of Ayscough's Shakespeare edition (see letter 235 n.13). Whatever the cause of disagreement between Joseph and Sammy, the son was "greeted with something of a 'prodigal's welcome'" in 1851, when he spent six months in England at the time of the Great Exhibition; "it seems that past differences were forgotten and all was well" (personal communication, based on family letters, from Richard Crosby, 3 Dec. 1976). Much later, in 1876,

Joseph wrote to his family with some small pride about his scholarly achievements (ibid., 27 Sept. 1976).

15. The records of Appleby School have been lost for the relevant years, but Crosbys have been Appleby scholars from a time before Joseph's to the present. Appleby, the school of George Washington's father and brothers, was established on its present footing in the time of Queen Elizabeth I. Joseph would have ridden to school from Powis House on a pony, down the Old Roman Road.

16. Norris F. Schneider in Zanesville, Ohio, *Sunday Times Signal*, 11 Jan. 1959, A Section, p. 7.

17. See letters 85 and 131 for lists of Crosby's favorite books on Shakespeare; other lists can be found passim in the letters. Isaac N. Demmon, curator of rare books in the University of Michigan Library, purchased some four-hundred volumes from Crosby's library in the fall of 1885 for the McMillan Shakespeare Collection. He speaks of the annotated volumes among them as "unique" and valuable in an article on the collection in *The Michigan Alumnus* 13 (1907): 375–77.

18. Even the rare and very expensive Halliwell-Phillipps folio edition (1851–65), which Crosby had coveted all through the years of his correspondence with Norris, eventually took its place in his library. He mentions owning this folio set in a letter to Halliwell-Phillips dated 10 May 1881 (Folger Shakespeare Library), though he may have been forced to sell it as his financial position deteriorated in the early 1880s, since it is not listed in the sale catalogue of his library (1886).

19. Crosby believed the latter to be the only copy in America. Both of these extraordinary books are now in the Harlan Hatcher Graduate Library, University of Michigan.

20. Letter from Crosby to I. N. Demmon (14 July 1883) in the Harlan Hatcher Graduate Library, University of Michigan. This first sale was only of duplicates of Crosby's Shakespeariana. The Wisconsin Historical Society added to them by purchasing about a dozen Shakespeare editions at the auction of Crosby's library in March, 1886. The Historical Society holdings were later transferred to the University of Wisconsin (Madison) Library, where they now are.

21. Crosby's correspondence with Demmon about this sale and Demmon's preliminary survey of the Crosby library are in the University of Michigan McMillan Shakespeare Collection, Harlan Hatcher Graduate Library.

22. John W. Velz, "Certification in 'The Basics' 100 Years Ago," *English Journal* 66, no. 7 (Oct. 1977): 32–38.

23. He gives an account (235) of one such reading, by James Murdoch, the actor.

24. See Index s.v. "Shakespearian performances."

25. Information from Cleveland City Directories and files of contemporary newspapers, Cleveland Public Library.

26. Frances N. Teague, "A Nineteenth-Century Shakespeare Reading Club," *Shakespeare Newsletter* (May 1977): 20.

27. Norris was unjustly resentful when Crosby accepted a retainer from *The Literary World* for Shakespeare articles.

28. Letter to Furness (25 Oct. 1879) in Furness Memorial Library; letter to W. H. Wyman (16 July 1882) in Wyman Scrapbook Collection, Folger Shakespeare Library; various letters to C. M. Ingleby in Folger Shakespeare Library.

29. In the early 1880s Crosby wrote to C. M. Ingleby about Shakespeare very much as he had once written to Norris (some fourteen letters survive in the Folger Shakespeare Library, MSS. C.a. 8, C.a. 9, and C.a. 10). It is instructive to contrast the letters Crosby wrote to a distinguished scholar his own age with those he wrote to Norris, nearly three decades his junior and very much an amateur. The differences in tone are subtle, but quite noticeable; the easy confident tenor of the Norris letters does not transfer to his letters to Ingleby. As he himself once said of Ingleby to Norris, "I always write to him with fear & trembling, expecting every minute I may be 'smashed' . . ." (161).

30. See various comments about Dowden, Snider, Brae and other scholars.

31. One of his tricks of style is quoting Shakespeare out of context and anachronistically to comic and sometimes acidulous effect.

32. Norris F. Schneider in Zanesville, Ohio, *Sunday Times Signal*, 4 Jan. 1959, B Section, p. 4, quoting Thomas W. Lewis, a contemporary historian of Zanesville: "We remember seeing him

reading from [a pocket edition of Shakespeare] as he walked along Main street oblivious to all things around." Cf. ibid., 11 Jan. 1959, A Section, p. 7.

33. Ibid., 11 Jan. 1959, citing Zanesville *Signal* 17 July 1884. The *Signal*'s estimate of indebtedness seems inordinately high. We do not find evidence in letters Crosby wrote in 1883 and 1884 of impending catastrophe, and Crosby wrote to W. H. Wyman in the fall of 1884 of having sufficient assets in Zanesville to cover his indebtedness.

34. In late April 1884 he wrote to Ingleby with clarity and leisurely naturalness about Shakespearian topics (Folger MS. C.a. 10 #26), and he was publishing prolifically in the new periodical *Shakespeariana* throughout the first half of 1884.

35. He discusses the motto in a letter to Norris (187 b1-2, 1 May 1877) that we have not reprinted. The history of the Muskingum County Courthouse was written for its centennial by Norris F. Schneider (Zanesville, 1977).

36. *Shakespeariana* 3 (1886): 520–22.

37. Letter to Henry Clay Folger (9 Mar. 1897) in Folger Shakespeare Library. Even Norris, his intimate friend in time past, was not aware that Crosby was living in Canada; a letter from Norris to F. A. Leo written 30 April 1885, nearly ten months after Crosby's departure, assumes that he is in prison in America (Norris Letters, Uncatalogued Autograph MS Collection, Folger Shakespeare Library.)

38. See letter 239 and note 1 to letter 240. It seems probable that Crosby took his unpublished notes on Shakespearian questions with him when he went to Canada; this part of his Collectanea is missing from the University of Michigan collection. See S. P. Cerasano, "Joseph Crosby's Green Boxes: His Shakespeare Collectanea," *Michigan Academician* 14, no. 1 (Summer 1981): 81–92; cf. S. P. Cerasano, et al., *A Bibliography of the Crosby Shakespeare Collectanea at the University of Michigan* (Ann Arbor: University of Michigan, 1979), 81pp. + addenda.

39. Some exceptions are notable: the long and vivid account of the rioting in Zanesville during the Great Railway Strike of 1877; the scattered discussions of the operation of the insurance business he was engaged in; the running account of the disputed Hayes/Tilden Election of 1876; the comments on his duties as examiner of teachers for the city schools in Zanesville. All these we have omitted, despite their interest. But probably 85 percent or more of the content of the letters as a whole is "Shakespearian."

40. There is a 251st letter to Norris (3 Dec. 1874) in the Furness Memorial Library, Philadelphia; Norris passed it on to Furness for use in a later printing of the *Variorum Macbeth* because it shows that a famous emendation claimed by Richard Grant White at *Mac*. 3.6.7–10 is attributable to Andrew Becket.

41. I.e., it happens, the style of the *MLA Handbook for Writers of Research Papers, Theses, and Dissertations* (New York: Modern Language Association, 1977), section 14f.

42. G. Blakemore Evans et al., eds., *The Riverside Shakespeare* (Boston: Houghton Mifflin, 1974) is our textual authority for Shakespeare. If Crosby's citation is off locus by more than five lines from the *Riverside Edition*'s lineation, we supply the latter.

43. See letter 77 in this edition; Furness also seems to have known Whiter, as he cites him on the fishmonger passage in *Ham*. without crediting Crosby, who had pointed out the relevant Whiter commentary to him.

44. See letters 75, 89, et passim. James O. Halliwell-Phillipps wrote a pamphlet in defense of Capell (see note 2 to letter 51), but the slanders of Steevens and Malone were still current in Crosby's generation.

45. Dewey Ganzel's attempt (1982) to exculpate John Payne Collier has not been widely accepted. It is noteworthy in the present context that Ganzel's argument postulates scholarly fraud by others. See *Fortune and Men's Eyes: The Career of John Payne Collier* (New York and London: Oxford University Press, 1982). Crosby believed Collier innocent, as few people did in his day; his theory was that Collier was Cunningham's dupe. See note 7 to letter 114 for an alternative to this theory.

46. A full account of transatlantic literary piracy in the nineteenth century remains to be written. When it is undertaken the Crosby letters will have something to contribute, as Crosby's detective work exposes several piracies of Shakespeare editions. For a preliminary account of one of these, see "New Information About Some Nineteenth-Century Shakespeare Editions from the Letters of Joseph Crosby," *Papers of the Bibliographical Society of America* 71 (1977): 279–94 (280–87 esp.). Cf. the *Index* to MS. Y.c. 1372 s.v. *piracy, literary.*

47. Crosby also throws light on the private lives of his fellow scholars. White's sexual

promiscuousness, Furnivall's vitriol and arrogance, Andrew Brae's embittered poverty, C. M. Ingleby's singing. Furness's deafness and his financial troubles with early volumes of the *Variorum*, and the sad disappointment of Hudson and Collier in their sons all are touched on in Crosby's correspondence with Norris.

48. Cf. Crosby's comments on the editors of Horace and Milton (35; 151).

49. Virtue and Yorston placed about one hundred subscriptions in Zanesville and prophesied a nationwide sale of one hundred thousand. The ethical implications of Crosby's role in marketing the edition, the distinction between wholesale dissemination of real culture and catchpenny fraud, and the impact that the Virtue and Yorston edition had on Zanesville's intellectual life all can be found passim in this edition. See "Virtue & Yorston ('Imperial' Edn.)" s.v. "Sh., William: Collected Edns." in the Index.

50. Samuel Crosby died in October 1878, after the existing correspondence with Norris breaks off. By that time Crosby's financial affairs may have been in serious enough condition to require that any legacy be applied to other purposes than a Shakespeare edition.

51. The phenomenon is not confined to the Victorians; as a check of lexical glosses in the Shakespeare editions published since World War II will show, an apt bit of interpretation and phrasing often shows up in several editors' work, even now.

52. Crosby was distressed about the allusive euphemisms of Shakespeare commentators. In letter 173 he says that "our 'chaste commentators' " ought to be forced into frankness—or silenced—about the meaning of Shakespeare's bawdy.

53. Some of Crosby's shrewdest interpretations (e.g., the "wappened widow" in *Timon* and the "overscutch'd huswives" in *2 Henry IV*—both in letter 55) eluded Partridge entirely. Some readings of this sort are seen as Crosby saw them by E. A. M. Colman in *The Dramatic Use of Bawdy in Shakespeare* (London: Longman, 1974). Others have, so far as we are aware, been made by no editor or commentator.

54. For a single list of the Crosby explications included in this edition, see the Index, s.v. "explications, Crosby's." For each play there is a seriatim listing of *all* passages in it that are in any way discussed by Crosby in our excerpts (see s.v. "Shakespeare, William: Works").

55. In our annotations we have taken the Arden (where published), Pelican, Riverside, and Bevington as representative of "modern editions."

56. A second instance is the use of the word *memorable* in *Henry V* (discussed in letter 241). Crosby offered to write further about this phenomenon for Norris, but he seems not to have done so. For the relation of Caroline Spurgeon's *Shakespeare's Imagery and What It Tells Us* (1935) to the methods of the New Criticism, see S. Viswanathan, *The Shakespeare Play as Poem: A Critical Tradition in Perspective* (Cambridge and New York: Cambridge University Press, 1980).

57. A dreadful blunder about the meaning of a passage in *Cymbeline* is discussed in letter 124.

58. Although he does not do so, Crosby might logically have leveled the same qualified charge at Edward Dowden, also a student of German Shakespearian interpretation. The periodization of the Shakespeare canon in his *Shakspere: A Critical Study of His Mind and Art* (1875) is another kind of schematic approach which equally threatens to take precedence over the plays themselves.

59. For a further account of the potential interest and importance of Joseph Crosby, see John W. Velz, "Joseph Crosby and the Shakespeare Scholarship of the Nineteenth Century," *Shakespeare Quarterly* 27 (1976): 316–28.

One Touch
of Shakespeare

11:* 8 January 1875

. . . I sent off a long letter to Hudson[1] this A.M. on a reading he wishes to introduce into the Tempest. It is altogether misplaced, incongruous, & un-Shakespearian; yet after all arguments, which appeared so plain he *could* not but see the inadmissibility of his conjecture, he still adheres to it, like an old hen to her one chicken. You cannot imagine what a pleasant time I have had, & am having, going through the "Tempest" in this careful & critical way. *If* I only had a *mate* like *yourself* to tell my discoveries & lucubrations to, instead of Mr. Hudson, I should be *happy*. He is simply an old *absorbent*: he grasps & takes all, & wants "more, more"; but gives nothing out when squeezed himself. . . .

[1] Hudson: Henry N. Hudson; C was supplying him with notes for his Harvard Shakespeare in preparation.

15: 16 January 1875

. . . Wouldn't it surprise you to know that Hudson *does not possess* any of the Clarendon Press Series of Sh's Plays, except *Macbeth*, & asks me for their notes on this & that in *Hamlet*, &c.—I told him he could get them for 60 or 75 cents apiece of Macmillan & Co. N. Y., & that they were *sine quâ non* to an editor. He had no *Camb. Edn.*, no *Heath*, nor many[a] others of the commonest works on Sh., until he got them from the Boston library. How an *editor*—a *lecturer*—a *tutor*, &c. of Shak. can manage without a *Cambridge*, or to only have a vol. at a time out of a public library, beats me.

—One thing in the "Phil. S. S.[1] Notes on Tempest" a little astonished me—the number of *typographical errors*. . . . Occasionally a *word*, is misprinted, as, e.g. on p. 60, *tenth* line from top, "fabric" is printed where the right word is "faded"; *fabric* having been caught by the compositor's eye from the line above, where it occurs twice. This shows how these errors came in the First Folio, & how excusable many of them are; as they had no proofreaders then beyond the foreman of the office. . . .

Have you read Prof. Elze's new book yet?[2] I have not had time to do so, but shall shortly. It looks very æsthetical, as German books on Sh. generally are. It would be a hard book to *review* properly; I don't mean by 'reviewing' simply telling what such or such a book *contains*, when & how it was, & is, *printed*, some notice of the *author*, &c., matters of which *reviews* so often consist, & which any scribbler could make up without reading a line of the work itself: but, after close careful reading & getting into the very *spirit* of the writer, to go along with his argument—giving (in brief) an intelligible synopsis or résumé of it, so that a scholar can get the "pith and moment" of it in a short compass, and be able, from the reviewer's exhibition, to point out its fallacies & defects, if they exist, and its accuracy & beauty and *adopt*ability, if *they* exist. *One* such review of a work is worth a dozen such as we get now-a-days; and makes me long for the good old times of Macaulay, Jeffrey, & Carlyle. . . .

I am real glad that you have taken hold of the Shak. Dept. of the *Bibliopolist*[3] in good earnest. It will do both yourself & all of us[b] good. I long ago suggested such a Dept. to Sabin; & he rec'd.[c] my letter, but that ended it— What you say of Halliwell's[d] Life of Shak. has somewhat dampened my ardour for the book. It's true[e] "one must have it": but, as my present finances are so low,[f] I believe I will wait awhile, & get it by & by. It is becoming a matter of doubt with me, whether to buy *every* new thing that has Shakespeare's name upon it, that comes out of the press; or to "wait a leetle," & see from the reviews what is *worth* buying, and then only buy the best. Much unquestionably that is now being published, during what may be termed the Shakespeare rénaissance, will be ephemeral, & except to fill up one's Catalogue, of no earthly use. I believe I would rather "go slow"; take a good thing every now & then, & *read* it, while it is hot, so as to have something in my *head*[g] as well as on my *bookshelves*. I know the temptations[h] of a different course mighty well, & how nice it is to get everything one wants; however, in my case, there is one invincible obstacle,[i] viz. the *want of the needful* to pay for them. . . .

---

[1]Phil. S. S.: Shakspere Society of Philadelphia. For a full account of the Society and its history, see Henry L. Savage, "The Shakspere Society of Philadelphia," *Shakespeare Quarterly* 3 (1952): 341–52.

[2]Prof. Elze's new book: Karl Elze, *Essays on Shakespeare* (1874); the book is a revision and translation of essays originally pubd. in *Shakespeare Jahrbuch*.

[3]Shak. Dept. of the *Bibliopolist*: N edited a column, "Shakespearian Gossip," in Joseph Sabin & Sons' *American Bibliopolist* from February 1875 until the death of the periodical with the April 1877 number.

[a]*Heath*, nor many] *Heath*, ↑nor↓ &many MS.
[b]of us] of [word illegible] MS.
[c]he rec'd] he [word illegible] MS.
[d]Halliwell's] Halliwell[illegible] MS.
[e]It's true] [word illegible] true MS.
[f]low] [word illegible] MS.
[g]in my *head*] [word illegible] my *head* MS.
[h]temptations] tempta[illegible] MS.
[i]obstacle,] obstacle [punctuation illegible] MS.

19:   31 January 1875

. . . So you have at length got your list of "Editions" complete—from
Rowe I to Dyce III.—I heartily congratulate you, and you should be very
proud & thankful.

. . . As for *my* "collection," I am a long, long ways behind you. I still
want, to complete even the *modern* edns.,—the Grand Folios of Halliwell,—
a Warburton,—& a Rowe II.[1] I want also a *better* J. & S.[2] 1773, mine being a
miserably-poorly-bound copy—I don't *count* it. Still, *considering* that my
means are fearfully limited,—Cash *always* "scant," and that I live at so great
a distance from all literary centres & opportunities for finding rare books, I
have to look on the result of my 10 years work of collecting with a good
degree of self-complacency.[a] I have nearly, now, 100 editions of the Complete Works, and not a scrabby one among them, except that 1773 copy.
Even the old 1733 Theobald, that I got from you, I have had nicely rebound
in Hf. cf, red polished edges, & you would be surprised to see your old
acquaintance in its new dress. Almost every one of my edns. is both
strongly and beautifully bound—mostly (during the last 3 years) in the
Parker Norris Shakespn style, of Hf. mor. or Hf. cf. or Hf russia, with gilt
tops, silk headbands, uncut tails & edges, &c. I have several beautiful
edns, that are not valuable for their *critical* notes, &c. such as 3 of the fine
Pickering Edns, 3 of the Chiswick Press Edns. &c. I have, too, *Six* of the
very best of Knight's Edns. My list of "Shakespeariana" is *not very far behind*
yours; some things I have, that you yet want; & some I yet want, that you
have. I have also considerably over 100 "Separate Plays," almost all *useful*
for something or other. So you see I also deserve considerable credit for my
industry in gathering up, considering my circumstances & situation. . . .

—When I read, some time ago, in a "Penn Monthly," that you sent me,
an article on "Some Helps to Shakespeare" (I think that was the title), by
Mr. *A. I. Fish*,[3] I was by no means *overwhelmed* with admiration. If he could
do no better than *that*, after 30 years study of Shakesp., God help his
poverty-stricken intellect! While it was as full of self-complacence, & pomposity, as a turkey-cock, it was as *bare* of any *matter*—either *useful* or *ornamental*—as a buzzard's backside![b] Mr. F. may be a good lawyer; but, as you
say, he is certainly no *Shakespearian*, as even the few pages in the "Penn
Monthly" very plainly show. *His* work ("*A. I. F.*") in the "Notes on the
Tempest," I long ago noticed, is, as Hamlet says, "Words, Words, Words";
but when you attempt to *fish* out the "matter, my lord, which you are
reading," you find it "*Vox*, et præterea *nihil.*"—

I am delighted with the 3 Quarto vols. from the *New Sh. Soc.* Mr. P. A.
Daniel seems to have done his work most carefully. These vols. are a real
boon to us all—beautiful & very **valuable**, As you well say, they will amply,
to most, supply the place of the old originals, or the Ashbee-Halliwell

facsimiles. H. R. H. Prince Leopold[4] should have a unanimous vote of thanks for his generosity. We have indeed had a mighty good guinea's worth from the Society for last year. To me, Dr Ingleby's "Still Lion" is abundantly worth the price of the year's subscription. I cannot *begin* to tell you how much I have been *delighted* and *instructed* by it. I always dislike exceedingly to differ with *you* in any opinion of books or men: but here I cannot help it. You say you found it "*dry reading*," but "persevered to the end,"—as though you were performing some laborious duty. I found it the very opposite of "dry": every line, every word, is piquant, and witty, at the same time that it is inculcating the *best* principles of Shakespearian inter- pretation, and *packed full* of the choicest bits of the most needed illustration. I will tell you what *I* did. I thought so much of it, & found so exquisite a gratification in its too few pages, that I would only permit myself to read a little bit at once, so as to make it *last longer*; and I was heartily sorry—"yes, faith, heartily"—when my dainty repast came to an end. I then com- menced it again, & have gone through it now *three* times, so as have it at my fingers' ends. Take only one exposition; and it is but *one* sample of a *dozen*, or a *score*, similar; that of the line in *As You Like It*, "One inch of delay more is a South-sea of *discovery*."[5] Here is a passage that has perplexed & puzzled all the edd. & commentators,—not one of whom has *understood* it, or if he did, he has[c] at least failed to explain it.—The Doctor in a few words makes it all plain—apropos—harmonious. And he is unquestionably *right*. You *know he is right*, as soon as he has told you, & you wonder how you have come *not to see* it before, & *why* so simple a sentence should have worried you so long. I merely name this as a *sample*: there are lots more just as *good*: and he not only gives illustrations and expositions of many of the worst twisted-up passages in Shak., but *classifies* them, and lays down rules for making similar expositions ones self. Dry reading!! It is **charming**. While it is plain enough that a vast amount of *thought* has been expended on these few short pages, yet there is a jocoseness, mixed with its sound, *good sense*, that makes it light, agreeable, & exceedingly pleasant. He is afraid of none of them, who may, or may not, adopt his views,—critic or criticaster,—he strikes right and left; if Staunton, or Dyce, happen to be in the wrong, he gets it as heavy as Zachary Jackson, or "Mr. Perkins- Ireland."[6] I have not been as well pleased with a book of Shak*n* criticism for a very long time. Arrowsmith's "Editors and Commentators of Shake- speare" is another favourite of mine, in this line; so is Mr. Brae's "Collier, Coleridge, & Shakespeare," and "Prospero's Clothes-line." These are all little unpretending books; but I tell you they *show the scholar*, & repay study. I am glad that I kept hammering away at Ingleby, until I got him started on a new edn. of the "Still Lion." In a late letter he says: "Thanks to you,[7] and one other friend, in England, I have been induced to revise & enlarge my "Still Lion," & hope soon to send you a presentation copy." He then goes on to call my attention to the use he has made of *modern authors* in the

illustration of Sh.'s Text, e.g. Sir W. Scott, Sir Joshua Reynolds, Thos. Carlyle, Dr Caird,[8] & Mrs. H. Beecher Stowe. This is indeed a novel mode, &
he makes an effective use of it. There are, indeed, *two* places where I am
compelled to differ with the learned LL.D. *in toto.* One is in his *reading* of
that vexed crux in the Tempest, "Most busy least when I do it,"[9] which he
(after Bullock)[d] would read "Most *busiliest* when I do it." In my "excursus"
on this line, I have satisfactorily proved, **(to myself,)** what the *reading* &
interpretation here should be: and I think "busiliest" is about as awkward a
word—(fancy, "Most busiliest"!)—as could well be invented. The other is
in that line in *Timon*—"In a wide sea of *wax.*"[10] This is the passage, you
remember, on the Doctor's explanation of which, (making *wax* a *noun,*
signifying "growth,") Mr. Dyce devotes three pages of his Glossary, (9th
vol. of his 2nd edn.)—and gives Ingleby such a terrible raking. Here, I
humbly think, Mr Dyce is incontestably right, and the Dr wrong. There
never *was* such a noun as *wax* in that sense, (altho' the *verb,* undoubtedly,
has such a meaning,) and never will be, either in Shakespeare, or in any
other Author, ancient or modern. The word "wax" I think is unquestionably corrupt; but I cannot tell what to substitute for it: Coll. MS. Corr.[11] has
"verse," which is as *flat* "as a cat's face"; Staunton's conj. "tax," for *taxation,*
in the sense of *satirical reproach,* gives the meaning that is required; but it is
very harsh. I think "taxing" would be better; and it occurs in exactly that
sense in "As You Like It," where Jaques says: (II.7.70 *seq.*)—

> "Who cries out on pride,
> That can therein tax any private party?
> X X X X X* if he be free,
> Why then my *taxing* like a wild-goose flies,
> Unclaim'd of any man."—

After all, the old fol. word *wax* [waxe] *may be right*; alluding to the ancient
English, as well as Roman, method of covering tablets with a thin coating
of *wax,* and so writing on them with a sharp pointed instrument—a "style";
and including at the same time, (a not uncommon thing with Shakespeare,) the idea of the *flexibility* of wax, as compared to the poet-speaker's
matter of his poem, which he could mould into any form he pleased. But I
see I am running off on my own *hobby,* and forgetting that I am, most likely,
boring you nearly to death with my verbal criticisms. . . .

It was very kind of Mrs. Norris to undertake that work for Mr. Grant
White.[12] I might have *attempted* it, to gratify him, but I did not relish the
very *cool* way in which he asked the favour. He said he had somehow
formed an idea that I was a "man of leisure"; & after some flattering
remarks on a letter I wrote him, several months ago, insinuated that I

---

*X's: Crosby's version of asterisks (throughout).

would only be too delighted to perform the task to gratify *him*, & do something for *him*, that he could, indeed, do very much better himself, only he was too lazy. I don't admire his condescending manner one bit; so I told him plainly that I had something else to do just now.

—I am glad you had so enjoyable a visit from Prof. Hart.[13] He sent me his photograph—a most excellent one by the by, made in Canada—and he looks like a very gentlemanly & well-informed person. As you say, a great many of these Professors *think* they know "all about Shakespeare," when if you come to pin them down to any particular point, they are often *fishy*[14] in their information. No doubt Hart thinks he knows[15] a great sight more about the "Portraits" than *you* do; & yet I'll bet a "ten" you could settle him on the third question.—I did not see that Birmn. paper containing the burlesque diary of Dawson[16] in the U.S.—No doubt the allusion is to *your dinner*, as the *menu* was pubd., you know, in a Birmn. paper. "The original *Bill* of Fare" is good. . . . In England it has been, & is, the most common thing to put Shakespearian mottoes to the *Carte*; witness the numerous Bills of Fare that Timmins[17] has sent us. None of them, however, could begin to compare with *yours*, either in aptness or originality.—. . .

[1] a Rowe II: i.e., a Rowe III (1714); see note 1 to letter 101.

[2] J. & S.: Johnson & Steevens.

[3] *A. I. Fish*: Dean of the Sh Society of Philadelphia and a charter member. The Dean presided over the biweekly meetings at which Sh was read aloud and commented on. The flavor of the Society is conveyed in the obituary eulogy of Fish pubd. in *Robinson's Epitome of Literature* 1 June 1879, p. 87. After he had been excluded for years from membership, N was proposed (probably by H. H. Furness) when his edn. of Boydell's *Shakespeare Gallery* appeared in 1874; later in this letter C compared the Society to Lord Chesterfield who, after snubbing Samuel Johnson, sought him out when the *Dictionary* appeared. But Fish and the other members declined to elect N in the end; one adverse vote would be enough to disqualify a candidate.

[4] H. R. H. Prince Leopold: patron of Daniel's New Shakspere Society edn. of *Rom.* quartos; see also note 1 to letter 232.

[5] "One inch . . . *discovery*": *AYL* 3.2.196–97. "Celia's *inch* of delay in answering Rosalind's questions has cast her upon a *South Sea*—a vast and unexplored ocean—of discovery i.e., revelation" *Still Lion* (1875), pp. 80–81—this explication is not in the original *Still Lion*, *Shakespeare Jahrbuch* 2 (1867): 196–243. The alternative is to interpret the phrase as "tedious as the long delays on exploratory voyages to the South Seas" (Bevington edn., 1980).

[6] "Mr. Perkins-Ireland": the "manuscript corrector" in John Payne Collier's "Perkins Folio," a copy of F2; C joins Perkins to Ireland to indicate Ingleby's belief that the annotations in the Perkins Folio are forgeries. C agreed about this, but did not ascribe those forgeries to Collier himself, as most contemporary Sh scholars did.

[7] "Thanks to you: See Introduction, above, p. 14 and note 5 to the Introduction.

[8] Dr Caird: probably Edward (1835–1908), Master of Balliol, a prolific writer on philosophy and religion.

[9] "Most busy least when I do it": *Tmp.* 3.1.15; "Bullock" is an error for Bulloch (John).

[10] "In a wide sea of *wax*": *Tim.* 1.1.47.

[11] Coll. MS. Corr.: Collier's "manuscript corrector"—see "Mr. Perkins-Ireland," note 6 above.

[12] that work for Mr. Grant White: the compilation of a Sh bibliography "for the last 10 or 12 years" (letter 15).

[13] Prof. Hart: John Seely Hart, at that time Professor of Rhetoric and English Literature at the College of New Jersey (Princeton).

[14] *fishy*: alluding to Asa I. Fish's inadequate Sh scholarship.

[15] Hart thinks he knows: H was to publish a somewhat romantic account of the portraits in the *Avon Shakespeare* (1879), an American rpt. of Clark & Wright.

[16] Dawson: George Dawson, Birmingham England man of letters and lecturer, visited America in the fall of 1874; N helped to entertain him at a Shn dinner (20 November).

[17] Timmins: Samuel Timmins, Director of the Shakespeare Memorial Library, Birmingham.

[a] self-complacency] self-| complacency MS.

[b] backside] back–| side MS.

[c] did, he has] did, ↑he↓ has MS.

[d] (after Bullock)] ↑(after Bullock)↓ MS.

20:   6 February 1875

. . . I read R. Grant White's note, & herewith return it. I can see from it, what you & Mrs. Norris have accomplished for him. I suspected the task would be no trifling job; and it is just like your kind, generous, disposition, to do this work for him, & he *ought* to be *exceedingly grateful*. I suppose he is. This "list," as a Supplement to Bohn's Lowndes (1862–1875)[a] is a very valuable document—invaluable to *all* Shakespearians, as it is *unique*—I know of nothing like it, that has been done, bringing up the list to present date; and it should be *printed*, in a small pamphlet; it would be greedily snapped up I tell you, at 50 cents or 75 cents a copy. Don't you think more than enough would be sold, even in the U.S., to say nothing of England, to reimburse the expense of printing, and leave a good balance for you? One thing, at all events, should be done, whether you publish it in pamphlet form or not, & that is, it should be printed, (a few pages at a time) in the "Bibliopolist." It would add a hundred fold to the value and demand for the Bibliopolist for 1875. Dont you think it a good suggestion? As you undoubtedly have a copy of your work, and it is now accomplished, I think more persons than R. G. White ought to be benefitted by it. Think of it seriously. . . .

I see that you have been getting some new books that I have not seen yet. Among them the "Shakespeare Argosy." How is it? Good, or nothing but another Compilation of quotations from the 'divine Williams'? I have so many of that kind of books, like Dodd's Beauties, Price's Wisdom & Genius of Sh., Routledge's, Clarke's, "Mottoes & Aphorisms,"—Shakspn Anthology, &c. &c. &c., and they are all so much alike, that I am about resolved to buy no more of them, unless they are on some novel plan—or very pretty—or have some distinguishing mark from the general "ruck" of quotation-books. I see this "Argosy" costs 6/_, & the same money might buy something better.—. . .

—I fully concur in every word you say about *Furnivall*. He is almost sublime in his *impudence*. Considering his very limited reading & knowledge of Shakespeare, it is amusing to see him patting old Sh. scholars on the back—patronizing them, as Dogberry does[b] old Verges, "a good old man, Sir, and he will be talking"; "he speaks a little off the matter, Sir; an old man, Sir, and his wits are not as blunt as, God help, I would desire they were"; "When the age is in, the wit is out: God help us! it is a world to see: an two men ride of a horse, one must ride behind."— —Did you read his "Introduction"? It is almost sickening to see a man who has just *crammed-up* on Shakespeare, within a few months, talking in the manner he does of the *Variorum editors*, and other Shakespearian scholars, who have devoted a life-time to the study. He thinks he knows it all. Owing to the "Gifts that God gives, Sir," he got himself appointed as the "most *senseless* and fit person" to be the Director of the New Shakspere Society, and he *alone* must "carry the lantern." He well sustains the parallel,[1] and all that is wanting is some neighbour Seacole, with his pen and inkhorn, "to specify, when time and place shall serve, that" he is "an *ass!*" If *ignorance* and *presumption* were the distinguishing marks of worthy "Master Constable," who had "had losses, go to," certainly Bro. Furnivall is as well entitled by nature to the *long ears* as his immortal prototype.—"Masters, remember that I am an ass; though it be not written down, yet forget not that I am an ass!"—. . .

I have . . . received two pamphlets from London, one "Irving as *Hamlet*" by E. R. Russell; the other O'Carroll's *Address* to a Debating Society of a College in Ireland.[2] You probably have these also: and I think you will be pleased with Russell's tract. His analysis of the character of *Hamlet* is very elaborate; and he speaks very eulogistically indeed of *Henry Irving*, the new Actor of the character at the Lyceum in London. It is a nicely-printed & well-written tract, and you will not fail to read it. I noticed a **new reading**, in one of his quotations, that I have no doubt is nothing more than a press-error; but it is a good illustration of some of the typographical errors in the *folio*. See p. 46, describing Irving's acting of Hamlet during the play-scene; how he flung himself into the chair that the King had vacated, his body swaying the while from side to side, in irrepressible excitement, and re-cited there—"though the roar of applause into which the audience is sur-prised renders it barely audible"—the well-known stanza, "Why, let the stricken deer go limp."[3]—Of course the text is "go *weep*" in every ed. of Hamlet from the year 1603 to the year 1875. I presume the type-setter[c] had never heard, or read, of Jaques' *deer*, in "As You Like It," "That from the hunter's aim had *ta'en a hurt*, x x x And the big round *tears*[4] coursed one another down his innocent nose In piteous chase"; and he undoubtedly[d] thought the most *natural* thing for a "*stricken* deer" to do was *to limp*; & so he set it up "*limp*," and thought *weep* a mistake in the MS., and that he had made all snug and right. And unquestionably, if we had found the word *limp* in the original, we should have retained it as a *natural reading*, and poured out our "vials of wrath" on some *Jackson* or *Keightley*, *Becket* or *Bailey*,[5] who, because the word in the corresponding rhyme was "sleep," *would* argue that the word here ought to be amended to "weep," and cite the above-named Jaques' deer as a proof of the weeping proclivities of a wounded stag, and of Shakespeare's intuitive knowledge of *Natural History*. Then, we should have had Charles Knight, and J. P. Collier (before he found his "*Corr. fo.* 1632"),[6] Malone, and Grant White, fighting to the bitter end for the "integrity" of the Folio; Dyce would have called the emendation "wanton and tasteless,"[7] but probably have adopted it, notwithstanding, in his 2d & 3d Editions; and *Hudson* would probably have "suggested" another word, very much more to the point than either; the "Commentaries" would have occupied about three pages in Mr. Furness' "new Variorum" *Hamlet*; and Brae, and Ingleby, and Corson,[8] & J. Parker Norris, and J Crosby, and all other lovers of the "Grand Old Folio" would have *limped*, with the "stricken deer," to the present day. "Dost like the picture?"—

The "Address" by the Rev. J. J. O'Carroll, **S. J.** is a curious production, & certainly ought to be *exposed*, & I have been greatly tempted to expose it. It purports to be an address on *Eloquence*, by the writer, to the "Historical Debating Society" of what I infer to be a *Jesuit* College in Ireland: but it is really a most *jesuitical* attempt to make out Shakespeare to have been a *Jesuit*; because, in writing his Henry VIII, he adapted a quotation, on the character of Cardinal Wolsey,[9] from a certain *Edmund Campion*, a Jesuit, who wrote a little History of Ireland, and was executed for Conspiracy against Queen Elizabeth, as a traitor, in 1581. Of *Father Campion* our author has great difficulty in finding language sufficiently eulogistic: "his name, though scarcely found in the annals of literature, is a Missionary's and a *Martyr's* name, the name of one of the *noblest heroes* of this earth; a name which there is at this moment hope to see solemnly pronounced Blessed by the Church";—"Mainly known by having very early died a *glorious death*— the death of a traitor, under Queen Elizabeth." He goes on to ask, "*Why* should Shakespeare have copied? And *why*, of all men under the Sun, should he have copied from Edmund Campion?" &c. &c. Then Mr. O'Carroll propounds *his theory*—here the cat jumps clear out of the bag—which is, that our Poet "copied" the substance of these lines, either, because he [Shakespeare] was an adherent of the "old faith," or that he directly or indirectly had intercourse with Jesuits, or the books of Jesuits; or, rather, that he had sometime seen in the library of the splendid Earl of Leicester, at Kenilworth, the little tract which Campion wrote on Ireland; that his keen eyes noted this very passage; and that the same bold arm which once, it is said, laid low Justice Lucy's deer, seized without hesitation on that obscure Irish tract, because it suited his purpose in the play to "cog" (as O'Carroll calls it), or as we say *to cabbage* this passage! Our Saviour said of the Pharisees that they compassed sea and land to "make *one proselyte*": but Father O'Carroll has a tougher job than that, when he attempts to make a Jesuit of our beloved Shakespeare.—Now the *fact* is, that Shakespeare found this passage, containing the character of Wolsey, in his old, trusty, stand-by, and authority for his history & facts, viz. *Holinshed*, who quotes it at length, and ascribes it to Campion. If O'Carroll had looked into the *Variorum*, or almost any edition of Shak. with Notes, he would there have found the whole matter, & seen where Shakesp. "copied" from. He could have seen too, at a glance, the *difference* beteen the *coarse* prose of Campion [where he speaks of Wolsey as being "some Prince's *bastard*," &c.], and the beautiful, eloquent, & natural lines of Shakespeare. There is probably no passage in Sh., where the remark *"nihil tetigit quod non ornavit"*[10] is more truly exemplified. Shakespeare used this quotation as he used any other fact of history that he needed for his Plays: he found it, in its exceedingly raw state, in his old favourite Holinshed, (Vol. II. p. 917, Ed. 1587,) where it was *common property*; he breathed into its nostrils the breath of life; put it into the mouth of *Griffith*, to speak to the dying Queen Catharine, and thereby made the miserable old defunct Cardinal *immortal!* You see now how perfectly absurd, and ridiculous, & groundless, is the basis of the Rev. gentleman's argument to prove Shakespeare a Jesuit. The Poet, in writing this grand passage, had no more thought of, or care for, *Father Campion,* or his "Martyr's Crown," than he had of the man in the moon. . . .

[1] He well sustains the parallel: Ignoring C's warnings, N later printed this portrait of Furnivall as Dogberry in "Shakespearian Gossip" (without attributing it to C); F responded angrily though he and N eventually made peace.

[2] a College in Ireland: Clongowes Wood College, Dublin; O'Carroll is J. J. O'Carroll, S.J.

[3] "Why, let the stricken deer go limp": Cf. *Ham.* 3.2.271.

[4] And the big round *tears* . . . chase": *AYL* 2.1.38–40.

[5] *Jackson* or *Keightley, Becket* or *Bailey*: Zachariah Jackson, Thomas Keightley, Andrew Becket, and Samuel Bailey all pubd. books of proposed emendations of Sh's text.

[6] *"Corr. fo.* 1632": the Perkins Folio.

[7] "wanton and tasteless": In the Preface to *A Few Notes on Shakespeare* (1853), Dyce referred to the emendations in the Perkins Folio as "ignorant, tasteless, and wanton," but in his second Sh edn. (1864–67), he adopted many of them without acknowledgement, as Collier pointed out.

[8] Dyce . . . Brae . . . Ingleby . . . Corson: Alexander Dyce, Andrew Brae, C. M. Ingleby, Hiram Corson; all, like C, were distinguished by their textual conservatism—Dyce was an editor, Corson a professor at Cornell University, Ingleby and Brae authors of books of explication of Sh's text. (N pubd. a revised version of this squib in "Shakespearian Gossip" June 1875, and C repubd. it in *The Literary World* 17 July 1880, p. 247.)

[9] a quotation, on the character of Cardinal Wolsey: *H8* 4.2.48–54.

[10] *"nihil tetigit quod non ornavit"*: Paraphrased from Dr. Johnson's epitaph for Oliver Goldsmith, Westminster Abbey (see Boswell's *Life* s.v. 22 June 1776).

[a] (1862–1875)] ↑(1862–1875)↓ MS.

[b] as Dogberry does] ~~like~~ ↑as↓ Dogberry does MS.

[c] type-setter] type-| setter MS.

[d] he undoubtedly] ↑he↓ undoubtedly MS.

28: 11 March 1875

. . . The only article you have published in *The Bibliopolist* in which I was the least disappointed, was that on the "Mask." This is *your forte*; & I expected too much. But sometime you must give us all your arguments *pro*

& *con*, à la Prof. Hart.[1] You could write a *better* article on the subject than his: & it is needed. While the brief one in the Feb. is nicely worded, & *good*, as far as it goes, it does not give us "outside barbarians" any clue to the *authenticity* or otherwise of the now famous Beckel Mask.[2] One of our newspapers wanted to copy it; but I told him to wait; we should have a longer one, & more satisfactory in *history* & *argument*, ere long, I was sure. The logic of your concluding sentence *seems* faulty: that is, it does not state the argument as you mean it. Your proposition is: the *Stratford bust* & the *Droeshout print* are unquestionably genuine; authentic likenesses of Sh.; they do not in the least resemble each other; the Becker Mask does not resemble either; therefore the "Becker"—what? *is* Sh.? or is *not* Sh? The same argument would apply to a portrait of *Geo. Washington*. E.g. the Stratford bust *is* Sh.; the Droeshout *is* Sh.; there is no *likeness* between them; the *Geo. Washington Port.* does not look like either one; *ergo*, the *Geo. Washington may* be *Shakespeare*. The way you want to state your argument, I think, is; that no fair argument can be drawn against the authenticity of the Becker Mask, *because* it bears no resemblance to either of the genuine Shn. portraits that we have, *inasmuch* as neither of these bears any resemblance to the other.—

Please excuse my *fun*. You are a dear good fellow; & have relieved my mind of a weight, by your only too kind & friendly letters.— . . .

[1]à la Prof. Hart: See *Scribner's Monthly*, July 1874.
[2]Beckel [i.e., Becker] Mask: a deathmask found in Mainz, Germany, in 1849 by Dr. Ludwig Becker, who proposed it as Sh's; N credulously accepted its authenticity. See S. Schoenbaum, *Shakespeare's Lives* (1970), 468–70, for an account of the mask and of the controversy that surrounded it in the last half of the nineteenth century.

29: 14 March 1875

. . . I have just finished—*and copied*—my last batch of notes, on the *Tempest*, for Mr. Hudson, & will send them to-morrow. I have thoroughly ransacked everything on the Play—including the new C. P. Edn.[1]—(read 3 times through)—the Phil. Sh. Soc. notes—(read 4 or 5 times); Jephson's, and everybody else's notes,—good, bad, & indifferent—not forgetting Wilson's "Caliban, the missing link." I see Wilson[2] makes that same conj. "shall *forth at* vast of night" for "Shall *for that* vast of night" &c., which a Mr. Thos. White proposed, & which Dr. Ingleby so strenuously advocates, & the C. P. Edn. condemns. I don't know who has the *priority*[3] of the conj.—*White* or *Wilson*, as I don't know when Thos. White pubd his. Wilson's was in 1873.—(Preface dated July 3. 1872, however.) It is very ingenious, but not sound, i.e. in my humble opinion. As Aldis Wright says, "*at* vast of night" is unnatural; & who ever heard of "*work exercise* on" anyone? . . .

—As soon[a] as your hand is well again, and writing comfortable, you

must not delay your work on the "Portraits." Really you ought to get it out by next Fall.[4] You have the *matter* all ready: all it needs is shaping up.—Let me thank you for the little cut from the *Droeshout*: it is excellent, don't you think so? I made it into a *frontispiece* to my working copy of the "Globe," where I shall see it, & remember you, daily & nightly. . . .

—I have 3 or 4 more of Wilkes' "Spirit of the Times," each containing a slice of his "Shakespeare, from an *American* point of view." I trust there are but *few* Americans who adopt his "point of view." I presume you have read them. They really are hardly worth mentioning. You know of the old Horatian proverb,[5] "Ne *sutor* ultra *crepidam*"; & Wilkes had better confine his pen[b] to what he understands,[6] dogs & horses, guns & gambling. He knows how to "groom" Heenan;[7] but the "Bacon" trade is beyond his *means*; and when he undertakes to write on Shakespeare—(like a fool rushing in where an angel would fear to tread—) his *ignorance* is only matched by his *egotism*. But enough of *him*!—"an ounce of civet, good apothecary."—

Mr. Timmins has sent me 2 papers; one, "The London Telegraph," contains a well-written editorial on *Shakespeare, Hamlet & Irving.* The other, "The Birmingham Morning Post," contains a notice, with extracts, of Mr. George Dawson's article, (pubd in the "Gentleman's Magazine,") "In Ohio." I suppose we shall get the Magazine from Smith,[8] as soon as it is out. The notice is from the proof sheets. It must be an exceedingly interesting article; and I am in a terrible hurry to get it. I had no idea that Dawson was so near me, as *Marietta.* He was there, I judge, quite a little while. I should surely have run down & met him, had I known it. Marietta is almost next-door-neighbour to Zanesville,—just at the mouth of our river, the *Muskingum*—not *Muskinghum* as they have got it. Of course you have these papers from Timmins. But, if not, let me know, and I will send you mine. I should like to know the *name* of the gentleman at Marietta, at whose residence Mr. Dawson was so hospitably entertained. "Newcomerstown" I know well—a little railroad, country, village; & I can imagine the kind of a breakfast he got at "the hotel." I am very sorry I did not meet Dawson, as from all I learn about him, from yourself & elsewhere, he must be a "brick,"—a real clever, genial, amiable fellow.—. . .

—I told you, I think, that I had bought a copy of *Chaucer*, edited by Tyrwhitt. I have since bought the two issues of Chaucer in the Clarendon Press Series; one, "The Prologue," "The Knight's Tale," & "The Nonne-Preste's Tale," edited by *Morris;*[9] the other, "The Prioresse's Tale," "The Monke's Tale," "Sire Thopas," and several others, from the *Canterbury Tales*, edited by *Skeat*. They are splendid little books, edited with the same care that the C. P. Edn. of *Sh.'s plays* is: the most accurate, revised, *texts*,— full Introductions & Notes, & a copious explanatory Glossary to each. All the books in this "C.P. Series," that I have seen, are excellent. What an immense amount of care, & scholarship, is expended on these works, for one or two shillings apiece. There were no such helps to acquiring a ripe

English education, when I was a boy. Latin, Greek, and mathematics: but if we boys had, or took, a taste for reading an *English Poet*, we had to take it as we found it, pure & simple. *Now* there seems to be the same care in *editing* an English Classic, as a Greek or Latin one; & why not? There certainly is a noble lot of scholars in England now, engaged on Old English, & middle English literature. Look at the new publications by Macmillan & others, every week,—educational—historical, &c. I am gradually picking up some of these valuable books, as I can afford the time & money. One grand acquisition I have made to my library is Masson's Edition of *Milton*, just issued by Macmillan, 3 vols., demy 8vo., uniform in size, type, paper, binding, with the *Cambridge Shakespeare*. It cost £2..2.., about $15..00 here. *It is a noble work*. I fully intend to go through it at an early day. It has 3 portraits of Milton; facsimiles of handwriting, &c. essays on his English; *bibliographical, biographical*, & *expository*, Introductions; copious Notes, &c., and a fine large type, accurate *Text* from the first & best copies & MSS.—I had already 2 editions, one the 4to *Baskerville* Edn., 2vols.; but this of Prof. Masson caps them all: decidedly the *best Milton* ever pubd.—But I must get *to bed*. It is away past "the witching time of night," & so I wish you "Good night & pleasant dreams."—. . .

[1]C. P. Edn.: Clarendon Press Edition of W. Aldis Wright. (W. G. Clark had collaborated in the first four vols. but withdrew after those had been pubd.)

[2]*Wilson*: Sir Daniel Wilson.

[3]who has the *priority*: White's "Notes on Shakespeare" were written in 1793, pubd. in 1853. The passage is *Tmp.* 1.2.327.

[4]you ought to get it out by next Fall: C continued to prod N; the book however, was not pubd. until 1885, long after the correspondence had broken off.

[5]Horatian proverb: Not in Horace. According to tradition, Apelles the painter quipped, "The cobbler should keep to his last," when a shoemaker, having criticized the depiction of footwear in one of Apelles's paintings, went on to comment on other elements of the picture.

[6]what he understands: George Wilkes's *The Spirit of the Times* was a sporting paper. Wilkes argued against the Baconian theory; he also attacked Sh as an advocate of decadent aristocracy and an adherent to Roman Catholicism (cf. letter 176).

[7]Heenan: John Carmel Heenan, a prizefighter.

[8]Smith: A. Russell Smith, the London bookseller C bought from most often.

[9]*Morris*: Richard Morris.

[a]. . .—As soon] —as soon MS.

[b]his pen] ↑his pen↓ MS.

32:   23 March 1875

. . . I remarked in one place that I had sent you "a corollary" of notes; and that reminds me to tell you something about the word 'corollary.' You know where it occurs in the Tempest?—Where *Pros.* tells *Ariel* to "bring a corollary, rather than want a Spirit—."[1] The word is derived from *corolla*, the diminutive of *corona*, a crown, garland, &c., and *corollary* was the name given to anything—generally a wreath, bouquet, &c.—given to anyone—

say an actress, e.g.—**over & above** what was due; it was an *extra*-ordinary token of applause for merit; that was not bargained for, hence, "a surplus." But "corollary" means, also, 'an inference or deduction from recognized premisses or facts,' and, more particularly, 'an *additional conclusion, drawn from a proposition already complete.*' This last definition you will readily recognize, if you ever studied *Euclid*, as I am sure you have. Hence it came to mean 'a surplus,' 'a superfluity,' 'a superfluous number,' as here in the *Tempest*, Pros. bids Ariel bring more of his "quality"—more spirits than enough—rather than *want* a spirit. And this makes good enough sense, tho' one has to go a considerable way around to get at it. In "Caliban, the missing link," Dr Wilson rather ingeniously proposed to read, "bring *a whole array*, Rather than want a Spirit.*"—What do you think of it? At the end of the line too, for "pertly," Wilson would read "presently." He thinks "pertly" very inapt here. Ariel had just inquired of Prospero whether he wished "the show" to commence "*presently*," and Pros. answered "Ay, with a twink." The Dr thinks that the line being a long one, the word "presently," at the end of it, had been abbreviated, & so got to be printed "pertly."—So much for that. Wilson at the close of his book ventures to make "some dozen or sixteen" conjectural emendations; but the bulk of them are very injudicious, & totally inadmissible, even in a note. Three or four are worth attention, but that's all.—

To day I received, from A. R. Smith, *Prof. Dowden*'s new book, "Shakspere, his mind and art"; and the March No. of *Macmillan's Magazine*, containing an excellent article by Mr. Fleay, on the *Sonnets*. You must be sure & read it. I intend to read it again. It is a capital & close argument, putting to rout all the notions of immorality, adultery, &c., supposed to attach to the *man* Shakespeare, as deduced from his *Sonnets*. Dowden's book looks well: nicely printed & good type. From the 'Preface' & 'Contents,' I judge it is a very readable & interesting work. I know you will like it: anything relating to the Poet's *life* you are well read up in: much better than I am. I am glad to observe that none of the recent works on Sh. adopts Furnivall's absurd spelling.[2] Wouldn't it be *nice* for you and me to read this book of Dowden's through *together*? I have not yet read Elze. The truth is, I have had "a corollary" of new books lately. . . .

—I have just recd. a letter from Leavitt Bros. Auctioneers, saying that they have bought for me M. Retzsch's volume of engravings, illustrating Shakespeare; also Fitzgerald's Life of Garrick in 2 vols., Hf. mor., uncut, gilt tops, & one or two others. I have no bill of them yet; but I will tell you about them, when they come. Retzsch's plates, (100.) are, as I understand, very different from Howard's. They are *pictures*—& not pen & ink scratches. They are everywhere spoken of in the *highest terms*, as being truly *illustrative* of Shakespeare. . . .

Smith has also sent me a copy of Furnivall's new edn. of *Gervinus*. I did not intend to buy this, as I have a splendid copy of the 1st Edn. in full tree-calf, gilt edges, that cost me $14.—But I observe that the *English* of the 2d. Edn. is improved a trifle here and there; and then you know it contains the Director's Introduction! That of itself is worth ten, or twenty, or even one hundred, times the value of *Gervinus*. I am somewhat surprised at Mr. F's modesty in incorporating his "introduction" with the German Author's book. Of course everybody will be so anxious to read this "introduction" that it will *lift*, as they call it, Monsieur Gervinus into good scholarly society at once, & *introduce* him into good respectable company; and thus make the heavy German book sell fast, & be profitable.—

I want you to do me a little favour; but *not*, mind, until your hand is entirely well, & you can write with ease again. You know I am hard at work on The *Two Gent. of Verona*; and I see by the advertisements that Mr. Halliwell's new "Illustrations of the Life of Shakespeare" says something on the *date* of the composition, and *sources of the plot*, of this play. Now I don't want you to "copy" anything for me; but only just tell me in a few words of your own what Mr. H.'s views are. I know what all the old authorities say on the subject; but I presume that Mr. H. has discovered some *new* matter, or he would not have introduced the subject into his grand new work. . . .

[1] "bring a corollary: *Tmp.* 4.1.57.
[2] Furnivall's absurd spelling: of English generally, not of Sh's name (Dowden did adopt that); C feared that F's position in the New Shakspere Society would disseminate the spelling reforms he advocated.

33:   28 March 1875

. . . I am glad you have got for yourself a copy of the last edn. of Webster's Unabridged Dictionary: and you got it *cheap* enough. I paid $15.00 for mine. You will find it of daily & nightly use & value. I have had one for several years; and I keep it on a little round table, with a revolving top, at my elbow, so I can turn to it, without the trouble of getting up & *going to it*, any moment. It is a *multum in magno*—tho' one might still say 'parvo,' compared with some others; *Latham's*[1] for instance. Altho' my copy is strongly bound in *full russia* (red edges), yet the wear and tear of the binding shows that it has been "Nocturnâ versata manu, versata diurnâ."[2] I confess, however, that the "dictionary of Noted Names of Fiction," &c, and all the various tables of pronunciation of *Scripture, Latin and Greek, biographical & geographical proper names*, have been more used than the great body of the Dictionary. I can always get better satisfaction, either in Etymology or Definition, & especially in *examples* quoted from various sources, from Latham, & Richardson,[3] than I can from Webster. . . . I am very fortunate in my stock of *Dictionaries*.[4] My library boasts of *all* the best. Did I ever tell you how many I had? . . . *and yet*, in none of these Dictionaries, Encyclopædias, or Glossaries, do I find the word "agnosticism," that you refer to; and I don't wonder you are puzzled. I never, as far as I remember, saw[a] it before. It is, I think probably, a coinage of *Ruskin's* fertile brain.[5] It is no doubt derived from α, *non*, and γνωστος, *known*. The term *agnostus* is one devised to express the *obscure nature* of a genus of trilobites (fossil crustaceans) to which it is attached. But what it means when applied to *Shakespeare* I have not the remotest conception; in fact, I might say I am in a blissful state of *"agnosticism."* Very likely the inventor of the term laughed in his sleeve at what he considered a good practical joke which he was perpetrating on the *ignorance* (ἀγνωσια) of his readers. It is just possible that it refers to the *obscurity* that surrounds many phases of Shakespeare's Life, Character, & Works. For instance; there is more or less *agnosticism* how he spelt his name; how *much* Latin & Greek he learned at school; what was his employment during 4 or 5 years of his early manhood; as the old Jews said of our Lord, "How hath this man letters, having never learned?" So, unless we suppose our Great Poet to have been *inspired*, we are all "agnostics" *how*, with his small amount of scholastic education, he could write those matchless, immortal, Poems and Plays, that surpass in natural and intellectual *wisdom*, all that ancient and modern literature had produced; to what *religious* sect or creed he adhered; whether a protestant or a Papist; what *political* party in the state he preferred; whether he ever travelled out of his native island, or even visited Scotland; what he thought of Pythagoras' opinion concerning wild fowl; what was his object and "motive" in writing the *Sonnets*; who "Mr. W. H." was, to whom they were dedicated as their "onlie begetter"; "what *Hamlet* means"; what was the cause of his last illness; what became of his voluminous MSS; whether the Stratford bust, or the Droeshout portrait, is the more correct presentment of his "feature"; or whether the *Becker mask's* claim to authenticity is sound: in fact this list might be almost indefinitely extended of matters relating to this great *fact* of the world's literature—*Shakespeare*,—on which the best informed of us must acknowledge our "agnosticism."—

I herewith return you Mr. Cuyler's letter.[6] It is a miserably poor, stiff, stilted note, and the writer has evidently had but little experience in writing to *gentlemen*. Were it not that this is Easter Sunday, and I have just returned from Church and Communion, where love to your neighbour, & charity for his failings, are inculcated as "inseperable" from the duty of a good Christian, I could make "a heap" of fun out of this note. The more I think of this whole business of your connection with the "Phil. Sh. Soc.," the *madder* I become. If "the Shakspere Society do not need or seek an increase of the number of their members," why, after making asses of themselves in postponing it to the eleventh hour, did they vote to receive you at all, and even urge you, against your better judgment, to consent to have your name submitted? But when they had the chance to *honour themselves*, & their Society, by enrolling you among the members, to instruct their Secretary to send you such a note as this! Ignorant pomposity, *gratui-*

tous insult, sheer *asininity*, could no further go. What sort of "Shake-spearians" are they, when their chosen representative Secretary writes such English as this: "It is of course out of the question that such a membership of the Society as your letter indicates a willingness on your part should exist."—Lord help us! They have studied Shakespeare I fear to precious little purpose. With his "little Latin & less Greek," he never put forth such a sentence as that. Mr. Cuyler should hunt up an old copy of *Lindley Murray*,[7] and "Study" *that* a year as a preparation for studying Shakespeare, and writing a plain sentence to gentleman in an ordinary note. I am very sure that my little boy, 10 years old,[8] would have thrown the paper into the fire, had he found he had penned such a sentence as I have quoted—to say nothing of the schoolboy penmanship, and erroneous orthography; or if he did not, he ought to be whipped. The words "a willingness on your part" have no verb to govern them—have neither object nor subject—*ungrammatical* in the very worst way . . . and yet he to be the Secretary of a Society to which Mr. Furness belongs, I can hardly conceive possible. I can imagine that Mr. Furness' chagrin and mortification at the whole transaction exceeded yours; and I can only repeat, be thankful you are clear of them. *They* could never have been of the least benefit to *you*.—. . .

I did notice the two articles in *Notes & Queries*, by Mr. J. F. Marsh, about his having a copy of the 1664 Fol., supposed from the MS. Notes therein to have belonged to *Pope*. (Wouldn't you like to own it—bad condition as it is in?) I intended to have mentioned them to you, but forgot.[b] They are the first articles in the Numbers of "N. & Q." for Feb. 6th, and Feb 20th./75.[c] They are really quite *curious*; & Mr Marsh writes a very modest note anent them. On one point, however, I humbly beg to differ with him, viz. that "*earlier*-happy" (M.N.D.) is a happy correction of "*earthlier*-happy"[9] of the folios & 4to. The following is my note on the term in my *Sh. Collecta*.[10] "The reading of the old copies is *right*. "Earthlier-happy" is *more* "earthly-happy," a compound word. The *virgin* is thrice blessed as respects the *heaven* for which she prepares herself; but looking only to the *present* world, the other is the happier lot, "*earth*-lier-happy."—Capell suggested "earthly-*happier*," and both Collier & Knight adopted the suggestion; but as Hunter (Jos.) well says, the objections to this are, (1) that it is against authority; (2) that nothing is gained by it; (3) that if there is any difference in the meaning, it is a deterioration, not an improvement; and (4) that it spoils the melody. *Pope* and Johnson proposed "*earlier*-happy"; Steevens "earthly-happy." "————That seems to me a conclusive note, if I did write it myself—in 1871.—. . .

---

[1] *Latham's*: Robert Gordon Latham's revision (1866) of Dr. Johnson's *Dictionary*.

[2] "Nocturnâ versata manu, versata diurnâ.": Varied from Horace, *Ars Poetica* 269; C plays with the literal meaning of *verso* here.

[3] Richardson: Charles Richardson's *A New Dictionary of the English Language* (1836–37).

[4] my stock of *Dictionaries*: C lists and describes more than thirty.

[5] probably, a coinage of *Ruskin's* fertile brain: *Agnostic* was coined by Thomas Henry Huxley in 1869 *(OED)*.

[6] Mr. Cuyler's letter: Theodore Cuyler, a prominent attorney, was Secretary of the Sh Society of Philadelphia 1875–86.

[7] *Lindley Murray: English Grammar* (1795), a standard school text.

[8] my little boy, 10 years old: Albert Crosby (Bertie) was actually twelve at the time, b. 27 December 1862; his twin, Edward James, died within a month of birth. Bertie's elder brother, Charles Fitch, b. 28 February 1860, died within six months. Their mother, Ellen Grosvenor Fitch Crosby, died two years after Edward; her family then adopted Bertie, and took him to live in Cleveland.

[9] *"earthlier-*happy": *MND* 1.1.76.

[10] *Sh. Collecta.*: "Shakespeare Collectanea," a potpourri of offprints, clippings, transcriptions, and original notes on Sh. The Collectanea is presently in the McMillan Shakespeare Collection, Harlan Hatcher Graduate Library, University of Michigan. Such original notes as this one lack from the Collectanea and were presumably retained by C when he sold the collection to Isaac N. Demmon, Curator of the McMillan Library, in 1883. A privately printed descriptive catalogue of the Crosby Collectanea compiled by Susan Cerasano et al. is available in the Hatcher Library.

[a] saw] ~~ever~~ saw MS.
[b] forgot.] forgot.* MS.
[c] They are . . . 75.] ↑*They are . . . 75.↓ MS. [written at top of page].

35:   30 March 1875

My dear Norris:

You must not get out of patience with me for writing you so many notes. But the fact is, I cannot *rest* until I have told you again how *delighted* I am with this copy of "Horace,"[1] which you gave me. I read in it last night till after midnight.—It is the *ne plus ultra* of book-making, in my opinion: a book to make a bibliomaniac go into extacies. Paper old and ribbed,— margins wide, & edges so nice & rough; and then the *typography*—it is simply **exquisite**! What taste you have! I can fancy your eye darting on this book, possessing all the conditions that the most fastidious bibliomaniac exacts, and which are so rarely met with. You should have kept it yourself, to adorn your own library, & gratify your eye and taste. *Here* it will be lost, **except to me**. There is one pair of eyes that will ever ever appreciate it, & never never forget to thank the kind generous-hearted friend who presented it to him. I am going to keep it, in its present state, for a while, before I get it bound. How well it has been preserved—so clean; and then what a splendid edition it is, intrinsically! The notes are admirable; anyone can read this edition, without a dictionary, who knows any Latin at all. How I shall enjoy it! and wish you were with me to enjoy it together. Horace was always my favourite Latin Poet; and I took a prize[2] for the best translation of the "de arte poeticâ," when I was 15 years old. Thanks;—a thousand thanks, for your most kind thoughtfulness. Now I shall say no more; but I *had* to say this much, I am so *delighted* with the book. Yesterday was a gala-day to me, in the book line. Your Horace; and a clean, perfect copy of *Retzsch*'s original edition of the "Shakespeare-Gallery" for Nine Dollars! I pledge you my word of honour, twenty-five dollars would not buy it from me, if I could not get another. I had no idea it was so *good*. I had always heard the work praised, & knew that it had a signal success, when issued, both in Germany & England. I shall never be happy nor content, until I know that *you* have a copy too. The plates of pictures grow on you, the more you look at them. I never saw so much *expression* put into faces—even the animals show it in their looks. They remind me more of Hogarth, and Kenny Meadows, than any other artist. What a *wonderful* imagination the German must have possessed!—He was a *Shakespearian Scholar* too. There are *eight* plays represented, about 13 plates each. I have only examined the "Tempest" yet. The plays are named in Lowndes. You must be sure to get a peep at these "illustrations" as soon as you can. I want to know what your opinion is about them. I want you to have as good a set as mine too. They were republd in Boston; but I fear the plates would not be as good & clear as the original. My copy is edited by an "*Ernest Fleischer*," Leipzig, May, 1847, for Westerman Brothers, New York. They are all the original German plates, & German letterpress, with English translation in German typography. These "Explanations" are written by *Ulrici*, and other German Shakespearians, for this work. They are very copious, & *intensely interesting* (worth the price of the work alone,) being *æsthetic comments*, running along through the whole play. *Schlegel* figures largely in them. . . .

[1] this copy of "Horace": N's Easter present to C; John Bond's work (1606) had gone through fifteen edns. by the early nineteenth century, and Bond was regarded in C's time as the greatest of the commentators on Horace.
[2] I took a prize: Probably at Appleby School near Kirkby Thore (see Introduction, p. 15); such prizes are still given at the school.

36:　7 April 1875

. . . Now to reply to your letters in order. I do not know of any references that I possess to the fact of our beloved Shakespeare's ever having been a *Free Mason*. I don't remember to have seen the matter mooted[1] anywhere, tho' I may be mistaken. Should I ever come across such a fact, or proofs, or allusions, in my reading, I will inform you. He has been *proved*, by his writings, to have been everything almost, from a *lawyer* up to a butcher, schoolmaster, printer, &c.—I am a *free Mason* myself—used to be called a "bright" one; but I confess that I cannot now recall anything in the Poet's works that even squints at *his* ever having been a brother of the "mystic tie." I never looked for them. Perhaps certain words & passages *might* be found that by twisting properly would give such an idea. As for the real facts, & recent discoveries, touching his *Life*, you are I think better informed than I am. Did it ever strike *you* that he was a Mason? Or have you merely seen such a conjecture raised somewhere by others?—

I am glad you have *Wilkes'* articles. But you *must* read them, if only to see the *perversity of man*. I am aware they will terribly try your patience. I cannot find language *contemptuous* enough to designate their Spirit, or their Ignorance. Do, for pity's sake, read the article in the No. for *March 27th*. I wont defile my paper by quoting any part of it: but he branches off from Shakespeare to abuse Religion, and especially the English Church, and to insult all Americans who observe the *Lord's Day*, which he says they do from flunkeyism to England & her Episcopal Church, which he calls an "industry." He says he never was so humiliated, as an American, as when in Paris, during their Great Exposition, the English Department closed their doors out of regard for *Sunday*, and Americans flunkeyly followed suit. Then he proceeds to connect this with Shakespeare, & the British Aristocracy, &c. &c. It will positively make your blood boil at the impertinence, & especially the gross ignorance, and weak illogical reasoning, of the fellow. What can anyone make of such an argument as that in the No. I mentioned? You never in your life said a truer or better thing, than when you happily interpolated the word "blackguard's" into his title page, "from an American [blackguard's] point of view." I trust, in fact *I know*, that there are precious few Americans who will not be *intensely disgusted* with his "point of view." In fact the more I write about *him* the *madder* I get, so I will stop short off. You ask me to write a "stinging review" of his book, when it is finished. No: my dear boy: anything but that. My *patience*, if nothing else, would never hold out: I had every bit as soon undertake to fight a dirty hornets' nest. "There is a thing, Harry, which thou hast often heard of, and it is known to many in our land by the name of *pitch*: this pitch, as ancient writers do report, doth defile."—So said Falstaff; and you know the homely proverb, "The more you stir up a"—necessary, or a skunk—"the more it will *stink*." That is not the worst. You cannot escape contracting some portion of the "stink" on your *own clothes*.

. . . R. G. White's "Story of the Forest of Arden," in April *Galaxy*, is quite interesting: but it is "R. G. White" all over. *He* knew it all, long before *Gervinus*[2] did, about whom there is so much fuss of late—a hit at Furnivall too. For the purest specimen of White's *egotism* & *conceit*, read especially his "Shakespearian Mares' Nests," in the Galaxy.[3] *He* knew everything that *they*—the Edinburgh Review, Mr. Dyce, &c.—found out, long before they did. Theirs are only *mares' nests*. Mr. W. waited, however, until after Mr. Dyce's *death*, before he told us all this. I could tell you lots of funny things[4] à la Grant White, and his edn. of Sh., if I could only talk to you, instead of writing. By the way, his edition, *in cloth*, brought $2.45 a vol. at Leavitt's Sale last week. Isn't that *above* the retail price in Philadelphia?. . .

—I have the *Atlantic Monthly*, *Lippincott's*, & *Scribner's*, Magazines all for April, & all containing also Shakespn. articles; but I have not yet had time to read them. Did you read a very good review of Schmidt's "Shakespeare Lexicon," in the *Academy* for Mch. 20th? Same No. contains also an excellent review of Prof. Masson's new edn. of *Milton*, which I told you I recently added to my library. I observed the notice in the *Nation* of Judge Holmes' new edn. of his crazy book.[5] It is first-rate.—The article in *Scribner* also refers to this "Baconian theory." Like you, I am tired—"yes 'faith heartily" tired of the "Baconian theory."—. . .

Yesterday I took *fifty-six* more volumes to the Bookbinder, mostly *Shakespeariana*: among them the lovely copy of *Horace* which you gave me. This goes into Hf. green Turkey morocco, entirely uncut; I won't allow the edges to be *touched at all*, except the *top*, which will be gilt. I wish you would write your presentation to me, please, on a sheet of note-paper, and I will have it bound up with the vol.—I like to see such things; in my eye they add to the value of the book.—I have such a host of *little* books about Shakespeare; sewed pamphlets; tracts of a few pages only, &c. I don't know what to do with them. I cannot bear the way some have of binding several all up together. And yet I have added some few together that *assorted right*. E.g. I have put Brae's "Collier, Coleridge, & Shakespeare," and his "Literary Cookery" into one vol., lettered "A. E. Brae." I put the Jennens' "Lear" & "Othello" together; Finnegan's "Attempt to Illustrate some passages in Shakespeare," and Tyrwhitt's "Conjectures and Observations" &c. together; Ritson's "Cursory Criticisms," and Malone's "Letter to Dr Farmer in *Reply* to Ritson's Cursory Criticisms" together; Warner's "Letter to Garrick," &c., and the "Three Essays on King Lear, by Pupils of City of London School" together; H. Mercer Graves' "Essays on Shakespeare," & Griffin's "Studies in Literature" together; "Shakespearian Anthology" & Evans' "Seven Ages of Man" &c. together; &c. &c. These are all of the same size, I mean the two put together; are not inharmonious in character; and by *lettering* can easily be distinguished, making *together* only thin volumes; & thus saving one-half of the binding. What do you think of it? I am gradually getting my books into good shape; but I have to go *very slow*, both in buying & binding, on account of being so *cursed poor*. Poverty is said to be no disgrace; but I tell you it is mighty *inconvenient*. Books are the *only* luxury I can indulge in, & only very sparingly in them. I deny myself many things often, to invest in a book or two that I want. . . . .

I was glad the "Independent"[6] had the good taste to copy your notice from the *Bib.* of Mr. & Mrs. Furness. They might have added your name, I think, and stated that you had undertaken the editorship of the "Sh: Dept." of the Bib., and it would not have hurt them. The notice referred to was much more than "pleasant"; it was, as I told you, just, appreciative, well-worded, & *true*, without flattery.—I have not opened "Dowden"[7] since you wrote me about it. I fear I shall not like it. Anything but a pedantic style. And yet he *ought* to be a good Shak*n* critic, as it seems he has read all, & is the *best posted* Englishman in, the German critics & commentators. I like *Gervinus*; tho' I have by no means mastered all his ponderous work yet. *Elze* is also good, substantial criticism. I am *behind* on him too. I read two *little* books lately, that pleased me vastly, viz. J. R. Wise's "Sh., his birthplace," &c, and S. Neil's Critical Biography. They are excellent, both of them. Wise's little beautiful vol. contains explanations of several Shakn. words—still provincially used in Warwickshire. If you have not already, you must be sure & get & read these two charming little volumes.—I am glad you have bought so nice a copy of "Taine."[8] You will be highly *amused*, sometimes a trifle irritated, often instructed, & generally well pleased, with his chapters on *Shakespeare*. It is a very hard matter for these Frenchmen to understand Sh.—The Germans come much nearer; but many of their theories are very wild; witness *Schlegel*[9] on the Spurious Plays. . . .

—I had to laugh at the slips you sent me from the Phila. newspapers about *you*, and the *Bibliopolist*. I knew exactly how, with your modesty, you looked & felt, when you saw your name coupled as "æquales" (our old College term) with Furness & Halliwell. It is astonishing how little the world generally, & newspapers in particular, know about Shakespeare, his students, editors, commentators, & critics. Sometimes *our* little city papers get hold of my name as a "Shakespearian Scholar" &c., and it always makes me blush. By the way, I wonder if our old friend Hudson is not offended at me, for something. He has not written me a line since the 3d of January: and I have sent him many a page of note and manuscript since then. He has never noticed, in any way, any of the notes (40 or 50 sheets) I wrote on the *Tempest*. He wrote me very flatteringly indeed respecting those on "Lear"; & urged me to go on, & send more—more—he could never have enough. In fact he *adopted* nearly *every one* of my suggestions & explanations of the Folio text; as he *had* to do, if he possessed common sense. I fancy he is engaged with his classes; and also in preparing a vol. of poetry,[10] with *notes* for Schools, similar to his "School Shakespeare." I am sure I am not conscious of having said or done anything to offend him; and you & Goddard[11] are the only friends who know I have been helping him.

In your letter of the 28th Mch, you ask me if I am willing to part with one of my large-paper Variorum editions of 1813? Yes, I will, to you; but no one else should have it; and you must not think *I want* to sell it; because I don't. It is the same copy we spoke about, you remember, before you recd yours; that I kept to let you have, providing yours did not come. I will describe it to you as correctly as I can. The contents are entirely clean; not a speck, or pencil mark, or stain, in the volumes, that I know of. The binding is *full light-coloured calf*, backs full gilt, contents well lettered, but *marbled edges*. It cost me $33..00 at first; but being large paper, the paper very thick too, the volumes are very heavy; and I found that in some of the volumes the heavy calf backs had sprung more or less, and cracked at the joints; so I took the volumes so cracked to the Binder, and had them very *neatly* and very *strongly* repaired; which he did by raising up the leather at the joints, and putting in a new piece of same colour calf underneath, & pasting the old leather down again over it, so as hardly to show, or very little at least; and while it did not injure the looks of the book in any way, made the binding about as strong for wear again as ever it was. I think I paid him $3.50, or $4.00 for these repairs, and it was money well spent. The whole set is a bright, clean, good-looking set of volumes. I have always looked on them, in my book-case, with favour, being as the merchants say, "good stock."— You know large-paper Variorums are by no means picked up every day, is the reason I bought 2 copies; and I have no doubt this set will be worth $50., in a short time, if not now. Bouton charged me $32..50 for my *small paper* copy of the 1803 Var.—If you really would like to have it, you shall have it for $35.00, and I know it is very cheap at that price. I only wish I were well enough off to make you a present of it: but I am so confounded poor I cannot do as I would. You are better able to keep it than I am; and I am sure you will like it, & should you ever wish to sell it, you cannot but make money by it. At any rate, I will always give you $35.—a standing offer for it. Now I have said all I need about *that*. Do not take it, unless you would really like to own it. If you do, direct me how to send it, whether by freight (much the cheapest), or express (the quickest). I could wrap the vols. in newspapers, & box them, & they would go by frt. for half the express chgs.—Now, goodbye, my dear fellow, & believe me, as ever, Your friend, Joseph Crosby. . . .

[1] I don't remember to have seen the matter mooted: It had been, quite recently, by J. C. Parkinson, *Shakespeare, A Freemason* (1872), and earlier by J. O. Halliwell, *Early History of Freemasonry in England* (1840). Parkinson was a member of the "Bard of Avon Lodge of United, Free, and Accepted Masons of England, Province of Middlesex."

[2] before *Gervinus*: White in effect accused Georg Gottfried Gervinus of having plagiarized his analysis of Jaques's character from White's *Shakespeare's Scholar*; see "the Tale of the Forest of Arden," *The Galaxy* (April 1875).

[3] in the Galaxy: October 1869. White attacked Dyce for "instability and lack of intellectual character and purpose" and he attacked *The Edinburgh Review* for praising one of Dyce's readings.

[4] lots of funny things: I.e., about White's own "intellectual character" as manifested in flagrant plagiarism; see "Index," s.v. *plagiarism*.

[5] Judge Holmes' . . . crazy book: Nathaniel Holmes, *The Authorship of Shakespeare* (1866; 3d edn. 1875; it went through five edns. by 1886).

[6] the "Independent": a Philadelphia newspaper. Such appropriation of published articles was widespread.

[7] "Dowden": Edward Dowden, *Shakspere: A Critical Study of His Mind and Art* (1875).

[8] "Taine": H. Van Laun's trans. of Hippolyte Taine's *Histoire de la littérature anglaise* (1863). This is the second edn. (1873–74).

[9] Schlegel: In his *Lectures on Dramatic Art and Literature* (1809–11, trans. 1815). See appendix to

Lecture XXVI; Schlegel enthusiastically accepted the apocrypha, calling *Cromwell, Sir John Oldcastle*, and *A Yorkshire Tragedy* "among [Sh's] best and maturest works."

[10] a vol. of poetry: *A Textbook of Poetry* (1875); it went through several printings by 1890.

[11] Goddard: See note 6 to letter 146.

38:   10 April 1875

. . . Mr. *J. Payne Collier* is a puzzle to me. I have considerable respect for the veteran commentator; and yet it is often marred by the *disingenuousness* into which his enthusiasm in defending his "Corr. Fo. 1632" leads him. Of one thing I am very sure; these corrections are *no forgeries* of Collier's. And of another I am also convinced, that many of them are *very clever*, and the work of a man who is no novice in his business, either as a *reader* or *actor* of Shakespeare: and had they been brought forth *piecemeal*, instead of over-whelming us, and rousing our opposition at their number and immensity, many more of them would have found favour in our eyes. Collier's *manner* of defending them, too, has been most unfortunate both for *them* and *him*. Let me give you just one illustration of what I mildly term his *disin-genuousness*, from the paper you have just sent me. In the line of T. G. of V. which he quotes, "To be of *wealth*, and worthy estimation,"[1] the word *wealth* is the Corr. Fo. 1632 correction of what in the Folio 1623, and in all subsequent editions, is printed, "To be of *worth*, and worthy estimation."— Now this emendation is very plausible, and corrects a palpable tautology. Still, such repetitions are by no means uncommon in Sh., who uses them in a *quibbling* way; for instance, a few lines further down, he says, "with all good *grace* to *grace* a gentleman."[2] And, besides, Mr. Dyce produces six or eight passages from other old authors, wherein *worth* means exactly *wealth*, and cannot mean anything else. But what I blame Collier for, is his defend-ing it in such a *tricky* & sophistical way. . . . I want you particularly to note the expressions: "Even *Walker, in his Critical Examination, entirely approves of the line, as it stands in the Corr. Fo., 1632,*" and, "*Walker heartily welcomes it.*" Is it conceivable that Collier did not know that *Walker died in Octo. 1846*, three years before he *found* his Corrected Folio in Mr. Rodd's shop, 6 years before he knew it contained any MS. corrections, and nearly 7 years before he gave them to the world in his "Notes and Emendations"? Or, did he *suppose* his readers of the "Trilogy" either so ignorant as not to know that fact, or so careless as not to reflect on it? How, in the name of sense, can a man who has been 6 or 7 years in his grave, "*heartily welcome*" a correction that he never saw? or "*entirely approve*" of a line as it stands in the Corr. Fo. 1632" that he never heard of?—How could a *live* man, let alone a *dead* one, "approve entirely of," and "heartily welcome," a thing *he never saw or heard of*?—It is true Walker conjectured "wealth" as an emendation of "worth"; but it is a conjecture of his own. He neither "approves" nor "welcomes" anybody else's conjecture, much less one that he had never seen. He simply uses the two words "probably, *wealth*," after quoting the line from the folio, and that is *all*, that the "entire approval," and "hearty welcome" of Mr. Collier's MS. corrector have to stand on. If one did not have implicit confidence in Mr. Collier's *integrity*, one might be much more tempted to say that *Collier* "entirely approves," & "heartily welcomes," *Walker's* emendation, than that Walker approves & welcomes that of the Corr. Fo.—Don't you see how he opens the door of suspicion on himself by such "windlaces and assays of bias"? How easily he could have said, and said *truly*, that *this* correction of his Folio had *also* been independently made by so sound a critic as Walker; and that would have made us more inclined to accept it as genuine; whereas by his **suggestio falsi**—that Walker *had examined* this correction, given to it his *fiat* of approval, and *endorsed* it by his "hearty welcome," he lays himself liable (when found out) to the irresistible mental conviction of his readers, that there is something *wrong* about this "Corr. Fo.," or it would not need to be bolstered up by such tortuous devices, and *disingenuousness.*—Goodbye, my boy. Ever Yours,

—Jos. Crosby.—

[1] "To be . . . estimation": *TGV* 2.4.56.
[2] "with all good *grace* to *grace* a gentleman": *TGV* 2.4.74.

39: 10 April 1875

Furnivall's letter is the most *insulting* letter I ever read from one gentleman (!) to another. Let me beg of you to keep away from him. He is a *skunk*, sure, and you won't get over the—odor for weeks. Do, my boy, avoid him severely. I think I am giving you the best advice. You will only have your feelings wounded, without any compensation.

Truly Your grateful friend
J. Crosby. . . .[a]

[a] Furnivall's . . . *Crosby.*] ↑Furnivall's . . . *Crosby.*↓ MS. [written in and around the letterhead of p. 1 of this cover letter for #38].

40: 11 April 1875

My dear Norris:

Sunday Night: after Church
I dropped you a note yesterday, briefly acknowledging the recpt. of your kind letter of the 8th, and also the three "rubbings" from Shakespeare's tomb & monument, & his wife's, in the Stratford Church. I cannot tell you

how much I think of these *rubbings*. To an old monomaniacal[a] Shakespearian, like myself, who so rarely sees such dear curiosities, they are trebly
valuable, and valued. And how *perfect* they are! In spirit one is standing on
the identical spot, looking on these hallowed relics. I am not exactly perfect
how they are made. Is the blackening substance an *India Ink*? How does it
happen, that in rubbing over the marble or brass, the surface of the paper
that covers the indented letters is not also made black? One of my *scientific*
friends here would persist that they were *lithographs*, until I showed him
the *print* of the letters on the back of the paper. . . . I must say to you with
Sebastian, (*T.N.* III.3,13, according to Dyce's text of the imperfect folio
line,)—

> "My kind Antonio,
> I can no other answer make but thanks,
> And thanks, still thanks: and very oft good turns
> Are shuffled off with such uncurrent pay:
> But, were my worth as is my conscience firm,
> You should find better dealing."

By the by, note Shakespeare's undoubted use of *worth* in this passage for
wealth; because it proves Mr. Collier's "Corr. Fo. 1632" correction of *worth* to
wealth, in the line in T. G. of V., to be unnecessary & consequently
wrong. . . .

   You never told me whether you took much interest in the *Sonnets*, or had
read them yet sufficiently to form an opinion on the various theories about
them. I did not until recently. Of course I had *read* them: but that alone
won't do. They require more study & thought than any other portion of
Sh.'s works, in order to settle in your mind any just appreciation of their
meaning & beauty. It is truly one of the hardest things I have yet encountered in Sh., to know *why* they were written; when; **to whom** they are
addressed; whether autobiographical, or dramatic; realistic, or
philosophic. Mr. Fleay wrote a good article on the first 125, in Macmillan
for March. I believe he is right. At any rate, his theory relieves Sh. of the
charge of adultery &c., & (what is worse) *writing about it*, in such poetry
too; and he does substantiate his argument with good reasons. I hope you
will take the pains to read & master it. In this connection, a writer in
Lippincott's Mag. for April, Kate Hillard, has an admirable résumé of the
various theories on the Sonnets. It is not very long, and I assure you, (if
you can trust my judgment,) it will repay you right well for your time &
thought on it. You will get from it, *condensed,* a statement of Armitage
Brown's, Henry Browne's, Gen. Hitchcock's, Herr Barnstorff's, Heraud's,
Gerald Massey's, & several others' opinions, about these mystifying
Poems. She writes clearly, & understands what she is writing about; & she
has none of R. G. White's self-importance either. . . .

I can well imagine, my dear fellow, how grieved & mournful you felt at the sight of the ruins & wrecks of Mr. Forrest's Library:[1] and I thought how differently it would have fared had the care of these ruins fallen into *your* or *my* hands. I think I should have killed myself repairing the damages—to have all done well, & tastefully, & neatly. I suppose many of the books rebound & *cut* were previously uncut, & only wet: they should have been carefully dried, & then bound right, by P. & N.,[2] à la *Parker Norris' Sh. Style*. Don't you think *some* of the invaluable vols. of Halliwell's Folio Ed. could be repaired or saved? Will they *sell* these ruins, or cart them away to the paper-mill? I *was* astonished at the *meagreness* of Forrest's stock of editions. Not even a "Variorum of 1821"—an indispensable requisite to a Sh library; nor hardly any of the *late* editions, Dyce, Collier, (except the worthless monovolume one,)[3] Singer, White, Hudson, Clarke, &c. &c. besides many of the best of the *old* editions, like Theobald, Capell & Johnson. He did not seem to have even so *Useful* a book as Booth's reprint;[4] tho' I think I understood you that he had a photolithograph, which was found burnt up nearly. . . .

I had to laugh at your list of "jawbreakers"—what Horace calls "sesquipedalia verba"—from *Dowden*. I fear his study of German literature has not helped his English style. I have not read any of his book yet. . . . I was pall-bearer at *two* large Masonic funerals last week,—both friends of mine—and I thought of your inquiry whether our Shak. were ever a "brother of the mystic tie." I do not recollect ever to have seen any conjecture before of the subject: & I cannot call to mind at present any scene—line—or words, in his writings, that would suggest such a fact, altho' there *may* be. Hereafter I shall look out (incidentally) for them, & if any occur to me, I will let you know.—

I never felt more disposed to *swear*, in my life, than when I read the copy of Furnivall's letter to you,[5] which you sent me. And the impertinent puppy had the audacity to ask your friend Mr. Furness *to publish* it!!—Well, that is about as far as asinine impudence could go; don't you think so?— What does the simpering snub-nose mean by "people of your level"? Does he suppose that because *he* is the *self-appointed*[b] Director of the "New Sh. Society," that no one is to *presume* to criticize, "in print," his doings, sayings, or writings?—Are *we all* "untaught knaves, unmannerly," that "come between the wind and *his nobility*"?—God deliver *me* from ever declining to his "level."—"*People* of your level"! and, "such courteous & cultivated men as professors Child & Lowell"![6]—Why, *he* is no more fit, as a **gentleman**, to be named the same day with Professors Child or Lowell, than *Nym*, or *Pistol*, with "glorious Prince Hal." In point of real fact, *his* "level" is exactly on a par with that of *"ancient Pistol,"* and I am not sure but, as a *braggart*, it is disreputable to *Pistol* to couple him with *Furnivall*. "Now, by Cadwallader and all his goats," I would we had another *Fluellen*, to make him eat his *leek*. But it takes a *Fluellen* to do it. The **Prince** could not have done it; he was too much of a *gentleman*.—"Pite, I pray you; it is good for your ploody coxcomb."[c]—"*Must* I bite?"—"Yes, certainly, and out of doubt, and ambiguities." "By this leek; I will most horribly *revenge*: I eat, and eat, I swear—" "Eat, I pray you: will you have some more sauce to your leek? There is not enough leek to swear by."—"Quiet thy cudgel: thou dost see I eat."— "Much good do you, *scauld knave*, heartily"—x "Leeks is goot!"—What a capital scene! I fancy that when Furnivall sneered & mocked at the leek in Bro. *Timmins'* hat, *he* tried to make him eat it; but his cudgel was not heavy enough to have any effect on Furnivall's rhinoceros skin of self-conceit, and so, I fear, my dear boy, it would be in your case. Such natures as his **you** *cannot* understand; nothing but a cudgel,—a heavy one, & repeated blows, will make him "*pite*."—He'll find his Fluellen someday. What I advised yesterday, I would earnestly repeat; treat him with *silent* contempt, or he will make you **unhappy**. . . .

[1] Mr. Forrest's Library: Edwin Forrest, the distinguished Shn actor, had lived on North Broad Street in Philadelphia; he died in 1872. In a letter from C to Ingleby (Folger MS. C.a. 14, 28 January 1873) there is an account of his romantic death—reading *Hamlet* in Halliwell's Folio Shakespeare while dressing—and of the fire a few months later.
[2] P. & N.: Pawson & Nicholson, a bespoke bindery in Philadelphia.
[3] the worthless monovolume one: Collier's edn. of 1853—"worthless" because it printed the readings of the Perkins Folio.
[4] Booth's reprint: Lionel Booth's type facsimile of F1 (1864).
[5] Furnivall's letter to you: Furnivall's rejoinder to N's harsh criticism of his quarrels with Fleay and other members of the New Shakspere Society. "Surely Mr. Furnivall must be a hot-headed fellow, and the sooner the new Society gets rid of him as its Director, the better it will be for the members." "Shakespearian Gossip," *American Bibliopolist* (February 1875): 32, col. 1.
[6] Child & Lowell: F. J. Child and James Russell Lowell.

[a] monomaniacal] mono-I maniacal MS.
[b] *self-appointed*] *self-I appointed* MS.
[c] coxcomb] cox–I comb MS.

42:   20 April 1875

. . . In your letter you say, "whether you like it or not, you *must* write a review of his [Wilkes'] book, when complete."—My dear fellow, I fear you will never see a review of that book from the pen of "Yours truly." Poor as I am, I am afraid to state what amount of money it would take to induce me to undertake the dirty job: or to undergo the wear & tear of *temper* necessary for the task: sixthly, it would do no good to anyone: as for convincing such an ignorant bullhead as he is, or any of his "friends" who believe in him, the thing is impossible: thirdly, if you were to read the articles once yourself, you would not, I am very sure, permit any allusion even to the disreputable & lying production to defile the fair pages of the *Bibliopolist*; Seventy-fifthly, and lastly; as the poor distracted Hamlet says, "why look you now, how unworthy a thing you make of *me*." You want me to read, mark, inwardly digest,[1] and then *review*, (as if once reading were not more than enough,) a *thing*, that you yourself will not even take the *trouble*, or have not the *patience*, to read once. "Whar my Chrissn bruddern, whar I say, am dar any *farness* about dat?"—"No," as the immortal Sairey Gamp[2] remarked to Mrs. Prig, who was reaching for the teapot (with *gin* in it)— "No; drink *fair*, Betsey, wotever you do."—In the case in point, instead of drinking *fair*, Betsey, you want more than your share of the *gin*; but it won't do, Betsey; "no, not while my name's *Sairey*."—. . . In one of my recent letters to you, speaking of George Wilkes, Esq. A. S. S., and his incapacity, owing to his *ignorance* (notwithstanding his title aforesaid,) to comment & write upon *Shakespeare*, you may remember I quoted his referring to a passage in *The Tempest*, where Prospero, addressing Ariel, says "Go, bring the *rabble*,"[3] &c.

This word "*rabble*" Wilkes seized upon, in his eagerness to depreciate our beloved Shakespeare in the eyes of the American people, to prove Shakespeare an *aristocrat* and a *flunky*, &c., because he, "speaking through Prospero," applies this "degrading" term to the *common sailors*. I showed that, in the instance he quoted, Pros. was not referring to the sailors at all, but to Ariel's attendant *spirits*—his "fellows," companions; and I stated that the word "rabble," in the Elizabethan tongue, was by no means *necessarily* a "degrading" term, but meant simply "a company," "a small party." I have since come across a line in *Shakespeare himself*, that perfectly corroborates this. In the "Merry Wives," (III. v. 76) Falstaff says, "the peaking Cornuto, her husband, dwelling in a continual 'larum of jealousy, comes me in, x x x and at his heels a *rabble* of his companions x x to search his house for his wife's love." Isn't it plain enough here what "rabble" means? They were Master Brook's, or rather Ford's, *friends*, "companions,"—"a *rabble* of his **companions**"—Mr. Page, Sir Hugh Evans, Dr Caius, &c.—As I said, there might as easily be a rabble of *gentlemen*, or *ladies* either for that matter, as a rabble of *blackguards*, as far as the meaning of the word *rabble* went, in Shakespeare's time. I have an old Dictionary, in which "rabble" is translated into Latin by the word *series*, i.e. a number, or succession of persons, without any reference to *quality*. The proper synonym for the term in that passage in the *Tempest* is '**a train**.' It shows the fellow's *animus*, & how hard up he must be for something to find fault with in Shakespeare, when he makes an argument out of this: no doubt many of *his* "rabble" believed it, & do believe all he says. To talk with such men is *worse* than "casting pearls before swine." Wilkes is spiteful & cunning enough to know that nothing will injure a man's reputation, in the eyes of the **average American democrat**, so much as to put into his mouth words derogatory to the "great unwashed," the *profanum vulgus*, among whom his paper has its largest circulation.—

Since I wrote you, I have recd. from Smith the 3d & 4th vols. of Percy's Fol. MS.—. . . One thing is *certain*, that Shakespeare was a constant reader

& studier of these old-time productions. You can scarcely read one, without noting traces where *he* got some word, or line, or idea, to incorporate into his plays. In Percy's tinkered "Reliques," Book II of his First Series is entirely devoted to "Ballads that illustrate Shakespeare," and has (prefixed) a valuable & well-written essay on the Early Drama, Shakespeare, &c. of nearly 20 pages. In the Ms., as now pubd., these ballads are all printed promiscuously; in fact the original is copied word for word, spelling &c. Nothing is omitted; only the *very coarse* ballads are thrown together into One vol. (a thin one), but edited with the same care as the others. Our *Prof. Child* was very instrumental in accomplishing this great work. The old Ms. was in hands that utterly refused to part with it to be edited & printed; & so desirous was Prof. Child, & other antiquarian Scholars, to have it done, that he gave £50., & your friend Furnivall, gave £100., to the owners, to *loan* them this precious MS. for a certain time. After editing & printing, it was returned to the owners. It commences in the early part of English annals, & comes down to Shakespeare's time. I have already found several words & phrases in it, corroborating my interpretations of the old Folio 1623; & I have sent some of these to Hudson. I have another batch of Notes nearly ready for him. You may think me enthusiastic about this Fol. MS., but it merits it. It is a work that one will always *want*; and it will last *forever*—as an aid in expounding Shakespeare. . . .

I should, *most decidedly*, have preferred to have these *literary & explanatory notes* in Masson's *Milton*[a] directly under the text; or, if not that, at least in the same vol.—As it is, one has to have always 2 vols. open, if wanting to read the *Notes* in connection with the *text*. This was the great bugbear that made Capell's valuable notes less known, & thence unpopular; he pub*d* them in 3 lge 4to vols, separate from the text, and they were not pubd either until after his death. My experience is, to always choose the *Notes* at the foot of the same page as the *text*. I would not have any letters, or figures, or signs, to disfigure the text; but let it be in numbered lines, and the Notes giving the line readily enough designate the place annotated. If any reader does not wish to be interrupted by notes, he need not be, in this way: while the student, anxious to comprehend everything in his author, finds it to his hand, without turning over the end of the vol., or still worse, turning to an entirely separate vol. I like the Variorum Shakespeares, & Singer's, & Collier's, (& Knight's & Staunton's partly,) on this account, better than White's, or Dyce's, or many others, that place their Notes either at the end of the Play, or end of the volume.—

I suppose Smith has sent you also a copy of the Gentleman's Mag. for April, containing an article entitled "In Shakespeare's Country." I want to call your attention to a noble Sonnet to Shakespeare, by Matthew Arnold, on page 472 of the same number. I think it is very fine; I made 2 or 3 copies of it, & sent to my friends in the West. . . .

—Did it never strike you, that the *very language* of Shakespeare's will was primâ facie proof of his having been a *Protestant*, and *not* a Catholic, in religion?—"I commend my soul into the hands of God my Creator, hoping & assuredly believing, *through the* **only merits of Jesus Christ my Saviour**, to be made partaker of life everlasting." This surely is not the language of a Romanist.[4] The latter would have *coupled* at least, if not given precedence to, "the Holy Virgin Mary, and all the Saints," with our Saviour, in being the meritorious cause of his salvation. A man's Will, made not to be seen until his decease has removed him from earth, gives no occasion for any concealment of his religious views: & had our Shak. been a Papist at heart, as is so persistently argued, the fact would have appeared in such a case as in making his *Will*. This has always seemed to *me* a good argument for his Protestantism. . . .

I was sorry you did not like Kate Hillard's Sonnet-article in *Lippincott*. I think, to be the production of a *woman*, it is very far above mediocrity. . . . As I said before, there is nothing especially *new* in it: and I am by no means a believer in the autobiographical theory she holds & advocates. . . . But I was glad to observe that a lady had the courage not only to *read*—to read thoroughly—the Sonnets & the different opinions thereon, but to write so good & well-expressed an Article on them. . . .

—By the by, did you notice another article in "N. & Q." by the Mr. Marsh, the owner of the 1664-folio with notes in MS. which he thought were *Pope's*? It seems that the experts of the Museum have decided that these notes are *not* in Pope's chirography. But they *may* be by the *real editor* of Pope's Shakespeare, nevertheless, as it appears that Pope did very little of this work himself,[5] but was in the habit of *selling* the use of his name to authors & publishers, for considerable sums of money. The article is *worth* your reading. The question now is, *whose* MS. is it that these notes are written in? as, in the answer to this question, depends the name of the genuine author of *Pope*. Did *Pope* write *Pope's Shakespeare*? Or did somebody else? If so, who?—It is of very little consequence, is *my verdict*.— . . .

The other matter is in regard to the kind project which you mention, of my sending to you notes on *Hamlet*, to pass under Mr. Furness' eye, & mayhap be printed in his New Variorum Edn. My dear Norris, I understand and appreciate fully your kind partiality for me, which induces the suggestion: and, truly, if I *had* any notes that were *worthy*, I would pocket my modesty, and adopt your scheme. You may be sure my human vanity would be overwhelmed with gratification at seeing anything—a line even—from my poor pen in such company. But there is no need of saying more: *I now have none*, i.e. none of any account. As fast as I wrote & studied out my notes on *Hamlet*, I sent them to Mr. Hudson; and, very foolishly, **kept no copy**. I did not begin to copy my notes, until I wrote those on the *last 2 plays* I worked on, viz. *Lear*, & *The Tempest*.—Mr. Hudson has some very fair interpretations, & explanations, & conjectures, on *Hamlet*, of mine: but they are gone now—out of my control. He very kindly has acknowledged them—very flatteringly indeed: so you see, I cannot give them to Mr. Furness *too*. Hereafter, I mean to retain copies of *all* my notes, such at least as deserve the notice of such men as *Hudson* or *Furness*. . . .

[1] read, mark, inwardly digest: From the Collect for Second Sunday in Advent, "Bible Sunday"; C perhaps alludes ironically to Wilkes's pontifical tone and to his attacks on the Church.
[2] Sairey Gamp . . . Mrs. Prig: *Martin Chuzzlewit*, Ch. 49.
[3] "Go, bring the *rabble*": *Tmp.* 4.1.37.
[4] not the language of a Romanist: On the other hand, Sh's father, John, may have made a spiritual testament in a form regularly used by Spanish Jesuits and English Recusants; see James G. McManaway, "John Shakespeare's 'Spiritual Testament,'" *Shakespeare Quarterly* 18 (1967): 197–205.
[5] it appears that Pope did very little of this work himself: John Fitchett Marsh's opinion (*Notes & Queries* 6 March 1875, pp. 199–200). It is now generally agreed that Pope "worked [on his Sh edn.] with paid and unpaid assistants, and a number of dabblers" (Bonamy Dobrée, *Alexander Pope* [1951], 76–77).

[a] *notes* in Masson's *Milton*] *notes* MS.

44: 29 April 1875

. . . I have received a very kind & pleasant letter from Mr. Furness, chiefly about Mrs. Dall's pamphlet,[1] & some things in it which I did not understand. He does not seem to have a very exalted opinion of the book, but terms it a "wild, incoherent, inconsequent affair"; and says, "now, I, in turn, will be thankful if you will tell me what possible connection exists between Shakespeare's gloves and Eliza Wharton."—By the way, he enclosed me a beautiful photograph of these famous *gloves*, which I presume you also have. Mr. Winsor, of the Boston Library, has it seems found a reference to them, which Mr. F. had not seen. "It is to be found in Garrick's Correspondence, Vol. I. p. 352, in a letter from Ward, the grandfather of Mrs. Siddons, who received these gloves as a payment from the descendants of Shakespeare for raising the fund for repairing the monument in the Stratford Church. This letter Boaden discredits."—This letter I confess only mystifies them the more to me. If Ward, Mrs. Siddons' grandfather, got them from Sh's descendants, how did *Garrick* become possessed of them?[2] *Ward* naturally left them to his famous granddaughter *Mrs. Siddons*, from whom *Fanny Kemble* inherited them, who gives them now to Mr. Furness. At any rate, whether the Great Poet ever owned or wore these gloves, or not, they have been in the possession of so many great actors & Shakespearians, who considered them as having been *his*, that they are an interesting relic & curiosity. . . .

I was pleased to read the list of books you have on your "reading rack." It indicates your train of reading, & looks right. If you would allow me to suggest, I would substitute Mrs. Clarke's Concordance, and Schmidt's

Lexicon, for *Crabb's Synonyms*. That last book I never got much *good* from, have you? I will make another little suggestion. For about $1..25, you can buy "Soule and Wheeler's Manual of English Pronunciation & Spelling," an exceedingly well-printed, neat & handy volume, which if you had at your elbow, you would find yourself using a dozen times a day. It is one of the *best* things in the business, for settling any hesitation in one's mind about spelling or pronouncing. I would not be without a copy for 5 times its cost. *Soule* was the Associate Ed. of Worcester's Unabridged, and Wheeler the Associate Ed. of Webster's Unabridged; & they do not confine themselves to Webster or Worcester either, but give *Smart's* & others' authority: & the book is so *reliable* too, that it is *invaluable*. There are no *definitions*, (or very few,)—only all the *words* of the language nearly, correctly spelt & pronounced, with the authorities where they vary. I have recommended it to several of my friends, and they all like it. . . . Another edition, that I have just received, I bought of Luyster, for $5.00; it is called "*Mansell's Pocket Shakespeare*"; . . . all the Plays are the *Acting Editions* only; it seems to have been entirely printed from *Stage copies*, containing numerous changes both of *addition* & *omission*, (& both in *Text* & *Stage directions*,) from Shakespeare. For instance, The Tempest is, I judge, *Dryden & Davenant's Version*; & the play commences by Prospero asking Miranda where her *sister* is? I read the play through; there is a *man* in it, who has never seen a *woman*, to correspond with Miranda, who had never seen a *man*, &c. &c. It is funny enough, but *not Shakespeare*. No doubt the Author, or Authors, supposed they were *improving* upon the original, & adapting it to the modern stage. Then, there is *Colley Cibber's* version of K. Richard III.; *N. Tate's* version of King Lear, &c. &c. I did not regret procuring this edition; as it is right one should have *all* the versions. It is marked "scarce," on the flyleaf; but I can find no account of it anywhere, either in Lowndes, Allibone, Thimm, Halliwell, or Mullins. Do you know anything of such an edition? Or have any of your bibliographies any notice of "Mansell's Pocket Shakespeare"?—

Some time ago, Mr. Timmins sent me a "Manchester City Times," (I think is the paper,) containing a 2 column article, a translation from one in German, by a *Dr Goedke*, giving a new theory of the *Sonnets* of Shakespeare. This "theory" is too long for me to detail it to you now; but I instantly recognized it as almost *precisely similar* to that of Mr. S. Neil, as published by him in 1861, in his admirable little book, "Shakspere; a *critical* Biography." I had only recently read & examined Neil's theory, & it was all so fresh on my memory, I could scarcely help thinking, when I read the German Doctor's, that it was not the *same one* I had read. But on comparing notes, I found the Dutchman had certainly *cabbaged* his "*New*" Views, that were so to "astonish" the students of Shakespeare; & I wrote a note to the Academy, stating the facts, & my surprise that the German had made no word of acknowledgement to the previous English critic. I had barely sent this off, when lo! & behold!, the very next No. of the Academy (Apl. 10th) contains, among "Notes & News," an item, that *Mr. Fleay* had written the Editor the very same thing. So my note will go into the wastebasket. You don't know how *mad* I was at Mr. Fleay for living nearer, & getting in his note ahead of me.—. . .

I was interested in your description of Halliwell's Folio Shakespeare. It seems very evident that he must have "hurried up" a good deal with the later volumes. *Four,* sometimes, of the best & most important plays in one vol., where *two* had previously been enough to fill a vol.; and the time between the pubn. of the vols. so much shorter too. I expect that he began to feel the tedium of his contract; perhaps his health rendered it necessary; so he hastened to the conclusion. I wonder whether he cleared much *money* by the work, or not.—. . .

[1] Mrs. Dall's pamphlet: Caroline Wells Healey Dall, *The Romance of the Association; or One Last Glimpse of Charlotte Temple and Eliza Wharton* (1875). The "Association" is the American Association for the Advancement of Science; *Charlotte Temple* and *The Coquette, or the History of Eliza Wharton* were late-eighteenth-century American novels, by Susanna Rowson and Hannah Foster, respectively.

[2] how did *Garrick* become possessed of them?: Sh had putatively worn the gloves onstage. In 1746 John Ward, the actor, was given these gloves by "a relative" of Sh in gratitude for the benefit performance of *Oth.* Ward staged at Stratford that year to raise funds for the restoration of the Sh bust in Holy Trinity Church. Ward sent the gloves to Garrick many years later when he heard that Garrick would preside as Steward over the Jubilee (1769). See Martha W. England, *Garrick's Jubilee* (1964), 7, 58.

45:   30 April 1875

. . . You did not say whether you still *determined* to print the Dogberry–Furnivall article. I hope, for your own happiness, your better & cooler reason prompted you to leave it out. You don't know what a "Master of fence" this Furnivall is. He will dip his pen in the blackest gall he has, & "have   at   you"   with   "words   of   thundering   sound,"— "honorificabilitudinitatibus"![1]—and *sich,—sesquipedalia verba,*[2] as Horace calls them. My dear boy, I fear for you. As sure as your name is J. Parker Norris, you *are in for it,* if you suffer that severe attack to go into print. I have tried to save you from what I know & feel will be a painful thing to you; & you must pardon my earnestness, because it is no joking matter. Indeed it isn't. I hope it is not now too late! You are in a "parlous state." . . .

I am glad you have bought the new edn. of *Gifford's Jonson:* and you bought it I think **remarkably cheap**. I saw the work advertised; and I don't think your description *any overdrawn.*[a] I don't think I can afford to buy it; as I have already a very handsome copy of the original edition of Gifford's in 9 vols. 8vo.; which is also a very *beautifully printed* work, (by Bulmer & Co.)— pubd in 1816. It cost me an *awful price,* however; £9.. or £9..9..0; more than double what you have got a really better book for; as yours contains *Cun-*

ningham's Notes &c. In the 1st vol. of my edn. is a very finely engraved Port. of Jonson by *Behnes*, engd by Fittler. Gifford's editions are all, as you say, the *best*: old Dibdin accords them the highest praise. It will amuse you to read some of Gifford's sarcastic notes: worse, if possible, (or better,) than your Dogberry onslaught on Furnivall. He rides roughshod over the preceding edd. & critics. . . .

[1] "honorificabilitudinitatibus": *LLL* 5.1.41.
[2] *sesquipedalia verba*: Horace, *Ars Poetica*, 97.

[a] overdrawn] over–I drawn MS.

47:   9 May 1875

. . . I now enclose you the article on "The puns of Shakespeare"; and I repeat what I said before; please overhaul it very carefully, before you send it:[1] undoubtedly you will find some *lapsus*, both of the pen & the sentiment. . . . It is by no means *easy* for me to write for *publication*. So long as I am only writing letters, or little matters for a friend's private eye, I sail along easily enough. But once the idea of printer's ink putting my effusions into preservable shape, for the public eye & criticism, gets hold of me, I feel nervous all over, lose my selfconfidence, and my ideas get knocked all endways. When sitting with a friend, I can *talk*, about what I know, well & passably enough: but once set me up on my legs to make a set formal speech, and I can positively say, or think of, *nothing*. Do you know why some men are so affected? I have often sat by fellows, at a public dinner for instance, whom I knew to be as conceited as well as *ignorant* asses as the globe carried on its surface, and seen them get up, with or without being called on, and run on for 15 or 20 minutes in a speech, giving the most perfect satisfaction to themselves & the others, & "setting the table on a roar," when I, altho' very likely a great deal better posted on the subject talked about, could not have opened my lips in a decent way for a million. It must be constitutional, I fancy. Anyway, it is a very unenviable infirmity. You lawyers, who are barristers in practice, can know nothing of this weakness of the knee–joints,[a] when called upon to make a speech; or if you do, you have learned to conquer it by long & patient practice, like Demosthenes with his pebbles.[2] The same feeling affects me, whenever I attempt to write a few lines for the press. "My muse *labours*: and my invention comes from my pate as birdlime comes from frize; it plucks out brains and all." For that reason, I have always *shunned*, what so many men deem an honour,—appearing in print: and I beg you earnestly, but sincerely, to accept this as my apology, both for *doing so little* for your department of the *Bib.*, and also for doing that little so feebly & inefficiently. . . .

By the way, I received a pleasant little letter from Mr. D. J. Snider, of St.

Louis, which I enclose you. He also sent me 3 nos. of the "Western." What a modest, *nice* fellow he seems to be; and yet what an excellent writer & thinker! I have carefully read all his papers; and received real enjoyment & instruction from them: more than I have from many more ambitious essays. . . . His scheme of *diagramming* (as I call it) each play, at the outset of his essay, is original & capital. He lays out all the outlines—the *warps* & *woofs* of the web—the "faithful" & the "faithless"[3]—lengthwise and crosswise—the connections of each thread thru' Family & State—just like a *mathematical* figure, and in this way succeeds in not only photographing the "scheme" of the characters as they existed in the Poet's *mind*, when he laid out his plan, but in presenting them to the reader in a comprehensive & *clear* way, that sticks to the memory, & that helps him in disentangling each motive & action, & following it up singly, from its inception to its end.—You will see by his note, that he intends doing with the Plays, as a *whole*,[4] what he is now doing with each individual play. I wrote him quite a long letter on the subject. I fear he will find it a much more difficult task. . . .

If one only lived in N. York, I fancy many splendid bargains could be had, at these *Auctions*. I presume that Bouton, Denham, Luyster, A. R. Smith, Sotheran, &c. all receive the bulk of their Stocks from these Auction-Sales; & put on enormous profits to the prices they paid. They probably make from 30 to 50 per cent off us. I have received some of the *best bargains* I ever got anywhere from the Auction-rooms; & you know how much *better* one could do by being there in person, than by *bidding* at random. I suppose you have recd. *Bouton's* new Catalogue. I observe that he offers a copy of Halliwell's Grand Folio Shak., like yours, for $550. It is very cheap, & I should dearly love to be able to buy it; but I must defer it yet a little longer. I suppose if one had $500. *in cash*, it might be had for that round sum. I should have supposed the Work would have advanced in price faster than it apparently has. . . .

I don't think you need be afraid to use Keightly's editions. In fact, for a *pocket edn.* I would prefer his to almost any other, for the reason that you know at a glance the *changes* he introduces into his Text, either by the references to the list at the end of the Play, or by being printed in *italics*. Altho' some critics are disposed to ridicule Mr. Keightly, he is a *good Shakespearian*.[5] His worst fault is his *egotism*, & that hurts no one. His little "Expositor" contains a mass of most useful & valuable matter; a real **multum in parvo**. Just for *use*—my own use—if I could not get another copy, $25.. would not buy mine. Like an old pair of breeches, however, my copy is so written over & *patched*[6] with my own notes in pencil, that you can hardly recognize the original printing.—Have you received your April No. of the Bibliopolist yet? I have not. I should like to have about 5 or 6 nos. extra, for my friends, each month, now, since you have taken charge of the Shn. Dept.—I presume I can get them from Sabin. I am glad to hear the publication will hereafter be more prompt & regular.[7] There is no *need*, one would suppose, of being so behindhand.—[b]

All that you say of English binders leaving out the "bastard title pages"[8] is *even so*. Not one of my Variorums has it in; and it is missing from a large no. of my other edns. that I have examined: altho' all my *finest* binding— that by Hayday, Rivière, Jenkins, and others—*has* it in. It is also left in in Matthews' work; he is a New Yorker, however, I believe. The man who has done a great deal of binding for me here, (now unfortunately gone away,) was an Englishman, who learnt his trade in London. He came near spoiling many of my finest edns. (the Cambridge, Dyce, Collier, &c. &c.) just in the way mentioned. I luckily caught him in time to keep them (the bastard titles) in; but I had a rough time with him, ere he would do it. He *determined* they should be left *out*, & I *determined* they shd be left *in*, & I won. But what a stubborn race bookbinders are anyway. They are fully convinced that "outsiders" know nothing about binding, and that what *they don't* know would make only a very small book. He told me that in England the bastard title was only to be found in cloth-bound books; & that it was right, & *fashionable*, to remove it from all books, when put into their last & regular binding. I could only convince him by taking to him "Power's Handy Book about Books," & showing him where it was recommended *always to leave this in*; and showing him *some* of Hayday's & Rivière's work, where it was retained.—. . .

You must tell me all about your 2d folio, when it comes.—Do you know, I was terribly tempted to order one, this Spring, that I saw advertised by *Sotheran*, in his *March '75* Catalogue. It is perfect, all but Ben Jonson's verses, which are wanting; *has* the portrait on the title, & is described as a "very fair copy in old calf gilt," for £15..15..0. . . .

---

[1] send it: I.e., to the printer; it appeared in "Shakespearian Gossip" June 1875.

[2] Demosthenes with his pebbles: According to legend Demosthenes strengthened his weak voice by declaiming with pebbles in his mouth (and on the beach, competing with the noise of the surf).

[3] the "faithful" & the "faithless": Possibly alluding to *Paradise Lost* V, where the angels are polarized, e.g. in the description of Abdiel, "Among the faithless, faithful only he" (V, 897).

[4] he intends doing with the Plays, as a *whole*: He did so in *System of Shakespeare's Dramas* (1877) a redaction of his essays on individual plays; C urged the project on him.

[5] he is a *good Shakespearian*: C elsewhere (161 c4, unpublished) contrasts K's Sh edn. unfavorably for N with his Milton edn. and calls the Sh edn. the work of K's dotage.

[6] so written over & *patched* with my own notes in pencil: C's heavily annotated copy of Keightley's *Shakespeare Expositor* is now in the University of Michigan's Harlan Hatcher Graduate Library.

[7] each month . . . more prompt & regular: *The Bibliopolist* was a bimonthly; it became even more "behind-hand" as time went by—and more slender, too (Vol. 7 is approximately twice the size of Vols. 8 and 9 combined); Sabin let the journal die in April 1877.

[8] "bastard title pages": half-title pages; the bastard title page precedes the full title page and contains only the book's short title.

---

[a] knee-joints] knee–I joints MS.
[b] behindhand] behind–I hand MS.

48:   11 May 1875

. . . I must congratulate you on securing the copy of the 2d Folio—imperfect as it is.—You got it **very low** indeed, I should say. One looks at an *imperfect Folio* of Shak. with different eyes than when we look at almost any other *imperfect* book. It is no *discredit* to it to be imperfect. What there *is* of it is all right, and we are thankful to have even that much. When bound, in the sumptuous manner you describe, it will be a valuable addition to your library, & you will look at it with pleasure & reverence. . . .

49:   16 May 1875

. . . I read a few chapters of "Dowden"; but it is *awfully dry & laboured writing*, so far as I read. It may get better further on. I will see what I can do with it in the shape of a little review; but I greatly fear that nothing very *interesting* can be made out of it. I hope you have bought Macready's "Reminiscences & Diaries." I have read a portion of it, and it is very interesting indeed. Apart from its personal history of the Life & Character of a true *gentleman* & *scholar*, you will find several bits of good criticism on Shakespearian and other dramas. It has made me *like Macready*: he was not alone an intelligent, conscientious, industrious, & popular Actor; but a deep student of *books* of all good kinds; and, besides, a true Christian. His private diaries show his genuine character. I know you will be pleased with the book.—

I see that Chatto and Windus, London, announce "an exact reproduction in reduced facsimile[1] of the first folio Shakspere"; a small folio, I suppose, by photolithography, like Staunton's contemplated one.—And I suppose you saw, also, that "Mr. Halliwell approving of the forthcoming pamphlet, 'Shakspere's plays: a chapter of Stage history. An Essay on the Shaksperian Drama, by A. H. Paget,' has presented 600 copies of it to the New Shakspere Society, for distribution to its members."—Good: cannot have too much of that sort of thing: don't you fully approve Mr. H.'s liberality? . . .

P.S. I suppose of course you have seen H. Sotheran & Co's Catalogue of *Shakespeariana* Apl. 30th.—I know how your mouth watered, by my own, reading over the list of so many things we both want. I have ordered about £10.. worth, through Sabin & Sons, & must *take my chances*, & be content with what I can get. As usual my luck will be like the poor cripple's at the Pool of Siloam,[2] someone will "step down before me." I ordered one book that I have long waited for, & which you have already, Wivell's Portraits, and Supplement.[3] £1..10..0 I think is the price, & it is *very low*. Did you not pay much more? I ordered, but without *any* hope of getting it, Capell's Notes & Various Readings, 3 vols. 4to.—£2..15.—Cheap enough. Most of the books are *very reasonable*, & apparently in *good new Hf. mor.* bindings.

Some, tho', are high.—£10..10..0 for an 1821 Var. in ordinary binding, cut, is a big price. It is the best list of "Shakespeariana" I have seen for sale for a long time.

[1] reduced facsimile: It appeared in 1876, and was a facsimile of Staunton's photolithograph, 1864–66.

[2] at the Pool of Siloam: The cripple was at the pool of Bethesda; C has conflated John 5:7 with John 9:7, where Jesus cured a blind man by having him bathe in the pool of Siloam.

[3] Wivell's Portraits, and Supplement: Abraham Wivell, *An Inquiry into the History, Authenticity, & Characteristics of the Shakspeare Portraits . . .* (1827) with *Supplement* (1827).

50:   29 May 1875

My dear Norris:

I arrived safely home again, yesterday, from a delightful visit to Cleveland, Ohio, where I have spent several days. I was pleased to see my dear little boy much grown, looking well, full of life & animal spirits, going to an excellent school, & learning quite fast enough. He has a good head on him, an open intelligent countenance; & (if I do say it myself) *good blood* in him, on both sides of the house. His great-grandfather (maternal) was an officer of distinction in the American Revolution. My ancestors have all been landowners in England, called there *yeomen* from time immemorial.—My boy is now 12 years old; & I hope he may live, & be a comfort to me, in my old age. He lives with his grandparents, and a maiden aunt; all of whom are devoted to him: & I only fear they will *spoil* him. In fact he is somewhat tainted that way already. It is astonishing how soon boys will find out their power. . . .

Thanks for the *May* No. of the "Literary Gem,"[1] and a thousand thanks for the "Cornell Review," containing Prof. Corson's admirable article on Ingleby's "Centurie of Prayse." How *well* he writes! Do you know I really admire Corson's terse, clear, sensible, style. While this review does justice to the "Centurie of Prayse," it is an invincible argument to the Baconite theory. Corson is certainly a scholar, & a clear-headed thinker; & he is *original* too. I read his "piece" over 3 or 4 times, & I was heartily pleased with it. It, and Mr. Spedding's letter to Holmes,[2] are two of the best refutations of that "pestilent heresy" I know of. I trust you also have carefully read them. I thought, as soon as I had leisure, I would write Prof. Corson a line, & tell him how greatly I was both *instructed* & *delighted* with his review. Do you think it would be an *acceptable* little courtesy, or not?

What a delightful evening you must have had among Mr. Furness' books, & in his, & his wife's company; & oh! *how* I should have enjoyed being with you in your jottings & notings, &c. I shall look with great interest for the article thereon, in the Bibliopolist.[3] I have long known of Cinthio's *Hecatommithi*, and its *rarity* & *value*; and I truly congratulate you on your good fortune in being now the owner of a copy. You are not only gradually, but rapidly, collecting a *complete* Shakespearian library. I had to laugh at your remark, "I have been making vigorous efforts to catch up to your collection, *and hope to do so.*" Why, my dear fellow, your collection now *far exceeds mine.* As I have often told you, my *means* will only permit me to go ahead slowly, *"festinare lentè"*; and I shall be an old man, should God spare my life, ere I have anything like a complete collection. Had I commenced my study of Shakesp. when I was younger, (when you did, for instance), I might now not only have been a good Shakespearian scholar, but had a splendid Shakespearian library. I have wasted many a hundred dollars on Novels, & *transient* literature, in my early days, that *then* (Shakespeariana were *then* less than half the prices they now are,) would have bought many a Shakn vol., now desirable & dear. But it is useless to regret. I must do the best in my power *now*, and tho' I can only pick up slowly, yet I think I study more what I do acquire, & certainly I appreciate them the more for the difficulty & self-denial requisite for their acquisition.—No: a library, like the noble one of Mr. Furness, must be the object of your ambition, & not *my* poor little collection.—. . .

When on the cars travelling, I read Emerson's Essay on "Shakespeare," in his book "Representative Men." I presume you have the book: & I can tell you his essays are all fine; of course I enjoyed that one on our favourite Poet the most of any of them.— . . . While travelling[a] I also read over again Goëthe's *Wilhelm Meister.* You have read this of course. It contains one of the best criticisms on *Hamlet* I ever read. Perfectly delightful. I have Bell & Daldy's nice edition of the work, & I enjoyed reading it greatly. . . .

I know you have given a good deal of attention to Shakespeare's *biography.* Did you ever read *De Quincey's* Life of the Poet? I did not, that is carefully, until lately; and it is really very clever & well done. He is a delightful writer anyway. This 'biography' was written for, & is in, the 8th Edn. of the Encyclopædia Britannica: and you will also find it, occupying 100 pp of the 2d vol. of De Quincey's Works, Ticknor & Fields' Edn., 1854, Boston.—Another charming bit of critical writing, that will delight you, if you have not already read it, is a short essay "On the Knocking at the gate, in Macbeth." It is in the beginning of the 3rd vol. of the Boston edn. of De Q's works. . . .

[1] the "Literary Gem": An eight-page periodical pubd. by the Crescent Literary Society of Philadelphia, beginning in January 1875. Two pages in each issue were reserved for Sh under sponsorship of the Philadelphia Shakespeare Society (not the organization that rejected N, but a younger and less prestigious rival).

[2] Mr. Spedding's letter to Holmes: James Spedding had edited Bacon's *Conference of Pleasure* in 1870; Holmes included in the 3d edn. (1875) of *The Authorship of Shakespeare* the letter Spedding had written him refuting the Baconian theory.

[3] the article thereon, in the Bibliopolist: It appeared in the June 1875 "Shakespearian Gossip."

[a] While travelling] while travelling MS.

51: 30 May 1875

. . . One book I ordered, which I *know* almost I shall not get, but I hope *you* may, as you have also ordered it, (of course ahead of me,) viz. "Capell's Notes & Various Readings," 3 vols., 4to. I forget the price, but I thought it very cheap. I shall be almost as glad if you get it, as if I got it myself. All the editors & Commentators roundly abuse that work, & yet it is very scarce, & hard to find. I have not heard of a copy for Sale in the U. S. since Burton's Sale. I have the 1st vol. (which is quite common,) & I prize it highly. Capell's notes are *always* right, scholarly, & perfectly explanatory; but couched in such obscure style[1] as often to be more inexplicable than the passage explained. But, when you once see the old Scholar's meaning, it sticks to you, & you can bet on it. What little I have of Capell has done me great good. I have often thought that anyone would do a *noble service* to Shakespearian students, if he would take Capell's 10 vols. of text, & 3 4to-vols. of Notes, & reprint them *verbatim et literatim*, only putting the notes *directly* underneath the text to which they belong. It should be done in good old faced type, on good paper, in about 8 octavo volumes. I would not permit a single *change* in any shape or form; but just to make an edition of *Capell*, that could be used with real pleasure, on acct. of good typography, & having the notes at foot of same page as the text. But I fear such a venture would never pay. None but Scholars, men who really knew the *worth* of Capell, would buy it: and altho' the notes are so terribly scarce & dear now, not over say 100 or 150 copies of a new edition could be sold. And yet, if Shakespeare is going to be studied the next generation, as he is in this, any gentleman, of leisure to superintend carefully the reprint, & of wealth to pay for a handsome edition, would be conferring an invaluable *boon* on his own & future generations. Did not Mr. Halliwell *dedicate* his grand folio edition to the memory of *Capell*[2]? I think I have read that he did so somewhere. I fancy poor Capell was the longest, hardest, closest, most industrious, & most conscientious, Student of Shakespeare that ever lived. I think it was 30 years, or perhaps more, that he kept digging away at the mine, & then *died* before his labours saw the light of print. Steevens & Malone stepped in, & used up the fruits of his researches without acknowledgment; or if they deigned to mention him, it was only to sneer at & abuse him. It always makes me feel sad, when I think of the pains & labours he endured, & the poor reward he reaped. . . .

I read about halfway thro' *Dowden*; and there I stuck fast. It was too dry for the cars, or to read at Cleveland. I tried to like it, but, truth to say, I did *not* very well. No doubt there are many good things in it—many fine deep thoughts, and some *excellent* criticism; but it is all too fine-spun, too elaborate, too **wordy**, too "high-faluting";[a] his style is anything but pleasing to *me*. I had rather have one page of Professor Corson's good, plain, honest, sturdy sense, than a whole chapter of Dowden's *Metaphysics*. I fear, feeling as I do now, I shall never be able to write anything about it satisfactory for the *Bib.*—I will not promise, as yet, however: I will give it one more trial; & then report progress.—I never *could* write about *anything*, unless the matter were *congenial* to my feelings, & Dowden's book is *not*. It *may be like some grand operatic air*, or other fine piece of music: *another* ear & taste might be charmed; but *mine*, I regret to say, are so uncultivated I cannot appreciate its superfine strains. The *thought* in the book is so strained, & spun out so supersubtly fine; and the *words*—the language—are so affectedly grand, & high-sounding, that I get *lost*, not in admiration, but in a German sort of haziness. You have undoubtedly heard people go off into ecstacies at a "grand Concert" of music, when the fact was, it was nothing but its unintelligibility that was dumbfoundering their ears: & it is on the same principle—*omnes ignotum pro magnifico*[3]—that men admire a book like this of Dowden's: I very much question whether the Professor understands much of it himself.— . . .

[1] couched in such obscure style: Samuel Johnson said of Capell, "he doth gabble monstrously" (Boswell's *Life*).
[2] Did not Mr. Halliwell *dedicate . . . Capell?*: C is mistaken, but correct in his recollection of H's high opinion of Capell; see H's *A Few Words in Defence of the Memory of Edward Capell* (1861).
[3] *omnes ignotum pro magnifico*: Tacitus, *Agricola* 30 (slightly altered).

[a] high-faluting] high–I faluting MS.

52: 30 May 1875

. . . It seems to me that you have been entirely too good-natured & generous thro' this whole transaction; & my *respect* for Brae is all gone. I am sorry, very; because I should not have looked for such conduct from *him*. I fear, indeed am almost *sure*, you, or Ashworth[1] will not dispose of a copy of the Astrolabe at *any price*. It is out of date; no one wants such a production revived in this age of advanced *science*. Even *Chaucer's* name will be of no avail. The other, "C. C. & S."[2] may probably sell. *Every* Shakespearian, who has not a copy, certainly ought to have it. I will take another one of you; but the "Astrolabe" you *could not give* me. Is there not some mistake about the *duty*? If the books were "invoiced," (as I understand your letter to Brae suggested,) at 1/- each, the duty could only have been 3d. on each, or 25/- on 100 books, & not £5..0..0, the total **value**. I don't feel one bit like "roaring" at your misfortune. I only see in it another instance of your extreme goodness, & liberality, & generosity towards your friends,— especially your *Shakespearian* friends,—a kindness of which *I* have received so many *instances*. The only thing I blame you for is this; you should have nipped the thing in the bud; told him plainly there was, nor would be, *no sale* for a book *here*, that was totally & provedly unsaleable in England, where, if anywhere, the demand for such a book would be likely to exist.

If, after that, he had persisted, & sent the books, you should simply have sent them back.—But he wrote you such a good criticism[3] on Corson's "Jottings," you thought he could not do anything wrong. As I before said, I can, hereafter, have *no respect* for a man that will so *use* (rather *abuse*) an incipient friendship. Whenever *I* do such a thing, I want you, & every friend I have, to *cut* me dead, & publish me from "Dan to Beersheba."[4]. . .

I hope your enthusiasm in the cause will be fully rewarded in obtaining large photographs of the Stratford Bust, taken from the right level. I remember, when I was in the Church, looking at this Bust, with a party of relatives & friends, in 1851, at my suggestion, the Sexton or guide brought me a step-ladder, which I used to get a closer & better view of the countenance: & you would be astonished at the vast *difference* it made. Altho' *then* I knew but little on the subject, & was no more than an ordinary sight-seer,[a] I remember well speaking of the necessity of anyone (who wanted to *see* the effect right.) getting on to a level with the face. The *large* upper lip all vanished; the nose looked better, and the effect of *fatness* in the lower part of the face was not noticed, as when below, & *looking up.*—The *first time* I ever was at Stratford was in 1840, a boy going through the town to Oxford. We stopped a few hours,[5] & looked at all the sights commonly seen. *Then* the old Birthplace had not been renovated; & I recollect a board over the door, painted "The immortal Shakspeare was born in this House." Happy, Happy, Happy days, never to return! . . .

[1] Ashworth: A Philadelphia bookseller.
[2] "C. C. & S.": *Collier, Coleridge, and Shakespeare.*
[3] he wrote you such a good criticism: N did not publish it in "Shakespearian Gossip"; the "Jottings" is a pamphlet, *Jottings on the Text of Hamlet* (1874).
[4] from "Dan to Beersheba": See Judges 20:1, etc.
[5] We stopped a few hours: They apparently did not sign the Visitors' Book for 1840, now in the Library of the Shakespeare Birthplace Trust.

[a] sight-seer] sight–I seer MS.

(This Note is *not* for the "Bibliopolist"; but for my friend Norris' private eye, and then for the *Stove*.)—[a]

55: 5 June 1875

Dear Norris:

You may have observed in *Notes & Queries*, during the last few months, a discussion on the meaning of the word "*wappened,*" in the line in *Timon of Athens*, (IV, 3.):—"this [*viz.* gold] is it

That makes the *wappened* widow wed again,"[1] &c.

i.e. be sought after in marriage, or get married, again: "wed" = wedded.
There have appeared at least a half-dozen explanations of "wappened,"
and I have been surprised at their being, often, so **very wide** of the meaning. A certain Mr. Brown says, it refers to the arms, or escutcheon, borne
by a widow; that the widow being "wappened," & therefore provided for,
has no need to marry again!—Another man says, it is from the Saxon
waepun, a weapon; & a "wappened widow" is a widow weaponed, or
wounded, & so waped, overcome,[b] dejected, or cast down!—And Dr Char-
nock says, it is from Saxon *wepan*, to weep, & means a weeping widow!

Steevens has a good note on the passage, which you must read. He
comes as *near* to giving the correct meaning, as he *dare*: and his examples
prove his point. Dyce simply explains it by "overworn"; and adduces more
examples, which, so far as I can examine them, all prove the same meaning. But his modesty forbade him stating *how*, or *in what way*, or *by what*,
the widow was "overworn."—

If you will look at the word "to wap," in Halliwell's "Archaic Dictionary,"
you will see he defines it, "a cant word, *futuo, futuere.*" [I presume you
know what *that* means.] And he quotes from an old "canting song," which
proves it. Under "wappen'd" he says, "Steevens is right in deriving this
word from *wap, futuo.*" Wright's "Dictionary of Obsolete & Provincial English," (1869,) gives "*To wap,*" and "To wappen, (cant) *futuere.*"—Is it, then
not plain enough[c] to see what "wappen'd" means?—The "wappen'd
widow" is one who is, (as we would now say,) **played-out, used-up,**—
debilitated by excessive **venery.** And this is what Dyce means by "overworn."—The argument also requires this sense, if you will look for a
moment at the context. Read what Timon says that *gold will do.* "This is it
which makes the wappen'd widow wed again"; if she only have plenty of
gold, no matter for her being "wappened," she will be wooed, & wedded
again. He then gives other instances of its power:

> "She, whom the spital-house, and ulcerous sores
> Would cast the gorge at, *this* embalms and spices
> To the April day again."

Steevens gives a quotation from Middleton & Decker's "Roaring Girl,"
(1611,) that one would think *ought* to settle the meaning:—

> *"Moll.* And there you shall *wap* with me.
> *Sir B.* Nay, Moll, what's that *wap*?
> *Moll. Wappening* and niggling is all one; the rogue my man can tell
> you."—

And from another old play, 1610, he quotes:—"*Niggling* is company-
keeping with a woman: this word is not used now, but *wapping*; and

thereof comes the name *wapping*-morts for whores."—After all this, (Steevens, Halliwell, Wright, & Dyce, & their **quotations**,) could one suppose any "critic" unable to see[2] that a "wappen'd widow" was one who had paid *so many* "bed-rites"; who had sacrificed *so often*, & *so long*, to Venus, that she was no longer desirable, or "any good," for that purpose?—& yet, give **her** *gold* enough, she would soon be married again.

While on this subject, let me explain what I conceive to be the meaning of another word in Shakespeare, "over-scutch'd."[3] You remember where it occurs, in II Hen. IV. III. 2. Falstaff, speaking of Justice Shallow, & his braggadocio of what he did when he was *young*, &c, says, "he came ever in the rear-ward of the fashion; and sung those tunes to the *over-scutched* huswives that he heard the carmen whistle, and sware—they were his Fancies, or his Good-nights," &c. This term is generally explained as meaning *whipt, carted*; & Johnson says it means *dirty, grimed*.—But it really means, *precisely* what I have explained "wappen'd" as meaning. There is no question about "huswives" meaning *strumpets, whores*. Shakespeare attaches this sense almost universally to *house-wives*, or *huswives*, with very few exceptions. Our words "hussy" & "hussies" sometimes have that sense *now*.—But for "overscutched," compare the *name* the Poet gives to the "bawd" in *Mea. for Mea. viz.* "Mrs. *Over*done," with a passage in the *Merry Wives,—*

"*Mrs. Ford.* Sir John! Art thou there, my deer? My male deer?
Falstaff. My doe with the black *scut*!"[4] &c.—

In the same way that "o'erparted,"[5] in *L.L.L.*, means 'whose part is *too much* for him'—above his abilities; so here, can there be a doubt[6] that *overscutched* means one who hath *scutched* too much, or used her *scut* to excess, and that "the overscutched huswives" meant *old, played-out* whores? I think not. And, besides,[d] it is the only meaning of the words that affords any sense to the passage & context. Shallow was "ever in the *rearward*" (mark that!) "of the fashion"; he was not the *man* to attack a new, fresh piece; but he sang old odds & ends of songs he had heard among the draymen to the old "rips," & *they* made *him* believe he was a fine gallant, and *he them* that these were *his* "Fancies" & *his* "Good-nights." Grant White reads "over-switch'd";[e] but what need of change, when the original word is so plain & expressive? Besides, "scutcherie" was an old & common term for *whoredom*. Malone has a quotation from "Bankes' Bay Horse in a Traunce," 1595, which "settles" it:—"The leacherous landlord hath his wench at his commandment, and is content to take *ware* for his money; his private *scutcherie* hurts not the commonwealth farther than that his whoore shall have a house rent-free."—

Did you ever examine Halliwell's definition of "*Sear*," in his "Archaic Dictionary"? If not, do so; it is curious. His 3rd definition is, "The touchhole of a pistol. Hence used metaphorically for the *pudendum muliebre*." But you must be *sure* to read the whole of it. He comes *very near* the correct meaning of "tickle o' the sere,"[7] in *Hamlet*. Instead of the "touchhole," it means the "trigger," or, rather, the *spring* that connects the trigger with the hammer, in a gunlock. He gives a quotation, (which I had never noticed until recently,) which I think entirely proves the meaning right, as given in the *Clar. Press Hamlet*, & by Dr Nicholson, in "N. & Q."[8]—It seems a wonder how he came to miss it, after coming so close to it. The quotation is:— "Even as a pistole that is ready charged and bent, will flie off by & by, if a man do but touch the *seare*." *Lambarde's Peram.*, 1596, p 452. Now "by & by" means "in an instant," (as it commonly does both in **Sh.**, and the **Bible**, and **old authors** generally.) But a "pistole" does not "flie off" by touching the "touchhole," but by touching[f] the "trigger," or rather the "*seare*," which releases the *hammer. Is'nt it plain to you, now?*—**Pardon**, & **burn up, this letter**. Yours ever,

J. C.—

[1] wed again: The grammar of *Tim.* 4.3.39 is ambiguous; *wed* can be taken as an infinitive or as a past participle; a man's gold may make her wish to marry though she is wappened, or her gold may make a widow attractive to suitors though she is wappened. In addition to the evidence C gives for the second interpretation, there are the immediately preceding lines in *Tim.* in which the accursed, the leper, and the thief all are made attractive by gold. Some modern editors (e.g., Bevington) make the other interpretation.

[2] could one suppose any "critic" unable to see: Partridge failed to recognize this meaning of *the wappened widow (see Shakespeare's Bawdy* [1947/1955]).

[3] "over-scutch'd": *2H4* 3.2.317.

[4] Sir John! . . . black *scut*!: *Wiv.* 5.5.16–18.

[5] "o'erparted": *LLL* 5.2.584.

[6] can there be a doubt: Partridge failed to see this meaning in the passage (op. cit.); *OED* does not relate the word *scutchery* to *scut* and glosses it "knavery."

[7] "tickle o' the sere": *Ham.* 2.2.324. *OED* supports C's interpretation; not in Partridge.

[8] Dr Nicholson, in "N. & Q.": 4 *Notes & Queries* 8 (1871): 62–63.

[a] (This Note . . . *Stove.*)—] ↑(This Note . . . Stove.)—↓ MS. [inserted between letterhead and salutation].

[b] overcome] over-| come MS.

[c] not plain enough] ↑not↓ plain enough MS.

[d] And, besides,] And, ~~in this passage~~ ↑besides↓, MS.

[e] over-*switch'd*] over-| *switch'd* MS.

[f] but by touching] but ↑by touching↓ MS.

56: 6 June 1875

. . . What you say about *importing* books, & the rascally Custom House swindling, I know well, practically, to be the case. I have suffered many scores of dollars, I know, that way.—I remember when I imported my old "Sh. Soc. Pub.," because *one* or *two* of the last vols. were within the *20 years*, they charged me *duty on the whole*: and so they did on my *1821 Variorum*, most unjustly; but not being there, I could get *no redress*, tho' I tried. In one bill was *one dollar & fifty cents* "postage," when *not one* letter was written; only they informed *Adams Express*, to whom it was consigned in N.Y., that a package of books had arrived! And as for "porterage," "brokerage," "insurance" (!), "custom-house *fees*," &c. &c., it is positively *disgusting* the *swindling* that is practised.—I see *gold* is going up, & I fear Sabin will not keep his promise to get me undutiable books for 30¢ to the 1/—. If he do, I will let you know, so you too can take advantage. I observe that, *by mail*, the shilling in England averages from 33 to 35 cents here, except on small & *costly* books.—. . .

58: 14 June 1875

. . . I think *sincerity* the first & main element in letter-writing: and how much more agreeable it is to read the free & easy epistles of Cowper & Byron, with every line & word warm from the heart-mint, and how much *more you know* of the writers too, than the polished correspondence of Pope. I hate a friendly letter that bears the appearance of being *studied*. Charles Lamb's (bless him!) are perfect specimens of good letter writing. He would just as soon as not make a big blot of ink on his sheet on purpose, and write *about it*; and why not? To write as nearly as possible what one would say face to face is a good rule, & leave the *style* to take care of itself. Who cares for a grammatical error, or a dozen of them, in a warm enthusiastic friendly conversational chat? They but show the mind is more intent on *convincing* another mind, of telling the truth, of conveying an idea or picture as it appears to one—rather than of making an impression of smartness, or eloquence.—. . .

I read with earnest attention, in your note of the 11*th* what you say of my recommending the Messrs. Virtue's new folio edn. of Knight.[1] I have thought it all over seriously, & the result is, I cannot for the life of me see wherein I have done anything wrong, or which I will "live to regret." I think if you had seen & examined the work, you would agree with me. In the first place, there is nothing "catchpenny"[a] about it. It is simply *what it professes to be*—neither more nor less. It is the *entire* text of Knight's "Second Pictorial," well printed in good heavy-faced type, on good paper. . . . The "Introductions" are on the same plan:[2] & the glorious "Supplementary Notices" are all entire. The forty-three[b] Steel Plates are from Paintings by Leslie, Maclise, Stanfield,[3] &c., the *best* English Painters of the day. . . . When you see & examine them, I feel sure you cannot but admire them. Most of the Plates comprise *several characters*, which are in the very spirit of the author who invented them. Now these are *not old worn-out*[c] Plates: they have been used once in the "Art Journal," & that is all. They are as *sharp &*

clear to my eye, as they could possibly be. Now where is there anything "catchpenny"[d] about all this? These admirable & beautiful illustrative Plates attract attention, & set people to reading the Text. And could they have a *better text*, one which is so close to that of the Folio 1623, that it is the *only objection* that has been made to it? . . . In the Notes & Introductions, everything needed for explanation is given: & as I have often said to you, the "Supplementary Notices" are beyond all of my praise. They are the *best general commentaries* on Shakespeare I have ever read. They first inspired me with the *love* I have of the Great Poet's Works, breathing as they do the very spirit of Shakespeare. I remember when I was young, a member of your profession, a true friend & a very learned man, advising me to read & study Bacon's Essays, told me to get the edn. with *Whateley's Annotations.* He says, "They are almost as good as old Bacon himself": & so I can say of the "Supplementary Notices" of C. Knight: they are almost as good as old Shakespeare himself. *As a rule* I am sternly opposed to *subscription books.* They are *generally* "poor & catchpenny." But in this case, there are advantages overruling my objections. How very few would spare the money to buy a full edition like this, at once? Or, if bought, to *read* it? Whereas, by taking it 2 Nos. a month, they not only *will subscribe*, & so become possessors of a thing all must own to be valuable, but hardly miss the price: and moreover, will *read* it, No. by No., as they would a Newspaper, & so get to know something about Shakespeare, they otherwise certainly would not know; &, maybe, be inspired to pursue the study further. Then it is *very cheap.* Fifty cents a No. (London, 2/—)—40 Nos in all—$20. for so *good* an edn. is very cheap: the *Plate* alone in each No. is well worth the Hf. dollar.

And now, what have I done? I *recommended* this edn. to my fellow citizens—the young men especially—who know little or nothing of Sh:—and they are buying it freely. Unfortunately, perhaps, people in a small place like this, place so much confidence in my judgment, "Shakespearianly," if I had withheld my support to it, not a half-dozen—hardly one—copies would have been taken. *Could* I, practically, have recommended a *better* thing? Tell me that. The agent will place, on the strength of my little note, from 75 to 100 copies, on the tables, & in the hands of young & old, of what? Why Knight's Shakespeare complete—Notes, Introductions & Supplementary Notices—of his revised edn., in a good large type, on white paper, & with 43 admirable steel illustrative engravings, 8 by 10 inches in size. Could these folks, not being *critical* students, have a better—a purer—text to read, or better popular Notes, & elucidations, & commentaries? If they could—no such edn. is *now* being published; & I thought it better they should have this than none. It may lead them, as it did *me*, to study Grant White, & Dyce, & Collier, & Halliwell, & Furness. Even under these circumstances, had I seen anything "Catchpenny" about it, I should have been the *last* man to recommend it. But I don't. If you do, please show me.

I'll tell you what I consider a "catchpenny" edn.—*That of Tallis*. It is neither one thing nor another. It professes to be Halliwell's. But is it? Read what he says of it in my 1 vol. Folio copy of his "Comedies." And the *Illustrations*! Pah! "an ounce of civet, good apothecary."

Then you think I did wrong to accept a copy as a present. Well, perhaps I did. But, you must know, I accepted nothing until *after* I had given Sangster my note of recommendation. *He* had no authority to present me with anything. I *subscribed* for the edn., was the first to enter my name; & gave him a short recommendatory Note, in which I spoke as I thought of Knight's edns. *Every word* was the exact & literal *truth*. He sent a copy of my note to the house in N. Y., or Cincinnati, I forget which; and I found, left on my desk afterwards, the first six Nos., with a very courteous note from the *publishers*, thanking me for the interest I had taken in the work, and politely begging me to accept these Nos. as a compliment from them. They further stated that I would be pleased to learn that this work had met with a greater *success*, both in England and America, than any which their house had ever published. They told me that the original *copyright* was sold by *Knight* to Routledge & Sons, & by them to *Virtue & Co.*, London, & that their *right* to issue this edn. was unassailable. That there was not a word in it, that was not from Mr. Knight's own pen: & that it had been endorsed by all Shakespearian critics, & scholars, & amateurs, both in England & America, wherever it had been introduced. Now would it not have been affectation, fastidious, silly foolishness in *me* to have returned their compliment in their face? I simply thanked them, & that was all. Mr. Sangster has since informed me that they wrote to him to instruct the deliverer of the Nos. not to receive any money from me for my subscription.—I have now written you all I know of it. When I got your note, I thought of going to him, & telling him I had done wrong to accept their present, & to pay him for the Nos.—But, after reflection I thought it would be a rude piece of presumption, & I dropped the idea. . . .

Two of my Shakespearian friends in Cincinnati, members of your profession, both *scholars* & *collectors*, wrote me some time ago, highly praising the work; & *they* accepted copies of presentation; not, "by no manner of means," as "hire & salary"; like myself, as I trust, they would be *above* any so low a motive; but merely as a testimonial from the Publishers of the value of their recommendation, in circulating the edition. I have written thus freely, & at length, about this, because I was pained you should have entertained[e] the idea that *any amount* of "hire & salary" could have tempted me to recommend a thing that was *not* what it *purported, & expressed itself to be*, & that is what I conceive to be the meaning of "Catchpenny." For 2 or 3 years there has been a Subscription edn. of Shakespeare, a N. Y. edn., carried round here. It is something like *Tallis*';[4] said to be *Halliwell's* & *Knight's*, & *Collier's*, with portraits (!) of American actors, &c. You may have seen it. Time & again, the agents have begged me to put down my name, & it should not cost me anything. But of course I never dreamed of doing so. . . .

I am glad you saw "Midsummer Night's Dream" on the stage. How I *should* have enjoyed sitting with you, & commenting with you on the passing scenes! I once saw it, at Laura Keene's Theatre,[5] in New York; it was a grand *pageant*, but not Shakespeare. Still I liked it: and my recollections of it are pleasant. I shall never forget *Bottom*. His Asses' head would *not* stay on right, & in pulling the string that opened the mouth to speak, he *would* pull the whole concern on one side: the applause in the pit was thundering.—. . .

[1] Virtue's new folio edn. of Knight: Marketed in America by John C. Yorston & Co.

[2] on the same plan: I.e., containing all of Knight's work except what refers to woodcuts omitted in V & Y, and adding no new material.

[3] Leslie, Maclise, Stanfield: Robert Leslie, Daniel Maclise, Clarkson Stanfield.

[4] a N. Y. edn. . . . something like *Tallis'*: A piracy issued by Martin and Johnson; for an account of the chicanery surrounding this edn. and Tallis', see our "New Information About Some Nineteenth-Century Editions of Shakespeare from the Letters of Joseph Crosby," *Papers of the Bibliographical Society of America* 71 (1977): 279–94.

[5] at Laura Keene's Theatre: This would have been sometime between 1856 and 1863; the production may have been a re-creation of the "notable" (*DAB*) MND which Miss Keene mounted earlier in San Francisco. Best known for having played in *Our American Cousin* in Ford's Theatre the night of Lincoln's assassination, Laura Keene is worthy of remembrance on other grounds, according to *DAB*.

[a] catchpenny] catch-| penny MS.

[b] forty-three] forty-| three MS.

[c] *worn-out*] *worn-| out* MS.

[d] catchpenny] catch-| penny MS.

[e] should have entertained] should ↑have↓ entertained MS.

59: 　15 June 1875

My dear Norris:

Since I wrote you yesterday, I have received your note of the 12th, covering Mr. Furnivall's epistle, which I herewith return. I am glad it isn't any *worse*. I hope now that he has relieved his bile by calling you irredeemably vulgar, and no gentleman, he has exhausted his stock of blackguardism, & feels better. "Hard words," however, as they say, "break no bones"; and as long as the Atlantic rolls between you, I have no fears of any "bloody or fatal end." I fancy he thought he was putting "vinegar and pepper in't," when he indited it; "brief shall it be, my lord, but very bitter"—"*Youth*, whatsoever thou art, thou art but a scurvy fellow"— "Wonder not, nor admire not in thy mind, *why I do call thee so*, for I will show thee *no reason for't*"—"Fare thee well; and God have mercy on one of our souls!"—I will "write it in a martial hand; be curst and brief"; "Tho' it be but little, it shall be fierce"; "I will taunt him with the license of ink," and there shall be "gall enough" in my ink, thought I write "with[a] a *goose*-pen, no matter."—As good old Sir Toby says, "therefore this letter, being so **excellently ignorant**, will breed no terror in the *youth*; he will find it comes from a *clodpole*."—

Of course, you will send no reply to this "missive," and I hope the "clodpole" will here let the thing drop. If he keeps from making any attack on you *in print*—dragging your name into some of his publications, in a scurrilous way, I shall be thankful: and, old as I am, may yet live to see you two shaking hands, burying the hatchet, and "hob-nobbing" like the best of friends; though your "incensement, at this moment, is so implacable that satisfaction can be none but by pangs of death and sepulchre."—I am such a coward myself, and have such a horror of literary quarrels, that, like Sir Andrew, "I'ld have seen him *damned* ere I'ld have challenged him," and, like poor Viola, "I care not who knows so much of my mettle."—. . .

I will conclude this note with a little "explanation" (for yourself,) from my "Collectanea." You know, in the *Two Gentlemen of Ver.*, the passage where Launce says to Speed "x x because thou hast not so much *charity* in thee, as to go to the Ale[1] with a Christian." This I fancy is not fully understood. "Ales" were merry meetings for drinking ale, and there were several kinds of them, as the "Whitsun Ale," the "Church Ale," &c. This last seems to have been the exact counterpart of our "Church Suppers," "Mite Societies," "Strawberry Festivals," &c. &c. When any extra repairs were needed, or contributions for charitable purposes, or other Church assessments, an "Ale" was given by the Church Officers; at which a very large quantity was brewed especially, and sold at big prices per drink, or per pitcherful, to the honest ale-loving parishioners; and so the funds required were raised, and the folks all pleased. Of course no *Jews* would be present at "Church-Ales"; and that is why Launce says "Thou art an Hebrew, a Jew, and not worth the name of a Christian"; and, afterwards, "because thou hast not so much *charity* (mark the word,) in thee, as to go to the *ale* with a Christian.—"[b]. . .

[1] to go to the Ale: *TGV* 2.5.58; a passage from Stubbes's *Anatomy of Abuses* quoted in OED confirms C's interpretation; modern edns., e.g., Riverside, explicate as C does.

[a] write "with] write with MS.
[b] Christian.—"] Christian.— MS.

62:   29 June 1875

. . . I will send you a notice of *Dowden*, in time. I am reading him carefully now. I bent down to the book, as you would read Blackstone or Kent; & do you know, the more I read, the better I began to like it. Excepting its "high-faluting" language, it is really an *able work*. Its scholarship is immense; his analysis of character, & skill in dissecting human nature is wonderful: but he has undertaken a difficult task; & it is very doubtful to my mind whether any of us will be any better for such works. There is a great deal of guess-work about it after all, and deductions are often made from very small & inadequate premises. It is unquestionably the *best* book on the *man*, & the *mind* of, Shakespeare, as gathered from his works, that has ever been penned, & a real acquisition[1] to our stock of Shakespeariana; but his style is too *rich*—his figures too gorgeous—& his combinations too numerous & often plausible only. A little more common sense, & a little less *ambitious* style, would have made a capital work of it.—I shall try & write what I think of it, with a short sketch of its method, in not exceeding two pages of foolscap. Will that suit you? Dowden is not the man to be thoughtlessly *attacked*: "he is a scholar, & a ripe & good one"; he has written a work that I would give my library to be *able* to write; he is no F. J. *Furnivall* "by a jugfull"; he is a real honour to the "New Sh. Society," altho' only *one* of its V.P.s—

Permit me to congratulate you on getting so fine a copy of F4. I think you are *right* in buying a *good copy*, once for all; then, you are not perpetually hankering after a *duplicate*. Now that you have a first rate one, you will not trouble yourself looking through catalogues to see what is offered: and you have the satisfaction of knowing you have a piece of property that will always *appreciate* in value.— It is real amusing to hear you talking of going into bankruptcy, & selling your books, & in the next breath paying $130. for a fourth folio!—If Quaritch's *third,* that he bought for £57. is *perfect*, I think it was a cheap bargain; but fancy asking £120. for the same book! He knows however what he is about, & will probably get it. The 3d. is almost as scarce as the 1st, for some reason; it is said on acct. of so many being burnt up in the fire in London in 1666, tho' that is disputed.—. . .

I am sorry you missed the "Croft's Annotations," because it was cheap, considering its **extreme rarity**. . . . It only contains 24 pp. of notes; but some of them, when you can make them out from the typ. errors, are very funny, & very *original*. For instance, you remember in the *Two Gent*. Julia tells Lucetta she has "a month's mind"[2] to something. The commentators give a round-about explann. of "month's mind," which is too long to quote, & you no doubt know all about it; it never satisfied me a bit; and Mr Croft, I believe, gives the *correct* interpretation, viz. the *longing* which (I presume you have discovered) pregnant women have[a] when about "a month gone."—The fact is, as I have said to you before, not only this, but scores of other simple explanations in Shakespeare are missed from *over-subtlety,* from an unwillingness to give them a plain, practical, common sense meaning, well understood by the Poet and the audiences of his day; from a wish to show extensive learning, & raking up some metaphysical or

transcendental allusion, that *he* probably never dreamt of, to print a long
note that is copied by each succeeding editor.—. . .

[1] a real acquisition: The book was very influential in the next seventy-five years: twenty-five printings by 1962.
[2] "a month's mind": *TGV* 1.2.134. Clifford Leech shows in the Arden Edn. that the original meaning was legal: "a religious commemoration of a deceased person on a day one month after his death"; by the late sixteenth century the idiom took on the meaning C assigns it here (though Leech, like the Penguin editor, speaks of the last, not the first, month of pregnancy).

[a] women have] women ~~to~~ have MS.

63:   1 July 1875

. . . Did you ever notice that *Stephano* is always pronounced with ă in *The
Tempest*, "Is not this Stephăno[1] my drunken butler?", and with ā in the *Mer.
of Venice*, "Stephāno is my name,[2] and I bring word," & "My friend
Stephāno, signify, I pray you"? After Sh. wrote the *M. of V.*, & before he
wrote the *Temp.* he became acquainted with Ben Jonson, who taught him
the correct classical pronunciation.—

[1] "Is not this Stephăno: *Tmp.* 5.1.277.
[2] "Stephāno is my name . . . "My friend Stephāno,: *MV* 5.1.28, 51.

64:   7 July 1875

. . . I am glad, indeed, to learn that Mr. Furness has agreed[1] to write a
critical review of Daniel's new revised text of *Romeo & Juliet*. As you well
say, no one is so well qualified; if he can only spare the time. It will be a
delightful treat, most unquestionably: and besides I think it is a valuable
compliment to you too, when so many of the most ambitious literary
journals would give their eye-teeth for an article from the pen of Mr.
Furness. Do you know how his *Hamlet* is progressing? And when he expects to go to press with it? Mr. J. P. Collier alludes to him as being *sick,*—
and unable either to work or correspond. That is not so, is it?—I am very
sorry to hear of Mr. Halliwell-Phillipps being so nervously afflicted.[2] The
world of Shakespearian letters can ill afford to spare him from work. There
is no doubt that he is better prepared to write the *Life* of Shakespeare than
any other man living. I do hope he will soon be all right again.—
What a truly wonderful old scholar Collier is! To think of his working
away on Shakespeare's *text*, at 87 years of age! . . .
I have no doubt these booksellers all speculate on the demand, from
such men as you and me, for Shakespeariana, & put up prices accordingly.—For my part, I shall just go along *slowly* & *quietly*, as I have done for

nearly ten years, and pick up a book now & then, as I can afford it, and as the *price* may correspond to the *value*, and not be dragooned, by any of them, into paying extortionate prices, just because they know I want their books. There will be "Shakespeariana" enough to meet the demand, no doubt, many years after I am dead and gone; and I cannot *bear* to be imposed on; I had much rather wait patiently, and read what I have, & acquire more by *slow degrees*. I cannot expect to live long enough to own *all* that has been written & printed on the subject, like the Shak. Mem. Library, at Birmingham. I *hope*, ere many more years, to obtain the *last 3 Folios*, & Halliwell's Folio Edition: but at present I have to regulate my ambition by the size of my "pile." I have a quite wealthy father living, in England, whose life may God long spare!—At his death, if he leaves me some money, I intend to put a few more hundreds, perhaps 2 or 3 thousand dollars more, into my Shakespearian books.—Then, again, I am 50 years old[3] myself, and may probably "shuffle off this mortal coil" before that event occur. So, I try to be *content*, & thankful for what I have; & leave the future to take care of itself.— . . .

I have finished *The Two Gentlemen of Verona*, in my course of study; and *As You Like It* succeeds. I don't think I was ever so *long* over one play, as I have been over that easy simple one. But I have been so interrupted, with travelling, outside reading, & other things, it is no wonder. I enjoy *nothing* so much as to read & study each Play, according to my particular way. When I once get through one, there is *not much* about it I don't know more or less of. What a saving of time, & repetition, the next generation will have, by being able to get *all* that is material about any one play in *one* of Mr. Furness' comprehensive volumes: for, of course, sh*d* he not live to complete the edn. some other editor will do it. I always *begin* with the pure & simple *text* in Booth's Reprint; then the *critical text* edns. (Cambridge, Dyce, Staunton, &c. &c.); then all the *explanatory* edns. (Knight, Clarke, White, Hudson, Singer, Rann, &c. &c. *beginning* with the 1821 Var.); Then all the outside explanatory, textual, *commentaries*, from Upton, Heath, Edwards, &c., down to *now*, so much of each as attaches to the play in hand, including Abbott's Grammar, (each item by the Index,) S. Walker's books, the first 2 vols., & *Vers.*, by Mrs. H. H. F.'s[4] Index [thanks to your great kindness], & the 3d by itself; Keightley's Expositor; R. G. W.'s[5] Shak. Scholar; Douce; Dyce's Remarks, Few Notes, & Strictures; Singer's Shak. Vindicated; S. Bailey's 2 vols; not omitting old Z. Jackson, or A. Becket; all the *little* works on the text, such as Cartwright's, S. Jervis', Hunter's, Nichols', P. A. Daniel's, Arrowsmith's, Ritson's, &c.; Hunter's New Illustrations; &c. Then I run through the *School* editions, wherever I have[a] any on the play, Hudson's, Clarendon, Rugby, &c. to see if I can pick up a stray crumb, and lastly, the great æsthetic critics, Ulrici, Gervinus, Schlegel, Hazlitt, Mrs. Jameson, Hudson, reading only so much of each as belongs to the play in hand. My *textual* books are all pencil marked "thick as leaves in

Vallambrosa,"[6] and you don't know what a comfort & help many of my own notes are to me, on coming to the play a second or third time. I often find my views & opinions on a reading or interpretation change, with more extensive study; but my *references* are very useful, & save much time. This work is vastly more easy & pleasant than it used to be at first; I can get over it more rapidly, & it becomes *more & more* delightful, the longer I study. Now this close, critical, textual, verbal, study by no means *hinders*, but rather *helps*, the enjoyment of Shakespeare as a *whole*; as Dowden well says, a person does not enjoy a delightful landscape the *less*, for knowing its history,—its geological formation, or the changes it has undergone, but rather the *more*.—**Hereafter**, I must curb all propensity for outside reading, & give my time, as of yore, to my regular course of study, or I shall lose my ground that I have conquered, & have to do it all over again. Talk about the *pleasure* of reading Shakespeare! No one knows anything about this pleasure *really*, until he has mastered every difficulty, (at least all that are *masterable*)[b] and can read it straight along, & understand it, with the ease & freedom with which he reads a paragraph in the newspaper. . . .

[1] Mr. Furness has agreed: F changed his mind about writing the review, and N insisted that C should undertake it; see letters 73 and 74.
[2] so nervously afflicted: James O. Halliwell-Phillipps's wife Henrietta lost her faculties in 1872 as a result of a horseback-riding accident; he was much affected and changed his style of life entirely; she died insane in 1879.
[3] I am 50 years old: C was actually nearly fifty-four; his idiosyncrasy is to shrink the ages of himself and his family (even his twelve-year-old son is "ten years old" in letter 33). C's father Samuel died in 1878 aged eighty.
[4] Mrs. H. H. F.'s: I.e., Mrs. H. H. (Helen Kate Rogers) Furness's; the allusion is to her index to the Sh commentaries of William Sidney Walker. *Vers.* = *Shakespeare's Versification* (1854).
[5] R. G. W.'s: Richard Grant White's.
[6] "Thick as leaves in Vallambrosa": *Paradise Lost* I, 302–3 (altered).

[a] wherever I have] whenever I have [?] [doubtful reading].
[b] are masterable] ↑are↓ masterable MS.

66: 10 July 1875

My dear Norris:

I have finished my "Review" of Prof. Dowden's Book, as you desired, and herewith mail it to you, hoping it will please you, and be suitable to your wants for the *Bib*. It is somewhat *longer* than I contemplated; but the work itself is really so excellent, and grew upon me so, the longer I studied & read it, that even now I fear I have not done it justice. I should have liked to have followed[a] up his method through the Plays at greater length; and also to have introduced[b] more in the shape of *quotation*, to show the richness of his style & imagery. I have only quoted one passage, & that I selected because I thought it contained so admirable a reply to those who say that close analytic students of our Great Poet are apt to *overlook his real beauties*, in their investigation of the minutiæ of style, words, readings, &c.—I gave him a very gentle tap indeed on the point of his *Grandiloquence*, & a still gentler one, (amounting almost, one might say, to a *compliment*,) on that of his signing himself *the* V.P. of the New Sh. Soc.—I don't fancy any offence will be taken by either the Professor, or his friend the *President*.[1] . . .

[1] the *President*: I.e., the Director, F. J. Furnivall; there were several Vice Presidents.

[a] have followed] ↑have↓ followed MS.
[b] to have introduced] ↑to↓ have introduced MS.

67: 12 July 1875

. . . —I notice your neighbour, Mr. Allibone, has another book of "Quotations"[1] ready for press,—*prose*, this time—all numbered and indexed, *more suo*. He is a most industrious gatherer-up of "unconsidered trifles." His wife, or some other lady, I think, acts as his amanuensis. He wrote me once, how he managed to get through so much work. It is by *systematizing*, & never losing a minute of time. His "Dictionary" is a very laborious work;[2] yet I have never *enjoyed* using it, so much as I have *Lowndes*. Have you? . . .

[1] another book of "Quotations": Samuel Austin Allibone, *Prose Quotations from Socrates to Macaulay* (1876); A was an indefatigable compiler of reference books. C strongly disliked florilegia.
[2] a very laborious work: *A Critical Dictionary of English Literature and British and American Authors* (1858–71); it contains in more than three thousand pages forty indexes of subjects and accounts of 46,499 authors.

68:   21 July 1875

. . . I felt pretty confident *you would not agree with me* in my estimate of *Dowden's* book. Now, I would say, don't publish it, if you cannot conscientiously do so. You can write a brief notice of the book yourself, which will suit you better, & have time yet do to it. I am sorry about it, but I cannot help it. I went at that book, almost *determined* to dislike, & abuse it: but, like Goldsmith's Church-goer,[1] when I went to scoff, I remained to pray. The more I read of it, the more I got into the author's *scheme*, & mode of developing it, the better I began to like it. Spite of its grandiloquence, it *is* a good book, a *great* acquisition to our literature on that subject. I wish I could sit down by you, for 3 hours, & pick out the choice thoughts & passages, & talk to you about them, I am sure I could make you like it better. It is wonderfully *learned*. I felt like a mouse nibbling at a mountain, even trying to *comprehend* it all, much more trying to *criticize* it. Now please don't be *mad* at me, for not adopting your views. Yours were my own, until I studied it, & then I could not *help* changing them. It is far in advance of any book I have read on Shakespeare's *mind*, or "true inwardness." I wrote to Mr. Hudson for *his* opinion. He told me, that what he had read of it prepossessed him highly in its favour; and that *old Mr. Dana*,[2] "who was an excellent judge," commended it in the very highest terms. I have not yet seen a notice or review of the work, that did *not* praise it; have you? But, (I am honestly telling *you* the truth now,) I did not go by anyone's opinion; I read it through, then went over most of it again; & I could not help but acquiesce in their judgment. I agree with you that it is very ambitious in *style*; but the *subject* is an ambitious one & deserves it.—. . .

—I told you, I think, I was deep into "As You Like It" now, in due course. It has been so hot, & I have been so used-up with sickness &c., I have made slow progress. But it is a *lovely* play, isn't it? An *idyl*, not a play.—This idyllic element, so worked out in "A. Y. L.," "The Tempest," & "Cymbeline," altogether proves *where* the Poet was when he wrote them, better than any *stopt* & *unstopt* lines[3] &c.—He was at Stratford-on-Avon,[a] a happy country farmer, and he could not *help* writing of the *country*; and these were his *last* idyls.[4] When he was a boy he had loved the *country*, & he came back to it to *die*.

I don't quite agree with your friend Mr. Law, in his estimate of Prof. Masson's *Milton*. I know all about Todd's edn. We used it at School. It is an excellent edition, a regular *Variorum*, and bears about the same relation to Masson's, that the Variorum Shakesp. bears to the Cambridge, or rather to Dyce's, or White's, or Staunton's editions. I had a *Todd* in 6 vols. I think; perfectly overladen with *Notes* by everybody. These notes of course are essential to learners; Milton is full of classical allusions, which need to be explained. But for a *critical* edition, I should say, with all deference, that Masson's is far ahead. His is intended for accomplished readers, rather than students. I think his essay on "Milton's English" is a capital performance. Also his Bibliographical, Biographical, & Critical Prefaces, are full of information of the choicest kind. The study of *Milton* is like that of *Shakesp.*, and a different kind of edn. is necessary for a more, or less, advanced student. I have two annotated edns; Keightley's & Cleveland's; the notes in the former are very full & useful. But they are altogether different from Masson's. Besides, I think, Masson's *text* is much nearer Milton's, than any other I ever saw. He went to the fountain-head, & prints from it. The very great objection I have to Masson's Edn. is that he prints his "Notes," not only *not* at the foot of the page, where I like always to have them, but *not* even in the *same vol.*, but in a vol. by themselves. Imagine the trouble of always having *two* big vols. open before you, to read and understand a hard place.—. . .

[1] Goldsmith's Church-goer: "The Deserted Village" l. 180.
[2] *old Mr. Dana*: Probably Richard Henry Dana Sr., the man of letters, who in 1875 was eighty-seven years old.

[3] *stopt & unstopt* lines: Alluding to "verse tests" applied by F. G. Fleay and other members of the New Shakspere Society in rationalizing the chronology of the Sh canon.
[4] his *last* idyls: *AYL* is now universally dated 1598–1600.

[a] Stratford-on-Avon] Stratford-on Avon MS.

69:   30 July 1875

. . . My letter to the publishers of the *Knight Imperial* Edition, respecting the misspelling of Claghorn's and Sartain's names, in their recommendations, made a wonderful row. They would not be satisfied nor content until Mr. Yorston of New York went on to the Philadelphia office, & got the *originals*, which he sent me from Philadelphia, in a *registered* letter. Of course they were all right. I saw at once *how* Mr. Sartain's name had been miscopied "Sattain." He widens it somewhat thus, "Sartain," the top of the 'r' is nearly as high as the 't,' & the copyist took it for two 't's.—He wrote me a very gentlemanly & courteous letter, thanking me for the interest (!) I had taken in the work; & told me he thought the edition would run to 100.000. He told me a great many interesting facts about their House. It is a *very old* house. They are the engravers of the plates in "Picturesque America," and most of the finest engraving done for the U.S. is done at their House in London. One of the Virtues, of London, has a "Gallery" of Paintings valued at £600.000.—The Mr. Yorston who wrote me I should judge was a *Quaker*, as he commenced "Respected Sir," & ended "Thy sincere friend."—He thought it not very *likely* that a House of the age, wealth, & standing of theirs, should undertake to *forge* a few recommendations, at this time of day.—

. . . I am still working away on "As You Like It." I will divulge to you what I intend to do, someday, if I live long enough, when my ship comes in, and I can spare $5.000 or $6.000 on the project. I will print an edition of Shakespeare—Plays and Poems, each Play in 1 small quarto vol., on the best Whatman ribbed paper (large), and in the most perfect style of old-faced typography, that I can have done in London. The *text* shall be *my own*—based chiefly on the Folio, of course, with many returns to it in passages that now vary from it quite needlessly. But it will be neither the Cambridge, nor Dyce's, nor Collier's, nor Knight's, nor the Variorum of 1821, nor anybody's, but a Text selected just to suit myself alone. It shall be most carefully proof-read, & punctuated, in fact as nearly perfect as can now be made. I will print short, original, "Introductions," giving the history of the Play, text, chronology, editors, &c, and "Supplementary Notices," at the end, giving original criticisms on the Characters, the "motive," and other æsthetic matters; but *brief*; only 2 or 3 pages,—condensed; & carefully & attractively written. I will print a few *Notes*, at the foot of each page, in a smaller type, but still large, & readable by an old man. These

Notes will be textual, & critical, & explanatory; but all re-written or original; & *only* explain such difficulties as the *Most advanced* Shakespearian
students want. I will have no figures, or letters, or marks, to disfigure the
text, but the references will be to the lines, which I would number, as in the
Cambridge Edn. Great care should be taken about these *Notes*. There
should be no *useless* reading, or display of learning by references to other
authors or editors. Plain intelligible explanations of *real* difficulties, where
explainable, & where not, to say so. In short, a well-read, classical, intelligent Scholar's Shakespeare: such a one as you & I feel the need of every
day; & different from any of the 100 I already have, in being more *satisfactory to myself*. Then I would print just **one copy**—no more, for my own
library alone: I would make up *one other* from the "clean proof sheets," to
present to *one* kind friend; but to all intents & purposes, it should be a
unique edition of Shakespeare. Then wouldn't I be *even* with old Mr. Collier,
& Mr. Halliwell,[1] with their limited editions of 50 or 100 copies? I should
say so. You know "Everyone who pretends to have a fine Shakespeare
Library must have this edition"; and yet it could not be procured "for love
or money," and I don't know of any other means than love or money for
procuring it. Then wouldn't I be in splendid shape to remind Mr. Collier of
the analogue of the "fox and the grapes." I would quote Touchstone to him:
"The heathen philosopher, when he had a desire to eat a grape, would
open his lips when he put it into his mouth; meaning thereby, that grapes
were made to eat, and lips to open"; or as old Lodge says in his
"Rosalynde";—"Phebe is no latice for your lips; and her grapes hang so
hie, that *gaze on them you may, but touch them you cannot*." Wouldn't I
chuckle, when I recalled to him that "All your writers do consent, that *ipse*
is he; now *you* are not *ipse*, for *I* am he."—. . .

[1] *even* with old Mr. Collier, & Mr. Halliwell: Collier pubd. his last edn. of Sh (in progress in
1875) in fifty-eight copies only, and C had difficulty obtaining a subscription; H pubd. his
elephant folio Sh in an edn. of 150 copies and his *Comedies* in an edn. of twenty copies.

70: 2 August 1875

. . . At Ironton, a small town in this state, on the Ohio River, a few young
men formed a "Shakespeare Reading Club," meeting once every two
weeks to read Sh., & each contributing some little essay on something
Shakespearian. They wrote me that they had elected me an "honorary
member"; and asked me to give them *a name*. I suggested "The Mulberry
Club," or "The Mulberries," & their little contributions could be called
"mulberry *leaves*"; and they have adopted the name. The idea was *not
original* with me, as I had somewhere seen that the original name of the
present "Dramatic Club," in London, was "The Mulberry Club," no doubt
from Sh's *Mulberry tree*.—

In Zanesville, the young folks, men & women, have instituted a "Murdoch Dramatic Club"[1]—a sort of Thespian, or histrionic Society, to perform Comedy &c., to their friends & honorary members only. They elected me "Critic" of the concern; but it would be a thankless & unpleasant office, and I shall decline the honour. I attended one of their rehearsals. Goddard is one of the club, & goes through his parts very well.—. . .

3 August 1875 P.S.[a]

I open my letter to tell you that my long-looked-for box of books came last night—all safely & in good order—*by express*, not having been shipped until the 31st ult. They are *more than satisfactory*, so far as I have yet examined them. I think Sotheran must have bought a library belonging to some *one person*; as about 20 of my vols. are *uniformly* bound & lettered; in real good, Hf. turkey mor., green, *extra*, neatly & tastefully bound, gilt panels on the backs, well lettered, &c. and all nearly new. The "Capell's Notes," &c. is bound in this way. It is a splendid copy—no mistake. *Very wide margins*, and clean as new, except where it has the *MS. notes* and references of "Robt. Nares." These are all through the vols, but especially thick in the "Glossary." I could not but think that they were made by Nares, *before* he compiled his own "Glossary"; as they consist of *additions, corrections* &c. to Capell's Glossary. Nares was a great admirer of Capell, as appears by his notes everywhere. They are written in a good plain hand; and he has added several *indexes*, that help the use of Capell's volumes. . . .

[1] "Murdoch Dramatic Club": Named for James E. Murdoch, American actor and teacher of elocution; he owned a farm near Cincinnati. (See letter 235 for an account of M's visit to Zanesville.)

[a] P.S.] [omitted] MS.

71:   7 August 1875

. . . By the way, I see that Nares[a] gave £3..13..6 for this copy in boards. He has written several very useful notes on words in the "Glossary." On the first fly leaf he has written:—

"Few authors or commentators have been more injuriously treated than poor Capell. But his fame has been nobly vindicated by the *Pursuits of Literature:*[1]

'O injured patron of our noblest Bard!
Capell, receive this tribute of regard;

And may this honest verse to life and light
Call forth thy name, and vindicate thy right.'

Part I. v. 245.—

The note goes still further, and calls him not only the patron, but 'the Father of all legitimate Commentary on Shakespeare.' Those who stole from him, and then condemned both his edition and his *School of Shakespeare,* (published after his death,) are also severely lashed.—

Robt. Nares"

I can hardly believe it possible that I should secure so *capital* a set[2] of this very rare work for $16..25!—a book I have watched for and written for during 10 years. Timmins says he had not seen a copy for sale since they got theirs for the Shak. Mem. Library: and Sabin wrote me that he believed the last one sold in the U.S. was at Burton's Sale. . . .

What a magnificent library Mr. F. must have, to be sure! With plenty of money—no business cares—fine health—& taste for truly enjoying his treasures, & communicating the fruits of his enjoyment & study to the world, in his Superb *New Variorum,* what a happy life his is! I know of few more enviable men. To make his happiness perfect, he has a "better half," who sympathizes with, and aids him in, all his studies & work. I presume one might vainly search the world over to find a similarly happy & accomplished pair. . . .

I have recd a long, & very flattering, & kind letter from D. J. Snider, in reply to one I wrote him on his late critiques. He agrees with me in condemning the *smart,* or rather flippant & *slangy* tone of Mr. Hudson's book on the characters &c. of Sh.—It is abominable to me; and hurts his otherwise good & readable & useful work.—Snider is a good fellow; and improves on acquaintance. His last letter is charming; but too flattering for me to send it[b] to you. He has one of his *best* essays—on "Othello"—in the *Western.* . . .

I have only *one* copy of Edward III, I believe, in my library, that in Capell's Prolusions: . . . In my last note to Mr. Collier, I offered to pay him any reasonable price for a copy:[3] but as you say it is *unobtainable* "either for love or money." I have given up all hope: *unless* some "manufacturer in the north" should fortunately discover his copy is too costly, and so return it to the old gentleman. Then I *might* have a chance, who knows? I have some scarcer things, in my collection, than that even; such as Halliwell's small folio of *Comedies,* of which only 20 copies were printed, at an awful price; and yet *one* floated over to the U.S.—even away West to Ohio.—. . . Do you think Mr. Hudson will be offended at my reference to him in that little squib in the *Bib.,* about his making Mr. Singer's notes *his own* by abbreviation, & affixing an "H."? It is no more than the truth, anyway, as one may see in scores of instances. However, I hope he won't see it.—. . .

[1] *Pursuits of Literature*: By Thomas J. Mathias. "A Satirical Poem in Dialogue" (1794 etc.).
[2] so *capital* a set: It is now in the Harlan Hatcher Graduate Library, University of Michigan.
[3] a copy: I.e., of Collier's edn. of *Edward III*.

[a] Nares] he MS.
[b] to send it] to send ↑it↓ MS.

73:   9 August 1875

. . . I have recd yours of the 6th inst. giving me a good "blowing up" for declining to review Mr. Daniel's R. & J. for you in the *Bib*:—As I expect to go away Wednesday, I did not wish to leave without telling you, as you take it so much to heart, that I *will* on my return, *try* what I can do to accommodate you. It was not from *indolence*, or carelessness, but from solely what you lawyers term *incompetence*, that I *shrank* from the task. You know how cheerfully I would do anything *in my power* to oblige you in any way: and that makes me think you a little bit unreasonable at getting "mad" at me in this case. You did not *realize* what you want me to do. I know of but three gentlemen in the United States[1] duly qualified to review such a work, Mr. Furness, Mr. R. Grant White, & Mr. Hudson. This is a work simply devoted to the *Text*; and that not a *textus receptus*, but the *revised text* of one of the Quartos only, that of 1599.—

Now what will any one of the authors and gentlemen I have named, or what will Mr. P. A. Daniel, or Mr. Brae, or Dr Ingleby (should they see the Bibliopolist,) think of **me**? Would they not say, 'here is an unknown fellow of the name of *Crosby*—what does *he* know of the text of R. & J.? How does *he dare* to set himself up to "review" a work by a scholar like Mr. Daniel, who is not only a fine *antiquarian*, & *textual critic*, but has devoted months on months to the preparation of this revised text—a text not intended for the *profanum vulgus*, but for scholars & critics alone—for reference?—We have heard of *impudence* before now; but this fellow's—*pushing himself* into print—presuming to write about one of the most *delicate* & *ticklish* subjects in the whole circle of literature—well, *his* impudence is sublime; & confirms our old adage that *"fools* rush in, where angels fear to tread."' . . . I *will* attempt to write a *notice*, I could not call it a *review*, of the "R. & J.," as soon as I come home again, God willing. But you must not expect much, then you won't be disappointed. I shall have to deal chiefly with the "externals" of the work—mention the *varias lectiones*, without daring to criticize them: make-believe I know lots more than I do; like the owl, not *say* much, but put on a devilish wise look; touch up a little here and a little there, and so get out of it as *gingerly*, and give as little offence, as I possibly can manage. My dear boy, I would like to know who there is, in the wide world, I would do this for but you. But mind, such work as this I don't call a *review*. When I take up a *review*, I expect to learn something from it. The reviewer is supposed to *know* at least as much of the matter in question as the author whose book he presumes to review; else how can he say whether it is *well* or *poorly* done; whether his *views, tastes, & readings,* are sensible, refined, & correct, or shallow, unpolished, & inadmissible? There is an old Roman maxim *"judex damnatur, cum nocens absolvitur"*;[2] and if a reviewer make a blunder or a mistake of judgment, he is liable to the severest penalty under the law for his impertinent & officious ignorance. If there is any class of man to be *pitied*, it is reviewers who *have to write for a living.*—

What you observe about "begging" for articles for the "Sh: Gossip" is exactly right; and your determination *not* to do so is, I think, cor-rect. If you have to "beg" for an article, you may rest assured it will not be "interest-ing." Men, to write an "interesting" article, must be "in the vein"; & not only so, but must *understand* what they are writing about. And, moreover, if there is not talent and *willingness* enough in the country to keep up a few pages of interesting & instructive "Shakespearian gossip" every 60 days, without "begging" for articles, it would be a pity for the country I say. But I think there will be no fear of *any such a result.* When the Bibliopolist gets a little larger circulation, and Shak: scholars see what is in the "Gossip" department, and read in it such nice, clever, & interesting articles as, e.g. yours this month on Mr. Furness' library, there will be no need to beg any more by the editor: his trouble will only be, which to retain, and which to discard. The *newspapers* will be republishing them all over the country, "and all our hearts will jump for joy."—. . .

[1] but three gentlemen in the United States: Hudson makes an odd member of the trio, as C elsewhere passes harsh judgment on his textual scholarship.

[2] *judex damnatur, cum nocens absolvitur*: Slightly altered from Publilius Syrus; it was the motto of the *Edinburgh Review*.

74:   13 August 1875

. . . I hope you have quite forgiven me,[1] ere this; and are in real *good humour* with me again. Your last letter reminded me very forcibly of a little circumstance that took place in my schoolboy days, when I was about 16 or 17 years old. Like many another boy, I had *two sweethearts,* two strings to my bow. One was a young, wealthy, pretty, witty, & very accomplished *belle*; the other I liked I don't know why; as she had nothing very remark-able to recommend her. On one occasion, I invited Sweetheart No I to accompany me to a Ball: whether from whim, or from having some other engagement, she declined my invitation. I then invited sweetheart No. 2; *she* was *really* unable to go; she was sick, and out of sorts; and had no *appropriate ball-dress;* so she declined too. I got most unreasonably "mad" at my disappointment; and sweetheart No. 2 being the last one that had declined, & being, moreover, the *handiest*, I let out on her all the vials of my wrath; and *vowed* that from that day until the end of the world *and after*, I would never more invite a girl to go with me to a Ball. If they came and offered their company, *all right*; but no more *invitations* for me!—The poor thing did not know what to make of me; she got frightened; but finally she got herself up *as nicely as she could*, and signified her willingness to "go along." I forgave her,[2] and all went "merry as a marriage-bell." That is over 30 years ago; but I have often thought of it since; and that it is not good to be too hasty in making *rash resolutions.*—

[1] forgiven me: I.e., for reluctance to write the review of Daniel (see letter 73).
[2] I forgave her: The story alludes to the affair of the Daniel review: the first girl represents Furness; the second girl represents C; the young C represents N.

75:   22 August 1875

. . . I enclose you a Postal Card received from J. Sabin & Sons, offering me their copy of *Wivell*, with Supplement, for $15..00, price 18.—I have *not* accepted their offer. I don't like to gratify them so much as to pay them so big a profit. No doubt it is a scarce & valuable book: still $15..00 is too much for what they only gave £1..10, *at most*. You will notice what they say about its being "grabbed immediately on issue of the list." You & I know *who* "grabbed" it.—I am in no great hurry about it. Another will "turn up" someday: and if I have to pay $15.., I would rather pay it to someone who was not such a "grabber."—

I am much obliged to you for sending me Ingleby's letter. . . . You will see what he says of my conjecture of "charter house" (originally *"chartreuse"*) for the terrible crux "charge-house,"[1] in L. L. L.—His word "clergy-house," spelt "clargie-house," I must say is not by any means as good as mine. It is not as near the folio, in the first place; and it has no *history* to recommend it at all. I must say it sounds very flat to me. I cannot away with it at all. Do you remember what I said of "charter-house"? It is an *educational* establishment in or near London, to this day. It was just being taken from the Carthusian Monks, and made into a sort of *poor boys college,* in Shakespeare's time; and it is quite probable that *Florio*,[2] with whom Sh. was at sword's points for abusing tragedy & comedy, &c., was a teacher or professor of philology in this "chartreuse," or *charter-house*, (as it then came to be popularly called,) and Shakespeare hits him off in his character of *Holofernes*, the pedant or *schoolmaster*:[a] "Do you not educate youth at the *charge-house*?" The difference between "charge-house" and "charter-house" is not very great. "Charge-house" has *no* meaning. In his 1st Edn. Ingleby wanted to read "Church-house" (not original with him however, as Brae & others advocated it); & now he wants to conjecture "clargie-house." I gave the reading "charter-house," with a long argument supporting it, historically, (which I hunted up,) & otherwise, to Mr. Hudson, and he has adopted it, *toto corde*. I think Ingleby would too, only he does not like to be indebted to a common critic out west, like me, for it. I can say to you confidentially, however, that I am almost *sure* I am right. It is not often I express myself with much certainty about conjectural readings. In this, it appears to me so plain & satisfactory, & explains *fully* an hitherto unintelligible & irreducible crux, that if no one else adopt it, I will save it for my *unique* new qto edn. of Shakespeare, 37 vols. A.D. 1925.—. . .

Among my letters are *two* very kind & polite notes from old Mr. Collier. In one he "deeply regrets" that he cannot *now* help me to a copy of his new Qto Shakespeare. He says, however, that *should* any one be returned, or offered for sale, I shall have the first chance at it. He says that A. R. Smith never applied to him for a copy for me, nor anyone else; which shows that the old gentleman's memory is failing; as, you know, Smith sent me Collier's *own note* stating that all the copies were taken up in a week. His "Edward III" he is going to *reprint*, to go with the Shakespeare; and he will send me a copy of that as soon as it is printed.—A few days later another note arrives, stating that he has "just recovered" a copy of his "Trilogy,"[3] and offers it to me free, if I will tell him how to send it. What a kind old fellow he is! I have just written him, accepting his present, & telling him to send it by "book-post." So you see I shall have the "Trilogy" and "Edward III" *sure*, and a good hope of getting the "Shakespeare" too: that is I am to have the first one obtainable. He is sending me these, because, as he says, he thinks I am "a very deserving gentleman"; and "is anxious to do what" he "can to promote" my "Shakespearian collections," in my "remote settlement." I wrote him as kindly & gratefully as I knew how. What a long & active life his has been! I have a work of his—a good & learned one too— called the "Poetical Decameron," 2 vols., 8vo, printed in *1820*, so that he must have been 55 years a working author.[4] He is now 86¾ years old: I sincerely hope he may live to finish this last ambition of his, to show the world—I mean 50[5]—what in his opinion a Shakespeare should be. Precious few men, at his years, would be worrying over the proofs—new readings—&c. &c. of a New Edn. of Shakespeare; and that not for necessity, or to make money, but from pure love of work, & of Shakespeare. In one of his letters to me he says "Your study and love of Shakespeare does you credit." Dr Ingleby's, & Mr. Brae's, & Mr. Singer's, & Mr. Halliwell's writings, which I eagerly read in my early study of Sh:, terribly prejudiced me against Collier—not against *him* so much as against his "Corr. Fo. 1632." I still think it a great pity he ever found that notorious volume. Still had he only given the old Corrector's Conjectures *as such*, (and many are very plausible,) and not tried to force them on the public as *Authentic*, no one I believe would have annoyed him; and *they* would have stood a tenfold better chance of being adopted, where deserving: they would have taken their stand among other conjectures, according to their merits, without prejudice. As it is, his *texts* will always be regarded now with *suspicion*. On his account, I feel that it is a pity this should be so: but it is too late now to remedy it; and even his new beautiful 4to edn. of 37 vols., or more, will never have the intrinsic value (I don't mean the collector's, or money, value,) that his excellent 8 vol. 8vo edn. of 1842–4 possesses.—

You laugh at me for buying a copy of *Bowdler's* Edn.—My opinion of that edn. is *not changed*. It is a perfectly useless book to me—a mere figure-head. I bought it because it was cheap—15/—for a well printed 6 vol., illustrated edn., pubd at £1..10; and I intend to give it to my boy the next time I go to Cleveland. You say I should now buy a copy of *Dick's* Shilling Edn.—Bless you I have one; have had a half dozen copies in my time; they are good to *give away*: a young friend comes to my room, & says—'Here you have all these edns. of Sh., and I don't possess *one*; you can afford to give me one': 'Will you read it, if I do give you one?' say I; 'Oh yes, indeed.' So I go & bring out a *Dick*, & for fifty cents perhaps induce some good young fellow to read Shakespeare. That is *all* the use Dick's edn. is of to me.—. . .

You would be surprised what a pretty copy of "Walker's Crit. Ex." &c., in 3 vols., I got for 15/—(abt $5.25,) in new Hf. green mor. extra. My own copy is so be-pencilled that it *cannot* be bound. When I die, I should like *you* to have it,[6] and my Grant White's Shakespeare, and a score of other volumes, or more, that are completely filled with notes & references. *You* would appreciate them, and they would be very useful to you, & save you lots of reading, & you would find many original readings & explanations, that of course *I value*; but they would only be considered by the booksellers as deteriorating from the value of the books at a sale.—But this is not a very pleasant subject to write about, is it?—I am *hugely* pleased with my *Capell's Notes*. No one, but such men as Furness, who have examined these invaluable vols., knows the immense amount of learning, patient toil, & love, which poor contemned Capell has put into these vols. on his favourite Shakespeare. Talk of studying Shakespeare! Think of Capell *transcribing* the whole of the Poet's works with his own hand, I cannot tell how many times! It always makes my heart ache, when I think of him, & the *luck* he had. But, then, he had the private enjoyment of the study; & God knows that is repayment enough: but *he* really merited *fame*, & was beaten out of it by Steevens & others, not half the men he was.—. . .

I am still at work on "A. Y. L. It." What a crusty old *bilious* character *Jaques* is; and how beautifully the Duke, and Rosalind, and Orlando, all put him to flight, when he wants to inoculate *them* with his "melancholy." The contrast of *his* sour, crabbed, disappointed, cross-grained *affected*, pride of opinion, with *their* fresh, pure, unsophisticated *love* of nature and their fellows, is simply charming. One breath from their true, heart whole, natures blows him to shivers, & routs him "horse, foot, & dragoons." Ulrici calls *Jaques* & *Touchstone* "the two fools"; but *Jaques* is infinitely the bigger *fool* of *the two*.

[1] "charge-house": *LLL* 5.1.83. See Richard David's note in the Arden Edn. ad loc. for a defense of F1 drawing from Erasmus's *Colloquia*. Modern editors generally read with F1.

[2] *Florio*: John Florio, the Italian teacher and lexicographer. There is no evidence or likelihood that F taught in the Charterhouse, and the belief of Bishop Warburton and Richard Farmer that he is the model for Holofernes is now generally discredited.

[3] his "Trilogy": A defense (1874) of the Perkins Folio in reply to the attacks on it by Alexander Dyce and other scholars; the book was pubd. in a limited gift edn.

[4] 55 years a working author: More nearly 65 years--Collier's career actually began in 1809 when (at the age of twenty) he joined the staff of *The Times*; he had been a paid assistant reporter six years longer than that.

[5] I mean 50: I.e., the fifty original subscribers to his fourth Sh edn.

[6] When I die, I should like *you* to have it: This pious wish, expressed several times about C's favorite and most heavily annotated books, was never carried out; his library was sold to pay his debts more than five years before his death.

[a] *schoolmaster*] school-| *master* MS.

76: 2 September 1875

. . . Setting[a] aside the genuineness of the *Mask*, as being a "true present-ment" of Sh., to make a *satisfactory*, pleasing, striking, handsome, *ideal* bust or likeness of the Poet, on the basis of it, and the Stratford, Chandos, & Droeshout, is something of which Mr. Page [and his wife], and America, may well be proud. We certainly have nothing of the kind at present. You remember where Celia (in *A. Y. L.*) speaking of her sex says, "for those [women] she [Fortune] makes fair she scarce makes honest; and those that she makes honest she makes very ill-favouredly"; I think we may apply her words to the portraits of Shakespeare, and say, "for those portraits [ideal] that are made handsome, or pleasing, are scarce authentic; and those that are authentic are made very ill-favouredly."—But I always feel myself treading on slippery ground, when I presume to speak of this subject: so I shall wait eagerly for your book, before I pretend to make up my mind "to any conclusion." . . .

I heard of a gentleman, named *Col. Thompson*,[1] living in *Flint, Michigan*, who is said to own 100 or more edns. of Shak. He is a lawyer by profession, and occasionally lectures on Sh.—From an abstract that I saw of his Lec-ture, I should guess that he is *no very great* Sh. *scholar*: it read very shallow, & pretentious, without any new matter or ideas. Did you ever hear of him?

[1] Col. Thompson: Edward Thomson. James McMillan purchased his 750-vol. Sh library in 1880 for $3500 and presented it to the University of Michigan; it became the nucleus of the present McMillan Shakespeare Collection in the Harlan Hatcher Graduate Library in Ann Arbor. See *The Michigan Alumnus* 13 (1907): 375–77.

[a] Setting] setting MS.

77:    4 September 1875

My dear Norris:

I have just come across an important and valuable Note on a "hard place" in *Hamlet*, which is entirely new to me; and as it may be so to you, I thought I would send it to you. I found it in *Whiter's* Book—the Second Part—"An Attempt to explain and illustrate Various Passages [of Shakespeare] on a new principle of Criticism," &c., 8vo, 1794, p. 152, *note*.

> "*Pol.* Do you know me, my lord?
> *Ham.* Excellent well; y'are a *fishmonger*."[1]

> "Why[a] should Hamlet mistake Polonius for a *Fishmonger*? Though I am not able to inform the reader respecting the full force and nature of the *exquisite reason*, which belongs to this denomination; yet I can certainly convince him that some reason (such as it is) existed in the mind of the Poet. In Jonson's *Christmas Masque* (595) *Venus* is introduced as a Tire-woman [misprinted in Whiter *Fire-woman*], and thus speaks of her son Cupid: "I had him by my first husband: he was a Smith, forsooth; we dwelt in *Do-little-lane* then: he came a month before his time, and that may make him somewhat imperfect: But I was a **Fishmonger's Daughter**." We see now that some opinion prevailed, which induced Hamlet, who is *still harping* on the *daughter* of Polonius, to mistake the father for a *Fishmonger*; though I shall leave others to discover the peculiar notion which was attached to this matter. Probably it was supposed that the daughters of these tradesmen,[b] who dealt in so nourishing a species of food, were *blessed* with extraordinary powers of *conception*. I am surprised that this passage has escaped the diligence of our Critics."

You know what trouble this word has given the Commentators on Hamlet; all sorts of reasons being given for it, the usual one being that Hamlet called the old Lord Chamberlain a *fishmonger*,[c] because he was always prying into, and trying to *fish out*, his secret. But in such a case, I should think he would have called him a *fisherman*, and not a *fishmonger*. You remember the context; in what coarse language Hamlet speaks of Ophelia, cautioning her father not to let her walk in the sun, as she might conceive, &c.: This reference to Jonson's *Christmas Masque*, in which *Venus* calls herself a *Fishmonger's[d] Daughter*, and assigns it as a reason for having so precocious a boy at *eight months*, I think, undoubtedly contains the reason why Hamlet used the term to Polonius. At all events, it throws *some light* on the passage. Don't you think so?—

In great haste, Your friend,
Joseph Crosby.

P. S. Do you think Mr. Furness would be offended if you were to mention this reference to him, sometime when in his company? You can do it casually: and as it occurs in such an out-of-the-way place, it is just possible he might overlook it;[2] and it is too good not to find a place in the "New Variorum Hamlet."

J.C.

[1] y'are a *fishmonger*: *Ham.* 2.2.174.
[2] he might overlook it: Apparently he had not done so, as he pubd. the Whiter material in the Variorum *Ham.* ad loc. without crediting C.

[a] "Why] Why MS.
[b] tradesmen] trades-| men MS.
[c] fishmonger] fish-| monger MS.
[d] Fishmonger's] Fish-| monger's MS.

78:   7 September 1875

. . . Being at home on Sunday, I wrote you the accompanying "critique" on Snider's Essays, for the *Bibliopolist*, if suitable & acceptable. I hope you will not think it *too long*, as you will perceive I could not well do justice to Mr. Snider, nor the Subject, in less space. . . . I made, as briefly as I could, a little synopsis of Snider's last essay, that on *Othello*. You will see it contains many new, original, even startling, points. I put in an extract also, to show his style, & which condenses his argument, so as to kill 2 birds with one stone. I have not done one bit more for his really excellent criticisms than they merit. Indeed they deserve a *much better review* than anything I can make: but I have done the *best* I could in my space, and I hope it will please you, as well as him, and induce him to persevere, and also to collect his clever essays into a readable volume, so more Shakespearians can get hold of them, & enjoy, and be profited by, them, as much as I have been. . . . They are full of thought & method, & are nicely[a] written: and why should we not award to our own American Critics their meed of praise (mind, only when they *deserve* it,) as well as the English, French, and German essayists? . . . You may mark my prophecy, that his Shakespearian essays will make their mark, when they come to be properly published & circulated; and we will gain some credit for having been the first to bring them into notice in the *Bibliopolist*. . . .

Like yourself, I also dipped into *Mercade's* "Hamlet," and soon saw what sort of a book it was. It will *not pay* to read such transcendental, trashy, speculation. It is evidently the production of a very *wise* lunatic! He undoubtedly, as he says, has spent *many years* of deep thought upon it; but *cui bono*? What is the good, or use, of such fanciful, *whimsical*, theorizing? Can anyone for a moment imagine that such outrageous fancies ever occurred to the Poet when he wrote the Play? I wonder what next the critics will make of *Hamlet*.—I don't know whether I shall waste any time reading this book, or not. I suppose I shall, just to see what lengths he goes to. I looked into the "Othello," at the end of the book, & saw the author making *Cassio* the representative of *science* because, forsooth, *sio*, the latter half of his name, is something like the Latin verb *scio, scire*, to know! *Iago* is to stand for *the past*, because you can take the "I" for a "1," separate it from "*ago*," and put one two, three, or 20 *oughts* between the 1 and *ago*; thus: 10 ago; 100 ago; 1000 ago, meaning, ten, one hundred, or one thousand years *ago*!! Did ever any Bedlamite beat that? Suppose you read it, and unravel yourself in a review of it, for the *Bib*.—It would be a better subject than opening Shakespeare's grave,[1] to photograph his bones or dust. Where I say, in the name of curiosity, did you ever get hold of that idea? From poor Delia Bacon? Surely I think so. But are you in earnest, or trying to perpetrate a huge *sell* on me? You cannot "whip the devil round the stump," by getting *a woman* to open *that grave*. Delia was a woman; and even the *thoughts* of such a desecration, while she hovered by the side of that monumental slab, extinguished the poor little balance of *wit* she had left. Remember the curse! Remember Delia's fate, and *Beware*! . . . Dearly as I should love to behold, to kneel down & worship, that venerated "dust," I would not be one of a party in Trinity Church, when anyone attempted to move "these stones," for all the gold in California. He need but to whisper Ariel, and "Lord, what a smell of brimstone!" he would have a legion of devils to whisk off every man, and woman too, into the infernal regions, as quickly and as "quaintly," as when, in the shape of a harpy, he cleared off the "banquet" from Alonso and his friends, when they thought they had such a *nice thing*. What is there he *couldn't* do with you, if you ventured to incur *his* curse? He might tie you all up as "prisoners, Sir, In that line-grove that weather-fends" the Church, where his consecrated remains repose.—He might set 'Mountain' and 'Silver,' 'Fury' and 'Tyrant' on you; drive you through "Tooth'd briers, sharp furzes, pricking goss and thorns," dance you, up to the chins, "i' the filthy mantled pool"; or

> "charge his goblins that they grind your joints
> With dry convulsions; shorten up your sinews
> With aged cramps; and more pinch-spotted make you
> Than pard or cat o'mountain."—

If he were in a merry mood, and only wished to *make sport* of you, for attempting to *make fun* of his epitaph, by setting a *woman* to "gammon" him,[2] what would be easier than to send Puck, "in likeness of a filly foal," to delude you
> "Over hill, over dale,
>   Thorough bush, thorough brier,

       Over park, over pale,
         Thorough flood, thorough fire."—

But if, worse than worst, bent on practicing "equivocation" on *him*, you really provoke his wrathful ire, Oh, beware of Hecate, and the "secret, black and mid-night hags"; the weird sisters, who might, with one wave of his magic wand, transport you to the "blasted heath," or "the pit of Acheron," and there delude *you* to your destruction, as they did the "Thane of Glamis." Remember *they* were *"imperfect speakers"*; they *lied like truth*; they *juggled*, and paltered *"in a double sense"*; but they kept the word of promise only to the *ear*, while they broke it to the *hope*. *They* too were *women*, at least they "should be women," but that their beards forbade them to be so interpreted. But the subject is getting frightful: methinks I hear now the brinded cat, and the hedgepig, and smell the cursed ingredients of that caldron! "By the pricking of my thumbs Something wicked this way comes!"—I dare not look round! My fell of hair is rousing and stirring, as life were in't, and each particular hair standing on end "Like quills upon the fretful porpentine!" Oh pity! pity and mercy! If you would save yourselves from the horrors of a scene like this, oh, forbear to practice "equivocation" on Shakespeare! If you would deliver me from becoming a raving maniac, down, down on your knees, and beg pardon for ever even entertaining the *thought* of disturbing his honoured dust. *Requiescat in pace*. Let him rest!—

You ask me for advice about publishing your Book on the Portraits. . . . If you would only[b] do *two* things: banish to the winds all apprehension of your ability, your style of writing, &c.; and *commence at once*. Write a chapter—anywhere in the work—on that portion with which you are most familiar—first; then you can correct, enlarge, cut out, re-write, & get it to suit you, *as nearly as you can*. . . . Don't try to write finely—but just write in your own easy, pleasing, *gentlemanly* style, as if you were writing to *me*, & giving me the best account of this, that, and the other portrait, that you could. In fact, it would be a good idea for you to keep *me* in your mind's eye all the time; because I am as ignorant about the portraits as any man you ever saw; and if you can post me on the subject, you may be sure your book will *have* to be pretty full of information. Don't be afraid of writing too much; & never mind because it is not all *original*. No one expects an *original* book on such a topic, because it is an impossibility. All you can do is, to *arrange* your store of knowledge on the subject so as to present it in the clearest manner. Your own good taste will be an infinitely better adviser than I, or anyone else, can be. Whether it is desirable to print a partial work only now, say on the Mask alone, and a fuller one by & by, I cannot for my life determine. My best judgment would say, print only one, & that a good, comprehensive, & *final* one: I fear to divide it up would spoil it, and so *divert* attention, that neither would receive the credit deserved. When you have the ice once broken it will be but little more labour to perfect the job, than to do it half. Then you have *now* all the material you probably ever will have, viz. *all there is*. Again, I am desirous of seeing the work *soon*; & because I suggest a complete work at once, & not a partial one, you must not think I counsel delay. Besides, just now, or within a year or so anyway, I think would be the best time to publish, & get subscribers. Page's new Bust,[3] the German Death Mask, &c. have given an excited impetus to public attention on the subject: if that die out, you would find it vastly harder to do your work, or to get the people *interested* again.—I notice your remarks on Page's article; and also (what I long ago predicted) your full committal to the authenticity of the Mask. Well, so be it! Perhaps, if I were as well acquainted with, & informed upon, the matter as you are, and had I had the same *opportunities* of forming an opinion, I might have been ere this equally committed. At present, I must be candid with you, and say that I am not. You must not get angry now at me, because I do not agree with you (**as yet**) in this point. You know I can only look on the whole argument as an outsider, & judge it as I would any calm matter of business, of *insurance* for instance. . . . I simply know that this Mask is found in Germany, and how it got there, unless made there, nobody knows. Again, its resemblance to any one, or all, of the pictures that Mr. Page calls genuine, has not impinged itself on my cranium; because probably I have *seen* nothing but 3 or 4 photographs of it as a dead man's mask. Unquestionably when repaired—eyes opened—&c. &c. it must possess a very different appearance. Then, more than all, I am *no artist*: consequently, through ignorance, I have no enthusiasm about it; none of that *intuitive* conviction that Mr. Page has to such a remarkable degree. . . .

There is . . . a capital letter from Boston, by a Mr. T. S. Perry, in the *Academy*, which refers to Holmes' book and says, (as I remarked at the time it was published,) that Mr. Spedding's (editor of Bacon's Works) letter to Holmes, refuting his positions, is the best thing in the book. In fact, this one letter is, I think, the *best reply* to all the arguments of the Baconites at once, that has ever been published. It is *multum*, one might almost say *omne, in parvo*. . . .

From my "Shakespeariana Collectanea," Vol. I. p. 35.

The following note on *Mea. for Mea.* I wrote to a young friend as a proof, not hitherto noticed, that Sh. was *au fait* in what he styles in the same Play (Mea. for Mea., I. 1,) "the *terms* for common justice,"[4]— meaning the *technical language of the Courts*: as it is not mentioned by Lord Campbell, in his book, nor by H. T. in his work "Was Shakespeare a lawyer?," . . . "*Duke*. That shall not be much amiss: yet as the matter now stands, he will **avoid** your accusation; he made trial of you only."[5] This is one of the numerous ellipses, for which this fine play is noted: and the words written within brackets must be *understood* to complete the meaning: "He will avoid your accusation"; [and he will say], or [and he will pretend that] "he made trial of you only." This long paraphrase is to introduce the word"avoid,"—"*avoid* your accusation." The phrase struck me as singular, and turning to "Webster's Unabridged" I find as follows:—

> "*Avoid*, (5th definition,) to defeat, or evade.
> (*Pleading*). Thus in a replication, the plaintiff may deny the defendant's plea; or confess it, and *avoid* it, by stating new matter," *Blackstone*.

This is simply the present case. Angelo, says the Friar-Duke, "will *avoid* your accusation," i.e. he will either deny it *in toto*, or confess it, and *avoid* it, by stating new matter, viz. "that he made trial of you only," the very words the Duke would put into Angelo's mouth. How simply & beautifully all these explanations run into one another, when you once get hold of the right end of the line. Here *the law* plainly is the right end of the line: but how did Shakespeare know so much? . . .

Another *crux*, in the same Act, is the word "delighted," in that awfully picturesque description that Claudio gives to his sister of the terrors of death:—

> "Nay but to die, and go we know not where;
> To lie in cold obstruction, and to rot;
> This sensible, warm, motion to become
> A kneaded clod! And the *delighted* spirit
> To bathe in fiery floods, or to reside
> In thrilling regions of thick-ribbed ice!"[6] &c. &c.

This epithet has long puzzled the commentators; as "to reside in thrilling regions of thick-ribbed ice" must be anything but *delightful* to the enfranchised "Spirit." It is generally construed as "*delighted*" for *delighting*, the passive form for the active, *ut sæpe apud veteres auctores*, and meaning, the spirit that has heretofore been accustomed to, or capable of, *delights*. Various substitutions have also been proposed; as 'benighted,' 'dilated,' 'delinquent,' and the word 'delated' in its two Latin meanings of "carried" and "accused"; "a spirit *accused* of sin, and *whirled* through space." But I think the Folio epithet is right, only it should be written "*de-lighted*," the prefix 'de' being used in its Latin sense of *deprivation*; "*the spirit* **deprived of light**"; referring thus distinctly to the *darkness* always supposed to be a concomitant of the place of future punishment: "The *blackness of darkness* forever."—I may add that the word "obstruction" in this sentence is simply a synonym for *death*, meaning the *obstruction*, or *stopping*, of the natural powers of the body; "cold obstruction" being thus synonymous with "a lifeless mass."—

Jos Crosby.—

Zanesville, 12 April 1872. . . .

---

[1] opening Shakespeare's grave: N proposed doing so, so that Sh's skull, if it survived, could be measured to help determine which portraits of Sh are authentic. Delia Bacon tried to open Sh's grave clandestinely in September 1856: her object was to search for documents showing that Sh had not written the plays; she went mad a few years later. C jokes about the doggerel on the gravestone: "cursed be *he* that moves my bones." C's strictures on the proposal are

stated more forcefully in a letter (30 September 1883—Folger Shakespeare Library MS. C.a. 10) to C. M. Ingleby, another advocate of exhumation, when his *Shakespeare's Bones* appeared.

[2] "gammon" him: Alluding to Delia *Bacon.*

[3] Page's new Bust: The American painter William Page had sculpted a composite from the bust in Holy Trinity Church, various portraits, and the Becker deathmask; it was a nine days' wonder in 1875–76. Forty letters (1873–77) from N to Page's wife Sophie are preserved in the Archives of American Art, Washington, D.C.

[4] "The *terms* for common justice": *MM* 1.1.10–11.

[5] "*Duke. . . . only*": *MM* 3.1.195–97.

[6] "Nay but to die, . . . ice!": *MM* 3.1.117–22.

[a] are nicely] ↑are↓ nicely MS.

[b] If you would only] if you would only MS.

79:   12 September 1875

. . . Since I commenced taking the *Academy*, I have given up the *Athenæum*, as I cannot afford both: and we have no Library, or Reading Rooms here, whether either is taken. I always liked the *Athenæum*; but I thought the *Academy* was to be the organ of the "N. Sh. Soc.," & so changed to it. I take "Notes & Queries," & have done since 1871. I wish I had all the preceding volumes. It is a very useful & interesting pub*n* to have bound and *keep*. . . .

80:   14 September 1875

. . . I have just received the enclosed kind letter from old Mr. Collier, offering me a full set of his new Qto Shakespeare, except the "Tempest"; and he *hopes* to get that too, ere long.—I have just written to him, telling him that I was only too glad to get them, & considered myself very fortunate to get *any* of the Nos.—I told you, I think, that he offered to present me with a copy of his "Trilogy," which he had "recovered"; and I am expecting it by every post. It appears another *Lancashire* subscriber has *withdrawn* his subscription, just in time for me; and Mr. Collier thinks he *may* by chance get a copy of the "Tempest," which is the only no. missing to complete a Series. I should think his Lancashire friend would be very willing to sell back his nos., as his set, of course, is incomplete; and I told Collier I would willingly pay double or treble for a No. of the *Tempest*, rather than not have a complete set.—I'll bet you a bottle of wine *I shall have a complete set* ere long: I believe the old gentleman can get them all right; only he wants to be well coaxed for them. Well, I shall be real glad of it. I thought a copy would "float over" sometime; but did not look for it quite so soon. . . .

I read with real interest what you say about *Othello*, and Mr. Snider's theories. . . . I think you are mistaken in one sentence, "I am sorry to see that you consider Othello an *African*. He was a *Moor*, and the Moors were not Africans."—Now surely the Moors **are** Africans. Mauritania, their soil, is *in Africa*, beyond all question. What you meant, probably, was, that Othello was not a *negro*, or an *Ethiopian*. I think this last is very likely. He was of a different *tribe of Africans* from the Ethiopian or *negro* tribe. But still Sh. pictures him with a very negro face, countenance, & skin. He calls him "thick-lips"—"an old black ram"—"a *Barbary* horse,"—speaks of his "sooty bosom"—"such a thing as thou, *to fear*, not to delight"; and Othello says of himself "Haply for I am *black*"[1] &c.—Now Snider does not say of Desdemona that she incurred her fate by marrying a *negro*, but an **African**; & *that* Othello surely *was*. When *I* spoke of a *"negro* Othello," it referred only to his representatives on the *stage*, which are mostly pretty near the negro; & that sight—one of them fondling a young, fair, lovely, white girl for Desdemona, on the stage, has always disgusted me. Did it never strike *you* as *improper*—to call it by a mild term?— I remember R. G. W's remarks on Othello & Desdemona; & they are good. Still there is unquestionably a good deal of room for a sound argument on Snider's side: and he puts it so well, & it is so novel, & striking, that I thought it the very thing for the "Gossip." But, as I said before, if you think otherwise; or that the view advocated would give offence; let us leave it out by all means. In fact, in *all* of Snider's critiques, there is something new, & spicy, & original; and he is *generally right* too, i.e. according to my notions. He argues his points so ably & clearly, that he is very *convincing*: and at the same time he does not bring them forward for the sake of affectation, but he *really believes them* himself; & they often aid in giving consistency & harmony to a play, that is hard to explain otherwise. In the present case, what reason can we assign for this lovely, pure, loving, & innocent woman's tragic end? Disobedience to her father? That, surely, is insufficient. And Sh. never lets his *love-heroines* get the worst of it, when there is a collision between *love & filial obedience;* or *love-heroes* either. . . .

As for "delighted"—"delighted spirit," I don't remember Sh. using that particular word in any other place, in the sense I gave it—*deprived of light.* But he uses other words, where the 'de,' in combination, possesses its Latin meaning of *deprivation*. Take the word "defeature," V. & A. 736,

> "To mingle beauty with infirmities,
> And pure perfection with impure *defeature*."

Here is a noun "feature" combined with "de"—meaning deprivation; *de prived* of *feature* or beauty—disfigurement.
Com. of Err. II. l. 98.

> "Then is he the ground
> Of my *defeatures*."

Ibid. V. l. 298.

> "And careful hours, with time's deformed hand,
> Have written strange *defeatures* in my face."—

In all such words as "despoil," "deflower," &c. &c. the *de* has this meaning "De-nationalize" = to *deprive* of nationality.

But the adjective "delighted," in the present case, *may* be simply derived from the substantive *delight,* and mean full of—rich in—endowed with—*delight*; the *spirit* that possesses the power of *giving* and *receiving* **delight**. For this joyous—delight*ful* and delight*ing* spirit—"to bathe in fiery floods, or to reside In thrilling region of thick-ribbed[a] ice, x x x x 'Tis too horrible!" As I stated there have been any quantity of conjectures and suggestions of new words for "delighted"; but not one that I have ever seen at all satisfies me any better, or as well even, as the old one. You know how common it is for Sh. to use the *past* for the *present* participle, and *vice versâ*: and here, if we take the last explanation, it is simply *delighted* for *delighting*; the delight-ing spirit; the spirit that is, *in its nature,* so capable of giving & receiving *delight*; or simply *rich in delight.*—Does this fill your idea any better than my other interpretation[2] of "the spirit *deprived of light,* & condemned to the blackness of darkness"? . . .

[1] Sh. pictures him: "thick-lips" 1.1.66; "an old black ram" 1.1.88; "a *Barbary* horse" 1.1.111–12; "sooty bosom" 1.2.70; "such . . . delight" 1.2.71; "Haply for I am *black*" 3.3.263.

[2] my other interpretation: This explication, *deprived of light*, was anticipated by corre-spondents in Knight's first Sh edn. and in 2 *Notes & Queries* 11 (1861): 358; Brinsley Nicholson later advanced the idea again, very learnedly: 5 *N&Q* 10 (1878): 83.

[a] thick-ribbed] thick-| ribbed MS.

81:   26 September 1875

"Trilogy" came in the nicest order. Only one part had been cut open. Collier says:—"They come out of the hands of a person who begged very hard for them, expressed the strongest interest in them, and evidently never read above ⅓ of the contents! I was glad to get them for *you*. There is on this side of the water a monstrous deal of pretension to interest as well as competence. My immediate neighbours are rich, but wondrously igno-rant; and one of them actually asked me the other day whether Shake-speare had not written a play upon the history of Julius Cæsar?!!!—. . .

82   6 October 1875

. . . I received a very kind letter from Collier, with the 3 parts of the "Trilogy," which I answered, thanking him heartily for his kindness; and I took the liberty of pointing out to him the mistake he makes all through that work about the *Globe* Edition, blaming it for adopting some few of the emendations of his "Corr. fol. 1632" without ackgmt. by the (†) obelus; whereas, had he read the Preface, he would have seen very plainly that, by their plan, the Edd. only place the obelus against passages hopelessly corrupt, or where no admissible conjecture has been made. I did not tell him of another terrible mistake, (I was afraid he would think me very ungrateful, or hypercritical, if I criticised too much at one time,) which he makes in, at least, half-a-dozen places in the "Trilogy," regarding *W. Sidney Walker*, whom he accuses of picking the Old Corrector's pocket, "with the most practised dexterity," of several of his best emendations, . . . In spite, however, of these, and some other little weaknesses, (pardonable in the *old* gentleman) he has made a very entertaining Dialogue, & certainly a very *beautiful* book; and I was glad to be the owner of a copy. I am looking every day for the Parts of the *4to Shakespeare*. I don't know how I shall succeed in getting the "Tempest"; the rest I seem to be tolerably sure of. I fancy the old editor will *find* an odd no. of *The Tempest*,[1] down in Lancashire, yet. I hope so at least. The "Edward III" I shall get with the Shakespeare.—

Mr. Hudson has sent me a[a] presentation copy of his "Text Book of Poetry," and I wrote him a long letter of thanks, & criticisms on it, & other matters, principally Shakespearian. Mr. Hudson's part of the new Text Book is much better done than the *printer's*. It is a thick p:[2] 8vo, of about 700 pp., and not as well got up, I think, as the "S. Shak."[3]—The text is in *two sizes* of type, which is abominable; the "notes" are at the foot of the page; "lives" at beginning, & "glossaries" at end, of each author, (Wordsworth, Coleridge, Burns, Beattie, Goldsmith, & Thomson.) His *selections* of Poems is excellent, and the work is well & *conscientiously* edited, and an acquisition to any library, as well as most useful for students & readers. But the paper is poor, and edges close cropped. I gave him a good lecture for not attending better to the *looks* of his book, & cautioning him to do so, very especially, in his new "Shakespeare."—

I was "kinder" *sorry* to read what you say about *Snider*. I am not *in love* with him, or his style of writing, by any means; but I think him a smart & *original* genius, & a deep student, & admirer, of our great Poet. I have never detected any approach to "conceit" in his letters to me; had I done so, there is *nothing* which would sooner make me *drop him* "like a hot potato." I hate *conceit*, even when a man, or woman either, has claims to superiority of any kind. . . .

I have *not* seen Bellamy's "New Dictionary of Shakespearian Quotations." Unless Smith send it to me, I hardly think I shall order it, as I have now so many "dictionaries of Shakespearian Quotations," &c. &c. and they are all about alike—not of much *use* to you and me,[b] but useful to men, who want to get a "quotation" to fill in & adorn their compositions. . . .

I want to tell you something anent that passage in *Much Ado,* referred to by Furnivall. You remember in *M. N. Dream*, IV, i, 47—"So doth the *woodbine* the sweet *honeysuckle* Gently entwist," &c. It has always been a controverted point whether the *woodbine* & *honeysuckle* were the *same*, or *two* different varieties of tree or shrub. The commentators, you know, have long notes on it, & R. Grant White strenuously argues that they were *separate & distinct*. But I think I have found a passage in Sh. proving indisputably that *he*, at least, considered them *one* & the same thing. Look at your "Globe Sh." *Much Ado*, III. i. 7, where Hero, Margaret, & Ursula are laying a trap to catch Beatrice. Hero asks Margaret to go to Beatrice, and

> "bid her steal into the pleachèd bower,
> Where *honeysuckles*, ripen'd by the sun,
> Forbid the sun to enter"; &c. &c.

and then a little further down, line 29, Ursula says of Beatrice, who had in the meantime gone into this same "bower":

> "So angle we for Beatrice; who even now
> Is couchèd in the *woodbine* coverture," &c.

Now does not this passage show that *honeysuckles* and *woodbine* are the same thing? I think so, unquestionably. And I am astonished[c] no one ever before saw this point, which "settles" it, as I think, & proves R. Grant White *mistaken*: at least it proves the *Poet* regarded them as one & the same. . . . I entered this in my *Collectanea Shakespeariana*, in 1871, and I have never seen it referred to by any of the Edd. or Commentators, whose long notes on the subject have always made me smile.—. . .

[1] I fancy . . . *The Tempest*: He had not done so by late summer, 1878, when the correspondence as we have it breaks off; but C eventually obtained the missing play, to judge from item ninety-one in Bangs's sale catalogue of C's library (March 1886), which describes the edn. as bound and implies that it is perfect.

[2] thick p: Thick paper.

[3] "S. Shak.": *School Shakespeare* (3 vols., 1871–75).

[a] sent me a] sent ↑me a↓ MS.

[b] to you and me] to ↑you and↓ me MS.

[c] I am astonished] I ↑am↓ astonished MS.

84:   11 October 1875

. . . Dr Ingleby has sent me a presentation copy of his new "Shakespeare Hermeneutics, or The Still Lion." Of course you have received one also. I am just delighted with it. It is a wonderful improvement, in external appearance, on the last edn.. A nice quarto, handsomely printed in semi-antique type, on good (tho' *not* Whatman) paper, with wide margins, & bd.

in Boards. It is a nice mate for his "Centurie of Prayse." I have not as yet had time to examine it much; but I observe several *new examples* of explained passages; & I notice also that tho' he has, I think, *finally settled* some hard points, he still sticks to others wherein he is wrong: e.g. to *church*, or *cleargie*-house, for the Fol. "charge-house," and to "wax," in Timon, that Dyce ridicules so felicitously. Still it is a most valuable & *clever* addition to our Shakn literature; well-written, & will do lots of good. I hope it may have a wide circulation. I shall write to him, after I have read it all carefully. Would it do to say anything more about it in the *Bibliopolist*? A brief notice, say a column, or two at most?

R. Simpson has a very witty review of Bellamy's "New Shakespeare Dictionary," in the last *Academy*; and the *Nation* one of Jacox's "Diversions." There was one of the latter book also in the "British Quarterly Review" for July, 1875. It corresponds in spirit with yours in the *Bib.*, but is more extended. I think you would like it. The same No. (Brit. Qtly) also contains a long, but most admirable essay[1] on "Shakespeare's Character and Early Career." I thought so much of this production, that I copied it all in a MS. book—60 pp. of close-written manuscript; but it repaid me for my labour well. It defends Shakespeare's *character* for morality, integrity, chastity, &c. nobly & convincingly; and is full of good *history*. One sentence contains a remark that may interest you. He says, "Between 1583 and 1586 he had been received into the Blackfriars Company as an Actor on the influential consideration that he 'was a country author passing at a moral.' These actors were 'allowed liveries and wages as grooms of the chamber'—in such a livery Shakespeare's Bust at Stratford even now presents him." I always thought the Bust dress,[2] or sleeveless gown, was the paraphernalia of some *character*, probably one in Jonson's plays, which he played in London.—You once asked me about the motto *"Non sanz droict,"* and I could not give you any satisfaction. This essayist says: "In the summer of this year [1596] he had busied himself in securing for his father the gratification of the long-entertained wish—that he should bear 'a shield or cote of armes,' and be written among the gentlemen of England. This on 20th October he obtained, selecting as the motto of that blazon which his father should display, and he should inherit, the words '*Non sanz droict'*— Not without right. Objection was probably raised by some who still envied the successful player and playwright, and in 1599 the grant, first tricked by Cooke, was ratified by Dethick and Camden."—. . .

---

[1] a long, but most admirable essay: A surprising response from C to this unsigned review, which accepts Collier documents unquestioningly and advances outright error as fact: e.g., the Globe was built in 1594.

[2] the Bust dress: Neither interpretation is mentioned in S. Schoenbaum's *Shakespeare's Lives* (1970). C has confused the Bust costume with that of the Droeshout engraving, which unfounded speculation had called Sh's costume for his role as Old Kno'well in *Every Man in His Humour*.

85:   24 October 1875

. . . A thousand thanks for offering to present to me a copy of "Roffe's Ghost Belief,"[1] &c.; I *have* a very nice, uncut, copy, bound in Hf. mor, gilt top, that belonged to the celebrated philospher *John Stuart Mill*, a presentation copy to him from the author.—. . .

I have met with one great disappointment, that I want to consult you about. Old Mr. Collier writes me, in a very kind letter, (I think, however, he had not yet recd that of mine noticing his errors *à la* "The Globe Sh.",) that when he came to get ready the Nos. of his new 4to Sh. to send me, he found "The Two Gent. of Verona" was *missing*, as well as "The Tempest"; and hesitated to send the rest, without advice. He says he will "do his best" to secure the 2 missing plays; but he has no sure thing of getting them. Now altho' I would dearly like to own the whole set, yet I "hesitate" too, when I fear it will be permanently *imperfect*. Shd the old gentleman die, I would *never* be able to secure the wanted nos.; if he live, it is very doubtful; and the work is so *costly* (£13 or £14)—an imperfect set would be a bore, & almost valueless, pecuniarly.[2] I don't know what to do. Can you advise me? The old editor does not urge me to take the other nos; tho' he says he would like to have my name as a Subscriber. As an instance of his wonderful forgetfulness, do you know he offers to send me, as a present, a set of his "Trilogy," having *forgotten* that he had already sent me one, only a few days ago! I am glad you mentioned his sensitiveness about being reminded of his mistakes; . . . I am obliged to you for the hint. But would not *you* be rather glad than "mad," if anyone told you of so gross errors in any of your *printed* publns., so you might correct them? I am sure I should, even altho' mortified at the same time. . . .

I told you, I think that Dr Ingleby had sent me also a presentation copy of his new "Still Lion." I am sorry he left out the very admirable preliminary essay, that was in his first edn.—I have not yet read it all, but enough to see that it is an improvement, in the way of *examples*, on the other edn. It is a *capital book* every way; & should be in the library & hands of every student of Shakespeare. He sticks like "wax" to some few errors, as I think; but there is *so much* that is true & valuable, I can easily pardon him. I love him for his conservatism of the old folio text.—It is one of my "favourites" in my library; & ranks, in my love, with Walker's books, P. A. Daniel's book; A. E. Brae's "C. C. & Shakespeare"; Arrowsmith's book; Mrs. Jameson's "Characteristics"[3]; and a few others, that I *never* tire of. . . .

What you say, regarding the stereotyping, I think is perfectly correct. In England they very rarely stereotype a work. Each new edition is entirely *reprinted*; and consequently the changes and improvements are incorporated in the text of each succeeding edition, & not, as often in this country, printed at the *end* of a new edition. I think it was a great pity & oversight not to stereotype the "Cambridge" Shakespeare, & all such valuable works. Knight's "Pictorial," I guess, is stereotyped, is it not? I don't know of any other English edition that is. Verplanck's, Hudson's, White's, & Furness', all are, I think. The plates of Verplanck's were burned up in Harper's great fire; & that is the cause it is so scarce now.—. . .

Your mention of the young actor who by antedating Juliet's *accouchement*[4] brought his own engagement to an early end, reminds me of a rather profane blunder that an Actor is said to have made in Hamlet; as follows:—

> "The spirit that I have seen
> May be the devil: and the devil hath power
> To assume a pleasing shape; yea, and perhaps
> Out of my weakness and my melancholy,
> As he is very potent with such spirits,
> Abuses *me too—damme!*"[5]

"The devil," that time, was too "potent" for *him*; and the mental association of his infernal majesty with an oath was very *natural*.—

Did you ever notice a *pun* in Rich. II. Act. II. Sc. iii, line 75, where Berkeley addresses Bolingbroke by his title of "Lord of Hereford." Bolingbroke replies, "My lord, my answer is to *Lancaster*," meaning that he will only answer when addressed by his title of "Duke of Lancaster." Berkeley rejoins:

> "Mistake me not, my lord; 'tis not my meaning
> To raze one *title* of your honour out:" &c.

Evidently, I think, punning on *title* and *tittle*.—. . .

[1] "Roffe's Ghost Belief": Alfred T. Roffe, *An Essay upon the ghost-belief of Shakespeare*. Privately printed, 1851, 31 pp.

[2] pecuniarly: *OED* does not give this form of the adverb after 1656; perhaps a slip of the pen, as the received spelling appears in the MS. at letter 116.

[3] Walker's books, . . . Mrs. Jameson's "Characteristics": William Sidney Walker, *Shakespeare's Versification* (1854) and *Critical Examination of Shakespeare's Text* (1860), both ed. posthumously by W. N. Lettsom; Peter Augustin Daniel, *Notes and Conjectural Emendations of Shakespeare's Text* (1870); Andrew E. Brae, *Collier, Coleridge, and Shakespeare* (1860); William Arrowsmith, *Shakespeare's Editors and Commentators* (1865); Anna Jameson, *Characteristics of Women* (1832 etc.).

[4] Juliet's *accouchement*: Evidently a blunder of some kind on stage which resulted in an unintended obscenity; but the story is no doubt unrecoverable.

[5] "The spirit . . . *damme!*": *Ham.* 2.2.598–603.

87: 1 November 1875

My dear Norris:

I have only time for a line or two, to tell you how kind Mr. Collier has been to me. On my return home, I found a note from him saying—"My friend[1] Mr. Ouvry has sent you, by bookpost, and through me, his Reprint of John Singer's[2] "Quips upon Questions," 1600. For an account of this curious book see my *Bibl. Cat.* II. 209. He has only 50 copies made, so that it is a *rarity*."—Has he sent you one too? It is a very curious & interesting Reprint of an old book of Poetical Quips, &c. &c., by *Clunnyco de Curtanio Snuffe*, which means, "Clown of the Curtain Theatre." It is beautifully printed in small 4to on thick paper, in old-faced[a] facsimile type, bound in Hf. mor, roxburghe, uncut; a dainty little vol.; & has written on fly leaf "Joseph Crosby, Esq., with the Editor's compliments, October, 1875." It contains the Editor's (Frederic Ouvry, Vice-Pres. Soc. of Antiquaries,) Book plate & arms. Mr. Ouvry says in his Preface, that he has reprinted it from the *only known copy* (in his own possession); and that "a careful analysis of this curious volume will be found in Mr. Payne Collier's *Bibliographical Catalogue*,[3] Vol. ii, page 209. Mr. Collier attributes the authorship to John Singer, a noted Actor of the period, who also wrote several plays, which have not come down to us. Besides the Fac Simile title-page, the Editor has a title page, saying it is by "John Singer, *Comedian in the time of Shakespeare*."—"London, privately printed, 1875."—I felt much gratified at Mr. Collier's kindness, & also Mr. Ouvry's, who is, of course, a stranger to me.—Do you know what Mr. Collier's *Bibliographical Catalogue* is? I thought it meant, of course, his "Bibliographical Account of the Rarest Books in the English Language," which you & I have, in 4 vols.; but I could find in that work nothing about Singer's, or the Clunnyco's, "Quips upon Questions," either in "Vol. ii, p. 209," nor anywhere else in the 4 vols.—There is no mention of it, either, in his "Poetical Decameron," 2 vols., 1820.—Mr. Collier says, that the author's name (John Singer) was written on the title-page of the unique book, in his own autograph; but it seems that it had been bound when Mr. Ouvry got it, and in cleaning by acid, the writing had disappeared.—There is not much in the book itself: its only *use* is it helps to explain a great number of Shakespearian words & phrases, or idioms; and Mr. Ouvry says "it is a highly curious volume, as illustrating the history of English Dramatic Literature."[b]—. . .

---

[1] "My friend: Frederic Ouvry was Collier's nephew.
[2] John Singer's: The Author is now thought to have been Robert Armin.
[3] Mr. Payne Collier's *Bibliographical Catalogue*: Collier's citation is to the London edn. (2 vols., 1865); C's citation is to the New York edn. (a piracy, 4 vols., 1866).

[a] old-faced] old-| faced MS.
[b] Literature."—] Literature.— MS.

88:   7 November 1875

. . . You may well imagine my reading & study are wofully broken up by my travelling about away from my books. I can only read little things—in a desultory hurried way. I read the new "Still Lion," however, with great care & pleasure; and have written the learned Dr a long letter about it. I took the liberty of pointing out some half dozen typographical errors, spite of his great care on it: also some criticisms on one or two of his explanations. But it is so capital—so glorious—so lovely—so covetable—a book for any true student of our dear Poet & admirer & conservator of the old text, & just interpretation thereof, that I gave him a sufficient allowance of sincere & congratulatory *praise*, to overbalance any annoyance he may feel at my little fault-finding. A curious typographical error is on p. 73, line 16, where the words "three fingers" should be "forefinger." The directions are, to hold the stock of the gun between the thumb and *forefinger*, and draw down the *serre* with the other three fingers[1] &c. The way it stands now, the man would need *six* fingers and a thumb, on one hand, to handle his piece.—. . .

[1] the other three fingers: *Pace* C's later statement (letter 95) that the error was Ingleby's, not the printer's, it would seem that the compositor erred in this reading by retrospective contamination; what is "curious" about the reading is the analogy to many passages in Fl which can be corrected by similar reconstruction of the process of error.

89:   14 November 1875

. . . I really envy your good luck in getting a copy of Mr. Collier's "Old Man's Diary." It must be intensely interesting. Poor old gentleman! As you say, his memory is fast failing. I have 4 or 5 letters from him, a few days apart, & all contradictory of each other. However, *I have got* 10 of the Plays, (including one yesterday.), & sent on my subscn. & got my *name* down; so I shall receive the rest, if he live to finish them; and must wait my chance to secure the first three.[1] I will adopt your advice, & keep on writing, and writing, until they come. With you, I regret his *New find*. He is so great on *finds*. He found the Corr. Fo. 1632 emendations, after having the old Folio on hand 3 or 4 years! He found his short-hand notes by Coleridge on Shakespeare & Milton, after they had been lost 40 years! And now he has found some of *Milton's* MS. notes in another old Book! He is lucky at finding. Yet probably they are all right. They may be so. He handles many old books, & could not be expected to examine each one thoroughly all at once. His memory, *to my knowledge*, is very treacherous. At first I could not have a "Trilogy" for love or money: then he "recovered" one, & sent it to me: and I had not had it over a month, (not that long,) before he asked me if I would not like to have another!—When I wrote for his 4to Shak., he regretted I could not by any possibility have it, & told me I shd. have applied sooner; & when I told him I *had* done so, through A R Smith, he denied that Smith, "or anyone else" had asked for one: and yet Smith sent me his (Collier's) *own note*, saying his "American correspondent could not be supplied, as all were taken up in a week." Then he "recovered" a set, all but the 1st Play; then all but the first 2; then all but the first 3; and so it stands now. Timmins made the same observation about him, in one of his letters, that he was always making discoveries, or recoveries, among his "remainders," of the most extraordinary kind.—After all, we owe him a heavy debt of gratitude, both for what he has done for Shakespeare, & also for his great kindness & generosity to us individually. We shall much miss him, when he shuffles off his old coil. . . .

I am glad that you have made a beginning now—and so *good* a one too—on your projected work on the Portraits. I always knew you *could* do it, if you only *would* make the attempt & begin. I suppose you have recd your "Romeus & Juliet" &c. of Mr. P. A. Daniel, from the N. S. Soc. I see it is the *last* we are to have for 1875. Well, we have had a good guinea's worth. Don't you think so? Do you hear any more of *Dawson's* coming again to the U. S.? Have Ingleby's eyes got well again. I wrote him last week; also Timmins, & Collier, & Ouvry. Did Ouvry send you also his "Quips upon Questions"? It is a queer book—but a great rarity. I have written 3 or 4 times of late to Hudson, with notes on readings & cruxes, new interpretations, &c, some original, some that I found; but I have not heard from him for a long time—never since he sent me his Book of Poetry. How is Furness getting on with Hamlet? Have you any idea *when* we may look for it out?—
. . .

As you desired, I have compared your collation of your Capell's Notes & Various Readings with my copy. They are alike very nearly. My copy has, in the 1st vol., which yours seems not to have,—after the Title page, & 2 leaves "To the Reader"—another Title page, and another 2 leaves "To the Reader." These last were what were prefixed to the "First Part" of *Notes & Various Readings*, which you know was pubd. several years before the whole Work was pubd. by *Collins*. I have long had this "First Part," in a separate vol.—It contains the *Glossary*, & *Notes* on the Plays to the end of II. Henry IV. This Title Page is nearly the same as the regular titlepage; only after the words "II Henry IV," instead of "Volume the First," &c. it has "With a General Glossary. London. Printed for Edw. and Chas. Dilly, in the Poultry." No date: the regular Title page has *no date* either. The remarks in the "To the Reader" are *not* the same as those in the general "To the Reader." They take up about the same space, & are signed "E.C.," and dated "Dec. 20. 1774."—After the remarks in the "To the Reader" (the regular advt.)—is a "N.B. The **Notes** *first Part*" was printed in 74 [sic], and publish'd then by itself; it's *Advertisement* different."—This is the "different" advertisement that is printed in my copy, after the regular one: and is the same as in my 1. vol. copy of the 1*st* Part.—

There is a little variation in the *arrangement* of our copies. In mine the "Dedication" to Lord Dacre, signed John Collins, is placed in the 1**st** *vol.*, immediately after "To the Reader," where I think it *ought* to be; as it is a Dedication of the *whole Work*, & not only of the "School of Shakespeare," as it would seem to be in your copy. You must read this Dedication by Collins carefully. It is not long, & throws a flood of light on Steevens' pilfering Capell's notes, readings, arrangement of Acts & Scenes, &c.—*Collins* shows Steevens up thoroughly as a dishonest editor, & is not mealy-mouthed in his language. Poor Capell! he got abused & pilfered on all hands, and no acknowledgment.—Be sure, if you have not done so, to read Collins' Dedication.—The rest seems to be just same as my copy.—I told you, didn't I, about mine being full of pencil & ink *notes & references*, (several hundreds, perhaps *thousands*, of them,) all through the vols. (but especially the Glossary, & Index of Words & Phrases,) by *Archdeacon Nares*, to whom it belonged. Many of them are very valuable, & all good, and nicely written in a plain oldish hand. They alone are worth what I gave for the whole work.—. . .

[1] the first three: See below in this letter.

90:   15 November 1875

My dear Norris:

I have just recd your kind note of the 13th, & "stop the press" to congratulate you, which I do heartily, on your good luck. One Hundred & Eight *more* Portraits of Shakespeare; & 350 in all!!—It takes one's breath away. I cannot realize it. Knowing how highly you appreciate these Portraits I can imagine your rapture at the valuable present, & your exquisite enjoyment examining them. I presume there is nothing, (in the U.S. at least,) to compare with your Collection[1] now. I am almost as glad you have them, as tho' they were mine; because you will make infinitely better use of them than I could, & they will give you more pleasure than I should know how to get out of them. Mr. Cosens[2] I have no acquaintance with at all; but he must be a fine fellow evidently.—I have a very fine "proof" (large size) of the "Somerset" Portrait; it is inserted in my copy of Hanmer, 1771; but if you would like to have it, I will detach it, & send it you. Perhaps however you have the same picture. It is a beautiful *engraving*.—

I have also recd a long & very flattering letter from Mr. Hudson to-day. He is preparing a vol. of *Prose*, similar to his Text Book of *Poetry*: it is nearly ready; will probably be out in January. Over half of the work is from Burke: the rest from Webster, Bacon, &c. He says: "I am sure you will like my Text Book of Prose; it is as rich a gathering of *wisdom* and *eloquence* as can well be made. Of course I sent the *Text Book of Poetry* to Furness, and am glad to find that he is an enthusiastic lover of Wordsworth. I did not know it before."

I want to ask you a question. Would there be any harm in Hudson's adopting in his next Text a reading or two from Collier's Trilogy & new

Quarto; of course acknowledging them as Collier's; I mean do you think Mr. Collier would be offended? I hardly think he *ought* to be, when they are duly acknowledged; but he is touchy you know. The reason is, I sent Hudson *two new readings*, that struck me as incontrovertibly right; one "manhood" for "malice" (which is a palpable misprint,)[3] in *Julius Cæsar*; the other "revil'd" for "defil'd" in the Quarto 1600, (the Folio omits it altogether,) in *Much Ado*. The "Corr. Fo. 1632" has "belied"; but *revil'd* is infinitely better, & has a close resemblance too to "defil'd" (a word which cannot be right).[4] Both these are Mr. Collier's *own*—not his Corr. Fo's—emendations. I wrote Mr. C. about the way they struck me, and he was highly pleased. He said I was the only person of the 50, who had his books, that had even mentioned them! Honestly I *do* think they are very valuable improvements, better than any yet suggested, of *corrupt* words of the old copies. Hudson adopts the latter, "revil'd" at once;[5] & probably will the other also; but as he had made one of *his own*, he hates to give it up. His word is "virtue"—where the Fol. has "malice," & Collier "manhood."—Hudson's "virtue" is awfully *tame*. "Our arms in *strength* of *manhood*" is away more forcible, & proper to the occasion, than "Our arms in strength of *virtue*." In fact the word *virtue* won't do at all.[6] Have *you* ever revolved the passage in *J. Cæsar*; if so, what do you think of the amendment? I believe in the old text where it makes *any reasonable sense*; when not, I want the *best* I can get, or make.—

Ever Yours faithfully, J. Crosby.

[1] your Collection: Present whereabouts unknown. The "portraits" were not sold with N's library in November 1922.

[2] Mr. Cosens: Frederick William Cosens, a British book collector.

[3] "malice" (which is a palpable misprint): Hilda M. Hulme defends the Fl reading at JC 3.1.174 in a way reminiscent of C's own philological method; see *Explorations in Shakespeare's Language* (1962), 274.

[4] "defil'd" (a word which cannot be right): *OED* (v., sense 6) gives the meaning sullied by slander; so modern editors, e.g. Riverside.

[5] Hudson adopts . . . "revil'd" at once: In the Harvard Edn. he retains Fl, but he does discuss the Collier reading in a note.

[6] *virtue* won't do at all: C has overlooked the root meaning of *virtue*, which is, ironically, manhood. (It is not obvious, of course, that Hudson was thinking of *virtus*; his reading in the Harvard Edn. is *amity*.)

91:   26 November 1875

. . . I also have added to my noble assortment or collection of "Dictionaries," Dr Johnson's, as revised by **H. J. Todd**; 4 large Quarto volumes, full calf, very clean, sound, neat, & perfect. I presume you know what a *valuable* work this is. It was published in 1818, in eleven parts, at One guinea each; £11..11..0 cloth; and I bought it in calf for less than $10..00.

Isn't that luck? It is worth $25.., if it is worth a cent. *Todd* ranks with *Nares* & *Richardson*, as one of our best etymologists & lexicographers. His Dictionary, like Latham's, & Richardson's, is exceedingly useful & valuable for the array of *quotations* from old & recent authors under each word. It is also a finely-printed work.—A. R. Smith sent me the VIIth vol. of *Dyce III*. To accommodate it to the new P. O. rules, which do not permit over 2lbs[a] in one parcel, he had to break it up, & send it in two parcels: but it was not much worse; & will be all right when bound. I suppose yours came in the same way. He also sent me *Macmillan's Magazine*, containing an article (good) by F. G. *Fleay* on the Authorship of King Henry VI. This makes the *fifth* theory we now have on this subject; *Malone's, Knight's, R. G. White's, Rives'*,[1] & *Fleay's*. Grant White's & Rives', however, are *nearly* alike.—He also sent me a *Cornhill Magazine*, containing a very readable short article on the *Macbeth* of Shakespeare, & that of the Stage. In the December No. of *Lippencott's Magazine* is a well written article, by Mrs Fanny Kemble, on the characters of *Queen Catharine* & *Cardinal Wolsey* in Henry VIII. You will be pleased with it; it points out the difference between the *pride of birth*, which can afford to be humble; and the *pride of power*, which cannot.—. . .

[1] *R. G. White's, Rives'*: Richard Grant White, *An Essay on the Authorship of the Three Parts of King Henry the Sixth* . . . (1859); George Lockhart Rives, *An Essay on the Authorship of the First, Second, and Third Parts of Henry the Sixth* . . . (1874).

[a] lbs] ~~lbs~~ MS. [not a deletion, but the British abbreviation]

92: 29 November 1875 Cincinnati, O.

My dear Norris:

"Here we are again," as Mr. "Clunnyco"[1] originally remarks when he comes jumping into the ring at the Circus. I sent you a hasty letter from *Springfield, O.*; since then I have been spending 2 or 3 days in this busy city. I was not in time, however, to see Sullivan[2] play "Hamlet," which he did to crowded houses, & gave very general satisfaction. A friend of mine told me that he made several innovations in his reading of the text; e.g. "*siege* of troubles" for "sea";[3] "I know a hawk from a *hern—pshaw!*," for "handsaw,"[4] &c. The newspaper critics, here, place his "Hamlet" above Booth's; but I have my doubts of their judgment.—I have bought a few books here which I wanted. Among them, a *lovely* copy of *Chambers & Carruthers'* Edition of Shakespeare, in 10 volumes 8vo. Did you ever see this edition? It is *expurgated*, slightly, for family reading; contains some good *introductions, notes*, &c. by the editors; and some woodcut illustrations by Halswelle. It is not a scholar's or critic's edition, tho' Mr. Furness included it among the edns. collated in his *Romeo & Juliet*. It is nicely printed; and the copy I have bought is *most beautifully* bound, in good Hf-dark-green-turkey morocco, *gilt tops, uncut edges.* It is a fine specimen of binding, contents lettered. &c. The price asked me was $35.00 for the set; but I got it for 20% off— $28..00—*cheap enough.*

They have a very fine "public library" here, containing, up to this time, about 100.000 volumes. I had a letter of introduction to the Librarian,[5] & he showed me his treasures. It is contained in a splendid large fire-proof building. I looked with most interest through the Shakespearian department; but I did not find much that I have not myself. The librarian told me they were negotiating with Quaritch[6] for a set of the *Four Folios*, which the latter has, & for which he asks about $2.000.—They have, however, one edition that I examined very carefully—as it was the *first time I ever saw it*—I mean Halliwell's Folio, 16 vols.—I don't wonder you are delighted with it, & proud of owning a copy. It is simply magnificent: & made me wish, more than ever, for the arrival of my *ship*, so I could order & possess a set of this invaluable work. There is a Mr. E. T. Carson of this city—a merchant—who has been a Shakespearian collector for many years, but has now given it up, & makes his specialty collecting works pertaining to "secret societies." He invited me to visit him, & see his *Shakespearian stores*, but I did not have time. I shall do so, however, next time I come here. He has some of the Folios—I think the three 1632, 1664, & 1685. He is great on *illustrated* editions. He bought a set at Burton's sale[7] in, I think, 38 vols, each play in a vol., and extended with *thousands* of pictures of all sorts & sizes—portraits, & views, & autographs, &c. &c. and he has greatly extended these volumes (or portfolios) since he bought it originally. It is said to be very valuable—many of the prints &c. being very rare proofs. He is quite wealthy, & spends large sums of money on his collections; but I should not set him down for much of a scholar or student of the poet's text.—I saw Miss Jane Coombs play Lady Macbeth, and Juliet, and Parthenia (in *Ingomar*).[8] In the latter piece she was tolerably good: in the two former I did not like her one bit. . . .

They have a remarkably *large* & fine copy of *Boydell's Sh. Gallery* in the Public Library here; 2 vols. very large elephant folio; and the plates seem to be beautiful early impressions. They have Boydell's *Edn.* also, same as yours & mine. This library is visited by over 1500 readers daily.—The librarian is at his wits' end, making a new Catalogue. . . .

---

[1] Mr. "Clunnyco": See letter 87.
[2] Sullivan: Barry Sullivan.
[3] "sea of troubles": *Ham.* 3.1.58.
[4] "I know a hawk from a handsaw": *Ham.* 2.2.379.
[5] the Librarian: Thomas Vickers.
[6] negotiating with Quaritch: Negotiations apparently broke down, as the Library has never owned the set. Records of Vickers's administration do not survive.
[7] Burton's sale: William Evans ("Falstaff") Burton, the Shn actor and theater manager, had a splendid library of Shakespeariana in New York; he died in 1860.
[8] *Ingomar: Ingomar, the Barbarian,* trans. (1872) from the German play by Eligius Freiherr von Münch-Bellinghausen. The Greek girl, Parthenia, tames her barbarian lover, Ingomar, by high-mindedly choosing honor over love.

93:   5 December 1875

. . . I told you, I think, that I had put in a "bid," at a New York book auction (Bangs & Merwin's), for a copy of *Dyce's "Beaumont & Fletcher,"* 11 vols. demy 8vo. You know of course how fearfully **scarce**, as well as **valuable**, this work is; rarer even, I think, than "Capell's Notes." I had great difficulty in procuring a set, some 4 years ago; & then it cost me about $75.00 to import; and the Bookseller said he had watched for a copy for 2 years. (I saw one advertised since, by Little Brown & Co., for $100..)—Noticing this copy for sale by Bangs, Merwin & Co.—a fine, superb set in new "tree calf, elegant," I bid on it, $5..50 a volume as a *speculation*, with no hope of getting it; but when I came home I found I *had*. I immediately remitted the Cash; & am looking for the parcel every minute. It will only cost me abt. $62.. here; & is represented to be a magnificent set, in the finest tree calf, full binding, clean & new. I think that is a piece of good luck I don't often meet with. I suppose of course Mr. Furness has a copy. It is an invaluable book for all Shakespearians,—most carefully edited,—full of Shakespearian information, & handsomely printed. There was a *reprint* of it published in Boston, in 2 large 8vo volumes; and I have a fine set of *that* also, in new Hf. brown morocco, yellow edges, that cost me $12.00. I have also a fine large copy of the 3d folio[1] (1679) that I picked up for about the same price. Some time ago R. Clarke & Co. of Cincti offered me $75.. for my first set of the 11-vol. Dyce's *B. & F.* for a customer; but I declined taking it. Such books as this, & the "Capell's Notes," are *good Stock*, as we merchants say; always (like diamonds) increasing in value: besides being indispensable *for use* in any Shakespearian student's library. . . .

I can well imagine the pleasure you enjoyed at receiving & owning a copy of Mr. Page's new *"bust."* I congratulate you sincerely on possessing a copy of what you so much admire, & what must be truly admirable. I could hardly repress a smile at your enthusiastic description of its *superhuman, extatic, etherial* beauty. You say "it is almost too *beautiful* to be **real**." That, I fear, is its only defect. I trust, however, it possesses reality & substance sufficient to keep it from "fading away like a beautiful vision." It would be a fearful calamity for you to wake up some morning, & find it *gone*,—faded away. Joking apart, it must be a very beautiful conception—a lovely work of art, with enough of Shakespeare in it to give it a *kinship* to the Stratford bust. You do not generally, or often, speak hyperbolically or extravagantly in praise of anything; and when you write of this bust in such rapturous terms I know that it deserves it. I am very anxious to see a photograph of it: and altho' my faith in its authenticity is, just now, no bigger than a grain of mustard seed, yet you know it may grow into a tree, big enough to shelter the whole feathered creation under its branches. . . .

What a *noble & beautiful* collection of "Shakespeariana" you are acquiring! I don't wonder that your friends love to come, & see, & admire them, even if they do occasionally *bore* you. I presume your stock of portraits, views, busts, &c. is unique in the U.S.—I am not troubled very much with sight-seers, for the reason that I have but very few *pictures*; and my *books*, altho' all the best in editions, good bindings, &c. are packed away, 2 rows deep often, in tight bookcases, & make no *show* at all. It is simply a *working* library; and I am unfortunately, as yet, too poor to fix up a handsome apartment for it, so as to display my treasures as they deserve. But I *love* them none the less, as I do many a true-hearted friend, who cannot afford to wear broadcloth, & fine jewelry.— . . . You are disposed to poke a little fun at me, calling my binding "gorgeous," &c. There is nothing gorgeous about it: but considering where it is done, & that I have no such binders as "P. & N." to work for me, my books are well, strongly, & neatly bound: many of them very well indeed, & much better than the generality of books we buy, bound in London or N.Y.—I watch my binder pretty closely; & he is very obedient now; tho' at first I had trouble with him. Most of my *editions* are now well bound, & most of my large vols. of *Shakespeariana*, but I have scores & scores of *pamphlets*, & small vols., unbound; & I got 2 dozen cases, made of pasteboard, & shaped like *books*, with lids or covers to them, labelled "Shakespearian pamphlets"; & these hold & keep clean the little valuable tracts, &c.—I intend, someday, to make me a *Catalogue;* and then I will consult you about the best way of doing it. I dread it, as it will be a fearfully tiresome job. I have a sort of one,[2] giving *brief criticisms* on most of the important works; but it is not in orderly shape, like yours. I have now, I believe, 102 or 103 *Complete Editions* (including some few duplicates, such as Dyce II, 1821 Var., 1793 Var., Capell, &c., &c.)— . . .

---

[1] the 3d folio: I.e., the 2nd folio.
[2] I have a sort of one: C's handwritten catalogue of his library in five vols. is in the McMillan Shakespeare Collection, University of Michigan.

94: 8 December 1875

. . . I dread travelling now, & especially stopping in small towns, & putting up at one-horse[a] hotels.—I *often & often* think of *you*, & your happy, cozy, comfortable *home*; surrounded by your wife & family, with your noble Shakespearian library in which to refresh your *mind*, when jaded with "the nice, sharp, quillets of the *law*." Do you ever think of *me*, and pity my *poor, lonely* condition?— . . .

---

[a] one-horse] one-| horse MS.

95: 10 December 1875

. . . I have . . . another very pleasant & good-natured letter from Dr Ingleby, which I enclose you to read. When he made out his slip of "er-rata," he had not received my letter to him, in which I pointed out to him a lot more, *two* especially of importance, one on p. 73, about the "fingers"; & one on p. 95, last line but one, where "Venus" ought to be printed "Adonis."—These are not slips of the *printer*, but errors of *his own* making. He says that my reading, "charter house," or "chartreuse," for the corrupt word "charge-house," is *very good,*" still he prefers "clergy-house." Of course every man likes his own bantlings the best. . . . What a fearfully *bad hand* Ingleby writes! I had the hardest work reading all of his letter. He uses one word that I never (I believe) saw before, "it *arrideth* not some others," meaning "it *pleases* not." It is, however, a good legitimate word, used by Ben Jonson, from the Latin *arrideo* (*ad* and *rideo—ridere*), but is now obsolete. Did *you* ever see it in your reading?

I cannot thank you *enough* for copying for me so much from Collier's Diary; or tell you how I laughed over, & enjoyed, all the good jokes, puns, bonmots, &c. by Lamb & the rest. What a glorious fellow C. Lamb must have been at a dinner or supper party! He seems to have been inexhaustible in his wit,—& so good & original too.—. . .

96:   14 December 1875

. . . I want to tell you about my "Beaumont & Fletcher," & *how* I came to let the Cincinnati booksellers have it. They had been begging me to sell my copy to them, & offered me $75. for it for a Mr. E. T. Carson, a wealthy collector. I had declined; but when I was there, a few days ago, I told them I had bid for another, & if I got it, I would sell them my copy. They said that Mr. Carson was supplied, but they would give me $65.. for it anyway. So when I found I was lucky enough to get the other, I sent them my first copy, & they remitted me the price. That you see is why I cannot comply with your request. Had I thought that you wanted it, I would have been glad to send it to you at cost. However it was not a very nice copy, tho' sound & good. It was *cut,* & well cut too; then it had marbled edges (a thing I hate in a nice book,) & besides, some previous owner had undertaken to point out the "choice passages" by pencil marks—to my infinite disgust. In my new copy there are *no blemishes* of this kind,—indeed it is "all my fancy painted" it. I notice in H. Sotheran & Co's Catalogue, for Nov. 29. 1875, a very similar copy—in full tree calf &c.—is advertised for *thirteen guineas,* which would be about 92$ or 93$ here. . . .

Like yourself, I am "disgusted" too with Sabin & Sons, and their *Bibliopolist.* I have long thought that you were throwing "pearls before swine" in attempting to *boost* their periodical. They cannot appreciate a good thing, when they have it. It is perfectly ridiculous the way they have been treating our articles; & the delay & irregularity in the publication make it entirely unreliable. Look how I hurried up that "Dowden review"; and there is no show for it to appear this year of our Lord. I had to laugh at their most contemptible criticism on your expression "as it were." To use a very mild phrase, they must be *fools*, as it were, not to know that this phrase is as old, as idiomatic, as well known & recognized among the best writers, as the Alleghany Mountains, as it were, or even the Rocky Mountains, or the hills of Sion. Anyone that has had, as it were, a common-school education, or studied the first principles of English Grammar, knows how common a phrase it is among all our best authors, meaning "in some sort"— and generally introduced to apologize, as it were, for something that might *seem* a little inappropriate. Thus, it is supererogatory, *as it were*, for me to fill up this sheet[1] writing about so well known—so well recognized—an English idiom. But it only shows the shallowness of the criticisers; and from all such hypercritics Good Lord deliver us!—I am glad to hear that you have determined to cut loose from the *Bib.*—as soon as convenient—and to make other arrangements. If the Galaxy, or Scribner, or any other well-conducted journal, that knows what *sense is*, accept your kind proposal, you can always depend on me—to the extent of my *ability* & *time*—to do my "level best," *as it were*, to assist you.—I enclose you a letter I have just recd. from Mr. Timmins, that you may see how complimentary *he* is on our *Bibliopolist* work. . . .

I have . . . received Skeat's new book "Shakespeare's Plutarch." This is a very useful book indeed. Mr. Skeat is one of our best critical and verbal English scholars: and his notes, so far as I have examined them, are capital—very explanatory & useful to learners of old English. The "Preface" is highly interesting, & gives a good bibliographical account of the edns. of North's Plutarch. I am only sorry that he had not a copy of the 1*st* or 1579 Edn. to make his "selections" from. It must be *very scarce* indeed, as he says he has never seen a copy. You are to be envied in having a copy. He thinks that the 1612 edn., in the Greenock library, was the one that Shak. owned, & that the writing, references, &c. are the Poet's genuine work: but of course Sh. *must* have seen, if not owned, one of the 2 previous edns., as the 3 Roman Plays were all unquestionably written from 3 to 6 years *before* 1612.—I wish too that Mr. Skeat had retained *all* the old spelling. It spoils the good it would otherwise do, I think, to modernize part of the spelling, & print part in the old style. Still the book is so well edited, the notes both marginal or glossarial, & critical at the end, are so excellent, & the Indexes so useful, one should be thankful to him for it.—

Do you observe that your old friends,[2] Gebbie & Barrie, are about to publish a *new edition* of Shakespeare? Their "prospectus" is a regular piece of *humbug*. From it, I should judge that their new edition is simply a reprint of *Valpy's Cabinet Edition*, 15 vols. They adopt the "pure, *uncastrated*, text of Malone, which has been *supervised* by an eminent Shakespearian" (who is it?); and they give the 170 plates from the Boydell Gallery &c., and 200 woodcuts, & say that with their 400 engravings (or nearly,) no other edition *extant* has so many illustrations. How about Knight's, or Staunton's illustrated edn.? Have you seen any "parts," or "volumes" of their new edn.?

Are their steel plates *outline* engravings, copies of those in Valpy, or line engravings? Their "life," "Preface by Johnson," "arguments," & "Glossarial Notes," all of which they brag about almost laughably, are copied bodily, I should judge, from *Valpy*. The size of the book, no. of volumes, even the name "Cabinet," are all "conveyed" from Valpy.— . . .

[1] it is supererogatory, *as it were*, . . . sheet: C reveals his reading habits as he brings together uses of *as it were* in St. Gregory, Lord Jeffrey, an *Academy* reviewer, and Charles Kingsley, all from "the last few days' reading" (letter 97); in letter 98, C provides thirteen Biblical citations, the results of "about a ten-minutes search."
[2] your old friends: This Philadelphia house had pubd. N's edn. of the Boydell *Shakespeare Gallery* in 1874.

97: 26 December 1875

. . . I have ordered, from Quaritch, a copy of the First Folio of North's Plutarch, 1579, advertised on p. 763 of his Cat. No. 300 (Dec. 1875.) It is represented as a fine *large* copy, in "full russia extra, gilt edges, with woodcut medallion portraits," and only costs £3..10.., very cheap I should think; as I agree with you from what Mr. Skeat says the book must be very rare.— I have a very fine copy of one of the later Folios; but I have always wanted to own the *1st edition.*—I hope it may be my luck to get it before someone else drops down on it. You got yours most remarkably low I think, only $12.—I shall be thankful to get this copy, especially if as fine & well bound as represented, for $25.00.— . . .

I notice that Quaritch advertises a set of the "Cambridge Shakespeare," in cloth, for *Nine Guineas*! Isn't that a brave price for it? But I presume it is very scarce now, & in great demand. I would not take, poor as I am, $200 for my beautiful copy, if I could not get another. . . .

No news yet of the Octo. No. of the *Bibliopolist*; & December is nearly gone. I return you Mr. Church's[1] note regarding a Sh. Dept. in the "Galaxy"; and I am sorry he is so blind to the interests of the Magazine. Have you heard from *Scribner* yet? You must let me know their decision. I hope they will accept, upon my word; and I will do what little I can to aid you, as far as time and ability will permit.— . . .

[1] Mr. Church's: William Conant Church.

98: 2 January 1876

. . . I have finished *King John*, which I have read most thoroughly, in connection with Rich. II. & Rich. III., "with all the appurtenances thereunto belonging." "Alls Well that Ends Well" comes next on my list; and it is (to me) one of the most crabbed & difficult of all the Plays, certainly of all the Comedies.—In *K. John* there are several "knots intrinsecate," very tough to unravel. What is a man to make of the following *torment*?

> "But thou hast sworne against religion:
> By what thou swear'st against the thing thou swear'st
> And mak'st an oath the suretie for thy truth,
> Against an oath the truth, thou art unsure
> To sweare, sweares onely not to be forsworne,
> Else what a mockerie should it be to sweare?"[1]

Do you know a Phila lawyer competent to disentangle this imbroglio without doing violence to the text of the Folio? If so, commend him to me; I want to know him.—I will not bore you by setting down the shape that I have finally decided to lick it into; as I know you would *skip* reading it; and I don't want you to skip anything I write you.— . . .

I have bought for $7..00, in N.Y., the new edn. by Chatto & Windus of *Dibdin's Bibliomania*, and I am quite well pleased with it. . . . What an *interesting & amusing* book it is! I have just revelled in it. It is *remarkably cheap* at £1..1..0; the 1842 edn I see was pubd. at £3.3.0, & is now very scarce. I have the "Library Companion"—a fine copy in new Hf. Cf. *uncut*, gilt top; and the "Reminiscences," in 2 vols. *ditto*. It is amusing to read over the Sales of Shakespeariana, & the *low prices* of many of the now awfully rare folios & quartos. See, e.g., pp. 430–437, for Dibdin's account of *Steevens*, and his sale of *Editions, Shakespeariana*, etc. and the prices. A *first* folio for £22..0..0; a *third* for £8..8..0; and a *fourth* for £2..12..6! And all those invaluable old Quartos—1st editions—where the prices are so *low* as to make one's mouth water for envy.—. . .

As Mr. Furness said, the *Bib.* is nothing but an advertising thing for the interests of J. Sabin & Sons; and they have not got sense enough to make even that interesting. I know how you feel, while your name is attached as Editor of the Sh. Dept.—You must just exercise your own judgment about continuing. I cannot advise you. If I write anything for publication, I want it to be worth reading, to be of some *use* to the reader; and you know I could not make those reviews much shorter, to have been of any service or account.—. . .

Your list of the "Old Dramatists" is much more complete than mine. I have only commenced lately picking them up; & will keep on gradually, until I have them all, if I live. You have, I think, all that I have, except perhaps 2 or 3 of the Dramatists that were pubd the last century. I have the *original* edn of Farquhar, 2 vols., and of Wycherley, 1 vol. &c; and the new edns. of Chapman, & Dekker; and the folios of B. & F. and Davenant; and *all* of Moxon's roy. 8vo "Old Dramatists." But I have neither the folio Ben Jonson (of which you have 2 copies), nor Halliwell's Marston, nor Dyce's Middleton, nor Heywood.—Neither have I Suckling, nor Lilly,[2] nor Randolph: all of which you own; & I hope to do so ere long. I am watching for the *best editions* in the Auctions, & putting in bids along: I have a Boston reprint of Dyce's B. & F., in 2 large roy. 8vo vols.—a fine copy in Hf mor., uncut. And I have a set of the *original edn.* of Gifford's Ben. Jonson, in 9 vols., lge 8vo., in full modern calf, a fine copy, that A. R. Smith charged me, I think, *9 guineas* for! The Plays are *not lettered* on the backs, & it is a bore. I think of having it done. Sometimes I take down almost the whole lot, to find a Play I want. The Binder who neglects to letter "Plays" on the backs of his vols. should be cowhided.—. . .

What are you *reading* now? I mean consecutively: any of the plays of Sh.?—What success has Ashworth had selling Mr. Brae's "C. C. & S."? Do you think he, or any other bookseller of Philad., could dispose of any copies of Ingleby's "Hermeneutics"? I sent some "prospectuses" of it to R. Clarke & Co., of Cincinnati, who are regular importers of English books, and begged them to order a small supply. It *ought* to sell: it is a beautiful, and cheap, and most valuable book to any Shak. scholar. But most readers would rather give their $2. for a copy of Mark Twain's fooleries, or Jules Verne's "Journey to the *Moon*."—

[1] "But thou . . . to sweare?": *Jn.* 3.1.280–85.
[2] Lilly: John Lyly.

99: 12 January 1876

. . . I enclose you a very acceptable & readable letter from our friend Snider. He is delighted with my notice of his essays; and I am right glad if I have been the means of encouraging him, or doing him any good. He is a most deserving fellow—a good Student—& an ardent & intelligent Shakespearian. He says he don't know what to write for you in the *Bibliopolist*. I'm sure I cannot advise him. Fancy one of his "essays" going to the Sabins! As for "Gossip" about the Poet, I imagine he is, like your obedient servant, *short* in that stock. Living, as we do, "out West," where hardly one out of one thousand has ever *read* a line of Shakespeare, & not one out of ten thousand read the Poet with any Critical care, how *could* we find any gossip? I imagine he might write some short *popular* critique, say on one particular "character," *Parolles*, for instance, as compared with *Sir Toby Belch*, or *Sir John Falstaff*, that would be suitable; if only the "wisdom could be compressed" into "a dozen or fifteen lines": but that is not an *easy* matter to do. If you think proper, perhaps you had better drop him a note, & suggest your views, & the "limits" allowed by the Edd. of the *Bibliopolist*.[1] How I wish there were Shakespearian devotees enough in the U.S., or among the English-speaking & reading Public, to support a "*Shakespearian Magazine*"![2] Say fifty or Seventy-five pages of well-printed reading, *Monthly*; with a leading dept. for short (but not *so short* as to be practically *useless* essays & critiques; a dept. for "hermeneutics," or explanations of text, conjectures, &c.; and one for brief, crisp, reviews of *all* the new books, & new editions. And I would add a page or so for *exchanges*, and *Sales* of Shakespearian books, between collectors. It should be printed on good paper, with l'ge margins for Notes; a neat wrapper; and cost not less than $500 a year. *Why* could not some such a periodical be sustained?[a] *Then* men like Mr. Furness, & Mr. Grant White, and Mr. Brae, & Prof. Corson, & Dr Ingleby, & Mr. Hudson, and the English scholars, like Mr. Minto, Mr. Skeat, Prof. Dowden, and (providing he would learn to *spell*, & behave as a gentleman,) Mr. Furnivall, *cum multis aliis*, would have a common organ for their scraps, & more important criticisms; & not scatter them among "*Notes & Queries*," "The *Athenæum*," "*Academy*," and a dozen other magazines, rendering it nearly impossible for one to get hold of all. An *Editor* like J. Parker Norris, Esq., to supervise his corps of correspondents, & write "leaders" himself, could make a delightful & most enjoyable literary monthly feast for his readers, & acquire honour, (& perhaps some money,) for himself. How many righteous men are there in Sodom that would subscribe, as *readers*, to such a "Shakespearian Magazine," do you suppose? I fancy there would be no trouble about subscribers, as *writers*.—As for any hope of doing any *good*, with the "Bibliopolist," I have given it up. Good writers won't waste their powder on such game, and I don't & cannot blame them. The Sabins have not *sense* enough to appreciate a good article.—

I have discovered by 3 or 4 "infallible proofs,"[3] that Grant White in editing his edition of Shakespeare did *not* have an original copy of the 1st Folio by him; altho' to read his Preface, & many of his Notes, you would suppose he had collated every *line, word, syllable, & point*, of it. . . .

I concur in every word you say of *Schmidt's Lexicon*. It is a very valuable & laborious production; & will be of daily use to the Shakn.. student. Of course it is more a *dictionary* than a *Concordance*; yet it answers the purpose of a concordance in a great measure. It does not contain *every word* as Mrs. Clarke's does; but all the most important words—words that require any *explanation*: and, as you observe, giving the no. of the line in the Globe Edn. is of great service. One of the most valuable features in the work is the *bringing together all* the passages where the word, or phrase, to be explained occurs; so one can see the varieties of usage given by the Poet. It must have taken an immense amount of work to compile; but the Germans are the most indefatigable lexicographers in the world.— . . .

I am now reading, *more meo*, "All's Well." It is a very corrupt Play; but my previous hard work & study on it render it quite easy to me now. This travelling about so much hinders my work on the regular study of the Plays very much. I always read the 1st folio edition through first, of each play, before I touch a commentator, or modern edition: putting myself in Rowe's place,[4] & seeing what *I* would have done with the tough passages. By the way, I observe in my copy of Halliwell's *Comedies*—the small folio edn. of 20 copies—he styles this Play *"Love's Labour Won*, or, All's Well that Ends Well": and the running title all through is **"Love's Labour Won**." This is the only instance I know of of any editor changing the name or title of a Play from the 1st Folio. . . .

[1] the "limits" allowed by the Edd. of the *Bibliopolist*: C quotes Sabin in a letter to Ingleby a few months after this: "Shn articles must be limited, as they did not bring in any new subscribers" (Folger MS. C.a. 14, 22 April 1876).

[2] Shakespearian devotees enough . . . to support a *"Shakespearian Magazine"*: Efforts to found such a magazine were made within a few years. N edited a Sh column in *Robinson's Epitome of Literature* from spring 1878 through mid-1879 (when *The Literary World* subsumed it and W. J. Rolfe carried on with a similar column through 1882). *Shakespeariana*, a monthly, appeared for a decade (1883–94); *The Shakespearean* followed 1895–98. Of greater staying power was *Poet-Lore* (devoted to Sh and Browning), founded in 1889—it lasted until 1932. *The Shakespeare Association Bulletin* first appeared in 1924; its successor, *Shakespeare Quarterly*, continues, though finding devotees enough to support a *"Shakespearian Magazine"* is as difficult in the twentieth century as it was in the nineteenth.

[3] 3 or 4 "infallible proofs": He goes on to give one of them—a word in *TGV* missing according to White is missing only in the 1808 type facsimile of Fl.

[4] in Rowe's place: I.e., without editorial precedent; Rowe, however, worked from F4, not F1.

[a] be sustained] ~~not~~ be sustained MS.

100:   23 January 1876 Alliance, Ohio

. . .It is anything but "nice" to lie over a dull Sunday, (raining all day,) in one of the dullest little towns, at a dull little hotel; with not a soul you care to speak to; no Episcopal Church, no public library; no nothing!— Fortunately I had a vol. of the 1821 Var. with me; and I read Dr Badham's essay on "The Text of Shakespeare," in the vol. of the *Cambridge Essays* for 1856, which I have only just been lucky enough to purchase at an Auction at Cincinnati.—

I have ordered from A. R. Smith a copy of A. W. Ward's book on the "Dramatic Poets"; the 2d vol. of Schmidt's Lexicon; W. A. Wright's "Lear"; Skeat's "Two Noble Kinsmen"; and some other books, which I will tell you about when I get them. He sent me the "Fortnightly" for Jan. 1876, containing the last part of *Swinburne's* essay on Shakespeare; but I never got the *first* part, pub'd in the No. for May 1875: have you these Nos.? I have not read any of this essay; but only notices of it. It seems to be "fornenst"[1] the views taken by some members of the "N. S. Soc." There is a very readable brief article in the *Cornhill* for Jan. 1876, on "A Stage Iago."—I saw a set of Dr Johnson's entire works, 11 vols, the celebrated "Oxford Classic" Edn., advertised by Sotheran for £3..10; and I have ordered it. You know all of this series are *lovely* specimens of typography; & the set is very low at that price. I think it is the same edn. as Mr. Furness has—1825—; The old Dr. is a special favourite with me; and I have long wished to get all his works in *this* fine edition. No word, that I know of, yet from the 1st edn North's

Plutarch. Did you ever read Dr Badham's essay in the "Cam. Essays"? It will repay you well for the trouble, tho' liable to considerable criticism *now*. I recd. an invitation to meet the Shak. club (of 25 gent*n*) of Wheeling, West Va.—I called on some of the Members, & had a pleasant time. They meet weekly, & *read* (not *perform*) Shakespeare. I am an hon. member,[2] & shall go to their anniversary on the 23d April.—Will write you more anon. This is only an *apology*, which please excuse the brevity & haste of, & believe me ever, Your friend, J. C.—

[1] "fornenst": A North Country expression: *OED* does not give the sense of moral opposition C implies by the term.

[2] I am an hon. member: Years later C twice gave the Shakespeare birthday address to the Club, "William Shakespeare" (1880) and "The Study of Shakespeare" (1881). Newspaper rpts. are in the Crosby Collectanea, University of Michigan McMillan Shakespeare Collection.

101:   27 January 1876

. . . The only "edition" I have added to my library,[a] since Chatto & Windus' Photo., is one published by one of your Philadelphia houses, Claxton, Remsen, & Haffelfinger. . . . This makes my list number (*including duplicates*) 104, all very good copies, except the following, which I want to get, in good sound binding:

> Rowe's 7 vols[1]
> Hanmer's 1st.—6 vols—
> J. & S.[2] 1773—10 vols.

and I have *no* "Warburton," & *no* Folio "Halliwell." If ever you come across any of the above, please post me, & I will be thankful. You have one also, by *Stebbing*, that I should like to get.—

I return you Furnivall's note, & your reply, with the notice of the "find" of a new Portrait. This is quite a change over the spirit of Mr. F.'s dream, since he wrote last: did not I prophesy all would ere long be serene between you two "distempered spirits"? But I had to admire the *curtness* & diplomatic style of your "notes"—the assurances each is so anxious to impress on the other of his "most distinguished consideration."—Better thus, than belabouring each other's head with such missiles as "*you* are an ass,"—and "*you* are no *gentleman*."

Hamlet remarked that there are "more things in heaven and earth than are dreamt of in your philosophy"; and there are more *Shakespearians* in the country than *I* had ever "dreamt of." The "Shakespeare Club" of Wheeling, West Va., is a real live institution. I spoke to you of my being an honorary member of this Club; & I paid them a visit. They are composed of 25 of the best men—merchants & professional gentlemen, & the Episcopal Rector—

of Wheeling. I gave them a good many useful hints; and they presented me a copy of their "proceedings" &c. It is a lovely little 4to[3]—handsomely printed, & contains the photographs (in miniature) of the members, the "Address" (really very good) of their president, at their dinner last 23d of April; their organization—casts of the plays for reading—some average Shakespeare Sonnets, & other poetry &c.—It is a brochure of 71 pp. & very creditable to their taste. Each member had 4 copies. Their weekly meetings are simply for critical *reading*—one play each evening, and discussion; and they enjoy it very much. . . .

---

[1] Rowe's 7 vols: The first (1709), or second (1709, i.e., 1710) of Rowe's three edns. (the difference between the first and second edns. was not recognized until the twentieth century).

[2] J. & S.: Johnson and Steevens.

[3] a lovely little 4to: It is in the Crosby Collectanea, McMillan Shakespeare Collection, Harlan Hatcher Graduate Library, University of Michigan (item VI, 16).

[a] my library] mine MS.

102: 6 February 1876 Cincinnati, Ohio

My dear Norris:

As I was on a trip in this vicinity I ran down here to spend my Sunday; & having a few spare moments concluded to tell you so. I had a very enjoyable treat yesterday, seeing *Henry V* played at the Grand Opera House, by *Rignold*[1]—exceedingly well supported. I presume you have seen this: it is a grand pageant, very well done indeed, & in good taste & harmony. They had a capital *Pistol* and a splendid *Fluellen*; & Rignold is a host in himself. I wish I could have sat by you during the play, & talked & laughed together. I also saw Mr. & Mrs. Florence,[2] in a new comedy "The Mighty Dollar," very well played. I laughed excessively, during the whole proceedings: it is full of capital hits & gags; & *Florence* brings down the house "by a large majority." While I was laughing at this play—a terrible & awful tragedy was being enacted at another Opera-house here. Ten persons killed outright, & many more so bruised & mangled, they will die; all women & children. Over 3000 persons were in the theatre, & some fool raised a cry of "Fire" (false alarm), & you can imagine the rest. I send you a "Cincinnati Enquirer" by this mail, containing the particulars. The same paper contains a well-written article from the pen of my new friend Dr Vance, of Gallipolis, on "Shakespearian Study." Read it carefully; he seems quite well posted in Shakn.. matters, & especially on the "N. S. Soc."; & Furnivall will be tickled to read it. An article like this, I fancy, is just about what you want for your "Gossip" column. I hope ere long to become better acquainted with Mr. Vance; and will interest him in this dept. of the Bibliopolist. I have found a member of the "N. S. Soc." here, a very nice gentleman, a lawyer, named

Moses F. Wilson. I had a pleasant tête-a tête with him on Shakn subjects. He is a modest fellow, well-read, and has a good collection of Shake-speariana. I spent 3 hours in the Public Library here—all on one book—(you can guess what it was)—Halliwell's Grand Folio Shakespeare. I commenced reading his valuable, interesting, essay on the "Formation of the Text," in the 1st vol., & was not half done when the rooms closed. Oh, what a treasure you possess, in this work. I have made up my mind[3] to "save up," & get it as soon as I can. I could only examine one vol. for want of time. "The Tempest" is nobly edited. . . .

[1] Rignold: George Rignold (1838–1912). *Henry V* was his most famous production.
[2] Mr. & Mrs. Florence: William J. and Malvina Florence were a famous team in comedy and melodrama; Bardwell Slote in *The Mighty Dollar* is said (by *DAB*) to be Florence's most enduring character.
[3] I have made up my mind: C's dream came true, if only temporarily; in a letter (10 May, 1881) to Halliwell-Phillipps now in the Folger Shakespeare Library, C speaks of his valued copy of the Halliwell Folio Shakespeare. But the edn. is not listed in Bangs's auction catalogue (March 1886) of C's library; he may have bought it and then been forced to resell it.

104:   12 February 1876

. . . Speaking of Mr. Forster's[1] biography of Dyce, in the "Fortnightly," I notice his *death*, in a late paper. Sad that good men should ever *die*: but "such is *life*." He was engaged, I believe, on a life of *Swift*, of which one or two volumes are issued. It will not, I presume, affect the publication of the remaining volumes[2] of Dyce's 3d edition of Shakespeare, that he was superintending.—

I read with great pleasure Swinburne's delightful, easy, *refreshing*, reply to Furnivall's attack on him, in the "Academy." I have often noticed that a real true *poet* was also a lovely composer of *prose*: as for instance Campbell in his Life of Mrs. Siddons; Southey in his Life of Nelson, &c. &c.— Furnivall setting himself up against Swinburne reminds me of nothing so much as a little ugly rat-terrier, running around, barking & snapping, at a big bushy Newfoundland. The noble fine old animal walks ahead, scarcely deigning to notice the *fiste*, except by a contemptuous turn of his quiet eye, until he gets too familiarly close with his snarls & his yelps, when Mr. Newfoundland gives a slight growl—"gently as a sucking dove," & fiste vanishes—" abiit, excessit, evasit, erupit."[3]—

As for getting hold of another copy of the "Proceedings of the Wheeling Shakespeare Society," I can only say, that I will *try*. I fear, however, the prospect is very slender. They only printed 100, 4 for each member; & they are all out in the hands & libraries of their individual friends. I only got my copy through the persistent influence of a kind *lady*, who married one of the members, & who formerly resided in Zanesville—a *very dear friend of mine* (when she was a young lady.) Still, you know *I* got a copy of the "Phila

Shak. Society's Notes on The *Tempest*," when I had given it up as hopeless; and it will be only because it is *impossible*, if I cannot manage to secure a stray copy of this for you. . . .

I have received my 2d volume of "Schmidt's Lexicon" from A. R. Smith. It came by post, in two parcels, & only cost 2/7 postage on the two. What a grand Work it is! No reader or student of Shakespeare can pretend to do without it. He wants it at his elbow, day & night. It is in itself a *Diction-ary*,—a *Commentary*, and a *Concordance*. Then, have you read the "Appen-dix"? The "Grammatical Observations"; the "Provincialisms"; the "Words & Sentences from foreign languages"? *Capital*. What an immense amount of labour, care, skill, scholarship, untiring industry, are in these 2 volumes! One good effect of this Lexicon will be, that it will·stop many needless *conjectures* & *emendations* hereafter. I cannot speak in terms high enough to express my admiration of this invaluable work. I only regret that the hon-our and credit of making it should go to Germany; and a plodding German lexicographer beat the English on their greatest & most favourite Poet. Nevertheless, all honour to him, & may his shadow never grow less! *Monumentum exegit, ære perennius.* . . .[4] I used to think Dyce's Glossary was *comprehensive*,[5] but what is that to this work of Schmidt's? Well; *laus deo*, and doctor Schmidt!—Like yourself, I was grievously disappointed with friend Snider's review of it. It really possesses only *one* merit,—its *brevity*. But then, perhaps, he did not think it necessary to do his *best*, as it was only for the "gossip." In my opinion, and I guess you have found it so too, it is harder to write "gossip" well, than an elaborate review-article. Snider's notice is so wretchedly *poor*: as the ennuyé remarked, when he looked into the crater of Vesuvius, "*there's nothing in it.*". . .

Smith has also sent me W. A. Wright's C. Press Edn. of *Lear*; & Skeat's Pitt Press Edn. of *The Two Noble Kinsmen*. They are both *excellent*, so far as I have read them. Skeat is an admirable antiquarian & English scholar. The great beauty and merit of all his books & editions is their *clearness*. He understands thoroughly what he is writing about; & has the faculty of expressing his thoughts so that everyone else can understand them. Maybe I won't enjoy reading & studying these little precious volumes, when I go out on my next trip—oh no! not *much* I wont!—Mr Collier has also sent me his *Edward III*; and a very characteristic, *kind* letter. The old gentleman celebrated his 87th (not 88th, as Ingleby says,) birthday on the 11th ulto. I hope he may celebrate many more. My feelings & sympathies towards him have very much changed the last 2 or 3 years: and I can, by no means, go the lengths that Dr Ingleby does, & call him "an old sinner," & speak of his "atrocious lies" going down to posterity, &c. It is unkind, & ungentlemanly language, I think; to say nothing of ingratitude for the great *good* that Mr. Collier did the cause, & is still doing it. He made a great blunder, I think, in so vehemently endorsing, as *authentic*, *all* the MS. changes in his "Corr. fo. 1632"; but *humanum est errare*. He has been a most industrious, persevering, ardent, life-long Shakespearian. In his early days he toiled, and dug out many a gem from the mine, that had been covered up for ages; he is now near his grave. I look every arrival almost to hear of "J. Payne Collier, the eminent Shakespearian scholar and editor, is *dead*!" Let us be charitable to his failings & weaknesses; & love him as well as we can, while we have him with us; and not call him a liar & an old Sinner, &c. We shall soon have only his *memory* to cherish. "Do unto others, as you would have others do unto you."—. . .

I had a very pleasant visit at *Cincinnati*; and I left the valuable "rub-bings,"[6] which you so kindly presented to me, to be nicely framed there.— In addition to Mr. *Moses F. Wilson*—a member of the N. Sh. Soc.—I became well acquainted with *Mr. Enoch T. Carson*, a Shakespearian collector, scholar, & *gentleman*. He bought largely at Burton's Sale in N. Y.; among other things he bought (from the administrators, I think,) the "illustrated Shake-speare," that Burton had gathered together with so much care, & industry, & *cost*. He bought both sets—the 4to or folio, & the roy. 8vo, Series: he paid $2.500 for these, then; and has been sparing neither money nor time in adding to the pictures ever since. He put the two together, by mounting the smaller pictures; & adopted the *Boydell Text*, for illustration. He has his treasures in some 45 *Portfolios*—a play in each one, &c.—It would do your heart good to see the *wealth of Portraits*, paintings, landscapes, photos., and every conceivable kind of illustrations, he has collected. He was one of the original subscribers to Halliwell's Folio Shakespeare. I think he said his *number* was 31, or 37. He has a fine collection of Shakespeariana, & edi-tions; but taking out this grand *illustrated* copy, & Halliwell's Folio, it does not begin to compare with yours, or even mine. He values his illustrated set of Portfolios at $10.000, & I should say it was *worth that sum*. He is rich, and has no compunctions of conscience about *despoiling* books of any or all the *pictures* that he wants. There are thousands of *prints*, many of them lovely proofs, & proofs before letters. He was much interested in my ac-count of *your* collection of *Portraits, busts*, &c. I wish you knew him; he is a real nice fellow; no pride or nonsense about him; and a genuine connois-seur. He has also a collection of *rare*, & *singular* books on "Secret Societies," 2.500 volumes or more; & is making a "Catalogue" for publication, that will make 250 pages of 8vo., of these works alone. He is in business in Cincin-nati, & a great *reader* as well as collector.—Another Cincinnati gentleman— a Mr. Probasco—has all the 4 Folios, I learn, good copies; but I did not see them, or him.

I have not yet received my copy of *Ward's* book on "Dramatic Poetry to the death of Queen Anne," but am looking for it daily. I saw the work at Clarke's, at Cincinnati, & I liked the *looks* of it very much. No doubt I shall be interested in it, as you have been. I have carefully read over your annotations on the errors in the Shakespearian Chapters, & they seem to me to be well & justly taken. Strange an *author* should not be better posted in the bare *bibliography* of the Dramatist. I suppose that what Dr Ingleby refers to, in Ward's book, is some endorsement of Collier's Mss. correc- tions, is it not? Why then don't he go to work, & write a proper reply himself?—Clarke asked me $12. for the book, & it is reasonable enough. I fear, as you say, that my copy from Smith will cost much more.—

I was amused & interested reading Dr Ingleby's 2 letters. They are queer things; not one word about your articles; & only some *hyper*criticism on my poor bantlings.[7] Then, if he wanted you to *publish* his "notes," why did he not put them in proper shape for the press? *You* will have all the *trouble* of licking them into shape, and none of the *honour*. Regarding their merit, *inter nos*, I don't see very much in them. The printing *chore* for *chare*, in the extracts or quotations from Sh., was, of course, a *typographical error*; as I knew well enough that the word in Sh. was *chare*, & not *chore*; but then everyone knows, and Dr Ingleby expressly *says*, that they are the *same word*—merely a slight difference of pronunciation—otherwise synony- mous. Why, then, any fuss about it? My object was simply to show that a word was commonly used *now* in New England, though obsolete in old England, or nearly so, that was to be found in Shakespeare. It is true that this word is still partly preserved in old England in *char*woman (pron. chārewoman;) but no English man or woman now speaks of doing *chores*, (the substantive,) tho' Shakespeare does; only he writes it "chare," (the same word, with the same A. S. derivation.) I wish you would please look at page 126 of Skeat's new edn. of "The Two Noble Kinsmen," and you will see whence Ingleby got the most of his "note." There is one portion, however, of Mr. Skeat's note that Ingleby did not copy. Skeat says, "the *Substantive* is used in America, but is pronounced *chore*." What does that imply? Why, that the substantive is *not* used in England, and is still pro- nounced (I mean the verb from which it is derived) *chare*, as spelled. Skeat gives, moreover, a good instance of the Yankee use of *chōre*, from Miss Wetherell's novel of *Queechy*.[8] (See the whole note.) Have we not, then, all I contended for, & which I thought worth a note; viz. *we* in New England[a] have a Substantive in common use, both in speech and in print, that is obsolete in England; yet it is used twice as a substantive by Shakespeare, altho' spelt as the verb is, "chare"; *we* pronounce & write it "chore" here; but Dr Ingleby says, what is evident enough, that it is the **same word.**— What he says about "orts" may be true. I cannot contradict him. Only, I lived in England until I was 18 years old, and never once heard the word, that I recollect. Yet it *may* be used in the South. I was born & raised in the North of England. . . .

A. R. Smith, in his last letter to me, speaking of my copy of "Capell's Notes," says "I should like to give you a handsome premium on it, whenever you wish to part with it." Perhaps you could save yourself *better* by returning to *him* the copy you have at Ashworth's. I tried to dispose of it, for you, at Cincinnati, but could not get them there to appreciate its

value & scarceness. They referred me to Mr. R. Grant White's very depre-
ciatory notice of the Work, in his Shakespeare—a most unjust notice to
Capell I think, especially from Mr. Grant White, who sh*d* have known
better. I don't believe *he* ever *read* the work, though he says "one must have
the book, and what is more, one must *read* it too." How different Mr.
Furness; & the Cambridge Editors! . . . I was afraid there was a trifle too
much laudation of *Furnivall*, A.S.S., in Dr Vance's articles, *to please you*. Still
I must think they are appreciative, & fairly well written articles. He has
been in Europe lately, & knows Furnivall personally I suspect. He married a
niece of Peter Cooper's, of New York; and once in his life, (I know not for
what reasons, but I think through excessive drinking,) attempted to commit *suicide*. He is a splendid scholar & linguist, & has applied for the
Professorship of Latin, Greek, & Hebrew, in Kenyon College, of Ohio.—
. . .

All's Well, IV, v, 38 *seqq*.

> "Clown. Why, Sir, if I cannot serve you, I can serve as great a prince as
> you are.
> *Lafeu.* Who's that? a Frenchman?
> *Clo.* Faith, Sir, a' has an English name; but his fisnomy is more
> hotter in France than there.
> *Laf.* What prince is that?
> *Clo.* The black prince, Sir; alias, the prince of darkness; alias, the
> devil.
>   X   X   X
> *Clo.* I am a woodland fellow, Sir, that always loved a great fire; and
> the master I speak of ever keeps a good fire. But, sure, he is
> the prince of the world; let his nobility remain in's court." &c.
> &c.

I don't believe the above has ever been fully understood.[9] "His fisnomy is
more hotter in France than there" (i.e. in England.)

Warburton says: "this is intolerable nonsense. The stupid editors, because the Devil was talked of, thought no quality would suit him but *hotter*.
We should read, more *honoured*." Steevens says, "this attempt at emendation is unnecessary. The allusion is, in all probability, to the *Morbus Gallicus*."[10]

Sam*l* Bailey conjectures that the Poet meant the prince aforesaid was
better *known* in France than in England, & says we should read, "more
noted."—But all this is entirely superfluous. There is a double allusion,—to
the *devil*, and to the *Black Prince of England*: and to the latter especial notice
should be paid in order to understand the passage. "Faith, Sir, a' has an
English name." Of course he has, viz. Edward Plantagenet, "the *Black
Prince*," so called from his wearing *black* armour; "alias, the *Prince of Darkness*," from the same cause; "alias, the *Devil*," from his courage, & invinci-

bility, and amazing victories, both in France & Spain. He defeated 100.000 of the *French* at the battles of Cressy & Poictiers; so the clown may very well say "his *fisnomy* is more *hotter* in France than there": and to make the term still more appropriate, it should be borne in mind that *cannons* were for the first time used by the English, under this Prince of Wales, to help gain the above victories. Surely his "fisnomy" was *hot* enough for the French; and moreover when the clown says, "the master I speak of ever keeps a *good fire*," the allusion is equally to the fire of the infernal regions presided over by the devil—"the Prince of darkness"—as he is called in Scripture; & the *fire* of artillery kept up by the Black Prince; & the towns &c. that fell a prey to the *flames* of war. Lastly, when the clown says, "But, sure, he is the prince of the world, let his *nobility* remain in his court," the reference is to the same victories; a reference that would always bring down the house in an *English* theatre. At Poictiers, all the princes of the blood, tributory[11] princes, & nobles of France, accompanied the King; as also the King of Bohemia, whose trophy, *three ostrich feathers*, with the motto *Ich dien* (I serve) was taken from him by this Prince of Wales, or Black Prince: and to this day this is the trophy & motto of our Princes of Wales (the king or queen of England's oldest sons). The clown says, such a display of "nobility" is unnecessary for the *Black Prince*; his name being sufficient to appal the enemy; and his "nobility" may "remain in's court." It is a memorable fact that at the battle of Cressy, the *English* lost but three knights, and one esquire; while the flower of the *French* nobility was destroyed.

———

———

The Clown's name is given *"Lavatch"*: & S. Jervis conjectures it should be *Lapatch*. Steevens says "this is an undoubted, and perhaps irremediable corruption of some French word." Unquestionably the French word, or name, was *La vache—the cow*; and it is possible that Shakespeare so named him, because the part may have been played by Richard *Cowly*, or John *Low*ine.[12] See "List of Actors" in 1st fol.—

[1] Mr. Forster's: John Forster, the biographer and friend of Dickens.

[2] the remaining volumes: They appeared in due course, but were mere rpts. of Dyce's second edn.; see 111 n.2.

[3] "abiit, excessit, evasit, erupit": Cicero, *In Catilinam* 2.1.1. C's sense of the ludicrous portrays Furnivall here as the conspirator Catiline and Swinburne the stylist as Cicero. The best account of the quarrel is Oscar Maurer's "Swinburne *vs.* Furnivall: A Case Study in 'Aesthetic' *vs.* 'Scientific' Criticism," *University of Texas Studies in English* 31 (1952): 86–96. Swinburne's objection was to the merely mechanical methods of scholarship in the New Shakspere Society; the acrimonious exchanges extended over some six years and resulted in mass resignations from the Society.

[4] *Monumentum exegit, ære perennius*: Horace, *Odes* III.xxx.1 altered slightly; in a revision by Gregor Sarrazin (1901) Schmidt's *Lexicon* is still in print.

[5] Dyce's Glossary was *comprehensive*: It occupies the whole of Vol. 9 of Dyce's second Sh edn.

[6] the valuable "rubbings": Of Sh's tombstone.

[7] your articles . . . my poor bantlings: In "Shakespearian Gossip" October 1875.

[8] Miss Wetherell's novel of *Queechy*: "Elizabeth Wetherell" was the pseudonym of Susan Borgert Warner. The passage in question (ch. 25 of *Queechy*) uses the term *chores* for household duties. It is not surprising that Skeat should choose *Queechy*: its popularity warranted at least six edns. in the 1870s.

[9] I don't believe . . . understood: The essentials of C's interpretation are generally accepted among modern editors, except that the play on *keeps a good fire* is not noted in recent edns. of the play.

[10] *Morbus Gallicus*: Syphilis, "the French disease."

[11] tributary: *OED* does not show the form after the early seventeenth century; it is characteristic of C to restore an Elizabethan word to usage. Cf. letter 218.

[12] played by Richard *Cowly*, or John *Lowine*: It seems unlikely that either Cowley or Lowin played Lavatch. G. K. Hunter argues in the Arden Edn. (1959) that Robert Armin took the role.

[a] in New England] ↑in New England↓ MS.

106:   22 February 1876

. . . I have finished "All's Well"—i.e. for the present; and my next *study* is the "Merchant of Venice"—a very easy one, as I have gone over the ground so thoroughly more than once before. "All's Well" is full of difficulties & obscurities; and I have accumulated quite a batch of *Notes*, similar to the one I sent you. (That was not designed to be printed; but only for your own reading.) I have no doubt that this Play was first written by Shakespeare about 1593 or '94, and then called "Love's Labour Won," as a counterpart to his "Love's Labour Lost." Afterwards, probably about 1605 or 1606, he rewrote much of it, and renamed it "All's Well that Ends Well." His two styles, or manners, are very palpable to anyone who has become familiar with his early & later work, & it would be easy to pick them apart.[1] There is no 4to you know of this Play; and I believe several of the difficulties arise from the Folio text[2] having been set up from a *corrected* MS. of the Poet's, in which the corrected places were not obliterated, and *both* were printed. (Look at lines 63, 64, 65, & 66 of Scene 3, Act V.[3] The first two were evidently written subsequently to the last two, and as an *improvement* of them; but the last two remained *uncancelled*, & so the printer sets up the whole; & there was no proof-reader to correct it.)[a] It is in this play that the celebrated "rope-scarre" occurs. You know the 1001 corrections that have been made of "scarre"; but the editors & commentators have uniformly, I believe, stuck to Rowe's change of "rope's" into "hopes." Fol. reads,

> "I see that men make rope's in such a scarre,[4]
> That wee'l forsake ourselves."

I presume you have carefully read A. E. Brae's "Prospero's Clothes-line." In that pamphlet the only correct meaning of "scarre" is given and proved. Add, in connection with that, R. G. White's note *ad loc.* in the

Supplementary Notes to his Shakespeare. "Scarre," therefore, is the same word as *scarce*, or *scarse*, and means a barter—a traffic—a deal—an *exchange*. Now I believe that we can accommodate this meaning of *scarre* with the folio text, by a very trifling emendation indeed, viz. "may rope's" for "make rope's." (Notice similarity of sound.) *Rope's* for *rope us* is a common usage; and (remember) the fol. text is "rope's," not "ropes." I need not to tell you how *in* is used for *into passim*, by Shakespeare. "But first I'll turn yon fellow *in* his grave"—(for *into*)—*Rich III.*; and see a whole *column* of instances on page 577. of Vol. I. of *Schmidt*. The meaning, then, would be, 'I see that men may draw us [rope us—"rope's"] into such an exchange, "that we'el *forsake*"—[forget—give away—] "ourselves" and our virtue for something else. This naturally leads Diana up to her main object, the getting possession of Bertram's "monumental ring"; and so she immediately says "Give me that ring." With any of the other explanations, her conversation would seem too **abrupt**. She *must* support her high ground as a virtuous girl; and yet she *must* get that ring for Helena. "All would have been naught else." In this way, while seeming to allow Bertram's superior powers of argument, she draws him on to the thought that something—and something very valuable—must be given in *exchange* for her yielding to his lustful desires: and this *fully accounts for her abrupt demand* (as it has always seemed) "Give me that ring." . . .I know it may be said that Sh. nowhere uses "rope" as a verb, in the sense of 'to draw': but that ought to be no valid objection, when on nearly every page he makes substantives into verbs,—adjectives into substantives, and adverbs into adjectives. He does, however, use the participle "roping": cf. *Hen. V.*, III. 5, 23, "Let us not hang[b] like *roping* icicles upon our houses' thatch": *roping* here, however, is used intransitively meaning 'running down & hanging together.'—But I fear you are yawning over this "rope scarre," and I will *wind it up*. I have written it more for *fun*, than for any confidence I have in it.

Take the play all through, I cannot say I like it as I do most of them. I agree with old Dr Johnson, that Bertram is a *despicable* character; "a man noble without generosity, and young without truth; who marries Helen as a coward, and leaves her as a profligate: when she is dead by his unkindness, sneaks home to a second marriage, is accused by a woman whom he has wronged, defends himself by falsehood, and is dismissed to happiness." What a sturdy old moraler Johnson was; and how *pointed* & yet *true* his words mostly are!—

As a proof that there's "nothing *new* under the sun," I may mention a *sub rosâ* emendation I made, *years ago*, in this play, II. v, 41;—

> "*Parolles.* I know not how I have deserved to run into my lord's displeasure.
> *Lafeu.*   You have made shift to run into't, boots and spurs and all,

> like him that leaped into the *custard*;[5] and out of it you'll run
> again rather than suffer question for your residence."

Here I had made a pencil query, "Should not this be printed *cow's–t..d*?" I
supposed of course *this* was original: but the other day where do you think
I found it? In *Nichol's Literary Illust. 18th Cent.*, Vol. II. p. 346, where
Theobald says that a friend of his had conjectured it to *him*. Of course,
custard is right; tho' it is just *possible* Sh. may have intended it as a dirty pun
in the mouth of Lafeu, who had "smoked" Parolles, & had the utmost
contempt for him. You remember afterwards, when Parolles offers the
Clown a paper to give to Lafeu, & says that he has been "muddied in
Fortune's mood,"[6] Mr. *Lavache* says to him, "a paper from the *close-stool*[c] of
Fortune to give to a nobleman!" &c. Poor Parolles says, "Nay, you need not
to stop your nose, Sir; I spake but by a metaphor." Mr. Clown rejoins,
"Indeed, Sir, if your metaphor *stink*, I will stop my nose; or against any
man's metaphor.—Prithee, get thee further. Prithee, allow the wind."—

I beg my dear fellow, you will excuse all this: and not think that *all my
notes* are as odoriferous as this one. . . .

Respecting Archdeacon Nares' notes in my copy of Capell's Notes and
Various Readings, they could not be printed, I think, to be of any use. They
are mainly in the "Glossary," in the First volume; and consist of additional
words—references—& explanations. One can easily see that Nares *liked*
Capell. He has a very eulogistic note of him indeed, over his signature, on
the flyleaf; and I imagine he used this very copy when compiling his own
"Glossary." He wrote a plain round hand, just a little old fashioned. Most
of the notes in the body of the book are in *pencil*; & were written before the
vols. were bound; & so are badly re-written on opposite pages (you know
what I mean,) by the *press* in binding. Still they are quite legible.—. . .

I cannot . . . coincide with you in thinking Mr. Skeat's book "Sh's
Plutarch" not a credit to him. Why do you think so? I have not read very
much of it; but I rather was pleased with it generally. The titles, notes,
glossarial & other, & the excellent index, seem all *useful*, especially to a
young student of the *Roman Plays*. I think, however, that he should have
waited until he could have used a copy of the 1st edn., & then he could
have given the very spelling of the words, & everything else, just as they
appeared to the eye of Shakespeare, when he read them to compose his
great Plays. I have always had a very high opinion of Skeat's *scholarship*. It
seems to be thorough, sound; & yet none of the Furnivall *varnish* about it. I
studied a book of his editing (Clar. Press. Edn.) "Vision of Piers the Plow-
man"; and another (Clar. Press Edn.) Several of Chaucer's Tales (from the
"Canterbury Tales")[d]; and they are excellent; so *clear*, & plain, & helpful to
beginners in "Old English," with such clever Notes, glossaries, &c., and
yet no boasting, or attempt to show off superior scholarship, tho' the
superior scholarship crops out everywhere. I learned all the little I know of

Chaucer &c. from these books, & Corson's "Legende of Goode Women"; & I like both Skeat & Corson.—

By the way, what do you think of Furnivall's last reply to Swinburne? Isn't it *Furnivall* all over & over! It is no use: "Master Constable" may try to hide his ears; but he will *not*, and no one can *make* him, rest satisfied, until he is written down An Ass. If others will not write it down, he will do it *himself*. Notice the air with which he couples himself with Tennyson, & Browning; "my friend Spedding, with the judge-like mind"; "my friend Ingram," and "my young friend Professor Dowden." It may be that his "cause" is all right; but it would ruin the best "cause" in the world to have Furnivall *advocate* it. They all seem to take his measure; notice Swinburne's gentle sidewipe[7] at his adversary's "Confidence." The fact is, he is no match for Swinburne; the latter carries so much *heavier metal*, that a shot or two is all that is needed to dismantle Furnivall's little yacht. . . .

Mr. E. T. Carson, of Cincinnati, a good authority in prints, pictures, &c. told me that he learned in London, among the connoisseurs, that the engravings, (the small set,) which are inserted in the *Text* of the "Boydell Edition" of Shakespeare, are *finer* than the copies often found bound in a separate volume, (making the 10th volume of the edition); those inserted in their proper places in the Text of the original 9-volume edition were the *earliest* and *best impressions*. Did you know this? . . .

[1] I have no doubt . . . apart: The identification of *LLW* as *AWW* was first proposed in 1764 by Bishop Thomas Percy and appropriated by Richard Farmer. Coleridge added the criterion of two styles, and by C's day the interpretation he makes here was orthodoxy; it has been widely challenged in the twentieth century.

[2] the Folio text . . . set up from a *corrected* MS. of the Poet's: This interpretation anticipates G. K. Hunter's view in the Arden Edn. (pp. xi–xii).

[3] [*AWW*] Lines 63, 64, 65, & 66 of Scene 3, Act V: We have not seen this interpretation made of these lines elsewhere; it is of interest, as the bibliographical approach anticipates modern thinking about numerous other passages in Fl.

[4] make rope's in such a scarre: *AWW* 4.2.38–39; some modern edns. read *may rope's in such a snare*.

[5] leaped into the *custard*: The pun on *cow's turd* goes unnoted in the modern edns. we have checked; it does not appear in Partridge's *Shakespeare's Bawdy*.

[6] "muddied in Fortune's mood": *AWW* 5.2.4.

[7] sidewipe: Another of C's many dialect words from the North Country.

[a] correct it.)] correct it. MS.

[b] not hang] ↑not↓ hang MS.

[c] *close-stool*] *close-| stool* MS.

[d] "Canterbury Tales");] "Canterbury Tales"; MS.

108: 1 March 1876

. . . Mr. "Rygenhoeg's" paper[1] I read with a good deal of pleasure & interest. It is very well written, & scholarly. But he is fighting an imaginary man of straw, as he would have seen if he had read Mr. Snider's criticism.

Neither Mr. Snider, nor I, ever said that *Othello was a Negro*: but simply that he was a *Moor* or *African*[a]—of a **different race**; & no matter how illustrious his ancestry may have been, still he & "all his tribe" were held in the utmost contempt by the Venetian grandees. This is abundantly plain all through the play: Desdemona's crime, or fault, consisted not in her marrying a Negro, but in breaking the prescriptive laws of marriage, & joining herself to a man of a totally distinct & *different blood*.—But I will not bother you with any reply to the "Erl"; and let Mr. Snider do that, if he think it will pay. By the way, why did not Mr. "Erl" send his paper to *you*, the Editor? He must have *known* that you were the Editor. Also, why did not Sabin send it to you, for your *licet*, or *non licet*, before he set it up in type, & said "*We* gladly publish" &c? Are *you* to be merely a "figure-head," to be consulted or not as convenient? Indeed, were I Editor, I would look for an apology, or at least some reason, or (as Parolles says) "*hic jacet.*"—

My dear fellow, there was no occasion for you to have said a word to me about not printing my papers. I knew how you were situated: and I know you would have put them in your department, had you been able. . . . You say, "Would it be asking too much of you to request an abridgement of them?," but I don't think you *mean* it. Would *you*, under the circumstances, have the *heart* to take the time & trouble to write an abridgement, or in fact re-write your papers? At present, I feel I must decline. I would do much to please *you*; but my *time*, you know, is very precious, and I need it all to improve myself & my understanding in Shakespearian matters. The more I study our dear Poet, the more shallow & ignorant I feel I am in comprehending the almost fathomless abysses of his wonderful wisdom. Every spare minute I want to utilize in digging in this mine. So, unless you insist upon it, I think it would not *pay*; especially as even if rewritten in one half, one-third, or one tenth, the space, still the MS. might be returned "Too long." When at College I remember, in writing our Greek or Latin *theses*, we were rigidly confined to "not less than 20, or more than 25 lines." And I have read of literary parvenus, who having fitted up a *library*, sent orders to the bookseller for 8 feet of octavos, and 13 feet, 6¾ inches of duodecimos. Now if Mr. Pumblechook[2] would only let one know the exact number of lines, or lineal inches, "small type," that could be properly adjusted to his measurement, one would have some encouragement to fill the order "as per sample," and some guarantee that the mechanical production would not be thrown on one's hands, at least for the reason that it was "Too long," or too short. Under all the circumstances, I concluded that the most satisfactory job of "abridging" my poor documents could be done by putting them within the affectionate embrace of my *stove*; and I had the pleasure of seeing all the "foul crimes" that "Dowden," "Paget" & "Ingleby" had "done in" their "days of nature" were "*burnt* and purged away." So ends my "share of dividends on the *contribution* plan" to the *Bibliopolist*.

When I was away, I had the pleasure of seeing Barry Sullivan play *Hamlet*, in Columbus, Ohio. He was fairly well supported, and I really enjoyed the treat extremely. I presume that you have also seen the performance: if not, & you have an opportunity, it will pay you well. He is unquestionably a *good Actor*, and has *read* the play very thoroughly. He brings out many points admirably, and in (to me) an original way. I wish I had time to tell you of several that were very interesting. One is, he keeps standing while the Ghost is telling the tale that makes "each hair to stand on end"; but when the Spirit has finished & vanished, nature gives way, & he falls to the ground. He does not fairly rise to his feet again, until he comes to the words "And you my sinews grow not instant old, But bear me stiffly up." This gives a *good effect* to the words. He makes several changes in the "business"; some I liked, others, being novel & startling, I did not like at once. I think altogether he puts more *feeling*, & less *subjectiveness* into the play than Booth does. In the scene with Ophelia, he treats her courteously & affectionately, until he catches a glimpse of the King & Polonius slipping in behind the arras; then, very rudely & coarsely. He does not, however, as Booth does, return at the close & lovingly embrace her, in a sort of heart-broken farewell. With his mother, the scene is grand, well conceived & played. Three times she approaches him as if to beg his pardon & "make up"; but he puts up the back of his hand, & makes her "keep her distance,"—"when you are desirous to be bless'd, I'll blessing beg of you." He gives a most effective & solemn feeling to such passages as "there's a special providence in the fall of a sparrow." I did *so* wish that you had sat by me, & we could have talked together of the many *points* he introduced. Since I saw *Charles Kean* play Hamlet, I have not been as well satisfied with any actor as Sullivan. I think Booth perhaps quite as *perfect*; but his perfection is like that of a fine piece of mechanism—a watch for instance; too steely, polished, & metallic: not enough of *feeling*: too much of Booth, & not enough of Hamlet. Sullivan can *project* himself better into the part, & so into his hearers' *hearts*, than Booth can, or does. He makes several very reprehensible changes[3] in the text, that I would like to tell him of, and get him out of, if possible. E.g. "Siege" for "*sea* of troubles"; "a hawk from a heron—pshaw!"—for "a hawk from a *handsaw*"; "I'll take the Ghost's word for *all the coin in Denmark*," for "a thousand pound." I suppose he thought because they did not reckon money by "pounds" in Denmark, he was justified in making the alteration; forgetting that Sh. makes all countries *England*, & all people (if he please) *Englishmen*. Again, he adopted Collier's Ms. Corrector's reading, "a certain convocation of *palated* worms are e'en at him," for "*politic* worms." By "palated" I suppose the old Corr. meant worms that were very nice & fastidious in their *palate*, and were enjoying a meal after their luxurious *taste* on the old nobleman & courtier. But this word "politic," it seems to me, has never been justly interpreted; at least I have never met any explanation that satisfied me: so I will make you a present of *mine*, & see how you like it. Sh. calls the worms "politic" because they were *bred out of*, & living-upon, a *politician*. What could be more in the Poet's manner, or *Hamlet's* on the occasion, than such a *quibble*? It is true there is also another reference, viz. to the Convocation, or *Diet*, held at *Worms*. See the Var. notes: but had the old Corr., or any of his followers, seen the quibble on "politic," he would never have thought of changing it into the tame "palated." Do you approve of this explanation? It seems to me irrefutable. The "worms" were not *brought to* the body of Polonius, but *bred out* of it—*part & parcel* of it,—hence, like the old chamberlain himself, they were "politic."—I'll bet you a nickel you won't find this "politic" note[4] *apud* Mr. Furness' new variorum *Hamlet*. . . .

Brome I have *not* yet; but it is on my slate, to get as soon as able. What you say of the obscenity & coarseness of some of the "Old Dramatists" is every word true. Did you ever read Wycherley's "Country Wife"? Is it possible *ladies* ever *patiently* listened to such abominable, disgusting, (even tho' witty,) plots & scenes?—and language?—

. . .—By the by, I am disposed to think Mr. *W. A. Wright* has no sympathy[5] with the new "metrical tests" of the "N. S. Soc." Please read the concluding sentences of his "Introduction" to *Lear*.

> "Nor do I wish to add to the awful amazement which must possess the soul of Shakespeare when he knows of the manner in which his works have been tabulated and classified and labelled with a purpose after the most approved method like a modern *tendenz-schriften*. Such criticism applied to Shakespeare is nothing less than a gross anachronism."—&c. &c. &c. . . .

[1] Mr. "Rygenhoeg's" paper: Erl Rygenhoeg, "Othello Not a Negro," "Shakespearian Gossip" December 1875.

[2] Mr. Pumblechook: The philistine corn-chandler in Dickens' *Great Expectations* (see esp. the first pages of ch. 8).

[3] several very reprehensible changes: Siege of troubles (3.1.58); a hawk. . . (2.2.379); the Ghost's word . . . (3.2.286–87); politic worms (4.3.20). Modern edns. print none of Sullivan's emendations; some eds. note the pun on the Diet of Worms and most point out that *handsaw* puns on *hernshaw*, heron.

[4] you won't find this "politic" note: See note 2 to letter 114.

[5] Mr. *W. A. Wright* has no sympathy: Anyone who publicly lacked sympathy with the "scientific" methods of the New Shakspere Society was liable to excoriation in print by Furnivall's virulence (see note 3 to letter 104). In a letter to Ingleby dated 14 September 1880, C comments on Furnivall's published attacks on Wright and Hudson (Folger MS. C.a. 8).

[a] or *African*] ↑or *African*↓ MS.

109:   10 March 1876 Lancaster, Ohio

. . . Have you read W. A. Wright's "King Lear" carefully? It is quite good, tho' I think not as carefully done as either his *Hamlet* or *Macbeth*. He gives R. G. White credit for a reading that H. J. Pye made half a century ago. But then you know Grant White *claimed* it as original. Nothing like *claiming*. It often passes muster whether just or not, through ignorance of readers. Several difficulties Mr. Wright passes over without any attempt to explain; & to several others he gives the old fashioned explns. made by Johnson, Steevens & Malone. He has expurgated largely of the poor old crazy King's explosions. He has taken considerable pains with the *text*, collating the several 4tos of the play. He introduces one new reading, made by Eccles, that I never saw in any edn. except Staunton's, and it is an improvement. Altogether I am disappointed with the book. Perhaps I expected too much, having studied the play so searchingly myself.—. . .

Do you recollect, in the *M.W. of Windsor*, where Mrs. Ford, having recd Sir John's letter, is telling her friend Mrs. Page about it, & says, "but for going," or I think it reads, "if I would but go to hell for an eternal moment or so, I could be knighted." Mrs. Page replies, "What, Sir Alice Ford! Thou liest! These knights will *hack*;[1] and thou would'st not alter the article of thy gentry." (I have no copy of Sh. handy, & cannot quote *verbatim*.)—What does she mean by "these knights will *hack*"? *To hack* was an abbreviation of *to hackney*, a term when applied to women that meant *"prostitute themselves."* Does she mean 'these female knights will be all prostitutes,—will be no better than common wh—es, & therefore thou should'st not alter the article of thy gentry'? I suspect there is also a quibble on "hack," a term that was used when knights were *disgraced*—their spurs were *hacked* off.

I wish I had a Sh. handy, so I could refer you to a passage in *Henry V*; but you will remember where, before the battle of Agincourt, in the night the French Prince and Gentlemen play dice for the poor miserable looking English, and crack all sorts of jokes on them—food for crows, &c. &c. The French Prince apostrophizes *his* horse very beautifully, & another gentleman compares it to his *mistress*, in regard to its *bearing* qualities—*throwing* &c. One says something of riding in loose hose or trowsers, and the other of riding [his mistress] in "strait strossers,"[2] having thrown off the loose ones. What does he mean by "strait strossers"? *Strossers* is the old word for trowsers or pantaloons, but by "strait strossers" I fancy he means the *naked skin*; as we would say he rode her *in buff*. Look up the passage, & see if you don't think this adds a point to an otherwise tame—very tame—joke. . . .

[1] These knights will *hack*: *Wiv*. 2.1.52. See letter 174 for C's later thoughts on the passage.
[2] "strait strossers": *H5* 3.7.54. C's interpretation was first hinted at by Edmond Malone (1790); it can be supported by the fact that the expression *straite strouses* appears in the 1620 translation of Boccaccio's *Decameron* (Seventh Day, Third Novell, p. 29b) with the meaning "naked from the waist down" implied. In *H5* the equation between horse and mistress argues that the intent is a barrack-room obscenity.

111:   26 March 1876

. . . I am much obliged indeed for your sending my crude guess about the meaning of "politic" in *Hamlet* to Mr. Furness, and for his view about it. . . . I wish that Mr. F. had given us *his* explanation of it. When a man says to me "your bank-note is a *Counterfeit*," I always want him to show me a *genuine* one, to compare it with. Mr. F. thinks that "politic" could not be used of old Polonius, because he was not a "politician"; & that Sh. always uses the term "politician" in a bad sense. But may not a man be "politic," without being a "politician" in the bad sense? I think there is a good deal of the "politic" element in Polonius' character. In the "election" that was just over, when Claudius "ran" for the crown against the regular heir of old Hamlet, I cannot but think that Claudius had used Polonius freely as his wire-puller; that he had got him to manage & manipulate the "primaries," and the "caucuses," and the "convention," and to stand and watch the "polls," and "leg for" him at the ballot-box.[1] We gather this from several indications. A man is not a very high-minded[a] "courtier," much more of a snobbish "politician" & office seeker, who will consent to play the spy on his own daughter & break her heart. . . . It has always seemed to me that when Hamlet stabs him for "a rat, dead, for a ducat," the plastic old "politic" *doughface* gets no more than strict poetical justice. We must remember too the state of Hamlet's mind when he used the expression "a certain convocation of *politic* worms are e'en at him," worms bred out of the very substance of the old chamberlain; he was filled "from the crown to the toe top full of direst," bitterest, *irony*: "If your *messenger* find him not there [in heaven], seek him i' the other place *yourself*." Surely, Hamlet's regard for the meddling old busybody—the "thorough courtier"—was not very exalted.—. . .

By the way, have you a copy of Warton's History of English Poetry? It is a sine quâ non in a Shak. library. If you have not, and should ever want to buy one, the edition of *1840*, in 3 vols. 8vo. is the *best*. It is not so handsomely printed as one pub*d* in *1824*, in 4 vols, 8vo, but it contains many more notes, and corrections, by Sir F. Madden, W. J. Thoms, and others. I was lucky enough to get a remarkably fine, uncut, copy, gilt tops, & most beautifully bound by Hayday in yellow polished calf. I bought it at auction for I think $450 a vol.—. . .

You ask me about Dyce's III edn. So far as I have had occasion to compare the 2 edns, I find but little difference. The greatest no. of changes occur in the earlier volumes.[2] He adopted several of Mr. Arrowsmith's conjectures & explanations. You will observe in the 8th vol., just recd., which contains The *Two Noble Kinsmen*, the same singular error remains uncorrected of stating that the Play was printed in the 1664 and 1685 Folios of *Shakespeare*; whereas the fact is, it is not printed in either of them. It was first printed in 4to., in 1634, and not again till the 2d Folio (1679) of Beaumont & Fletcher. It is not in the 1st Folio of B. & F., viz. 1647. Is not it remarkably strange that a man like *Dyce* should make such a blunder? and isn't it almost more strange his posthumous & now deceased editor, Mr. Forster, should have permitted it to remain? Had Dyce been only a Shakespearian editor, or only a Beaumont & Fletcherian editor, one might have perhaps overlooked such an oversight; but being the editor of *both* the works, and the *facile princeps* editor of both (certainly of B. & F.), it is to me unaccountable.—I entirely agree with you about the *printing* of this Dyce III. It is not as well done as either Dyce I or Dyce II. It is a money-making speculation of the Publishers entirely. The few revisions & corrections of text & notes, made by Mr. Dyce, could easily have been put into a thin 8vo volume.—. . .

I enclose for your perusal a note just received from Dr R. A. Vance, which may amuse you. He is now in Washington City, and I was greatly disappointed at not meeting him at his home in Gallipolis, where I was last week. He has been writing to Furnivall, to make *me* an Hon. Sec. of the "N. Sh. Soc." for the Western States. It is ridiculous; and I have written him to-day, and begged him to let the matter drop. What service can *I* be of to the N. S. Soc., living out here? Had my domicile been in Cincinnati, or Chicago, I might possibly have been able to drum up some more subscribers or members. But as it is, I have neither time, ability, influence, or opportunity, to do anything for them. I appreciate his kindness & partiality however. . . .

I also enclose you a letter to read from John C. Yorston (Virtue & Yorston), about compiling a "Shak. Dictionary" in a small 8vo vol., "on the basis of Schmidt's Lexicon"! And asking me to write a Life of Shakespeare & sketch of his Plays and Characters, &c. (The letter will explain itself; it is the 2nd or 3d I have had from them.) Of course I declined the whole thing *in toto,* tho' as politely as I could. I shall keep clear of publishers, unless they pay me for my work. Very probably, after I had written or compiled some such Life or Sketch as he describes, if it contained 3 more words than the prescribed number, these accommodating publishers would find it "not appropriate to the limits"[3] of their Preface, or what not.

I never have read Beaumont and Fletcher's *Custom of the Country;* but I will do so the first leisure I have. I have always known it was fearfully obscene. The "custom of the country" was for the King to have the "virginity" of all the young maidens who got married, was it not? Or was that the "custom" of some other country? I wonder what would be thought of such a "custom" now-a-days.[b] The King would need to be a "lustful Turk" to keep it up. When one reads of such filth & indecency in the works of the *contemporaries* of our dear Shakespeare, one may well admire the purity both of thought and language in the writings of the latter, especially taking into account the great temptation of *fashionable popularity* that such indecency acquired, and that filled[c] the houses of those days. No one should ever prate for a moment about the odd word, or occasional sentence, of that character, that we find in Shakespeare.— . . .

I had almost forgotten to refer to your question about *"miching mallecho"*[4] in *Hamlet.* You are unquestionably right. Dr Farmer is the author of the conjectural emendation, (if it is one,) of "mimicking Malbecco"; but he puts it as though it might have been, or had been, made by someone else. Dr Farmer's language, in my opinion, amounts to this: "May not some private friend of the theatre, or of the Poet's, someone who was acquainted with *Malbecco* and his story, have written on the margin of the MS., or playhouse copy, of the play these words—'This is mimicking Malbecco'; and so the words have subsequently, through accident or ignorance, become incorporated into the text?"—Thus, although Dr Farmer's *supposed* "private friend" is really the "first hand," yet the Doctor is really the *author of the conjecture*, as the whole thing is *his* from first to last. This *Malbecco*, it seems, was known as a *prolocutor* in some old play. . . . By the way—how do you pronounce *mallecho*? I have always pronounced it *mal' le ko*. But Barry Sullivan pronounced it *mal etch' o*. Is *ch* hard, like *k*, in *Spanish*? I think it is in Italian.—Wheeler[5] pronounces Borachio— Bo räk' io; but I have always heard it Bo rät' shio on the stage. See especially Steevens' note on the name, "like a true *drunkard*," in the Var. notes to *Much Ado*.

[1] In the "election" . . . at the ballot-box: C's electoral imagery perhaps results from the fact that this was being written in March of a Presidential election year.

[2] The greatest no. of changes occur in the earlier volumes: Dyce died in 1869 having prepared only the first four vols. for the press; his literary executor, John Forster, saw them through the press and merely rptd. later vols. from the second edn.; the publisher continued rpting. the second edn. after Forster's death (see letter 104).

[3] "not appropriate to the limits": Alluding to the Sabins, who had complained of the inappropriate length of C's contributions to "Shakespearian Gossip."

[4] "miching mallecho": Ham. 3.2.137.

[5] Wheeler: William Adolphus Wheeler, *Noted Names of Fiction*.

[a] high-minded] high-| minded MS.
[b] now-a-days] now-| a-days MS.
[c] that filled] ↑that↓ filled MS.

112:   31 March 1876

My dear Norris:

   Last night I read B. & F.'s "Custom of the Country"—the first time I ever did so. In spite of some of the most obscene and filthy scenes & passages I almost ever read, it contains some good poetry—a good deal of wit—and several fine passages. This Play, like all the contemporary writers of Shakespeare, helps one, more or less, to understand some word or sentence in our own dear Poet. E. g., when Clodio says to Charino (Zenocia's father), "I'll ha' your life, you villain, You *politic* old thief," there is no reference to a *politician*, in the good or bad sense, in the epithet. He merely means *cunning, time-serving*, exactly in the sense in which Hamlet may have used it of Polonius, in the passage we were discussing the other day; and in the sense in which Shakespeare does use it in, "I have trod a measure; I have flattered a lady; I have been *politic* with my friend,[1] smooth with mine enemy."—. . .

I have just received a letter from W. J. Smith, the second-hand bookseller[a] in Brighton, informing me that he had sent me the *Warburton*, 1747, 8 vols. cf. £1..5..0; and the *Johnson & Steevens*, 1773, 10 vols. full calf, fresh, yellow edges, £1..8..0. . . . They are in New York now—came by Steamer; and I had to send on an affidavit of the Invoice, in order to clear the box out of the Custom House. I hope the expenses of transit may be reasonable, thus the books will be cheap enough. . . .

A gentleman in Cincinnati has a copy of Davenant's *Gondibert*, which evidently belonged to Davenant himself, and contains a MS. poem by the Poet, over his signature. The poem itself does not amount to much, & is so poorly written as to be nearly unintelligible. The book also contains many pen-marks[b] & corrections "which no one but the author could make." The book is a rare curiosity,[2] and is for sale; I do not know what is asked for it. I enclose you the account of it, and the Poem, so far as it can be de-cyphered.—Please return it when you are writing. I want to *scrap-book* it. . . .

[1] I have been *politic* with my friend: *AYL* 5.4.45.
[2] The book is a rare curiosity: Nearly all the copies of *Gondibert* in the Folger Shakespeare Library have MS. notes by Davenant; this copy (location unknown to us) is not among them.

[a] bookseller] book-| seller MS.
[b] pen-marks] pen-| marks MS.

113: 11 April 1876

. . . I received a very pleasant note from Mr. Furness, in which he says:— "In *Hamlet* (II. ii, 307)[1] the Cam. Ed. cites a conjecture of Staunton's: *escoted* for 'coted.' Can you find out where this conj. is to be found? It is not *ad loc.* in Staunton's edition, as far as I can see." I hunted for it everywhere, in vain; and as it does not seem to me to have any sense in this place, I wrote Mr. F. that, in the language of the illustrious Mrs. Betsey Prig, I don't believe there ain't no sich a conjecture; and that it is either a misprint or a myth. I took the liberty of calling his attention to an admirable note on this word "coted," in Hales' essay "New Shakespearian Interpretations," in the *Edin. Rev.* for Octo. 1872.—. . .

I have read over—three times—*Edward III*. It is a splendid play,[2] and almost justifies Teetgen's rhapsody & "indignation."[3] Every page contains beautiful—very beautiful—poetry: and often I was inclined to say 'this is either by Shakespeare, or his brother,'—"*aut Shakespearius, aut diabolus.*" And yet there are some things about it hard to reconcile. I cannot tell in what stage of the Poet's life to place it. It is not a bit like any of his early productions; and yet it contains none of those *condensed*, or *inverted* sentences & passages, that are so prominent in his later works. It has not one single *crux*, or hard or knotty passage. All is smooth as oil. No place here for *conjecturers* or *emendators*. And then it is *too tame*, I fancy, for genuine Shakespeare: not any *passion* in it. And yet the question arises, if not Shakespeare, who else *could* write so beautiful a play? Again, it is a hundred times more like Shakespeare's work than *Titus Andronicus*, which is *in* his collected Folio; while there is about one-half of *The Two Noble Kinsmen*, which is *not* in the Collected Folio, that is more surely Shakespeare's than *Edward III*. There seems to be positively *no external* evidence to fix its authorship. It seems too, to me, to be written all by one hand; tho' the play is divided into two parts, there is but one same style; one lovely rich garden; flat & prospectless, but full of sweet flowers; and not a single slough, or ravine, or rough place, or crag, or hill, to wade through, climb over, & vary the scene. You have read it, what is your opinion? Don't you miss the *fearfully condensed passages, the inversions* that nearly drive you wild, the scarifying & dissecting of *motives*, the tempests of *passion*, that everlastingly meet you in Sh.? I do.— . . .

[Scraps[4] from the *Mer. of Venice.*]

I think there cannot be a doubt that Lorenzo's *pun* on "steal," in *M. of V.* V. 1, is genuine, and is intended as a sly reference to the "ducats" that his fair Jessica had "gilded" herself with, and the "stones" that she had "on her," when she made her elopement. "*Steal* from the *wealthy* Jew, and with an *unthrift* love," &c.; the words *wealthy* and *unthrift* confirm it: and Jessica appreciated her husband's joke and allusion, too, by forthwith retorting, in effect: "*Steal*, did I? for whose benefit, may I ask? Who first taught me to *steal*? Who *began* that business? Did not "young Lorenzo," on such a night, *steal* my soul with many vows of love, and ne'er a true one?"—

This play is full of conceits and word-quibbles. Cf. the following:—

> "So is the *will* of a living daughter
> curbed by the *will* of a dead father."—

> "We all expect a *gentle* answer, *Jew*."—

> "If e'er the *Jew* her father come to heaven,
> It will be for his *gentle* daughter's sake."—

> "Then *must* the Jew be merciful.
> On what compulsion *must* I? Tell me that."

[Note the difference in meaning between Portia's and Shylock's use of the word 'must.']

> "What *say you*, then, *to* Faulconbridge, &c?
> You know I *say nothing to* him," &c

> "I would you had won the *fleece* (*fleets*)
> That he hath lost."—

"In law, what plea so *tainted* and corrupt
But, being *season'd* with a gracious voice," &c. . . .

"It is no *mean* [small] happiness, therefore, to
be seated in the *mean* [middle]."

"If I serve not him, I will run as far
as God has any Ground."

This is witty for a Venetian to say, remembering that the *streets* of Venice are all *canals*, and "ground" to "run" or even walk on is fearfully limited.[a]

"As I have set up my *rest* to run away, so I will not *rest* till I have run some ground." . . .[b]

I have a whole batch of verbal notes on this beautiful play, but I refrain to bore you with any more *at present.*—

The character of *Portia* is a charming study æsthetically. She evidently does not desire to get Antonio clear by means of the legal quibble with which Bellario has armed her, and holds *it* as a *dernier ressort.* Her wish is that Antonio may get off by the Jew accepting the money—even three, or thirty, times the just amount—given him by Bassanio—*her* money; so will she have her new husband under *obligation* to her. She hopes all along to effect this end by her eloquence. It would be a real study to see her *watching the effect* of her words on the Jew, as she proceeds with the trial in court; and it is a noble part for a fine actress. At first she appeals to his *mercy*, in that noble, immortal burst of eloquence, which the Jew gives her a chance to introduce, by wilfully misconstruing her meaning of the word 'must.' She does not heap upon him a whole lot of vile epithets—'cur,' 'dog,' 'wolf' &c, like Bassanio and Gratiano. But, like every true woman who has an object to effect, she begins by rather flattering his sagacity, and fully acknowledging the *justice* of his claim in the eye of the law.

"For the intent and purpose of the law
Hath *full relation* to the penalty." . . .

Portia, with her heart full of the woman's tenderest emotions—every fibre of sympathy and antipathy[c] strained to the utmost,—yet never once loses her temper, or abuses or insults the Jew. She keeps the Duke, the Court, the spectators, in a fever of intense suspense and agony; as it seems certain she is going to decide in favour of the plaintiff. Keenly watching the effect of her appeals to his *self-love*—the *justice of his cause*, and his *mercy*, and seeing with pain that her eloquence cannot even *touch* his stony heart, she tries it on his *avarice*: "Shylock, there's *thrice* thy money offered thee"; and when this is fruitless, she joins the two—*mercy* and *avarice*; "*be merciful; take thrice* thy money; bid me tear the bond." Oh, the effect of these words in the mouth of a feeling woman and actress! They should be uttered in a pleading, coaxing, loving, heart-broken, sobbing voice, and with imploring *tears*, so far of course as this could be made consistent with her assumed character of Civil doctor. "*Be* merciful: *take* thrice thy money: *bid* me tear the bond": and thus will *you* have the vantage ground over Antonio; thus will *you* be the master of the situation; thus, instead of being execrated for cruelty, will you be lauded for clemency, and respected by all "on the Rialto"; thus will even your greed for gold be satiated; thus, instead of being spurned, footed as a cur, and spit upon, hereafter you will have Antonio *under obligation to you*,—"**bid** me tear the bond." When, however, she sees all her eloquence wasted upon, and her feelings disregarded by, "the inexecrable cur"; when he says, "there is *no power in the tongue of man* to alter me," then, more by way of tantalizing her hearers than from any hope of the Jew's granting her request, she says, "Have by some surgeon, Shylock, on your charge, To stop his wounds, lest he do bleed to death." She knew he would refuse this; "I cannot find it; 'tis not in the bond"; but she put it to him, that so the rod of vengeance, which she knows *now* must fall on him, may seem the more deserved. Had Shylock not been *mad*, and *blinded* by his hatred and revenge, one would have thought he would have seen the pit he was approaching, when Portia spoke of "wounds," and "*bleeding* to death."—To close the scene, which is becoming too painful to bear, and as a final effort to "change this currish Jew," she bids the Merchant speak for himself. After this, coolly and with the nerves of iron, she proceeds to let fall on Shylock's devoted head the full stream of the law; but not all at once; her pent-up indignation distils itself on him, drop by drop. The remorseless sinner begins to see the mistake he has made, the trap he has so wilfully & securely walked into; but his day of grace is past; it is now useless to wriggle and writhe. He hopes, at first, to get off with "thrice the money"; then, "with barely his principal"; then, to escape out of court; but all his props are knocked from under him; and the *manner* of Portia here is inimitable: "Soft! the Jew shall have all justice; soft! no haste": "tarry, Jew": "tarry a little; there is something else": "Why doth the Jew pause? Take thy forfeiture":

> "For as thou urgest justice, be assured
> Thou shalt have justice, more than thou desirest."

The imperturbability of the "doctor," as she be-nets the Jew in the law's meshes, loop by loop; the vain attempts of the latter to escape which only fasten his cords tighter around him every moment; the irrepressible irony of Gratiano; and the final breakdown of the Jew, "I pray you give me leave to go from hence; *I am not well*"; are all too exquisitely drawn almost for the mind to contemplate.—

During the whole of the Fourth Act, the emotions have been so worked up, and so agonized between hope and suspense, between pain & joy, that the *glorious* Fifth Act becomes an absolute necessity to relieve them, to tone them down again, and to bring them back to their normal, unexcited, condition. This Act is a lovely, beautiful, *musical* and *romantic* **interlude**, by moonlight. The well-managed pleasantry of the interchange of the rings; the unalloyed happiness of the newly-married Bassanio and Portia, Gratiano and Nerissa; the serene joy of Antonio—that pure soul of honour and benevolence—first at his own escape from a terrible death, next at the overflowing happiness of all the dear friends around him, lastly at the return "to road" of his argosies in safety; the "deed of gift of all he dies possessed"[5] to Lorenzo and his "infidel"; the "concord of sweet sounds"; the "floor of heaven inlaid with patines of bright gold"; the "sweet wind that did gently kiss the trees, and they did make no noise"; the night that was but a little "paler than the day"; with the moonlight softly *sleeping* "on the bank"; all together make such a melodious diapason of joy, such a harmonious scene of romantic peace and love, that there is no heart but must feel it touchingly in contrast and relief to the recent agitating and soul-sickening passages in the Court of Justice. Never, never, ought this charming Fifth Act, the sweetest of all closing "Good-nights," to be omitted in the representation[6] of the *Merchant of Venice.*— . . .

[1] (II. ii. 307): I.e., 2.2.317.

[2] It is a splendid play: The performance of *Edward III* in the "Vivat Rex" series on National Public Radio in the Spring of 1980 would support C's judgment of the merit of the play.

[3] Teetgen's rhapsody & "indignation": Alex T. Teetgen, *"King Edward the Third" Absurdly Called and Scandalously Treated as a "Doubtful Play": An Indignation Pamphlet* (1875). In "Shakespearian Gossip" February 1876 N had expressed the opinion that "indignation" was misplaced, as the scholarly consensus was that the play was Sh's, in whole or in part.

[4] Scraps: "steal" (5.1.14–20); *will* (1.2.24–25); *gentle* 4.1.34; 2.4.34); *must* (4.1.182–83); *say* (1.2.66, 68); *fleece* (3.2.241–42); *tainted . . . season'd* (3.2.75–76); *mean* (1.2.7–8); *Ground* (2.2.110–11); *rest* (2.2.103).

[5] all he dies possessed: *he* = Shylock.

[6] omitted in the representation: In the nineteenth century it was regularly omitted by producers whose object was to portray Shylock as a tragic figure.

[a] limited.] limited.* MS.

[b] "As . . . ground." . . .] ⋀*"As . . . ground." . . .⋁ MS. [written perpendicular to main text at top of page].

[c] and antipathy] ⋀and antipathy⋁ MS.

114: 23 April 1876

. . . I have just got home from the binder about 45 volumes of my books, and I am well pleased with them. For a country workman, this binder does a good job, strong, well sewed, good leather, & neat lettering; and he works quite cheap, I think, for the pains that he takes with my books. He bound me the "Annniversary" Edn., that I spoke of, beautifully, in Hf. turkey, gilt edges, extra, for $200, and other books in proportion. Someone will reap the benefit of my care in putting all these old & cloth bound valuable books into substantial, durable binding, that will preserve them one generation longer, at least.

I received a kind & pleasant letter from Mr. Furness, which I enclose you.

The nearest I could come to finding any of Ingleby's conjectures was in a letter to me, in which he speaks of the "noble substance"[1] of this passage as unquestionably meaning *gold*. I hunted one whole night, through everything I had, without any success in finding the conjectures that Mr. F. wants. I was very sorry at my want of luck: and I have since written Dr Ingleby to let me know, as soon as possible, the whereabouts of those assigned to *him* in the Cam. Edn. Mr. Furness mentions my notion of the meaning of "politic," & says it "grows in favour" with him. Glad of it. He speaks of squeezing it into his new Hamlet;[2] that surely would be "honour enough for one day." . . .

I was exceedingly amused & pleased with Mr. Swinburne's burlesque[3] on the "Newest Sh. Soc."; it is admirable; both clever & witty; *bitter* yet with enough of *truth* about it to make the caricature *biting* & *intelligible*. I have taken the liberty of copying it out into my *"Sh: Collectanea"*; and I herewith return it to you. If Furnivall's hide is not more callous than the hippopotamus', I should think this parody would touch his sensibilities. Note the date too, *April 1st*, "All fools' day"! How well Swinburne writes too! So apt his quotations: and he ends up with Armin's **"Nest of Ninnies,"** as a nickname for the managers.[a] Did you notice how he introduces Furnivall's *very expressions* & *similes*? I think it is capital all through.— . . . Mr. Furnivall sent me from London a paper containing his Prospectus of the *N. S. Soc.*, with list of Members to this date; also two slips containing his two articles anent Mr. Swinburne that appeared in the *Academy*. He can go to work now and write another on this keen burlesque of Mr. Swinburne's, and print that; but he will have to be up very early in the morning, & practice other accomplishments than conceit & egotism, if he expect to become a decent antagonist of Swinburne.[4]—I should have been delighted to sit with you at the Theatre[5] & see *Julius Cæsar* well "enacted." I never saw it on the stage. . . .

Do you ever conjecture who *could* have been the forger of so many of these papers?[6] I fancy old *Peter Cunningham*[7] must have done some of them. The brains that devised, and the hand that executed them, are now like those of poor Yorick, and we shall never likely know to whom they belonged. Though I confess, guided by Brae & Ingleby & Singer, I *used* to have hard thoughts about Collier, of late years I have learnt better, and I now entirely acquit him of anything but being *duped*. I recently read over again Dr Ingleby's "Complete View," with my present *lights*, and it certainly does bring forward some *queer* matters. . . .

---

[1] "noble substance": *Ham.* 1.4.37.

[2] squeezing it into his new Hamlet: C's interpretation of *politic* (4.3.20) had been made by Delius, who is credited by Furness ad loc.

[3] Mr. Swinburne's burlesque: N rptd. it (from the Birmingham *Examiner*) in the April 1876 *Bibliopolist*.

[4] to become a decent antagonist of Swinburne: Furnivall resorted instead to gross vilification

and silly name-calling, and Swinburne followed his lead; see O. Maurer (104 n.3) and also S. Schoenbaum, *Shakespeare's Lives* (1970), 429–30 et passim, for accounts of Swinburne's quarrel with the New Shakspere Society and of F's capacities as a controversialist.

[5] with you at the Theatre: The Jarrett-Palmer revival of *Julius Caesar*, a spectacular, played Philadelphia (Academy of Music) April 3–8; the Philadelphia *Evening Bulletin* damned E. L. Davenport's Brutus, Lawrence Barrett's Cassius, and Milnes Levick's Caesar, but had high praise for Frank C. Bangs's Antony.

[6] these papers: Papers pubd. by members of the original Shakespeare Society.

[7] old *Peter Cunningham*: Cunningham was accused in the 1860s of having forged entries in the Revels Accounts which he pubd. for the Shakespeare Society in 1842. In 1928, S. A. Tannenbaum argued that John Payne Collier was the culprit in the Revels forgery (see *Shakspere Forgeries in the Revels Accounts*, Columbia Univ. Press). Elsewhere C expresses the belief that Cunningham may have taken in an innocent Collier with the forged Perkins Folio. Dewey Ganzel has recently argued at length for Collier's innocence of the Perkins forgery (see Introduction above, note 45).

[a] the managers] ↑the↓ managers MS.

116: 3 May 1876

. . . I have just received a very kind and pleasant letter from Mr. Furness. No wonder I could not find any of those conjectures on which he wanted light. They all, except Bullock's, appeared in the Cam. Ed. *for the first time.* The Edd. carelessly (I think) omitted to append 'MS.' to the citation of them. Mr. Furness says his notes on this passage, "the dram of eale" &c., cover 42 MS. pages! and he calls it his "dram shop." He speaks quite flatteringly of Prof. Corson's explanation[1] given, you recollect, in his "Jottings." He says it is "singularly ingenious, and not a little convincing." You remember the contemptuous way that Ingleby treated it, and I quoted it for Mr. F., and in this letter he answers the learned Dr very well.—I dare not tell you what he says about the conj. of "our dear old friend Mr. Hudson,"[2] as he *deposes* me not to mention it, but to "burn the letter." He concludes, however, by saying, "Hudson has done grand work in æsthetic criticism— the best ever done on these shores—but his strength does not lie in verbal correction."

Isn't it about time we were getting something from the New Sh. Society? I wonder whether Furnivall will make any reply to Swinburne's burlesque. I see, by the *Academy*, that he is making his Shakespearian studies (?) pay pecuniarily, by giving *Lectures to ladies*, at a good round price for tickets. His position as *Director* of the "N. S. Soc.," and that conceited smirk of his, stand him in good stead. I see that even the *Nation*, in an article on the spelling of the Poet's name, calls 'Shakspere' *Furnivall's* theory. I believe it was so spelt, in Bell's edition, in the last century; and Sir F. Madden wrote a pamphlet[3] on that mode of spelling—advocating it: and it is adopted in all of Charles Knight's editions; so Furnivall has no claim to *originating* it. The Nation says that *Shakespear* was the first "fashion," then Shakspeare, then *Shakespeare*, until recently, when *Shakspere* is "all the go." . . .

[1] Prof. Corson's explanation: In *Jottings on the Text of Hamlet (First Folio versus 'Cambridge' Edition)* (1874), 13–14. It appears at length in the *Ham.* Variorum—*noble* is a noun and *substance* a verb: i.e., the dram of evil alters the essence of what is noble. Corson had pubd. an earlier form of this interpretation in *Notes & Queries* October 1862, pp. 269–70.

[2] the conj. of "our dear old friend Mr. Hudson": "The dram of leav'n / Doth all the noble substance of 'em sour."

[3] Sir F. Madden wrote a pamphlet: Sir Frederic Madden, *Observations on an Autograph of Shakspere and the Orthography of his Name . . .* (1838). C is incorrect about Bell's edn.; there *Shakespeare* is used regularly.

117: 6 May 1876

My dear Norris:

I am confined to my room all this day with that terrible *neuralgia*, in my right foot; I can neither walk, read, write, nor eat; and I am as cross as a bear with a sore head. I am afraid my letter will be as cantankerous as I feel; but it *always* does me good to write to *you*—next *best* thing to receiving a letter from you: so you must pardon my selfishness this time; I hope next time I write I may feel in a better humour.

I enclose you to read a letter from our old friend Mr. Hudson. Poor old dear gentleman! he is in trouble about his son. Who knows whether you & I may not, some day, have a similar anxiety! I have been keeping a sharp look out for some suitable situation for him, but, as yet, unsuccessfully. Business of every description is now most ungodly dull, "flat, stale & unprofitable"; and Zanesville is only a small place, and already many of our Mercantile firms, bankers, & manufacturers are discharging clerks & bookkeepers, & cutting down salaries, &c. to curtail expenses in every possible way. Last time (some 2 or 3 years ago) that Mr. H. mentioned his son to me, the young man was just entering Harvard College; and his dear father's & mother's anxious care in his behalf induced them to leave Boston, & take up their domicile at Cambridge, to be near their son, & only child. And this is the reward of their care—a big crop of wild oats! Too bad, too bad! . . .

I have been working away at *Richard II.* and shall soon *finish* it. How I do wish that you & I, together, could have an evening, or 2 or 3 evenings, over a play, after I have gone through it in my exhaustive way. Each to read a passage, "ride and tie" fashion,[1] and give each other the benefit of either's *collectanea* on the *loci impediti*, textually & æsthetically. Wouldn't it be *nice*? I know that for *one* I should enjoy it hugely. As Byron says,[2]

> "He that *joy* would win,
> Must share it: *happiness* was born a *twin*." . . .

I am very glad that you wrote Prof. Ward, and gave him a statement of the *errata, addenda,* & *corrigenda,* in his Shakespearian Chapters. If you had not done it, I should have been tempted to do so. It is a pity that so *excellent* a work should have any disfigurements at all; & his are mostly the faults of *carelessness in revising* for the press. I notice he does not think Sh. had much (if any) hand in "The Two Noble Kinsmen"; and his arguments are quite good. The most that Sh. did, I think, was probably to *help* the young Fletcher towards the beginning of the Play, & perhaps in some other places. Some passages are, to my ear, almost *certainly* from Our Poet's pen. But I fancy that Sh. did not *finish* the Play, or even see it when finished, before it was pubd or acted, otherwise he would never have permitted his name to such bald[a] imitations of his own grand work,[3] as there are from *Hamlet* (Ophelia), *M. N. Dream*, & *Love's Labour's Lost*. . . .

[1] "ride and tie" fashion: I.e., explicating it by turns; ride and tie was an arrangement in which two men could ride the same horse by turns, one walking to where his partner had tied it, mounting, overtaking the partner, and tying it for him some distance down the road.

[2] as Byron says: See *Don Juan* 2.172.7–8.

[3] imitations of his own grand work: Some of these may be by Sh himself; e.g., the Jailer's Ophelia-like daughter is introduced in a scene usually assigned to Sh, though her plot is developed in Fletcher scenes.

[a] bald] bold [?] [doubtful reading].

118:   7 May 1876

. . . You ask me to give you "a reference to the book where Hazlitt is criticised as an editor by Lowell"; and you add, "I want to read it, as I thought Hazlitt had a reputation for accuracy of his texts, tho' not distinguished for any great amount of labour in his notes and introductions." The book you want (and I have no doubt you have it in your library) is Lowell's "My Study Windows," pp. 290–374, in a Review of J. Russell Smith's "Library of Old Authors." It is one of the most severe critiques on Hazlitt's *ignorance* as an annotator, and unpardonable *carelessness* as a reproducer of Old Texts, that I ever read on anyone. I used to think Macaulay, in his reviews—e.g. of Croker's Boswell, &c. was about as bitter as anything in the English language; but Lowell on Hazlitt throws Macaulay into the shade. . . . On page 337[a], he says—"Of all Mr. Smith's editors, Mr. W. Carew Hazlitt is the worst. He is at times positively incredible, worse even than Mr. Halliwell, and that is saying a good deal. Worthless as Lovelace's poems were, they should have been edited correctly, if edited at all. Even dulness and dirtiness have a right to fair play, and to be dull and dirty in their own way. Mr. Hazlitt has allowed all the misprints of the original (or by far the greater part of them) to stand, but he has ventured on many *emendations of the text*, and in every important instance has blundered, and that, too, even where the habitual practice of his author in the use of words might have led him right. . . ." He then proceeds to give page after page of instances where Hazlitt has changed the text through *sheer ignorance* of the old language, or some idiom, or custom. It is almost sickening; and one begins to pity the scarified editor under Mr. Lowell's merciless, but deserved, rod. . . .

I need not to tell you that I shall be *most glad* to read your article on the opening of Sh's grave, or anything else from your pen. When you spoke of it once before,[1] I thought you were in jest. I ought to tell you, however, in advance, that no arguments whatever—not even from your convincing pen, can have any weight with me, in regard to the propriety or *becomingness* of such a—proceeding. Not that I care a straw about the doggrel verses you allude to; but from other reasons, that affect *my* mind, tho' they might not another's; and are much[b] too long & important to be given at the tail end of this letter. I am, My dear fellow, Ever Your friend,

Jos: Crosby.

[1] When you spoke of it once before: See letter 78.

[a] On page 337] on page 337 MS.
[b] are much] ↑are↓ much MS.

120:   20 May 1876

. . . I can well appreciate the pleasure & interest you have from your visits to the "Exposition." I attended the *first* of these Expositions, that was ever held—the "World's Fair," in Hyde Park, London, in 1851: and it was a truly magnificent affair. The treasures of the world seemed to be gathered into that beautiful & fairy-like Building, which covered 21 acres of ground itself. Still I presume the present one is vastly superior: I know it is in magnitude. If spared until Sept. or Octo, I hope to spend perhaps a week in Phil:; but I fancy more than half the time I shall put in talking to you, and looking at your nice Library, & Pictures, &c., as well as those of Mr. Furness. I have little taste for machinery, agricultural, or horticultural productions, &c. My principal delight will come from the "Fine Art" & "Memorial" Halls. . . .

I enclose you also a letter from friend Hudson, that you may see what he is about, and what he wants me to do. He is at his old tricks,—itching to *change something* in the text. In that notorious passage in *Macbeth*, "Who cannot want the thought how monstrous," &c., he wants to change "cannot" to *can now*, which will not do at all, for more reasons than I will bore you with now, tho' I hope to convince him to let it stand as Sh. wrote it.[1] . . .

I have finished *Richard II*, and am now engaged on *Cymbeline*, a much more difficult play. It is nearly 3 years since I went through it last, i.e. in my close, critical, course. Like you, I have a good deal of pleasure from reading the old dramas of Jonson, Fletcher, Massinger, Dekker, &c., but hitherto they have not done me that *good* they ought, because I have only *rushed* through them, for the sake of the plot, or to pick out the meanings of a few words, here & there, or phrases, &c. that are **Shakespearian**; what I mean is, that my *reading* of *them* has been entirely *subservient* to my *study* of Shakespeare; and that, you know, is hardly fair to the "Old Dramatists." But I intend, if I live, to *study* them, more or less carefully, by and by.—. . .

—I saw the account of our friend Swinburne's antics[2] in a London paper, some days ago; and was real sorry for it. He had become quite a favourite of mine by his able Shak: articles, & his inimitable burlesque on the N. S. Soc.

I must not forget to tell you how nearly I came to having a *2d Folio Shakespeare.* On coming home from a trip I found a Catalogue of Bangs & Merwin's Auction Sale—next day but one. It contained a 2d Folio Shakespeare, a *good sound* copy, all perfect & genuine except verses & title-page, which were in facsimile, and splendidly bound in full crushed levant morocco, by Bedford, gilt. Also a copy of Ben Jonson, the *First Folio*, 1616, Portrait, 2 vols, calf.—

I immediately ordered these to be bid in for me, if the former did not go over $100, & the latter 20$: but I *ought* to have *telegraphed*: as it was, I got a letter from Bangs & Merwin that my bid was not received in time: and that the 2d folio Shakespeare sold for $75.., and the 1st fol. Jonson for $16..— Now was not that provoking? I was hugely mortified. . . . These figures don't indicate so great an *advance* in prices as one would suppose. Perhaps "hard times" have some effect.—. . .

You say that you expected more from me regarding your idea of opening Shakespeare's grave. The reason I did not then, & do not now, wish to broach the subject at all is, that my mind is so made up about it, I feel you could not convince *me*; and I know you so well I am quite sure I could make no impression on *you*; . . . As Mr. Furness says, "Is it *pretium operis?*"[3] *Cui bono?* What good could come of it? It probably is only a matter of *feeling* with me: but did I know, for certain, the skull of the great Bard could be taken out entire, I should *abhor* to handle it; to apply calipers, & compasses, & measuring tapes;[4] it would be the very *bathos* and grave of all *sentiment*; and I should regard it as quite as much of a *desecration*, as if he were my own father or grandfather. **Requiescat in pace** is my advice; & so farewell to this *grave* subject.

Yours again,
J. Crosby.

[1] I hope to convince him to let it stand as Sh. wrote it: *Mac.* 3.6.8. C's hope was a vain one.
[2] our friend Swinburne's antics: In the spring of 1876, Swinburne was involved in a sensational libel suit. At this time his personal behavior was as notorious as his literary controversies were; not long afterward he suffered a major breakdown. See Donald Thomas, *Swinburne: The Poet in his World* (1979), chs. 7, 9, et passim.

³ "Is it *pretium operis?*": Cf. Horace, *Satires* I.ii.37: "Audire est operæ pretium."
⁴ to apply calipers, & compasses, & measuring tapes: C here associates exhumation with the pseudo-science of phrenology, perhaps remembering E. T. Craig's pamphlet, *Shakspere's Portraits Considered Phrenologically* (1864).

121:   28 May 1876

My dear Norris:

Your two welcome favours of the 25th & 26th are duly to hand, the latter to-day. I am very much obliged to you for the information regarding the fol. *Ben Jonson.* I made indeed a lucky escape. I think it is shameful to advertise a book as perfect, when it is not; and houses that make a practice of so doing will soon, I should suppose, lose their business. Men living at a distance cannot be expected to be on hand personally to examine every book they want; they *must* depend on the Catalogues; and when these are deceptive, what is to become of confidence & honour? . . .

When Mr. Furness asked me to hunt up the interpretations by different actors of passages in *Hamlet,* although I could not bear to refuse to attempt it, I had *two* fears,—one, that being absent so much from home & my library, I should not be able to do it for him *in time,* or as soon as he needed it; the other, & more important, was that I did not possess several of the books that I would want to collate for such interpretations. I thought that, probably, *you* would not be hampered by either of these things; and that made me respectfully suggest that he should ask you instead of me. I did *not* ask him "why he did not apply to you?" I fancy he was jesting when he told you that. I should not have thought, or dared, to address him, regarding you, so bluffly as that. However, my dear fellow, I am real glad that you agreed to do as he desired. . . .

Mr. Fleay, in his new "Manual," makes some singular errors for so accurate a scholar as he is. He is perpetually saying "the two first," "the three last" (p. 28, l. 18), &c., instead of "the first two," "the last three," &c. This is a mistake in phraseology that Prof. Ward is never guilty of. How can there be *two* both *first?* Or *three* all *last?*—On p. 7, in the "Biography," he calls "Thomas Quiney the future husband of *Susanna* Shakespeare," instead of *Judith* Shakespeare. On p. 52., l. 9, he prints "Act V. sc. 1" for Act V. Sc. 3, and line 24 (of same page) "Act VI," instead of Act V.—(whoever heard of a play of *Six* acts in Shakespeare?)—On page 34, he has a singular criticism. Speaking of *Romeo and Juliet,* he says "In Act 1, Sc. 3, line 23, Q1, the Nurse's speech probably alludes to the earthquake in 1580, as Juliet's weaning day; and as Juliet is nearly fourteen years old, this brings us to 1593. The Nurse's miscalculation that fourteen less one makes eleven, adds to the humour of the passage." Now do you see any "miscalculation" by the nurse, or any "humour" therefrom, here? Nurse says it is now "a leven yeares since she was weaned," but she nowhere says that the child was only *one year* old at the earthquake, or when she was weaned. On the contrary, as she says Juliet is now within "a fortnight and odd days" of being fourteen, she must have been 3 *years* old at this famous earthquake. It is true that children born under Italian skies are more precocious than those of a colder clime, yet a girl baby that at *one year old* could "stand alone"—"nay, by the rood, could have run and waddled all about"; one that when she fell and broke her brow, and was asked by the merry husband, "Yea, dost thou fall upon thy face? Thou wilt fall backward when thou hast more wit: wilt thou not, Jule?," the "little wretch" with "a bump upon its brow as big as a young cockerel's stone," should leave crying and say 'Ay'; must have been more than precocious; she must have been a *miraculously* smart year-old. The fact is plain enough, she was *three years old*, or nearly, when she was weaned; and as the earthquake was in 1580, the date of this conversation is 1591, & not 1593.

122: 11 June 1876

. . . —I have . . . recd. the *Jour. Spec. Phil.* containing Snider's essay on "The Two Gln. of Verona"; *The Western,* with essays on "The Com. of Errors" & "Taming of the Shrew": and I have written him a long letter anent the same. His style is *improving*—vastly, I think. Read that one on "The Two Gentlemen," and I will guarantee you will be pleased with it. It is only *short*; and the analysis is very well done. In his letter he says he has none of the great editions of the Poet—Dyce, Knight, Collier, Staunton, Clarke, Halliwell, White, &c.; but uses Mr. Hudson's "School Shakespeare" for such plays as that edn. contains; & Delius' edition, (English text with German notes,) for the rest. He has *one* great advantage over us,—he reads *German* like a native;[1] and has read all the German critics, Gervinus, Ulrici, Kreyssig, &c. in the original. He is a teacher in the High School at St. Louis; I saw his name "Denton J. Snider" among the list, in one of their publications. He is one of the *Editors* of "The Western," and wants me to write him some Shakespearian articles for it, guaranteeing that they shall be printed—"the longer the better." I have not *promised* to do so; but if I find the steam getting up too high, I shall have a safety-valve to let it off by now. I have been concocting a paper on Shakespeare's use of the conjunction "though," which I think may be made interesting. If I finish it, I will show you the MS. first. A friend of mine—the editor of a Cincinnati paper—has also written me asking me to prepare for his paper short notices of the new Shakespeariana &c. &c., and he "will *pay me well* for them"; but I fear it will be too much trouble; & my time is so fearfully limited.—. . .

I am still working away at *Cymbeline.* Did you ever observe what a capital edition of *Lear* & *Cymbeline* that is by *Eccles?*[2]—I have read it every word, and it is an excellent Variorum to the date, & contains a great amount of valuable *original* matter—conjectures & explanation by the Editor. I had no idea, hitherto, it was so *clever* an edition. I possess a very fine copy of it, that formerly belonged to "James Orchard Halliwell," having his autograph at the bottom of the Title-pages. . . .

Like you, I cannot help *resenting* so many changes of authorship in the Plays of our dear Shakespeare. Let Fleay, & such *counters* & *testers*, go on much farther, & we shall have *nothing left*[3] as from the pen of the Great Poet himself. I am adverse to, (& cannot help it,) believing that *Middleton* manipulated *Macbeth*, and that Ben Jonson "Johnsonized" *Julius Cæsar*, abbreviating it one-third, correcting its rhetoric, and interpolating classical allusions into the Play. This may be *old fogyism* in me; but my natural disposition is *conservative*; I am slow in making friends, but once made, I stick to them like wax. . . .

[1] he reads *German* like a native: Snider was a member of The St. Louis Movement, a group of Hegelian philosophers centered in St. Louis in the late nineteenth century; the Hegelian method is dominant in his Sh criticism. There is a substantial Snider collection in the Missouri Historical Society Library, St. Louis.

[2] a capital edition of *Lear* & *Cymbeline* . . . by *Eccles*: Ambrose Eccles's *Lr.* and *Cym.* (1793) are now regarded as important edns. He edited *MV* in 1805; his projected *AYL* was never completed.

[3] Let Fleay . . . go on much farther, & we shall have *nothing left*: Fleay, a mathematics teacher without literary gifts, applied statistical methods mechanically to Shn prosody and diction and then rejected from the canon whatever did not fit his mathematical models. The excesses of his "scientific" method in the early months of the New Shakspere Society's existence drew strong opposition—even from Furnivall, an advocate of the method—that led to Fleay's withdrawal from the Society in July 1874. Here C is referring to Fleay's paper, "On Two Plays of Shakspere's, the Versions of Which as We Have Them are the Results of Alterations by Other Hands," *New Shakspere Society's Transactions* (1874 Part II), 339–66.

123:   27 June 1876

My dear Norris:

Your pleasant and welcome letter of the 14th inst. is not yet acknowledged. My apology is that I have been corresponding with the Cincinnati folks regarding the "engagement" you mention, of writing for a paper on Shak. matters. I soon learned, what I had presumed was the case, that it *would not suit you at all*, any more than it would me: They have not any idea of what we mean by a "department"; they would print about what suited *themselves*, how & when they pleased, not allowing *any liberty* of saying what one thought proper at all. They would give the names of the books to be "reviewed," & these chiefly, or entirely, such as might be imported by the Cincinnati booksellers for sale. An indiscriminate system of **puffery**, is about what they require, & **nothing else**. So, learning this, I did not mention your name at all; but simply declined the whole affair. A large daily political newspaper, always on the *qui vive* for news, and items of a "sharp,

short, and decisive" character, is no place for *our* pens on *Shakespeariana*.
"What will *pay*"—"what would add *subscribers*"—is all their aim. So there
ends *that*. I don't know whether "The Western" would add "a department"[1] on *Shakespeare*, or not: if they would, it would be a nice medium, as
the Magazine goes into the hands of a goodly number of cultivated people.
Would you like to ask Snider about it? Or would you desire me to do so?—
. . .

Half the year gone, nearly, and nothing yet from the *New Sh. Soc*. "Great
cry, and little wool"[2] ought to be Furnivall's motto. I fancy it is not so much
the lack of funds, as the lack of workers, and harmony among the
editors.—At all events, this is not the way to increase the number of Subscribers.—. . .

[1] whether "The Western" would add "a department": Nothing came of it; finally in spring
1878, N found a publisher for his column in *Robinson's Epitome of Literature* (cf. note 2 to letter
99).
[2] "Great cry, and little wool": Proverbial in the Renaissance in the expression "Here's a great
cry and but little wool (as the fellow said when he sheared his hogs)" (Bergen Evans, *Dictionary of Quotations*).

124:   14 July 1876

. . . Many thanks for sending me Snider's letter to read, which I herewith
return. I should never have thought "The Western" was so small an affair
as he represents, judging from his letters to me, and the *urgent* way in
which he asked me to write for it. Literary periodicals, in this country,
seem to be wretchedly supported. Were I an editor of "The Western,"
however, I believe I could add to its subscription list, by organizing a
clever, trustworthy, "Shakespearian Department," contributed to by the
best Shak. scholars in the U.S. & England. There is no such a Dept. in *any*
literary publication that I know of. The consequence is, we have nothing
but *scraps*—here, there, & everywhere—*Athenæum, Academy, N. & Q., Bibliopolist, Nation*, &c. &c., and one can never hope to see *all* that is issued on
the subject. Such a periodical ought to be self-supporting, and not cost the
Editor anything more than his labour, at least. I presume if I had to pay
$100 a year towards keeping a Magazine alive, I should feel, as Snider says,
that there was no great necessity for its existence. . . .

I have just completed *Cymbeline*, and completed it most thoroughly. In
addition to my regular study of the Play; I wrote out *78 pages* of close MS.,
containing probably over 100 of *original notes*; and sent off the package to
Mr. Hudson. It is the result of long & hard study; the notes are, almost
entirely, explanations of the old text—so as to save it from many wholesale
alterations. In all those notes, (and they are all textual or critical—*not*

æsthetical,) I did not make but one *new conjecture* of my own. I will tell you what it is; and I wish you would give me your opinion of it. In *Cymb.* I, vi, 32, seq.:—

> "What, are men mad? Hath nature given them eyes
> To see this vaulted arch, and the rich crop
> Of sea and land, which can distinguish 'twixt
> The fiery orbs above, and the twinn'd stones
> Upon the number'd beach?"—&c. &c.

In the second line of this passage, what is the sense of "the rich *crop* of sea and land"? With the meaning of *produce*, as usually explained, it is exceedingly harsh; "the rich *crop of sea*" seems to me neither Shakespearian nor English. Warburton read *cope*, which is a mere tautology of "vaulted arch"; and S. Bailey conjectured *prop*, which is still worse. Now I believe that the correct word here is *scope*, and I made this emendation on the margin of my *Variorum* several years ago. *Scope* is a word frequently used by Shakespeare; and in its sense of *prospect, expanse*, seems to me to have been the word used by the Poet,—the very right word in the right place. There is some sense then in the line, "the rich *scope* of sea and land." *Scope* is literally a *view, prospect*, from σκοπεω, to *view* or *see*. The conjecture appeared to me so palpable, that I presumed it must have been proposed by someone before; but it is not in the Camb. Edn. collation, nor can I find it suggested in any other edition or commentary, that I possess. It is a mistake that might be very easily made by the old printer.—Will you, sometime soon, please look over your authorities, & tell me if you find it anywhere? I made a brief note of it, and sent it to *N. & Q.*, about 2 weeks ago; but I presume that will be the last of it.[1] Does it not strike you as being a wonderfully easy, & unforced improvement over "crop"? . . .

In III. iv. 80,[a] *seq.* of this play:—where Pisanio, having shown to Imogen her husband's letter to him, telling him to take her away to Milford-Haven, & kill her for adultery, the poor fellow's heart softens, and he refuses to do it: Imogen, laying open her breast to his sword, finds her husband's beloved letters concealed there. She says:—

> "Come, here's my heart.
> Something's afore't. Soft, Soft! we'll no defence;
> Obedient as the scabbard."—

Would you believe it, that Mr. Hudson here makes *soft* an adjective, referring to the *letters*, viz. the package of letters, which was "afore" her heart, and was only *soft*, & consequently could be easily stabbed through!?—This is my note: "Here, again, I am compelled to differ with you in your explanation of "soft," which you think to be the adjective, referring to the "scriptures of the loyal Leonatus." Surely it is only the adverb "Soft!," that Sh. so commonly uses for hold! Stop! Wait a little!—A few lines farther on we have,

> " 'Faith, I'll lie down and sleep.
> But, Soft! no bedfellow!"—

[this, according to his way of interpreting, would mean a *soft* bedfellow!!][b] and, again,

> "Soft, ho! what trunk is here." &c.—[2]

The poor princess, in her readiness to die at the command of her husband, offers her breast to Pisanio's sword; but finding "something afore't," she says, 'hold on a moment! we'll no defence; there shall nothing intervene; my heart shall receive your sword "obedient as the scabbard" ';[c] then, proceeding to remove the obstacle, finds it to be her husband's letters. This, I think, is more natural than that she should call the package "soft," and so seem to apologize for it; besides, there was to be "*No defence,*"—not even a "soft" one.[d]—

If I were not afraid to *bore the life out of you*, I would love to point out dozens of mistakes of explanation, as palpable as this, by Hudson, C. Knight, R. Grant White, and the rest. And, *most generally*, it is the *misunderstanding* of the plain reading of the dear old Folio, that causes so many so-called "emendations,"—alterations, which are not merely un-necessary, but which pervert the sense. . . .

Did you ever notice the very curious way in which Sh. sometimes uses the verb *to appear*, viz. as a verb *active*. In Cymb. IV. ii, we have,

> "This youth, howe'er distress'd, *appears* he hath had[3]
> Good ancestors,"

i.e. *shows* to the world, Cf. also III. iv,

> "and but disguise
> That which, *to appear* itself,[4] must not yet be,"

where it is also a verb active = to shew, present. For want of understand-ing this usage by the Poet of *to appear,* Knight even thinks the first passage I have quoted is a *misprint*, and transposes it thus:—"This youth, how e'er distress'd *he appears*, hath had Good ancestors." And several other modern edd. read—"This youth, howe'er distress'd, appears, he hath had," which is simply unintelligible. For a convincing instance of this peculiarity, Cf. *Coriolanus* II. 3,

"Why in this woolvish toge should I stand here,
To beg of Hob and Dick, that do appear,[5]
Their needless vouches?"

So this passage is always punctuated; but it is *wrongly* so; as the correct sense is thereby destroyed. What force is there in the clause *"that do appear"*? Strike out the comma after "appear," and read:—

"To beg of Hob and Dick, that do *appear*
Their needless vouches,"

i.e. who *present* or *offer* their needless attestations of my worth. And another, in the same play, IV. ii, is similar:

"You had more beard when I last saw you, but Your favour is well *appeared*[6] by your tongue."

Here "appeared" certainly (I think) means "shewn," "represented"; and not (as commonly explained) "rendered apparent." His voice, which was *unchanged*, "represented," and **stood surety for**, his favour or face, which, by age and loss of beard, was hard to recognize.—. . .

You remember that difficult passage in V. 1,

"You some permit
To second ills with ills, each *elder* worse,"[7] &c.

(This *line* is only a small part of the trouble; the passage is full of hard places). Hudson, of course, runs after Collier's MS. Corr., and reads *later*, for "elder." My note to him is this:—

"Here Rowe read each *worse than other*; Capell, each *younger* worse; Singer (1856), each *alder-worse*; and Collier, from his MS. Corr., "each *later* worse," which text I observe that you have adopted, and defended in the notes of the "School Shakespeare,"—But did you never notice the Poet's peculiar use of this word "elder"? Cf. *Rich. II.* II, iii, 41,—

"*Percy.*—My gracious lord, I tender you my service,
Such as it is, being tender, raw, and young;
Which *elder* days shall ripen and confirm
To more approved service and desert."

What does "elder days" mean here but *later* days? It cannot mean anything else. By a sort of *hypallage*, the poet applies the epithet to the "days" that belongs to the person; the man himself is *elder* each day he lives, but the days are really *later*. So, again; *Rich. II.* V. iii, 20, &c, where Bolingbroke is speaking of his son, the prince:

> "As dissolute as desperate; yet through both
> I see some sparks of better hope, which *elder* years
> May happily bring forth."

What is the sense here of "elder" but *later*? With these instances before us of the Poet's way of using *elder*, so plain that "he who runs may read," why need we change it in the passage in Cymbeline? I am convinced he wrote, as in the *Folio*, "To second ills with ills, each *elder* worse."—. . . ."[e]

(Copy of one of a batch of notes on *King Lear*, sent by me to Rev. Mr. Hudson, in the Fall of 1875.)—[f]

King Lear, IV. ii, 62, seq.:—

> "Thou changèd and self-cover'd thing, for shame,
> Be-monster not thy feature." &c. &c.

What "changed" means here, we all know from Snout's remark to Bottom, in *M. N. Dream*,—"O Bottom! thou art *chang'd*!" But I have never been at all satisfied with any of the explanations given by you editors of "self-covered." Clarke's is perhaps the best:—"Thou perverted creature, thou hast covered thyself with the hideousness only proper to a fiend.". . . I have long thought that we should perhaps read, "Thou chang'd and self-*discover'd* thing," or, "Thou chang'd and self-*uncover'd* thing," &c. From what her husband says to her, it seems plain that Goneril had thrown off all disguise, and openly exposed her conduct. . . . But there is another emendation of the term which has struck me. "Covered" means *shielded, protected*, and I have thought the reading perhaps should be:—

> "Thou changèd and *sex-cover'd* thing, for shame,"

i.e. 'Thou devil in woman's garb, nothing but thy *sex protects* thee, or I would tear thee to pieces.'[g] This harmonizes exactly with what Albany immediately says:—

> "—"Wer't my fitness
> To let these hands obey my blood," i. e.

were it becoming me, as a *man*, to lay hands upon a *woman*, and follow the natural promptings of my passion,

"They are apt enough to dislocate and tear
Thy flesh and bones:—how e'er thou art a fiend
A *woman's shape* doth shield thee."

The last line is an exact paraphrase of "sex-covered." Either of the above conjectures I think is better than Theobald's reading "self-converted," which is mere tautology. Dr. Cartwright proposed "self-discover'd" in 1866.—

J. C.

[1] I presume that will be the last of it: *Notes and Queries* pubd. it (2 September 1876, p. 185) and likewise F. J. Furnivall's astute defense of Fl (16 September, p. 226).

[2] But Soft! no bedfellow! . . . Soft, ho! what trunk is here: *Cym.* 4.2.295, 353.

[3] *appears* he hath had: *Cym.* 4.2.47.

[4] *to appear* itself: *Cym.* 3.4.145.

[5] that do appear: *Cor.* 2.3.116–17 (slightly misquoted).

[6] is well *appeared*: *Cor.* 4.3.9.

[7] each *elder* worse.": *Cym.* 5.1.14.

[a] In III.iv.80,] in III.iv.80, MS.

[b] [this, . . .bedfellow!!]] ↑[this. . . .bedfellow!!]↓ MS.

[c] scabbard"';] scabbard"; MS.

[d] one.] one." MS.

[e] worse."—. . ."] worse."—MS.

[f] (Copy of one . . .1875.)—] [follows *J.C.* at end of this letter] MS.

[g] to pieces.'] to pieces. MS.

125:   18 July 1876

My dear Norris:

I wrote you quite a lengthy epistle last week; after which I started out on a trip; but I was only gone two days, & I assure you I was glad enough to get back home again. The weather out here, as I see it is with you, is, & has been for 3 weeks, simply intolerable. I can neither work, read, write, eat, drink, nor sleep comfortably. On Sunday at Church, when everybody was sweltering with heat, & mopping their faces, & fanning for dear life, our parson, I believe for pure devilment or tantalization, gave out the hymn "From Greenland's icy mountains"; and a broad smile came over the countenances of his parish. It is positively dangerous to go out on the Street without a couple of green cabbage leaves & a wet sponge in one's hat. I sometimes think this weather would have suited poor despondent Hamlet to a "T," as his "too too solid flesh" would have melted, thawed, and resolved itself into a dew, without the least trouble or ejaculations on his part. If I only had plenty of money now, and nothing to do, I would put a pocket edn. of Shakespeare into my satchel, and betake me to the Northern Lakes, or Alaska, or some other Northern point, where the thermometer had not quite so centennial an aspiration, and recline at my ease, careless of the world and *business, sub tegmine* of some cool *fagi.*[1] But alas! that "if."—I am so ungodly *poor*, that in heat or cold, no difference, I *must* keep grinding away, as some poor devil in Dickens[2] says, "like a dem'd old horse in a demnition mill." . . .

I have also been skimming over a charming book of Hawthorne's—"Our Old Home," I hope you possess this delightful volume. One chapter in it you should by all means read—"Recollections of a Gifted Lady"; the lady being *Miss Delia Bacon*. It is exquisite to see how delicately Hawthorne tells the story of this poor monomaniac on the subject of Shakespeare. She was no vulgar sentimentalist, but a bewildered enthusiast, who got beyond her depth. His description of his visit to her in London—her residence at Stratford—& especially the night when she got into *the* Church, containing the remains & grave of the immortal Bard—her wandering round with a dark lantern, watched by the clerk—her examining & trying the crevices of the flagstone that covers the grave; &c.; and then her getting angry with Hawthorne, and her despair & death; are all very, *very* beautiful. This, I believe, is the only case that has ever occurred of anyone attempting to infringe the Poet's wish about "moving his bones"; and surely never could his *anathema* have been more fully realized than it was in the case of this poor misguided woman.—Reading Hawthorne's *charming* sentences makes one regret that so sweet, true-hearted, a writer should have died so soon! . . .

[1] *sub tegmine . . . fagi*: Virgil, *Eclogues* I.1.
[2] some poor devil in Dickens: M. Mantalini in *Nicholas Nickleby*, Ch. 64.

126:   22 July 1876

. . . I wrote out my note on the emendation "Sex-cover'd," for "self-cover'd," in *Lear*, changed it somewhat, and sent it to the *Nation* to-day. I hardly expect they will publish it.[1] If they do not, I will give it to "N. & Q.," *perhaps*. I have just received two long eight-page, closely written, letters from Rev. Mr. Hudson, with reference to the 78 pp. of my notes on *Cymbeline*. He says many very kind & flattering things of the annotations. He says "some of your explanations I have *substituted* for my own, some I have *added* to my own."—"In regard to"—[about a dozen instances given]— "you have completely backed me down from where I stood, and I thank you for it. The same on"—[some 6 or 8 more].—But in spite of all I can do or say, he *will* hold on to "*falsing* it" (for "*telling* it")[2] in the *Tempest*. I have only, as yet, read his letters over once, & that hastily, but I observe that he has laid out for me a vast amount of *hard work*: enough to keep me close at it—comparing, thinking, arguing, quoting, & writing—for 2 weeks, this hot weather. His maw is perfectly insatiable. . . .

[1] I hardly expect they will publish it: They did not. C placed it more than three years later, in the 22 November 1879 issue of *The Literary World*.
    [2] *"telling* it"; *Tmp.* 1.2.100.

127:   15 August 1876

. . . I really wish you *would* send Rev. Mr. Hudson one of your copies of Ingleby's "Hermeneutics." You have *four*, and would not miss it. I only have one, & cannot afford more, or I would send the old gentleman one. I'll tell you, I really believe he is *very poor*; and that is the reason his Sh. library is so scantily supplied. Of late, I have got to like him better—much better—that I used to do: perhaps from having so much Shakesp: correspondence with him. I am to-day[a] in receipt of a long letter from him, anent one of some 60 pp. of MS. I sent him on a lot of *varias lectiones* scattered through Sh.—He has some peculiarities that perhaps are not very *loveable*: still I like him very much more than I do Grant White, with all the latter's *style*, and smartness, & real ability. I have copied for Mr. Hudson several long notes from the "Hermeneutics"; from Mr. Arrowsmith's book;[1] and various other sources; that I thought he **ought** to be familiar with, before he published his new edn.—. . .

I have received little or nothing new, in the way of books, since I wrote you last, except a pamphlet on the (everlasting) "Study of Hamlet," by "E. B. H."—It is mainly a reprint of those portions of the text in which *Hamlet* appears, with a running comment on almost every line, for the *guide* of *readers* and *actors*. It contains a rather good Prefatory Essay on the *madness* of the Prince; is quite well printed; and rather interesting altogether. It seems to me that books & tracts on *Hamlet* are like Banquo's issue; the line will "stretch out to the crack of doom." "Another yet! A seventh! I'll see no more: And yet the eighth appears. Horrible sight!"—

I have received the two *Bibliopolists*—April and June: and read the "Gossip" with interest & pleasure. It is all so good and well done, that, like Oliver Twist, one cannot help wishing for "more." . . .—Your charge against Furnivall,[2] of having last year lighted all his candles at once, & now having none left to light us through the gloom of 1876, will, I fear, again bring all the "fat into the fire." Look out for something very severe, in the shape of a *small note*, soon, from the irritable Director. Hold on to your nose and your hair; your scalp is in eminent danger I tell you. The Sioux[3] are nowhere to Furnivall, when once his *blood is up*.—. . .

When I was in Columbus, last week, I called on our Governor—the next President of the U. S.—His Excellency Rutherford P. Hayes: and had a very pleasant hour's *tête-à tête*. He is a very agreeable, educated, courteous, gentleman. I told him of a little incident,[4] connected with his family, or at least his family *name*, that he was not familiar with heretofore, viz. that it is immortalized in *Shakespeare*. You recollect in the 5th Act of *Cymbeline*, Posthumus describes[5] to a "Lord" the fight between the old Britons & the Romans; how the latter had gained a complete victory, & were routing & slaughtering the British pêle-mêle; & had got them in a *lane*—"ditch'd & wall'd with turf," and were driving them headlong to death &c.—Belarius [Morgan], and his two adopted sons Arviragus & Guiderius [Polydore & Cadwal]—had joined the Britons, & in this lane completely turned the tide of victory, by crying "Stand, Stand!," in favour of the Britons. Never was a greater change in the state of affairs than they effected, or a more complete rout and destruction of their enemies, all caused by their noble heroism. Now this is a *historical fact*. Sh. got it from his old stand-by, "Holinshed's Chronicle"; the names of these three brave fellows were *Hays*, or *Hayes*, father and two sons, and their deeds deserved, & have received, eternal renown in Shakespeare's immortal page. The Governor laughed heartily, as I recited the incident. I expect, you know, to go to the Court of St. James for this, when he is President: and I want *you* to devise something withal to do *yourself* good,—"be what thou wilt"—"I am fortune's steward, and blessed are they that have been my friends"; "get on thy boots"—"the laws are at my commandment; we'll ride all night, and woe to my lord" Furnivall!—. . .

[1] Mr. Arrowsmith's book: William R. Arrowsmith, *Shakespeare's Editors and Commentators* (1865).
[2] Your charge against Furnivall: In "Shakespearian Gossip" June/August 1876, pp. 63–64. The New Shakspere Society had pubd. nothing for the year 1876 up to that time. N was continuing his vendetta against F; this time he mocked his spelling and criticized his high-handedness with other members of the N.S.S.
[3] The Sioux: Possibly alluding to the Battle of the Little Big Horn, fought a few weeks before, 25 June 1876; Sitting Bull was a Sioux.
[4] I told him of a little incident: In a letter to Hayes, dated 13 August 1876 and now in the Rutherford B. Hayes Library, Fremont, Ohio, C writes that he "forgot to mention" the incident when he called on Hayes a few days before and he recounts it at length in the letter. H replied (in a letter that does not survive) asking how a passage in Holinshed found its way into *Cym.*; C wrote back 18 August (letter in Hayes Library) discussing Sh's use of Holinshed and pointing out that Milton also had a special interest in this story of Scottish heroism. Actually, the name itself (*Haie* in Holinshed) is not mentioned in the play.
[5] Posthumus describes: *Cym.* 5.3.1–58.

[a] to-day] to-l day MS.

129:   18 August 1876

. . . I have received a very pleasant & courteous letter from *Gov. Hayes*. I told you that I had mentioned to him the incident of his family *name* being immortalized in Sh.; and he wanted me to give him the quotations. &c. respecting it.—I did so, in as polite a note as I could write. He says— "Accept my best thanks for your very interesting letter. There has been a tradition in the family of the origin of the name of *Hayes* similar to the one you give, but I do not remember to have seen the account you give from

Holinshed. I certainly never heard that Shakespeare's description of the fight between the Britons and Romans was founded on the incident told by Holinshed. How do you connect them?"[1] x x x So you see I am likely to get into a correspondence with "His Excellency."

Some time ago I bought a copy of R. Grant White's Sh.—the thin paper edn.—for $10.—*very cheap*. I had it bound in Hf. russia—brown pol. edges—contents lettered; and to-day I sold it to a friend, who pestered me for it, for $3500.—You told me that you had come across one of the *thick paper edns* for $18.—in cloth. If you ever see *another* as cheap, please buy it for me. I have one, but it is written all over with my *annotations*; & I want one for *show*.

Yours Ever, Very truly,

J. Crosby.—

[1] How do you connect them?: Sh certainly encountered the incident (in the account of a battle between the Scots and the Danes in King Kenneth's time) while reading for *Mac.* four years before writing *Cym.* The account appears on pp. 154–55 of vol. II of Holinshed's *History of Scotland*; the materials for *Mac.* extend from ibid. 149–80.

130: 22 August 1876

. . . Dr Ingleby's letter[a] will explain why he has been so long silent: also the prospect of his new book. But it is most valuable because it contains a *critique*—equally as good as any in the "Shak. Hermeneutics," on the following fearfully hard knot in *Cymbeline*, IV. 2, 109,

> "*Bel.*" (referring to Cloten)—"Being scarce made up,
> I mean to man, he had not apprehension
> Of roaring terrors; for defect of judgment
> Is oft the cause of fear."

(*Textus receptus* here is, "for th' *effect* of" &c. Theobald's emendation of "defect" in the Folio.) See what a noble exegesis[1] he gives of the passage, confirming fully the old text. When you once get it clearly into your head it will stick there, & never trouble you again. You should, by all means, copy this admirable note and explanation into your scrap-book. Like Columbus and his egg, again, how easy it all seems, *when one once knows how* to do the feat. I feel positively ashamed of my ignorance hitherto on this passage; and of the many fruitless hours I have spent thinking over it, and trying to solve the difficulty, or cure it by cutting the Gordian knot with an "emendation"!—The other "crux," that he speaks of, refers also to a passage in *Cymbeline*, V. 4, 17—"take no *stricter* render of me than my all"—where I gave *him* an *original*, & I believe a correct explanation of the term "stricter,"[2] as Sh. here uses it. And I assure you, I am very proud of what he says of it;

as the whole passage is, you remember, the subject of one of his longest & best notes in the "Hermeneutics," pp. 99–102. I will write out for you a synopsis of my argument and explanation on a separate paper, maybe in my next, anyway as soon as I have time. What makes me most pleased & proud to receive the learned Doctor's approval of my note is, that Hudson & I have had (not a furious, but) a warm discussion over it. My Rev𝑑 friend would not hear to it at all, when it seemed so very evident to me as giving, to use Dr Ingleby's expression, "greater *consistency* to the passage." You may be sure I sent a copy of the Doctor's remarks to Mr. Hudson with no little glee and satisfaction.

You will note, also, what Dr Ingleby says of Fleay's "Manual," and also what Mr. Fleay himself says of it. It is curious too to watch the growing enmity between Ingleby & Furnivall. They are not exactly yet enemies, but there is a coolness approaching. Mark it, these two will be at swords' points ere another year is gone.—[3] I know you will be pleased with Mr. Fleay's kind, modest, note.[4] I am sorry he is not rich, & cannot publish his productions. Spite of Dr Ingleby's strictures, his Manual *is* a useful, nay, *valuable* little book, don't you think so too? . . .

[1] a noble exegesis: See note 1 to letter 178.
[2] a correct explanation of the term "stricter": *Stricter* = more narrow, less inclusive. C's full explication is in a letter dated 25 July 1876, now in the Folger Shakespeare Library (MS. C.a. 7).
[3] ere another year is gone: Ingleby's patience was greater than C predicted; despite provocation from Furnivall, Ingleby did not resign as Vice President until 1881—he left the organization altogether in 1883. His resignation is discussed in letters C wrote him 17 June 1881 and 30 September 1883 (Folger MSS. C.a. 9, C.a. 10).
[4] Mr. Fleay's kind, modest, note: This was a reply to C's letter to Fleay 24 July 1876, (#1 in Folger MS. Y.c. 1372) which praised Fleay's *Manual* warmly, but demurred at his attempt to disintegrate *Mac.* and *JC*. Further correspondence followed in summer 1877 about prospects (unfavorable) for getting a proposed F edn. of Sh pubd. in America

[a] Dr Ingleby's letter] Dr Ingleby's MS.

131: 30 August 1876

. . . Thanks for copying for me the extract from the *Dispatch* à la the exhumation of Sh.'s remains. It is a well-written article, and no doubt you were glad to see it, and so am I. Nevertheless—nevertheless—well, if *you* could not convince me of the propriety and *comme il faut* of so doing, I do not believe anyone else can. But it is useless, I imagine, to talk about it; as *the experiment will never be made.* Dowdall, in "Traditionary Anecdotes of Shakespeare, Collected in Warwickshire, 1693," reprinted by Rodd, 1838, says, "that the Poet's *wife* and *daughters* "did earnestly desire" to have his grave opened, that they might be "laid in the same grave with him"; but "Not one, for fear of the curse abovesaid ['Good friend,' etc.] did dare to touch his gravestone." If the "superstitious" curators of the "grave-stone" aforesaid were so insensible to the wishes & appeals of the Poet's own wife

& daughters, I hardly believe their successors would now yield merely to gratify common curiosity. Poor Delia Bacon's fate is sufficient warning. What must have been her feelings during the long night she spent by this grave-stone in that lonesome Church, watched as she was, though unknown to her, on her unhallowed errand. . . .

—Have you not in your mind's eye, among your list of critics, textual & otherwise, some that you especially *like* & *trust*? I have; and among the textual list I may name Walker, Ingleby, Brae, Arrowsmith, Badham,[1] and P. A. Daniel. Some 3 or 4 weeks ago, I mustered courage to write to Mr. Daniel, especially on some of his proposed emendations in his little book. I have not yet heard from him in reply; it is hardly time yet. . . . Of all the English Shakespearian Scholars and Commentators, &c., I have never had the courage[2] to address Mr. Halliwell, or try to make his acquaintance, or correspond with him. And yet he is, as you say, *facile princeps* of them all now living. On the contrary he has been rather *your favourite* from your first attack of the Shakespearian mania; and you have probably the finest collection of *his productions* in America. I have several, & I prize them highly: but I have sometimes thought that the very scarce vol. of his "Comedies" that I have would be more appropriately on *your* shelves than *mine*. So I will say that if you would like to have it, and would give me a *fair* price—I don't mean any *extravagant* price—for it, you shall have it. I presume it is the only copy in the U. S. . . . It seems Mr. H. commenced to issue an edn. of Sh. in America, which was "pirated"[3] by Mr. Vickers, London. On this account it was discontinued. This was in 1850–51. He says:

> "I have only the opportunity of issuing *twenty* copies in the present form . . . I somewhat regret my inability to make a more extensive publication, not merely from the fact of the pirated edition by **Messrs. John Tallis & Co.** being replete with oversights not to be ascribed to myself, but also because many of my notes have been almost literally adopted by an American editor—the **Rev. Mr. Hudson**—without the slightest acknowledgment. The system of editors of Shakespeare adopting the notes of their predecessors, and availing themselves of the results of their reading, as if it were their own, cannot be too strongly deprecated. Whatever is worth taking does, at least, also deserve a line of recognition. . . ."

It is singular that Halliwell's *Comedies*[a] is not mentioned, or any way referred to that I ever saw, either in Lowndes or Allibone, Mullins or Thimm, Mr. Furness or the Camb. Edd.—

I have also a couple of other *very rare books*, that (I think) you have not yet found, & which you may have, at a reasonable price. They would do you more *good*, in the completing of your noble Library, than they will ever do me, out here: and I could use their price to advantage in buying some others that I want, & cannot spare the money for. I mean "Hunter's Disquisition on the Tempest," 1839; and "Croft's Annotations," 1810. You know how exceedingly scarce these books are, and how almost *impossible* it is *now* to get anyway near a copy of either. The former is a *privately-printed*[b] book, pp. 151, beautifully printed. Only 100 copies were printed. It is nicely bound in *Hf. mor.*, clean & all right. Croft's book is still *more rare*. It is a little bit of a thing, pp. iv, 24, called "Annotations on Plays of Shakespear, (Johnson and Steevens Edition)." John Croft, the author, was "S.S.A.S."[4]— It was pub*d* at York, 1810, and is bound in Hf. calf. Dedicated to the Soc. of Antiquaries. In the binding, a half a line has been carelessly cut off in some 4 or 5 pages at the bottom, by being cut too close. It is a very *interesting* book, owing to the originality and *wit* (sometimes too coarse) of these "Annotations." It is miserably printed, full of typographical errors, and the author makes many mistakes, but also many *excellent* suggestions and interpretations of abstruse passages. I expect few of the Commentators have ever seen Croft's annotations, as they are not noticed in the Variorum notes; but they are of material help to the student, and one cannot often help smiling at their force & originality. Halliwell, in his "Shakespeariana" **1841**, says "This little book, being *very rare* and difficult to meet with, I may mention that a copy is in the Society of Antiquaries." Mr. Hunter says: "This pamphlet consists of twenty-four closely-printed pages, and I venture to say contains more valuable remark than is to be found in the volumes of Zachary Jackson and Andrew Becket, or even those of John Lord Chedworth, or Henry James Pye." . . .

By the way, I have this evening received a nice, pleasant, long letter from Mr. Hudson. He has got a copy of the "Hermeneutics"; found one at Little, Brown & Co's, Boston. So I ask pardon for my impudence (which I was *ashamed* of at the time) in asking you to "donate" the old gentleman one of your copies; and I withdraw the motion. He is very much pleased with the book, as of course he must be, and is "adopting" several of Ingleby's readings & explanations in his new edn.—I told you that I had had quite a fight with him in regard to my view of the Poet's meaning of "stricter" in the aforesaid passage.[5] He now says: "I rather think you have pretty much knocked me over in regard to "stricter." Your quotation from Hooker is exceedingly apt and telling. For almost thirty years Hooker has been one of my household gods; but I had never noticed his use of that word. So I intend to make a note[6] on the passage, giving your explanation"—There, I think that is very complimentary; and he has also accepted my suggestions on several other passages, in this letter, receding from his own, which is no easy matter for anyone to do, as I know myself; so that[c] I have nothing but the kindest words for the veteran editor. If I have been able to do him, or his new edition, any *good*, as I trust I have, he is surely *welcome*, heartily welcome, to it. It has done *me* quite as much, & more, good studying up in the work. I am now getting ready my notes on *Much Ado*; but this *travelling* so interrupts me, that it is almost impossible to make fast headway, or do anything satisfactorily.—. . . The only new book I have got since I wrote you last is the Sh. Mem. Lib. Catalogue of English "Shakespeariana." As you directed,[7] I had sent a P. O. order for a copy: but this copy[d] must have been mailed before my letter reached there. Mr. Mullins sent me a very polite note, asking my acceptance of it "for my library": and the book itself is inscribed: "To Joseph Crosby, Esq., Zanesville, from the Birmingham Free Library Committee, (by J. D. Mullins.)"—So I suppose I shall get another copy soon. What a grand production it is! How intensely interesting those bibliographical notes are! And how complete and comprehensive & valuable! Mr. Mullins must have devoted both long time, & no ordinary talents to its preparation. Shakespeare scholars everywhere will thank him for these useful catalogues. Taken altogether, it is far in advance, both in interest, completeness, & accuracy, of any Shakn. Catalogues heretofore published. Dr Ingleby calls it "one of the wonders of the world." That is a trifle hyperbolical, but is partly true. And what a Noble Library that is becoming! Mr. Timmins, and the other Officers, deserve much credit, both for the *design*, and for carrying it out so well. . . .

[1] Badham: Charles Badham, "The Text of Shakespeare" in *Cambridge Essays* (1856).

[2] I have never had the courage: C did not muster the courage until Furnivall's vilification of H-P caused him to express his sympathy and disgust in a letter dated 10 May 1881 (Folger Shakespeare Library); H-P's reply dismissing F as "a vulgar lunatic merely" is in the McMillan Shakespeare Collection, University of Michigan Library.

[3] an edn. of Sh. . . . which was "pirated": For an account of this sordid affair see our article, *Papers of the Bibliographical Society of America* 71 (1977): 279–94.

[4] S.S.A.S.: "S.A.S." (Societatis Antiquariorum Socius) is the normal title, which Croft used to sign another of his books. He was an eccentric given to word games; our best guess at the superfluous *S.* is *Shakespearianus*.

[5] the aforesaid passage: See letter 130.

[6] I intend to make a note: He did make a note, and a generous one, ad loc.

[7] As you directed: N was "Voluntary Assistant for America" of the Shakespeare Memorial Library. C had a similar honorary relationship to the Library, but N played the larger role in its affairs.

[a] Halliwell's *Comedies*] it MS.

[b] privately-printed] privately-| printed MS.

[c] so that] ↑so↓ that MS.

[d] this copy] this ↑copy↓ MS.

133:   6 September 1876

. . . You are[a] very much mistaken about "Halliwell's Comedies" being the *same in matter* as Halliwell & Tyrrell's edition. I also have that edn., 4 vols. roy. 8vo: and their vol. of "Comedies" is no more like my vol. of "Halliwell's Comedies," than chalk is like cheese. . . .—This Halliwell & Tyrrell edn. seems to me a regular fraud; "a thing of shreds and patches." It has Mr. Halliwell's name in large type on the titlepage, and yet all of Halliwell's work is a surreptitious copy of his Notes & Introductions to *four* Comedies, & the Introduction to the fifth. That is all. But where is the *American* edn. that Mr. H. speaks of? It would seem that he began to edit one in this country; that these English publishers pirated it, that he stopped them somehow on the fifth play, while they got H. Tyrrell to make a show of writing Notes & Introductions for it, & called it "Halliwell & Tyrrell's." It appears, however, from Mr. Halliwell's preface, that the *American* edition went on to the end of the Comedies, and into the first of the Histories; and then he stopped all connection with it. I presume the American edition was also continued to the end by another editor or two. I wonder if the one that I have, pubd. by Martin & Johnson, New York, n.d., but about 1852 or 3, in 3 volumes quarto, is not the one. If so, it was continued & finished by **Grant White**, as I learned from a letter of his to me, in which he said that he collated it; but was not responsible for the text, nor would he allow his name on the title page. . . .

ᵃ You are] you are MS.

135: 11 September 1876

. . . Somebody, I think probably A. R. Smith, sent *me*. . . . a copy of the pamphlet that you speak of "Furnivallos Furioso." I cannot think *who* can be the author of it;[1] but surely never Mr. Collier. It is not in his style a bit. Besides, just now he is too busy finishing his Qto Shakespeare to be writing *squibs* like this. I fancy it more probable that Swinburne had a finger in it; tho' it is not good enough scarcely for him. There is not a great deal in it. The rhymes all jingle well enough; but the *wit* appears to me a little *thin*; and the hits are neither particularly clever nor witty. It is a passable little ephemeral squib, that will flicker a few minutes, and die a natural death, & be *forever* buried, unless some future exhumationist resurrect it in a couple of centuries hence or so. It *may*, however, be preserved among "Shakespeariana" in the "Sh. Mem. Lib.," and in Collections like yours & mine; and be a source of deep puzzlement to the Sh. scholars of 1976 to discover its "true inwardness" & meaning. The "notices of the Press" are the best part of the burlesque; they are real good, and take off the different critics & journals to a 'T.'—On the cover is a capital little woodcut of a "fool" in full dress investing the Bust of our Great Poet with his own cap and bells. Did you notice this *fool's* face? I fancied that the smirk on the countenance, uplifted eyebrows, & conceited expression, intended the picture for that of the bully Director "Furnee." You have a photo. of him, have you not, or is it Furness who has one? I never saw a picture of his phisiognomy. . . .

I am very greatly obliged to you for taking the trouble of sending me the long newspaper articles on "ye Exhumation." I was deeply interested reading them; and they are both, (esp. the *Telegraph* article,) well-written,—i.e. from *their* standpoint. I should not be surprised if there were more of them. It is just the kind of a subject for newspaper-scribblers to *expatiate* over. They can dilate so freely on 'Yankee curiosity and impertinence,' 'bone-grabbers,' 'Philad. osteologist'—'body-snatcher,' 'resurrectionist,' &c. &c., until they have exhausted the dictionary of opprobrious vocables & epithets. That was a new idea of caravanning the skeleton around, as a raree-show, for coppers; also of analyzing a pinch of the dust of the immortal poet, & recording the analysis in a 2 vol. 4to work, to be deposited in Mullins' Library! He also has to give "the pestilential heresy of that Yankee woman *Delia Bacon*" a dig or two:—Did it make you *laugh*, or *mad*? Do you intend to *notice* either or any of these attacks in the next *Bib.*? Will you pardon me offering a word of advice? I would let the whole thing drop. It is thoroughly *impracticable*. To ruffle an Englishman's *prejudices* touches him very much more nearly than to pick his pocket. . . .

I have just received a very pretty letter from a young lady in Milwaukee, Wisconsin, asking me to tell her the best edition of Shakespeare "for parlour reading," in a Club they are forming to read Shakespeare. I knew her by reputation only, as the principal of a large ladies' Seminary in this County, some years ago. She must now be 25 or more. She was reputed very pretty, & very highly accomplished: so I took *pains* and replied to her letter as "nicely," you know, as I could. If she wanted an 'expurgated,' or 'household,' or 'family' edition, which I thoroughly abused "for people of as good sense as she," then Chambers' and Carruthers' was the best. But an edition of *Shakespeare* to read & enjoy—especially where a person did not care to go to the expense of buying more than one edition—one that would every way suit her purpose—such a one I told her was "The *Chiswick* Edition," by S. W. Singer, recently reprinted by Bell & Daldy, London, in 10 vols., 12mo., and published cheap, only 2/6 a vol. there, just to meet the demands of Clubs, and branch Shak. reading societies. The text is thoroughly trustworthy: type large and clear, & good paper, from the Chiswick press. Introductions well-written, & contain all the historical information regarding the plays; and the Notes are excellent, not too long, nor very critical, but mainly explanatory of obsolete words, phrases, & idioms, old customs, allusions, &c.—Then I offered, if she met with any textual difficulties, which of course she would, & would note them, & send me a line or two anent them, to do my best to help solve them for her, & her club.—Wasn't that clever? Would *you* have done it? How do you like my selection of an *edition* for such a purpose? Lippencott & Co. have imported quite a no. of copies of this newly reprinted Chiswick, or Singer's Edition: but they ask too much for it: $125 a vol. is too much for what is pubd at only 2/6 retail price. I told my lady friend not to give over $100 a vol. for the set, *in cloth*. I have seen it very beautifully bound in *limp* French morocco, various colours, full bound, gilt edges, contents lettered, in a French morocco case. I got a copy for a friend of mine here, in that style for $20.., altho' they ask $25. My own copy (i.e. the *1856 edition* of this Singer) cost me $2500 first in Hf. roxburghe, & $200 a vol. for binding afterwards, in Hf. green *real Turkey*, polished brown edges, contents lettered, & in a new box. It makes a lovely set, and is a favourite edn. with me, for handy reading. My 1826 edn.[2] is also nicely bound, in *full light calf*, contents lettered: but it has marbled edges, a style I never admire. I wish I was as young, and especially as *well off*, in this world's pelf, as you are. I should have so much pleasure in getting my dearly loved volumes beautifully bound by Pawson & Nicholson. I am a regular dandy about my books. I dearly love a well & tastefully-bound book; and I love to *superintend* clothing my precious volumes in a nice substantial dress. But as it is, I have to put up with many disappointments. I have had a very fair binder here for some time, & he does as I want him, & works cheap too, considering. Once he went away, & another took his place. I had left some 35 or 40 vols. to be Hf. bound, & was gone 10 days or 2 weeks. I almost *cried*, when I came back, & saw how vilely the rascal had treated them. He had *cut* them, contrary to all orders; the pasteboards[a] were thick & clumsy;—*common* end papers; *cotton* head-bands, &c.—you know about how I felt. . . .

Do you ever read any of *Tennyson's* poetry? He is a prime favourite of mine. Many of his lyrics & poems are very, *very* beautiful. Did you buy A. Smith's "Life-Drama" yet? It is very fine, and will please you. *Cowper* is another *loved* poet of mine. When I was a school-boy I committed the *whole* of his "Task"—6 books—to memory! Think of that "*task*," will you. I also committed the whole of the Gospel of *St. Matthew* to memory—28 chapters, some of over 70 verses! That was when I went to Sunday School—probably about 10 years old. What would our "boys" here think of having a thing like *that* to do? I had a most retentive memory: the more I used it, the more it held, & the easier it was to commit to it. I was always a rapid reader; but my memory now often fails me; what I read years ago I remember better than what I read recently:—natural effects of **old age**.

Much Ado, V. 2, 104, Benedick says to Beatrice:

"I will live in thy heart, die in thy lap, and be buried in thy eyes."

Don't you think it permissible to transpose two words, and change one letter, in this pretty sentiment, and read so:—

"I will live in thy *eyes*, die on thy *lip*, and be buried in thy *heart*"?

P. A. Daniel proposed the transposition of 'eyes' and 'heart.'—What a vast improvement it makes in the sense; so much more poetical,[3] too, to die "on her *lip*," than "in her *lap*"—. . . .

[1]*who* can be the author of it: The work is generally attributed to John Jeremiah.

[2]My 1826 edn.: I.e., the first Singer Edn.; C has been describing the second Singer Edn. 1856.

[3]so much more poetical: C has overlooked Benedick's genial obscenity; this is a rare instance in him of Victorian blindness.

[a]pasteboards] paste-| boards MS.

136:   2 October 1876

   . . . By the way, when I was at Cincinnati, I made[a] a delightful visit at Mr. E. T. Carson's, the collector of Shakespeariana, &c. of whom I before told you. I asked him to let me have a Catalogue of his *Portraits of Shakespeare* for you, some time ago. He told me, he had delayed for the reason that he is making up a Catalogue for himself of them, and other Shakesp. engravings, &c. &c., and that as soon as he has completed it, he will send it on to you at Philadelphia by express, so you can examine it. He is a charming gentleman; a man of taste; and he has plenty of means to gratify it. He began his collections many years ago, when these things were ¼ or even ½ cheaper than they now are. He bought the celebrated "Burton" Shakespeare (in some 45 or 50 portfolios), and has been adding to it ever since. It is almost invaluable now. He is well acquainted personally with Quaritch, Sotheran, J. R. & A. R. Smith, &c. He has several times been in Europe, collecting books, pictures, &c. He came within a trifle of getting the celebrated "Mazarin" Bible,[1] that was sold at the Perkins Sale. He has just had a beautiful set of the "Percy" Soc. Publns. bound by your friends Pawson & Nicholson. He was a great friend of the late Henry Bohn, of whom he speaks in glowing terms. Mr. Carson is now deep in the collections of "Secret Societies," & his Catalogue of these queer books, not yet finished, has got to the 242d page: so you can imagine its extent. I should not think he was so much of a *reader* or student, as Collector. He knows all about editions, unique copies, large paper books, &c., but shies off when one begins to talk Shakespeare a little critically. He has a magnificent set of "Dibdin's Works" complete. Altogether he is capital company; and I hugely enjoyed listening to him on his favourite hobbies. I wish you knew him; I am sure you would like him.

   I was very tired when I got back home, and I assure you I was glad enough to be again among my books, in my rooms. While travelling, however, I generally continue to do more or less reading, evenings. This trip, I gave *Antony and Cleopatra* a careful study. It comes next on my list of exhaustive reading of the plays *seriatim*. It is one of the hardest plays in Sh., full of *knots*, that beat my skill in unravelling. Besides this, I read a capital novel by Blackmore, called "Lorna Doone." The Reviews all spoke very highly of it, & justly so. It is no common or mediocre work, and it did me very much *good*.—I also re-read dear Mr. Hawthorne's 3 books, "The

Scarlet Letter," "The House of Seven Gables," and "The Blithedale Romance." Of course, you have read these works; and I need not speak of
their merits to you. There is a weird glamour about all of Hawthorne's
writings that makes him an especial favourite with me. And his style is
purity itself.— . . .

While riding on the cars, or sitting at night in a lonely "hotel," I have
managed to read, in addition to other things two or three of Sir W. Scott's
novels, for the 10th or 12th time. What a glorious writer he is, to be sure! I
often trace an affinity between his genius, and that of our Immortal Poet
Shakespeare; so that while reading his works, I get a better knowledge of
the latter, & the time is not wasted, to say nothing of the gratification
received. Every time I re-read a book of Scott's I am more deeply impressed
than ever with his vast superiority over all the novel-writers that have
turned up since his day. Scott did not rank novel-writing very high, nor did
he undertake to use it for any moral effect: his tales were merely the free
and natural overflow of a most fertile, happy, healthy mind; and therefore
they are to me always fraught with wholesome delectation; instructive,
too, as communion with a good, manly, and genial soul cannot but be
instructive.— . . .

I have just recd. a letter from Mr. Hudson, to whom I communicated Dr
Ingleby's explanation of "defect of judgment," in *Cymbeline*. I will copy for
you what he says anent it:—

> "Touching the passage in *Cymbeline*,—"For defect of judgment,"[2] &c., I
> am not at present able to see Ingleby's explanation just as you do. . . .
> The chief fault[b] I find with Ingleby, and several other commentators is,
> that they seem to prefer readings and explanations which none but
> themselves can understand. Perhaps I have said this to you before. I
> was myself, at one time, a good deal possessed with a fondness for
> recondite and fine-drawn explanations; and am something on my
> guard against it now."—

Now it is just such notes as this that have so often made me out of
patience with the old gentleman. Because *he* does not himself "see" an
explanation at the first glance (and the "gods" do not provide everyone
with the due amount of *brains* for seeing things), then, forsooth, the explanation must be "occult," & "recondite," and inadmissible. Remembering
how often, within my experience, Mr. Hudson has peremptorily refused to
hearken to an explanation or suggestion, which when more fully
elaborated, he subsequently not only *saw* but "*adopted*," I cannot say that I
have much faith in what he says above, regarding Dr Ingleby's very clever
& learned note. *His* way of getting over the difficulty is by cutting the
Gordian Knot in two, and *changing* the plain reading of the folio, "*cause* of
fear," to the bald & unShakespearian expression "*cure* of fear."— . . .

I fully applaud & approve of your decision to confine your reading as much as possible to literature illustrative of *Shakespeare*. Next to the Great Poet's writings themselves, a thorough course of Elizabethan & Jacobean reading[c] is of the greatest service in obtaining a correct understanding & appreciation of them. My *forays* among modern poets & novelists are mostly desultory; and more for the sake of relaxation for the mind than any other purpose. I find that after long study of Shak., and the old dramatists, & books appertaining thereto, in the *close* way that I have formed the habit of studying, my mind becomes fatigued, and sometimes flaccid, as it were, needing a change of diet for a short spell. Fresh modern air helps to brace me up again, & I go back into the old traces invigorated & refreshed. Another habit I have is never to waste a minute of time. I always have some book or other[3] in my pocket or satchel, into which I dip, while waiting for a train, or even while breakfast is getting ready. In this way I get through a great amount of *outside* reading: and I contrive, along with the pleasure & amusement of even the lightest literature, to pick out some crumbs of nutritious value; it may be only a single word, or some un-thought-of illustration, that I *fit in* as explanatory, or corroborative, of some place in *Shakespeare*. Thus, you see, Shakespeare, our favourite Shake-speare, is, after all, the great *sea* into which all minor streams pour their waters. I have somewhere seen a proverb 'Beware of the man of one book.' I do not think there is much in this adage. If it mean anything, it must be that men of "one book" are apt to become narrow in soul, feeling, and idea. But we may well make an exception of the "myriad-minded" Shakespeare. The more of *him* we read, the more noble & generous, and all-embracing, & *ingenuous*, the mind becomes. . . .

[1] "Mazarin" Bible: The Gutenberg Bible. The copy in Cardinal Mazarin's great library in Paris first drew the attention of scholars to the Gutenberg—hence the name.
[2] "defect of judgment": *Cym.* 4.2.111.
[3] some book or other . . . even while breakfast is getting ready: As noted earlier, C was regarded as an eccentric by the townspeople of Zanesville; he was said to study Sh out of pocket edns. even while walking down the street.

[a] I made] I ~~had~~ ↑made↓ MS.
[b] The chief fault] the chief fault MS.
[c] Jacobean reading] Jacobean ↑reading↓ MS.

138: 9 October 1876

. . . I have received a letter from bro. F. J. *Furnivall*, in which he says he has sent me a half-dozen copies of his "Introduction to Gervinus," in hope I may distribute them, and get some additional members to the New Sh. Soc. in the Western States. A long time ago, when writing to him, some-thing about being an Hon. Sec. for the West, (which I positively declined,) I asked him to send me a copy of his *carte de visite*, to add to my album of

Shakespearians. In his present note he tells me "I haven't a photo. on hand. *Perhaps I shall put an autotype of myself in one of our books someday.*" There; isn't that last sentence characteristic of vanity, to say it very mildly?—Don't mention it, however, outside: I should not like even *him* to think I retailed his vanity out of a private letter. I see by the *Academy* that his "2d book" is ready. But where is it?—Where is the 1st?—Echo answers 'where.' Have you read "George Elliot's" *Daniel Deronda* yet? It is said to be a grand production. I liked her "Middlemarch" exceedingly; but have not yet had time to read this one. Hudson wrote me he had read *Middlemarch*, three times. I see, in some paper, that a foreign nobleman—I think a *King* of some German country—wrote to the authoress, asking for an interview; and stating that he had read *Middlemarch eight* times over. Did you see it?—

141: 6 November 1876

. . . You remember I promised to send Mr. Fish my note on "Affection! thy intention"[1] &c. I have re-written it from my *Shak. Collectanea*, and enclose it to you. . . . Poor old Hudson picked my pocket of it; but I have forgiven him the *petty* larceny. After he had "given it up"—"was at his wit's end," &c. &c.—I sent this to him. In a week or 8 days afterwards, he writes me that the same thought had occurred to him, & that he was glad to find that he *agreed* with me. The whole thing was so plain, it was almost ridiculous: and I really *blushed* myself for him when I read his letter, & saw the cool way that he appropriated somebody else's work. I knew then that Mr. Halliwell was right in his strictures[2] on the old reverend.—When you have read it, please give it to Mr. Fish, sometime when you meet him.—

What a funny old gentleman Fish is! He reminded me very much of *some* of the old College *dons* we used to have at Oxford; great eaters—mighty fond of good wine, & good judges of it too; & always having some of the younger students & undergraduates up in their rooms to impress them with an *awful* sense of their own reading and learning & importance. But Fish is really very *industrious*; & tho' perhaps not very deep, or original, he does an immense amount of *Variorum* work. Witness these huge "Studies" on each play, and on the poems of Milton, Tennyson, &c. No one could do all this grubbing, collecting, pasting, copying,[3] &c., without *knowing* more or less of his authors. But how different his *work* from Mr. Furness'!—His library is a curious mixture. Many most valuable as well as beautiful books, got together regardless of expense; yet it is not a *library*, such as yours, or Mr. Furness' is. There seems to be less order about it than even about mine. And his books were all so dirty & slovenly. I should like to have those MS. volumes of his. Whatever does he intend to do with them? Keep them I suppose, to entertain his "young ladies," and the "Society." He was very kind & obliging, and gave us a real nice "tea"; and I am greatly obliged to your goodness for making me acquainted with the old Shakespearian. There are plenty of worse men than Mr. Fish, with greater pretensions; I fancy he is a kind-hearted[a] man, a trifle conceited, but nevertheless a scholar, a gentleman, & a good neighbour. . . .

Well, do you know I have let Corson have one of my Variorums of 1821, after all. After much hesitation, "resolved and re-resolved,"—I sent it to him yesterday (Saturday). I gave him the cut, full russia-bound, gilt-edged, set; and I never parted with anything that I so much regretted to lose. When I took the vols. down, they looked so sweet & clean—the whole set were so nice & new, & so handsomely bound, they would have delighted even *your* fastidious taste. I hope that he will take *good care* of them. They were bound in that *heavy, solid* way we talked about—beaten almost *thin,*— so nicely lettered, with gold *bands* in rows, inside & out, and gold *squares* on the backs; and the *double, worked* head-bands that you like so well. There could not be a prettier set, and I hope he has the taste to appreciate them. The margins were wide too; still, after all, it was a *cut* copy, & I preferred to keep the uncut copy, tho' not so lovely in looks. I must take my chances of getting *paid* for it. I gave him 4 *months;* & he says the University will have money in July next, & will then take it off his hands. . . .

Did Geo. A. Leavitt & Co. send you a copy of the Catalogue of a *Mr. Wm. Menzies,*[4] of New York, whose books they will sell at Auction on the 13th inst. & following days? It is a beautiful Catalogue, & the Library to be sold must be a magnificent one. The Cat. is printed by Joel Maunsell of Albany, on type cast for the purpose, & on good paper. It is very handsomely printed; contains nearly 500 pages, & is priced at $200, in paper cover, uncut. The books all seem to be picked copies, in elegant bindings by the most celebrated binders in London & The United States. It is not very rich in *Shakespeariana*, but mostly in *Americana*. It was prepared by Joseph Sabin, & he brags very highly about it, *ut suus est mos*. It contains a *large paper* copy of Grant White's Shakespeare, uncut, Hf olive mor. crushed, gilt tops, 48 copies only printed; and the "Shakespeare's Scholar," Book of the Biography, Essays, &c., and the vol. of the essay on Henry VI., all *large paper,* & uniformly bound. It must be a most desirable & lovely set of books. There is also an uncut copy of *Knight's* original edn. of Sh., with I forget how many inserted portraits, views, &c. The vol. of the Biography extended to 2 vols. with new title-pages, similarly bound with Grant White's edn.; Clarke's Concordance, & Fairholt's "Home of Sh." being also bound to match this set. I notice also an 1808 *Reprint,*[5] a very large copy, 15-in. by 9¼ in. *on the leaf;* bound in Hf. red levant, gilt top, uncut. . . . Do you know anything of *Mr. Menzies?* He seems to have had unbounded wealth as well as excellent taste in his command, to get up so large & valuable a library. Almost every book is "rare," "excessively rare," "scarce"—"of the most excessive rarity," & now & then "unique." It seems odd that he should bring this beautiful & costly library to the hammer *now*, when everything is so dull in trade, & money, especially for luxuries, so fearfully scarce. I read to-day in the New York Times of a recent Sale at Auction (on the 1st inst. & following days) at Bangs, Merwin & Co's, where several very valuable & desirable books went for almost nothing. . . .

[1] "Affection! thy intention" &c.: *WT* 1.2.138.
[2] Mr. Halliwell was right in his strictures: I.e., in the Preface to Halliwell's *Comedies*—see letter 131.
[3] all this grubbing, collecting, pasting, copying: A. I. Fish's papers are now in the Folger Shakespeare Library in a very extensive set of boxes.
[4] the Catalogue of a *Mr. Wm. Menzies:* A copy is in the Folger Shakespeare Library.
[5] an 1808 *Reprint:* i.e., of the First Folio of Sh.

[a] kind-hearted] kind-l hearted MS.

142: 12 November 1876

. . . I have many a night retired to bed, after spending an evening "out," and felt ashamed of the poor, sorry, figure I made in society. I *think*, very rapidly; but when I come to express my thoughts I *hesitate & stammer*, and lose my head, and get excited, and make a general *fiasco* of my conversation. No doubt, much of this arises from the cause you so kindly state—my utter loneliness of life. Only think of it, how many years I have lived a hermit's life almost, reading & studying Sh. and the commentaries, but without a single congenial spirit to speak a word to, about them or him. Then I have never, as many do, *committed to memory* fine passages, for the sake of extemporizing them in company. I wish I could remember & *quote* better. I *know* exactly *what* a passage is, & *where* it is, & most of what is to be known about it; & I detect an *error* of quotation, in another, *instanter;* yet I cannot, offhand, quote it[1] myself. . . .

I am glad you enjoyed your other visits at the *Theatre.* I fancy Mr. Walcot[2] would make a good *Falstaff.* He was the best *Mercutio* I ever saw; perhaps a trifle over-acted, but very good, capital, nevertheless.—. . .

I will trade with you, as you suggest; viz. my "Croft's Annotations," and "Hunter's Disquisition," for one of your cloth copies of Grant White's Shakespeare. In some respects I shall get the *best of the bargain;* as these two small books are not intrinsically worth Eighteen Dollars, nor one-fourth of it. But their being so *rare* gives them a fancy price or value: and of course a Shakespeare Library is not complete without them. They may not turn up again, for sale, in 10 years or more, & they *may* in a week. I think, however, that if offered for sale in London, they would be snapped up before you could get an order in now, as so many are collecting Shakespeariana. If you are not in any great hurry, I should like to keep the "Croft" a short time, in order to *copy* the Notes.[3] They are only 24 pp., 12mo, and I can soon copy them, when I get a little time. Some of the Notes are really valuable, and many of them are *queer*, and very broad. E.g., in *II Hen. IV.* II, 2,[a] "Because the rest of thy Low Countries have made a shift to eat up thy Holland,"[4] he explains "thou hast not a rag to thy a—e."—"The rump-fed ronyon,"[5] in Macbeth, he calls "the fat–a—d jade." Still, looking over the book, I am surprised to see how much *he knew* about the poet, & his times. He was a capital, well-read, antiquarian, & quotes from all sorts of old books.—It is a wretchedly-printed book, full of typographical errors, mistakes in punctuation, &c. And to make it worse, the binder (it is in Hf. calf) has cut into the print, in 3 or 4 of the leaves at the bottom of the page, & hurt the book. It has the book-plate of "John Adolphus, Esq."; and I find the same book-plate in several others of my Sh. books. The "Hunter,"[6] 1839, is a very nice copy; clean, & good as new, in every particular. It is in Hf. morocco. Both of these books you *ought to have*. You are a great deal better collector than I shall ever be; and out here such books have no value, as there is no one to ever see them, who knows anything about a *rare* Shakespearian treat. *Useful* books are more in my line: and I am glad that you are getting these two rare things;[b] as you can afford to have them, & need them to help make your noble library complete. You can send the "Grant White" by "*Adams'* Express," the only express that has an office here: and I will send your books by any way you advise, after I have copied the Croft.—. . .

Prof. Corson . . . is highly pleased with the *Var. 1821,* as I knew he *must* be. I only hope he will take good care of it, & not abuse it. He encloses me his note at 4 months for it; and says:

> "The books have come to me all safe. It's a **lovely** copy—I am **delighted** with it. If my limited means allow me to hold on to it, the University sha'nt have it.[7] Accept my best thanks for your kindness in letting me have it on such terms. I wish I could have gone to Philadelphia while you were there.[8] But I am held here with adamantine chains. My son has written me about his call on Mr. Fish and his meeting you. . . . What a pity Mr. Furness is so deaf! Fortune gave him everything that is desirable in this world, and then, the cruel jade, deprived him of his ears, as an offset to her favours. . . ."

I have got home from the binder my Warburton's Shakespeare, and I am right well pleased with it. He has made as neat and tasteful a job of it as almost anyone *could do*, considering that the vols. were *cut* to begin with. It is in Hf. dark green morocco, with polished red edges, & very nicely & fully lettered. I have given him my new *Dyce III* to bind, in Half *brown* levant, gilt tops, and entirely uncut edges. They have received a new article for binding purposes, called *leatherette,* an English patent, and really a capital invention. It is made of *paper*, but is a perfect imitation of leather— morocco generally, in all the various colours, beautifully *grained*, and *tough* as real leather. It is said also to be very *durable*. They use it for the *sides*, instead of agate paper, or cloth. It takes gilding beautifully, and looks exactly like a fine quality of the best leather. Have you seen it yet? I shall have it on my Dyce vols.; when the same colour is used as the morocco on the backs, it gives the books the appearance, and they say the durability, of being bound in full morocco. The difference in cost between it & the ordinary agate paper is only a few cents on a volume. . . .

Have you got *Rolfe's* new edition of *King Richard II*? It is, like the rest of these edns., very nicely edited & printed, perhaps a little fuller than his earlier edns.—I like his books better than either Hunter's,[9] or the "Collins' Series"; but not nearly as well as the "Clarendon Press Series." Rolfe has too many *references*, & not enough **originality**. In fact, I do not see one single *new* thought, reading, idea, or explanation, in this Rich. II.—

You speak of Snider. I have received a nice long letter from him recently. I am trying to get him to give his essays to a publisher, to put into one vol. He probably will, when he gets through the list. I got him to import a copy of *Delius' Shak.* for me; the last edn. in 2 vols., same as Mr. Furness uses so much.—He sent me a long and very amusing critique on *Fleay's Manual*. You can imagine how he *would* write of Fleay's book. The two critics are the very antipodes of one another—one is the nadir, the other the zenith of criticism; one all for counting, & mechanical or *scientific* criticism; the other is at the extreme end of the *æsthetic* pole. Fire and water are not more hostile than Snider is to Fleay, and his school. They both miss Horace's excellent maxim[10] *"in medio tutissimus ibis."* I dislike extremes in anything. . . .

[1] I cannot, offhand, quote it: Actually, C could quote from memory rather well when not in company, as letters written while travelling, far from his library, attest.
[2] Mr. Walcot: C. Melcot Walcot the Younger, who played at the Walnut Street Theatre in Philadelphia regularly in the 1870s. He had worked with Edwin Booth, Laura Keene, and Charlotte Cushman.
[3] to *copy* the Notes: The transcription C made is now in the Folger Shakespeare Library.
[4] "Because . . . thy Holland": *2H4* 2.2.21–22.
[5] "The rump-fed ronyon": *Mac.* 1.3.6.
[6] The "Hunter," 1839: Joseph Hunter, *Disquisition on "The Tempest."*
[7] the University sha'nt have it: The copy of the Variorum of 1821 in the John M. Olin Library at Cornell University is not this one; presumably Corson was able to keep his purchase.
[8] while you were there: C spent a week in Philadelphia in October 1876 combining sightseeing at the Centennial Exposition with scholarly social life in N's circle.
[9] Hunter's: John Hunter's school series.
[10] Horace's excellent maxim: Not in Horace; the quotation is from Ovid's story of Phaeton, *Metamorphoses* II.137 (slightly altered).

[a] II, 2] I, 2 MS.
[b] two rare things;] ↑two rare things↓; MS.

143:   15 November 1876

. . . Old Mr. Collier has just sent me *Coriolanus*, to hand in good order. Only eleven plays more now—or twelve, including *The Two Noble Kinsmen*, which I suppose he *will* include in the edition. Do you observe how "few and far between" the Notes are becoming in the later issues? He does not adopt *all* the "Corr. fo. 1632" emendations in this edition either. It is really a *better text* than the 1858—6 vol—edition. And what a lovely-printed book it is! I told you that he had sent me *The Two Gent.* and *Merry Wives*, in sheets. Now all I need, to perfect my set, is *The Tempest*; and from what he says, I am tolerably sure of soon getting *that* too. I have just sent him a remittance, and a nice long letter of encouragement. I told him that Mr. Hudson had adopted two of his recent emendations, and would print them in his new, forthcoming, critical edition—of course with the proper acknowl-edgements. I told him also that I had taken the liberty of communicating *one* striking emendation of his—that of "revil'd" for "defil'd," in *Much Ado*—to his countryman Dr Ingleby, and in what high praise the learned Dr had spoken of it, and adopted it at once. And yet Ingleby had written one of the severest criticisms in 1860, on the Old Corrector, 1632, in his "Com-plete View."—I wrote for the purpose of **cheering up** the old gentleman, and I hope I succeeded: he has been very kind to me.—Do you notice how *rapidly* the later plays are coming out? I fancy he is hurrying up his work, as fast as he can—lest *Death* overtake him ere it is completed. Poor old fel-low!—I hope that *you* write him, kindly & often, too. Any cablegram now[1] may bring us the message, "Mr. Collier, the Shakespearian editor & critic, is dead!"—. . .

---

[1] Any cablegram now: Collier lived on another seven years, until September 1883.

146:   4 December 1876

. . . Let[a] me **thank you cordially** for the *Grant White*, which came in the nicest order. I am highly pleased with it. It is every way equal to *new*. As soon as I can part with the money, I will have it nicely bound, in Hf. turkey mor., gilt tops, uncut, contents lettered; and keep it for my *show copy*. My own, as I have told you, is literally covered with pencil notes "from title-page to colophon." These annotations are of course very useful *to me*, but make the volumes look very unpresentable. I want *you* to have my copy of Grant White's Sh.,[1] if you survive me. The notes, tho' in pencil, are gener-ally my maturest thoughts on hard passages, and criticisms on White's egotistic readings & expressions. They are neatly & legibly written too, & will help a reader, & save him much time by the references, which I have made very full.—. . .

Mr. D. J. Snider has sent me the *Delius Shakespeare*, that I spoke to you about. I am very well pleased with it—should be more so, if I only could read German. It is in 2 vols., roy. 8vo, rather commonly bound in Hf. mor., marbled edges, pp. 1088, 858, closely printed, text in double column. So far as I have examined the book, the text seems a very *conservative* one. It is fully up to the latest date. The edition is that of *1876*, & Delius seems to have read **everything** on Shakespeare, & is *well posted*. Altho' there is a great deal of English in the *Introductions* and *Notes*, yet not being able to read German almost makes me wild, when, e.g., he gives his own interpretation of some difficult passage. The notes are very copious, and are at the foot of the page. Almost every line has a longer or shorter note. I shall get me a good German Dictionary, & try to make out the sense as well as I can. The German is in English letters you know, that makes it a little easier.—What wonderful readers & scholars these German professors are! I can see from Prof. Delius' numerous quotations that he is *au fait* in everything pertaining to Shakespeare, not only the editions, but other literature, Magazines, Reviews, &c. being called *in aid*. It only cost me about $9.— carriage and all. You *must* have it. I expect to consult it regularly—make out as much as I can—and get some Dutchman to translate the rest for me. It is a *standard* edition; &, Snider says, the *best* German one; indeed *he* thinks more of it than of any of the great English editions; but he is prejudiced in favour of the German critics. . . .

—Smith . . . sent me a photograph of Mr. Halliwell-Phillipps,—like yours—sitting in his library; and one of Charles Knight. I do not remember yours of Knight. This I have is that of a *very old* gentleman, with a kind expression, very white hair; sitting, hands clasped on his lap; pantaloons much "too wide for his shrunk shank"; a plaid vest buttoned up high. Is it same as yours? It is a very excellent & very striking picture. Knight looks "fourscore and upward, not a day more nor less," as poor old *Lear* says. A. R. Smith also sends me his own photo.—just like yours. In his letter he says:

> "I see your signature in *Notes & Queries*, and your emendation of "scope" in *Cymbeline* strikes me as being quite appropriate. With reference to many disputed words handed down from the early Quartos and from the Folios I am persuaded that the printers of those editions have a great many sins to answer for in these respects, as anyone who has had to do with printers can testify, by the way have you got Beckett's "Shakespeare's Genius Justified" and that still more ingenious book of Zechariah Jackson[2] who was himself a printer and consequently well understood the devil's tricks, did you read the article in the Telegraph anent Mr. Parker Norris's proposition to exhume the body of Shakespeare."

Above is *verbatim* & *punctuatim* extract from Smith. His *criticism* on the "Quartos and on the Folios" is as sapient and owlish as Jack Bunsby[3] himself could have enunciated; and note, too, how *business* crops out; he cannot "sink the shop"; he has to insinuate that he has two "ingenious" *books* [for sale]—Beckett, and "that still more ingenious book by *Zechariah* Jackson".—*Ne sutor ultra crepidam*, which being interpreted means "let the cobbler stick to his last."

You are a little hard, I fear, on my old friend Rev. Mr. Hudson, though I must allow there are many grains of truth in your strictures. Won't he open his old eyes, when he reads[4] what Mr. Halliwell says of his "appropriations." "*Convey*, the wise it call." I don't suppose he has ever seen it before. Did you direct a copy right to him, in your own hand? Won't he be "mad" at you? But you are a "*bold* gamester, Lord Sands." I could not refrain laughing at one remark of his in his last letter. Referring to my note on "the top of question,"—"There is no occasion for you to return it to me, as I at the time embodied in my notes on *Hamlet* most of its contents." That's another good word. "Embodied" is good, as old Polonius would say. He says further: "The truth is, I have been prodigiously busy the last seven or eight weeks. My publishers wished me to prepare the matter for a *Classical English Reader and Speaker*, to be made up of miscellaneous selections in prose and poetry. I set right about the work, and have already got it pretty much done." Now how do you like that *style*? Especially in a man preparing a "*Classical English Reader*":—"prodigiously busy"—"set right about"—"got it *pretty much done*." Not very *elegant*, is it?—"Priscian a little *scratched*; 'twill serve."—

I told you I had made up all I could find of actors' readings, &c., and sent it to Mr. Furness before I went away. He sent me a most delightful little note, saying,

> "I am vastly obliged for the trouble you've taken in looking up actors' points. Whether I use the material you've collected, or not, your kindness has saved me ever so much time. I am now anxious to get in time your note on 'the top of the question.'—Unless I get it by Tuesday, it will be too late I'm afraid.[5] The printers made a larger stride this week than ever they made before, and so we have come upon the passage quicker than I thought. The printers have accomplished thirty pages this week—which is perhaps harder work for me than for them. Ten more weeks of such progress, and the play (i.e. the text) will be about done.—I am very glad we caught a glimpse of you. It afforded both Mrs. Furness and myself great pleasure. I hope you'll come soon again—don't wait for a Centennial.
>
> Yours Cordially."

Now, isn't that kind and nice? Who would not do *anything* for such a man? I am real glad he has given you a chance to help him. I know that you will do the work carefully, in the first place; and that it gives you pleasure to do it, in the second. . . .

Goddard has just been up to see me. He begs me to give you his best love, and sympathy in the loss of your dear young brother. Charlie is behaving quite well lately.[6] He saw Neilson[7] in "Twelfth Night," in Cincinnati, I think; and again in *Juliet* and *Rosalind*. In *T. N.* she takes the part of *Viola*. I hope also to see her in this character. I have never seen "Twelfth Night" on the stage.—. . .

You say the writer of the article in the Review is enthusiastic over Retzsch's illustrations of Shakespeare.[8] He cannot be *more* enthusiastic in the praise of them than I am. I have looked at them for hours Together with increasing delight. I told you, didn't I, that I have a very fine set of the *original* drawings, that "I would not take too much for." The characterization, and the just & exact appreciation of the characters, and all done by a few strokes of a pen, are simply marvellous. There is no comparison to be made between the drawings of Retzsch, and Frank Howard's outlines. The Dutchman beats the Englishman all to pieces. I cannot attempt to describe to you a quarter of the beauties of Retzsch. He is like Hogarth; every little thing—every accompaniment is there, and just as one could expect. His faces—the *expression* of the characters—*speak out* like living beings, all done so easily too. Now will you oblige me, by just taking down your Hartley Coleridge's *Marginalia*, Vol. I, and turn to page 172, and read to page 178, inclusive, and you will see what *he* thinks of Retzsch, and his pictures. It is a critique on Retzsch's drawings of one play only—*Hamlet*—written for the *Noctes Ambrosianæ* of Blackwood; and I concur with every word, reading it with the pictures before me.—But *Fuseli*—I do *not* like,[9] nor his "Ghost" in the Boydell series either. . . .

I shall look anxiously out for the December *Bibliopolist* No doubt it will be an interesting "Gossip." I wish heartily for *two* things—one, that Sabin would give you more room—more "scope & verge"—so that you could make the department something more than a "Gossip"; and secondly, that his periodical had a wider circulation. But I suppose it is of no use talking to him. He thinks it his interest to publish only a small *advertising* tract only, and that a larger one would be a loss. Now, it seems to me, that like everything else, to make a venture *pay* requires some *enterprise*. Let him enlarge, instead of contracting, the "Bibliopolist"; if necessary, charge more for it; but give subscribers value received. Your department is the only good thing in it; and you really deserve great credit for working on so long, under such cramping & difficulties. Then it is so irregular too. I noticed we had only *one no.* for 4 months, instead of two. Why is this thus? How can he *expect* subscribers thusly? and if *no subscribers*, how can it *pay*?—As it is, I *cannot* help you any at all, because, you know, I have no "gossip" *out here*. . . .

I am compelled to think that you are a little too severe on the *Clarkes*, in your strictures on their edn. pubd. by Cassell. You must recollect that they had pubd. 3 editions of Shakespeare, with *perfect* text before; . . . There is no "expurgation" in any of these editions. They are intended for the Scholar & the Shakespearian reader & student. Then, the Cassells wanted to issue an edition—to be *popular*; to be a subscription-book, published in weekly parts, with cheap woodcuts, to go into the hands of every Tom Dick & Harry in the country—into thousands & tens of thousands of families— to be read by[b] boys & girls, and men & women, who did not know *Shakespeare* from Robinson Crusoe, or Jack Sheppard. They applied to the

Clarkes to prepare such an edition. I do not see how they could do otherwise than they did. "Expurgation" was the word of command by the men who held the "sinews of war," the purse-strings.ᶜ They (the Clarkes) were to edit, expurgate every word, phrase, or allusion, not fit for *modern* ears polite, and write *notes* or commentary, in order to make the Poet intelligible to *that class* for whom the edn. was designed. My only surprise is, that they have done the work so well. . . . And what I particularly like & admire, is, the *love* of the poet so evident everywhere throughout the work. His beauties—his characterization—his insight into that complicated machine called *man*—his miraculous command of language—his wit & humour—his jokes and his puns—his sublime flights of poetry, and his philosophy, are all pointed out and dwelt on, in a way to interest their readers whether high or low—learned or illiterate—young or old. Now don't they deserve credit for this? It is for very much the same reasons that I so dearly like old *Charles Knight.* He loved Shakespeare himself—his whole soul was imbued with him—and he did his very utmost, by publishing *lovely* volumes, to make Shakespeare *loved*, and attractive, to the world of readers. Honour to his memory! and honour, too, to the Clarkes, for their life-long devotion to the Great Bard, and for their share in making him *known, understood, loved*, and *remembered!*—. . .

What an accumulation of sad news you gave me in your three present letters: 1*st* the sad & mournful death of your beloved brother[10]—so young—so happy—taken away from his family so awfully suddenly: 2*d* the death of our friend George Dawson, a man who seemed to be in robust health but recently; 3*d* the derangement of Mrs. Halliwell,[11] and her consignment to an insane asylum; and Mr. Halliwell's own voluntary abandonment of all further work on Shakespeare; a work in which he has taken an engrossing interest for a long series of years, devoting to it all his time, thoughts, energies, reading, and a large fortune. "There is, indeed, a Power over us"; "there's a divinity that shapes our ends, Rough hew them how we will!"—I trust, with you, he will reconsider this determination. It will be much better for him, to continue his interest in Shakespeare, & "Keep on the even tenor of his way" and work. It will do more to quiet and soothe his own mind, than to do nothing but (as Enobarbus says) "*think and die.*" To stop so suddenly the work of a long life, for the sake of brooding over his unhappy fate, may cause insanity in his own case. Let us hope his friends & physicians will not consent to it: so both for his own safety, and *our profit*, he may be induced to go on again. Did it ever strike you, that there is a skeleton in everybody's closet? We look at people, & imagine them perfectly happy. Yet who knows but God, how they feel, or where the skeleton is concealed? . . .

Like yourself, I am as glad as I can be to know that Mr. Furness, after taking a rest from his severe labour on *Hamlet*, will proceed with *The Mer. of Venice*[12]. Do I understand you, that *Hamlet* will be ready *for sale* by the 23d of

April, 1877,—in abt. 4½ months?—If I were to advise, I should say put it into two volumes, wouldn't you? One vol. of 800 pp., or over, would be very unweildy. In two, we could have the text, &c., in one vol., and the appendixes, Index, &c. in the other, and it would be so much easier to handle.—. . .

¹ my copy of Grant White's Sh.: Its whereabouts is unknown to us; see note 6 to letter 75.

² Beckett's "Shakespeare's Genius Justified" . . . Zechariah Jackson: Smith has tangled both orthography and authorship; Zachariah Jackson wrote *Shakespeare's Genius Justified* (1818); Andrew Becket's book is *Shakespeare's Himself Again* (1815).

³ Jack Bunsby: Cf. *Dombey and Son*, ch. 23, where Bunsby utters a logical mish-mash when asked for an opinion in a dark matter.

⁴ when he reads: In the *Bibliopolist*, October 1876; N pubd. Halliwell's preface to the edn. of the fourteen Sh comedies from C's transcription—the book was so rare that Hudson would not, likely, have seen it otherwise.

⁵ too late I'm afraid: C's note does not appear in the Variorum *Ham.* at 2.2.327–28 (340 Riverside).

⁶ behaving quite well lately: Charles Goddard, an attorney and officer in the Ohio Militia, was a friend of both C and N. He had recently given up drinking to excess. His highly romantic elopement is described in detail in letters not rptd. here.

⁷ Neilson: Adelaide Neilson (ca. 1848–80) was acclaimed for her portrayals of Sh's romantic heroines in several American tours in the 1870s.

⁸ Retzsch's illustrations of Shakespeare: The 3d edn. of F. A. Moritz Retzsch's *Outlines to Shakespeare's Dramatic Works* appeared in Leipzig in 1871; the illustrations are line drawings, grotesque and witty, of scenes from *Ham., Mac., Rom., Wiv., Tmp., Oth., 1,2H4*, and *Lr.*

⁹ *Fuseli*—I do *not* like: N would not agree; he described Fuseli in "The Painters and Engravers of the Boydell Shakespeare Gallery" (preface to his 1874 rpt. of selections from the 1805 Boydell Gallery) as "The greatest genius, in some respects, of all the Boydell contributors, great as a scholar as he was great as an artist, and as versatile in style, in Art, as he was comprehensive in capacity in all intellectual pursuits. . ." (p. ix). The pop-eyed Ghost of Hamlet Senior is Plate XCIII of Norris's reprint.

¹⁰ your beloved brother: William P. Norris died 14 November 1876 leaving his wife and an infant.

¹¹ the derangement of Mrs. Halliwell; See note 2 to letter 64.

¹² Mr. Furness . . . will proceed with *The Mer. of Venice*: Actually, the next play to appear (1880) was *Lr.; MV* appeared in 1888.

ᵃ Let] let MS.

ᵇ to be read by] ↑to be read by↓ MS.

ᶜ purse-strings] purse-ǀ strings MS.

148: 10 December 1876

. . . "Thus *conscience* does make cowards of us all."¹—Hamlet. Can you define what the Prince means by *conscience*, in the above line? It is not easy to get it exactly; but I think the following comes near to it. *Conscience*, in this context, is *an internal sense of right or wrong*; and is synonymous with *consciousness*, i.e. the *knowledge* of what passes in the mind. Our definition of *conscience*, **now**, is "the faculty within us, which *decides* upon the lawfulness or unlawfulness of our actions."—Hamlet's meaning is, 'it is the *consciousness* that we would merit the ills or condign punishment that may be reserved by the Everlasting for such as commit forbidden acts, (e.g. *suicide*,) that makes cowards of us all.'—. . .

[1] "Thus *conscience* does make cowards of us all": *Ham.* 3.1.82.

149:   12 December 1876

My dear Norris:

I wrote you Sunday evening; and, last evening when I went to my Office, I was surprised to see a box left by the Express Co., on which I *thought* that I recognized the direction. Addressed to me, and marked "Glass—with care," I wondered and wondered *what* it could be. I opened it carefully, unfolded wrap after wrap, & at last I got to it. You can imagine my delight! So, I thought, I *was not* disappointed in the address—it *is* from *him*,—no one else would have had the kindness and generosity to send me this beautiful mask. I wondered then *who* it represented; I knew it was *not* Shakespeare—nor you—nor Furness; and yet I fancied the head and hair were somehow familiar; I had seen it in a portrait somewhere. Do you know I could not determine who it was, until I read your kind—most kind—letter of presentation.—It came perfectly safe: just as when you packed it. Now to say that I am *delighted* with it poorly expresses my feelings: and to say 'I thank you for the gift' still more poorly. You could not have selected a more lovely or more appropriate ornament for my room. It is a splendid head; I did not know that "Davy"[1] was so *handsome* a little fellow. The *expression* is wonderfully sweet and benign, yet full of intelligence. I held it up—then hung it up—and looked at it for an hour or more. Then I went to a cabinet-maker, & am having a "shield" made of black walnut, such as you describe. It will be done tomorrow, & then your kind and beautiful Christmas Gift will take its place, with so many others from the same generous source, on the walls of my lonely domicile. . . .

Do you remember a conversation that you, and Leighton, & I, had in your Library anent Shakespeare's not taking care of, and publishing, his own works during his lifetime. You thought it attributable to his laziness. I took the liberty to differ with you. The following brief extract from Dr Badham's Essay (*Camb. Essays*, 1856) is *àpropos*.

After giving various *other* reasons, Dr. Badham says: "It is also not unlikely that a mind so essentially dramatic never seriously brought itself to look upon a play as a thing *to read*, but considered its only real publication to be—in its living utterance upon the stage; so that, looking upon his vocation as quite distinct from mere authorship, he would regard all printing and revising as a curious niceness which in no way concerned him."— . . .

[1] "Davy": David Garrick.

151:   16 December 1876

. . . Regarding that idea advanced by Dr Ingleby, in his "Chapter" on "The Portraiture of Shakespeare,"[1] I think you have not exactly understood me. Long before I saw the Doctor's pamphlet, it had often occurred to me when seeing the date of the death of the Poet's widow, 1623, and knowing that that was the date of the 1st folio, that it might have been possible that Messrs Heminge and Condell had waited for the old lady's decease, in order to be able to correct their proofs by the poet's *original* MSS., which it seemed probable still remained at Stratford. I thought of this, when trying to assign some reason to myself for their waiting so long—seven years— after Sh's death, before publishing their volume; and the date of their publication tallying with that of Mrs. Shakespeare's death. I don't think the fact of there being in existence one or more copies of this folio, with the date 1622, instead of 1623, had any effect on my mind. It is not necessary to suppose that the old lady, as being a Puritan, refused to allow the MSS. to go out of her possession, because she was *ashamed* of them, being *Plays*; it might have been that she regarded them with so great *love* and *veneration*, she would not part with them, lest they might be *lost* or destroyed. Be that as it may, if these distinguished publishers *did* obtain them, as you justly observe, they made precious poor use of them. I think the probable facts are, that the Poet did not leave any of his own MSS., i.e. in a clean, revised form. When he wrote his plays, he sold them, or gave them, to the Theatre, with which he was connected as Stockholder; these of course became dirty, defaced, and dilapidated, by constant use for study by the actors, and Sh. himself may have revised, corrected, and re-written more or less of them, as required; I think that these were *all* the copies there were in MS.; that when the Theatre was burned down in 1613, (*The Globe*), a great portion even of these were destroyed by fire; and that the publishers, Heminge & Condell, used what were left, in their worn-out[a] & dilapidated condition, for their folio vol., as far as they would go; & used the surreptiti- ously printed copies of the Quartos, as far as *they* would go; probably correcting, and augmenting or revising these latter from the actors' MSS., or from memory. Their *work* shows plainly enough that their boast of having the author's original "writings," "without blot," &c. to set up from, was all sham: and we know that some of the plays were set up from the actors' copies, by the original *names of the actors* being set up & printed *in the text of the folio*, instead of the names of the characters of the play. All this helps to account for the wretched condition in which we have the Folio text printed. Had they had the Poet's original writings to work from, it would have been very different: but they had not and moreover I believe that there were none *in existence*, i.e. in clean, revised, correct, undilapidated condition, and fit to set up from, as *copy*: and if they thought it probable that Shakespeare had retained, or prepared, such "perfect coppies," and that they were at Stratford, and waited (for some reason) until the death of the possessor of them, in order to get them to correct their proofs by, then they were *disappointed*, that's all.—. . .

Another new book I have got, since I wrote you, is the *Clarendon Press* Edition of *Milton's Poems*, in 2 nice, handy, vols., 12mo, edited by[b] R. C. Browne, M. A., Oxford.—This is a *truly*[c] excellent edition of Milton. It is most ably edited, as all the "C. P. Series" of editions are, with Life, Introductions, accurate Text from the original editions, Notes, Various Readings, and Indexes. For scholarly reading I think it by far the *best* edition of Milton. There is no "expurgation" of course; it is all here; and the Notes are admirable, containing a great deal of matter illustrative of *Shakespeare* also. So far as I have read & examined this book, I cannot speak too highly of it. It only costs 6/6, about $12..50. I intend to read it all carefully; it is just the thing to take in one's satchel on a trip. *You ought* to have it, & read it; there's lots of "Shakespeare" in the Notes.—I have now *five* good editions of Milton's Poems: (1) Cleveland's edition, 1 vol. thick 8vo, with Notes, and Verbal Index, or *Concordance*; (2) The **Reprint**, by Pickering, of the *First* edition of *Paradise Lost*; a lovely facsimile volume, 4to., with facsimile of Milton's contract with his publisher to sell copyright of "P. L." for £20., &c. &c. (3) The celebrated *Baskerville* Edition of the Poems, in *beautiful*, large type, 2 vols. 4to, with portrait; (4) Masson's edition, 3 vols. 8vo, an excellent edition also, to match the "Cambridge Shakespeare"; & (5) The C. P. Series edn. by Browne, 2 vols. 12mo.—There is *one* more that I would like to have, viz., *Todd's* **Variorum** edition, the *last* one, in *4 vols.* 8vo, used to be in 6 vols.—It is very copious in Notes, something like our Sh: Variorums. *Boydell* also published a sumptuous edition, in 3 vols. folio; and Pickering, a very beautifully printed one, of all the works, *prose* & *poetry*, in 8 vols. 8vo. . . .

I am very glad . . . to know that you are reading *Romeo & Juliet*, critically, in Furness' edition. It will do you "lots" of good. I think I have gone through that book at least *four* times. You have it *all* there, i.e. all that is worth reading, and are not compelled to read the same thing over, and over, and over again—in the different editions & commentaries. The time & labour that is saved the student, in this alone, is wonderful, as I can well testify. I have had so much *outside* reading to do, of late, that I have somewhat neglected my regular routine of Shakespeare. But I will get at it, again soon, D. v.—I have been reading some of Littledale's new edition of *T. N. K.*, ("N. Sh. Soc."). It is a *Masterly* edition and no mistake. The care and labour spent, both on *text* & *notes*, are simply immense. It is very, *very*, instructive reading I can tell you. Just read the "Bibliography" of the editions of the play, that Littledale prefixes to the "Reprint" of the 1634 Quarto. It will interest you amazingly, as it did me: tho' I think him a little too severe on Mr. Skeat. He refers to the singular mistake that Dyce made (and which is repeated in his posthumous, 1876, edition) in saying that the play (*T. N. K.*) was printed in the 1664 and 1685 Folios of Shakespeare, whereas it is in neither; being first printed in Qto 1634, & not again until it appeared in B. & F.'s *2d Folio*, 1679. It seems that W. C. Hazlitt repeats the same mistake (no doubt copied from Dyce) in a Note in his new edition of his uncle W. Hazlitt's book, "Lit. of the Age of Elizabeth." I referred to this book, which I have, & found it even so. Note, too, what Littledale says of W. C. Hazlitt's *accuracy* in general, p. ix, *note*. . . .

[1] his "Chapter" on "The Portraiture of Shakespeare": This would be the prepublication rpt. (1876) of ch. 5 of *Shakespeare: The Man and the Book* (vol. 1, 1877). Ingleby sent both C and N offprints; N's is now in the Folger Shakespeare Library.

[a] worn-out] worn-| out MS.
[b] edited by] edited ↑by↓ MS.
[c] is a *truly*] ↑is↓ a *truly* MS.

152:   27 December 1876

. . . Thanks for the list of *errata* in Mr. F.'s 2 vols. of Shakespeare. It is very complete indeed, & must have been made with great care and pains. I append a few errata, in *Macbeth* only, that I had pencilled on the fly leaf; but they are only such as happened to strike me when reading. I did not go through the work to discover them. Mr. Furness has secured a most accurate and valuable coadjutor in you, for the revision of the proofs of his *Hamlet*. Whatever you undertake to do, you do well and thoroughly; and this is a work of no slight comprehensiveness and responsibility. I wish I lived in Philadelphia, so I could help you evenings. It would be to me, as no doubt it is to you, a real labour of love, such as Ferdinand describes so well in the *Tempest*. . . .

—I have just finished a long, closely-written letter of some 12 large pages to *Snider*, reviewing his 3 last essays—*M. A.*; *Troi. & Cres.*; and *Merry Wives*. That on *T. & C.* is the best of the three. This is a favourite play of mine, and I have studied it, textually & critically, with the greatest attention. I think it one among the Poet's *greatest* works; yet it is less read, & less understood, than probably any of the plays; and I *never heard* of its being acted on modern boards.[1] . . .

I bought Mr. Weiss' new book—"Wit, Humor, and Shakespeare"—in Zanesville, for $200; took it with me on my last trip; read about a third of it, on the cars; got out at a little town called Benwood to get supper, and left the book under my satchel in my seat; and when I returned, and expected to continue Mr. Weiss' amusing lectures on Falstaff, &c. &c. lo! & behold! it had vamosed, gone where the woodbine &c. In a word it was *stolen*, & I was both disconsolate and *mad*. However I hoped it would do somebody good; perhaps make some poor[a] fellow *laugh* who was over head and ears in debt; or make somebody a student and lover of Shakespeare, who had never before heard of the Poet, so I made a virtue of necessity, reconciled myself to my loss, and when I got to Wheeling went to the first bookstore, and bought another copy; and the proprietor, in consideration of my bad luck with the other copy, threw off 25¢, & only charged me $175. This copy I brought home all safe; and learned not to leave a nice new book on a car-seat, while I go to supper. It was a case that exactly fitted the old Latin adage:

"Nunc[b] mea, mox hujus, sed postea nescio cujus."[2] If I could only have known who the 'hujus' was who had so dexterously *translated* my book— from my seat to his, I should probably (?) have recited to him the words of that consummate rascal Iago:

> "Who steals my *purse* steals trash; 'tis something,
>   nothing;
> 'Twas mine, 'tis his, and has been slave to thousands;
> But he that filches from me my good *'Weiss'*
> Robs me of that—which he might have had honestly
>   for a pair of dollars,
> And makes me *mad* indeed."

Like Jaques, I sat and *ruminated*; I looked out of the window, but could discover no "*books* in the running brooks"; I looked in the faces of all my neighbours in the car, trying to make out which of them was laughing in his sleeve at so easily making me the victim of misplaced confidence. I compared myself with all the ill-used mortals I could recollect, & concluded that I was in not quite so bad a plight as poor old Lear; finally, "Tired nature's sweet restorer, balmy sleep" crept over my troubled senses, and I slept the sleep of the just.— . . .

---

[1] I *never heard* of its being acted on modern boards: The play was not produced in England between 1733 (the last production of Dryden's adaptation) and 1907. The first American production was in 1916.

[2] *Nunc mea, mox hujus, sed postea nescio cujus*: This loose paraphrase of Horace *Satires* II. ii appeared in William Camden's *Remains Concerning Britain* (1605), 107. C would have seen the line in the note on *Oth.* 3.3.157–58 in Boswell's Malone (1821). See T. W. Baldwin, *William Shakspere's Small Latine & Lesse Greeke* (1944), 2:513–15.

[a] some poor] ↑some↓ poor MS.
[b] "Nunc] Nunc MS.

153:   29 December 1876

. . . I don't like Dr. Ingleby's supercilious & very dogmatic way of speaking with reference to the *Droeshout*. I am not connoisseur enough, nor well enough read in this branch of Sh. literature, to argue with him. But it *does not stand to reason* that Shakespeare's editors would publish an "abomination" in their book, as a portrait of their dear friend and fellow; neither, unless it had *some merit* as a resemblance, would Ben Jonson have given such pronounced & exalted praise to this engraving; certainly he would not, if it bore (as Dr Ingleby says) "no resemblance to the Poet," no matter how much it was the fashion to print such "compliments." I must say, with all deference to our learned friend, that his illustration from the endings of two letters is very weak and far-fetched, and very much like begging the question. Again, he says, "we know that Jonson *did not mean* the praise," &c. &c, and refers to *Notes & Queries*, 5th Series, Vol. VI, page 276. I have the No. before me, and I can find *absolutely nothing* at that reference to warrant such an assertion. It is possible his "amanuensis" has made a mistake in the No. or page; but I have been a pretty faithful reader of N. & Q. for many years, and I recollect nothing like what he states. Had it been there, I think I should have remembered so striking a fact. The Doctor is very ready to criticize others, but I have noticed that he's fearfully conceited & **touchy**, if anyone presume to ruffle *his* hair the wrong way. His chapter on the "Portraiture of Shakespeare" is really a very poor performance indeed. Little as I know of the subject, I could almost have written as good an account. One naturally expects something above mediocrity when a LL.D. reads a paper on a *special* subject to the "Royal[a] Society of Literature."—. . .

[a] "Royal] ↑"Royal↓ MS.

154: 3 January 1877

. . . I have been reading over again Grant White's three chapters (all yet written—one more to come) on Sh: in the Octo, Nov., & Jan '77 Nos. of the *Galaxy*. There are many good & noteworthy *points* in these papers, and they are written in an easy & popular style that is attractive. Note his remarks on the reasons why *women* generally don't admire Shakespeare as much as men. Note also his excellent distinction between male and female *jealousy*. I cannot, however, think that Imogen ought to be classed among the poet's instances of female jealousy. Adriana, Regan, & Cleopatra, may very well; but it sounds cruel almost to attribute (at least much of) jealousy to dear, sweet Imogen, or even to Julia. Again, among his instances of unalloyed villains, monsters of baseness, what does he mean by enumerating the character of the "Duke" in *Measure & Measure*, alongside of *Iago* and *Edmund*? Does he mean *Angelo*? There surely is some mistake here.—Is it a fact (it is new to me) that previous to 1854, in the line in King Lear (*ad finem*) "and my poor *fool* is hanged,"[1] the term "fool" was supposed by all edd. & commentators to refer to the Fool of the play—the "boy" who accompanied the King? We all know now that it means his daughter Cordelia; & I knew that it had been mistakenly supposed by some to allude to the Court Fool; but that the correct interpretation was not conjectured until 1854 (does he mean that *he* made the discovery?) astonishes me.—I intend to look into this.—Note what he says regarding the *sex* of *Ariel*: "It is disturbing enough to see Ariel, sexless, but, like the angels, rather masculine than feminine, represented by a woman dressed below the waist in an inverted gauze saucer, and above the waist in a perverted gauze nothing."—He cannot get over the weakness of constantly referring to "my edition"—"my notes on this subject"; & in one instance giving us a long quotation from one of his "Introductions." But spite of this, the papers are very readable, and will do good, and should be read carefully by everybody.

Do you remember when we were looking over your album of Portraits of Shakespeare, you showed me one which you remarked was very rare? It was a *round* picture, a *profile*, with a chin whisker. I told you I thought I had one. I found it today. It was printed as an ornamental centre-piece on the wrappers of an edition of Shakespeare, that I have, which was pubd. in London, *in parts*, and called the Commemoration Edn., because pubd. in 1864, in commemoration of the Poet's Tercentenary. It is in 12mo, well printed, and an *excellent edition*. The text seems a reprint of the Lansdowne Edn., and it contains Barry Cornwall's *Essay on Sh.*—This round vignette is on the covers of the parts. I have had mine (the *parts*, not the *covers*)[a] bound up into 1 volume, and a nice portly 12mo it is, in Hf. d'k green mor, gilt edges, extra.—. . .

Have you read Weiss' book yet? I have, the greater part of it. I cannot say that I like it very much. . . . I think, some of his criticisms are *unsound*: e.g. his view of the purport of the grand play of *Troilus & Cressida* being a *burlesque* on Homer's Iliad & his *heroes*. Oh! gammon! The character of *Ulysses* alone in T. & C., might have shown him different. He (Ulysses) is more[b] replete with utterances of the sublimest philosophy, of true states-manship, of *conduct in life* generally, than almost any other of the noble galaxy in the Plays. Weiss sees little more than the "indecency" of the play, as exhibited by poor old *Pandarus*. I'll bet he does not know the *meaning* of that proverbial line in one of Ulysses' immortal speeches,—

"One touch of Nature makes the whole world kin."[2] In fact, very few persons indeed *do* know its true meaning. . . .

---

[1] "and my poor *fool* is hanged": *Lr.* 5.3.306. White is badly wrong; Steevens first proposed that *fool* = Cordelia, and Malone and the tradition endorsed him.
[2] "One touch of Nature makes the whole world kin": *Tro.* 3.3.175; see note 1 to letter 171.

[a] (the *parts*, not the *covers*)] ↑(the *parts*, not the *covers*)↓ MS.
[b] He (Ulysses) is more] He ↑(Ulysses)↓ is ↑more↓ MS.

156:   8 January 1877

My dear Norris:

Doubtless you remember on that interesting evening we spent together with Mr. Furness, in his charming library, quite an animated discussion we had on the lines in *Hamlet*:

> "Or e'er those *shoes* were old,
> With which she followed my poor father's body,
> Like Niobe all tears."   (I, ii, 147.)

Mr. Furness and I contended that "shoes" was a probable misprint in the folio, for *shows*,[1] and you opposed the idea. Since that time I have often thought of the subject, and I am now more convinced than I then was that the Poet wrote *shows*. Let me say, however, that were I editing a "Hamlet," I should unhesitatingly print "shoes," for the reason that my rule is to let the Folio text alone, whenever it supplies a decently intelligible meaning. But this does not prevent one from speculating on the goodness or badness of proposed conjectural emendations. In this case, the context, as well as the construction of the sentence, favour the alteration. Hamlet had previously spoken of the "Formes, Moods, and *shewes* of griefe," which were the usual concomitants of death, and which he called "the Trappings and the suites of woe." It is evident that these "shows" were the mourning apparel, the "inky cloak," crape hatbands, and "customary suits of solemn black"; the external evidences of woe, worn by the relatives and friends of the deceased, to *show* their grief to the world; and it is these that Hamlet refers to, when he says he has "that within which passeth *show*." Observe, too, the phraseology, "*With* which she followed my poor father's body." Had *shoes* only been meant, I think Hamlet would have said "*In* which she followed"; *with which* suggesting the idea of carrying them with her, not on her feet. You will remember that Dr Ingleby first suggested this change of *shows* for "shoes," in *N. & Q.*, 1855, and afterwards in his "Shakespeare Fabrications," 1859. He supports it by several quotations from Warner, and Drayton, to prove that *shoe* is but an obsolete form of spelling *show*. One from *Albion's England*, III, 17, will suffice:

> "But what! shall Caesar doubt to fight against so brave a foe?
> No! Caesar's triumphs, with their spoils, will make the greater *shoe*."—

This is one of the passages which gave Voltaire a handle to ridicule our Poet, taking offence at the vulgar familiarity of Hamlet's alluding to his mother's *shoes*; and I am almost inclined to say, 'Is it any wonder he should?'—Mr. Dyce, in the Preface to the Second edition of his *Shakespeare*, is very bitter on Dr Ingleby, for, as he says, deliberately depriving the

Danish Queen of her world-famed "shoes"; but I confess I do not see much point to his sarcasm. The learned Doctor deprives her of "shoes," (which, no matter how black they were, have never been considered a "trapping of woe,") only to confer upon her a full suit of funeral appointments, *"with which"* she might very properly follow her deceased lord, "like Niobe all tears." Moreover, this reading is singularly confirmed by a similar typographical error in *King John*, one which is acknowledged to be such by Mr. Dyce himself, and by most of the best editors. In Act II, Sc. i, when Blanche says—

> "O, well did he become that lion's robe,
> That did disrobe the lion of that robe!"

the Bastard replies—

> "It lies as sightly on the back of him
> As great Alcides' [*sub.* lion's robe] *shows* upon an ass."[2]

In the Folio, "shows" here is misprinted "shooes"; and the Variorum commentators adduce numerous instances where the allusion to Hercules' immense shoes is judiciously introduced. But in this passage it would be simply ridiculous. What possible connection is there between the lion's robe now on the back of Austria, and the big shoes of Hercules on the back (!), or even "on the hoofs," of an ass?—The preterite of show—*shew*—was formerly often pronounced, as spelt, *shoo*, and it is so to this day by many New England people.[3] I never heard my mother-in-law, an educated lady, by the way, pronounce it in any other way: "the man *shew* (*shoo*) me a beautiful shawl." This pronunciation may help to account for the misprint of "shoes" for *shows*, in the Folio, which Theobald first corrected, making the sense plain: "The lion's robe on the back of this man Austria is about as becoming and sightly, as that worn by the great Alcides would look on the shoulders of an ass." This leaves the Bastard's contemptuous allusion perfect and appropriate.

All which is respectfully submitted by,

> Dear Norris,
> Your obedt. friend,
> Joseph Crosby.

---

[1]"shoes" was a probable misprint . . . for *shows*: Halliwell-Phillipps lists *shoe/show* in his *Dictionary of Misprints Found in Printed Books of the Sixteenth and Seventeenth Centuries* (Brighton: privately printed, 1887).

[2]O, well . . . ass: *Jn.* 2.1.141–44.

[3]The preterite of show . . . New England people: This pronunciation of the word was recorded late in the nineteenth century in the dialects of northern Scotland, Norfolk, Suffolk, Essex, and Leicester. In those dialects (as in modern West London Cockney) the present tense is identical to the preterite. (Private communication from Prof. Ian Hancock.)

157: 10 January 1877

If any of my notes or explanations will fill a crevice in the *Bib.*, when you have nothing better, use them: but I only wrote them for *you*.—[a]

My dear Norris:

I received your welcome letter of the 3d inst., and had a good laugh at your reception of Mr. *Virtuous* (!) Yorston's Irishman. I hardly think after that, that old Mr. Virtuous himself will be very apt to trouble you with his "letter of introduction." I am sorry enough that I gave it to him; but you know they *asked* me for it, and with my usual impetuosity I did it *without thinking*. It is well said that a man is never too old *to learn*; and I think I have learned not to run my head into a trap of that kind again soon.

Respecting the book itself,[1] however, I cannot say that I sympathize with you very deeply in being "humbugged" into subscribing for it; because I not only told you, but, as Burns says, "I tauld ye *weel*," I told you in the strongest language I could command, *not* to subscribe for it. I often think of those noble words of Othello, when Iago was trying to distil into his pure, unsuspecting heart the first bitter drops of poison, insinuating to him that because he was "black," perhaps his beloved Desdemona had become tired or disgusted with him, when compared with her former suitors—"the wealthy curled darlings of the nation,"—"*No, Iago, she had eyes, and chose me*." Changing the subject, I might say, you had eyes, and saw the "humbug"; and if, after seeing it, you chose it; if, after all the caution and warning I gave you that it was a "filthy-mantled pool," you still deliberately walked into it, dancing up to your chin, that the foul lake o'erstunk[b] your feet, and came out with your "nose in great indignation" because you smelt "all horse-piss," I must say you had no one but yourself to blame; you had *eyes*, and *chose* to do it. I know I ought, and would *like*, to sympathize with you and Mr. Fish, in getting so fearfully *stuck*; but truly I cannot see where any sympathy from me would be either legitimate or *acceptable*. . . .

[1] the book itself: Virtue and Yorston's rpt. of Virtue's Imperial Edn. of Knight's Shakespeare.

[a] If any . . .for *you*.—] ↑If any . . .for *you*.—↓ MS. [written above salutation and dateline on p. 1].
[b] o'erstunk] o'er-| stunk MS.

158: 10 January 1877

> . . . "*Ant.* You do mistake your business; my brother never
> Did urge me in his act: I did inquire it;
> And have my learning from some true reports,
> That[a] drew their swords with you. Did he not rather
> Discredit my authority with yours;
> And make the wars alike against my stomach,

Having alike your cause? Of this my letters
Before did satisfy you. If you'll patch a quarrel,
As matter whole you have to make it with,
It must not be with this."[1]

It is the last sentence to which I refer: and many of the best editors, from Rowe down to Dyce, have interpolated the word "not" into the text—"As matter whole you have *not* to make it with," thereby seriously injuring the metre. The whole trouble is from not taking the Poet's meaning of the little conjunction "as." In instances, "thick as leaves in Vallambrosa," he uses it for *as though*, or *as if*. Open your Shakespeare almost anywhere, and you will meet with this construction. *Tam. of Shr.* II, i, 160:

"with twenty such vile terms,
As had she studied to misuse me so."

Haml. IV, v, 103:

"And, *as* the world were now but to begin."

Ibid. IV, vii, 88:

"*As* he had been incorpsed and demi-natured."

With this use of "as," let us paraphrase the passage: "If you wish to get up a quarrel out of shreds and patches, as though the matter were whole and sound that you had to make it out of, it must not be with this flimsy complaint; this patch will show; anyone can see that it is patched up merely, and not the whole and sound substance for a quarrel that you desire it should seem to be made from."—

"If you'll patch a quarrel
As [though the] matter [were] whole you have
to make it of,
It must not be with this."—

Is not this plain and sufficient?[2] And any emendation or interpolation not only superfluous, but impertinent? I think so.—
Ever Yours,

Very Truly,
Joseph Crosby.

The only editors who retain the Folio reading are *Knight, Hudson, Grant White,* & the *Clarkes.* All others from *Rowe* down, including *Camb. Edd.* & *Globe,* insert "not."—

All's Well V, iii, 65.

> "Our own love waking cries to see what's done
> While shameful hate sleeps out the afternoon."

Here is an exceedingly tough passage. The *Globe* marks the first line with an obelisk (†), denoting it to be corrupt; and reads the last line—

> "While shame *full late* sleeps" &c.

I think the correct meaning and paraphrase is this: "Our true, just, conscientious love, waking to the worth of the lost object, laments "to see what's done"; while our former hatred, of which we are now justly and thoroughly ashamed, is laid to sleep for the rest of our days, and forever *extinguished*." You know the context; it is in the King's speech to Bertram, when he comes to his senses regarding his lost Helena. Singer explains the last clause thus: "Our shameful hate or dislike having slept out the period when our fault was remediable." But, if you will pardon the egotism, I infinitely prefer my own. It is more congruous with the rest of the King's train of thought; and besides it is easy & intelligible, and necessitates no change of text: and a reasonably sensible interpretation of the old Folio text is far preferable to any emendation. Don't you think so too? Of course, many passages *must* be amended, but the above, I think, is *not* one of them.

J. C.

[1] If you'll patch . . . this: *Ant.* 2.2.52–54.
[2] Is not this plain and sufficient?: One might object that the subjunctive signifier C's interpretation asks is not here as it is in the other Shn uses he cites.

[a] reports, / That] reports, That| / That MS. [deliberate use of catchword].

159: 11 January 1877

. . . I have this day recd a long letter from Dr Ingleby, which I will send you in my next. He has just discovered (he says) the true expln. of that very passage in A. & C. that I wrote you about early this week, "If you'll patch a quarrel" &c. But he will not send it to me, until I have first "studied" the passage, & sent him *my* elucidation. He flatters me highly for some others of my explns—especially that on "stricter,"[1] which he *adopts in toto*. He says if I fail to give the right solution of the A. & C. "quarrel" passage, my mind will be in better condition for *his*. Then he wants his *printed*, at least so I deem it, by what he says; but *you* must judge when you see his letter & his expln. He is also great on the word "imperseverant"[2] in *Cymb*. Altogether it is a very interesting letter, as soon as I have replied to it, you shall have it, as his elucidations on "crux"es are always admirable. . . .

[1] "stricter": *Cym.* 5.4.17.
[2] "imperseverant": *Cym.* 4.1.14.

161:   18 January 1877

. . . What you observe of the beauty of the typography of the Cambridge Ed. is every word true. It is just exquisite. I always admire it, whenever I use the book. *If only*, as you say, the *ink had been blacker*. I have in my library a work that I think is still more beautifully printed than the Boydell Sh., I mean Bowyer's National Illustrated Edn. of Hume's Hist. of England. It is the most superb specimen of printing I ever laid my eye on. The title-pages are magnificent; and *all* the letters are so *large*, & *fat*, and clear-cut, and *black*—black as jet itself—and on the best of thick paper, that a blind man could *almost* read it. It is in 10 vols. imperial folio, & has some 200 splendid steel engravings. And yet I bought this grand work (in Hf. russia, extra, sound and clean as new,) for $100.—It was pub. in 1806 in 70 Nos. at a guinea a No. The type is somewhat larger than the "Boydell." Altogether it is a sumptuous book; and one of the most striking peculiarities about it is the glossy *blackness* of the *ink*. Real black ink in print is one of the greatest *comforts* to the reader. As you say, it seems of late years to have been *lost*.—
. . .
I cannot say that I admire the "Sunday Press" conj.[1] in *Cymb*. I, i,—

<blockquote>
"O disloyal thing,
That should'st repair my youth, thou heap'st
A *Lear*'s age on me," for, "a *year*'s age."
</blockquote>

It does not *sound* like Shakespeare to my ear. Besides, why shd the poet be *thinking* of *Lear*, when composing *Cymbeline*? Lear was not a *historical character*, as was the case in "Cato's daughter,"—Æneas, Anchises, Brutus' Portia, &c. There really needs no change, as the old text is intelligible. "A year's age," at Cymbeline's time of life, like an extra inch added to the end of a man's nose, was "quite an item." And yet just look at the ingenuity of the edd. & Commentators:

Thou heap'st a yare age,	Theobald (Warb.)
" " " meer "	Do[2] conj.
" " " hoar "	Do conj.
" heapest many A year's age,	Hanmer
" heap'st Years, Ages,	Johnson conj.
" heap'st instead. A year's age,	Capell

```
"    heapest A year's age,      Steevens
"    heap'st A sear age,      Becket conj.
"    heapest— Ay,—years' age,      Jackson conj.
"    heap'st An age of years upon,      Long MS.
"      "      A Lear's age—Albany S. Press.
```

and no doubt many more, not recorded in the Camb. Ed.—

What you say of Dr Schmidt's definition of "medlar"—& "et cetera," is all "just so": only I think you are mistaken when you say that by 'arse' he means 'ass.' An *arse* is not an *ass*, by a jugful; and what *could* he mean by an "open-*ass*"? "Open-arse" must be the common, vulgar *name* of the "medlar" in some parts of England; tho' it is all news to me. As for 'c—t,' it is a well-known term for the *pud. mulieb.* in several languages, both ancient and modern. Horace, you remember, uses it in his Satires, as a *synonym* for *woman*, speaking of "teterrima *cunnus*"³ being the cause of the Trojan war. By the by, if you have the 1st edn. of *Minsheu* (1617)—look at it, and you will be amused. He has a long article on "cunt" (which was all omitted in his second edn. of 1627).ᵃ He gives (principally in Latin) a full, exhaustive etymology both of this word and "fuck," which he spells *fucke*—tracing them from the Oriental Hebrew &c. down through the Greek, Latin, &c. to his own day and language.

While on this forbidden subject, I will tell you, that I once wrote quite an essay on the word "*prick*," in Shakespeare. Another on "*overscutch'd* hus-wives," &c. Did I ever send you them? I remember illustrating the for-mer—the *prickly*, or rather, the *precarious* one—by a passage in *Romeo & Juliet*. Several of the poet's allusions to the *time of day* are explainable only by understanding this pun. *Priapus*, you know, (called commonly the "god of gardens,") was the god of *large and stiff pricks*. At school we were told that the Romans set up his image in their gardens as a scarecrow, to frighten off the birds. I have seen some of these *Priapuses*, still existing, in the "British Museum," and they all have this monstrosity—an enormously long, thick, & rigid *penis*. But it is not commonly known that the Romans made this divinity . . . do duty in the manufacture and erection of their *Sun-dials*, which being *garden* ornaments, perhaps gave Mr. Priapus his title to the "god of gardens." The circular dial-plate, engraved with the hours, was placed on the top of a pedestal, and on this dial-plate Priapusᵇ stood erect with his hand upon his enormous p—k, which said p—k thus became the *gnomon*, or *pointer*, of the dial; and when the sun shone out, thus gave the chaste Roman dames the correct "time of day." Now Sh., who seems to have known everything, must have been familiar with this little item in Roman horticulture. Notice how clearly it brings out the exact sense of Mercutio's banter with the Nurse⁴ (II, iv). . . .

> "*Proculeius*: Let me report to him
> Your sweet dependancy; and you shall find

> A conqueror that will *pray in aid* for kindness,[5]
> When he for grace is kneel'd to." (*A. & C.* V, ii)

In talking over this passage, you remember we found it difficult properly to harmonize the law-term with the sentiment of the speech. I now think I see how it was meant. *"Kindness"* is personified, and is the *outside party* for introduction to the suit. "You will find a conqueror, who, when kneel'd to for "grace"—*pardon*, will not only grant *that*, but will pray you—the court—*in aid*, viz. that "kindness" may be introduced as his (Caesar's) Co-suitor[c] in the action": he will be a conqueror who will not only grant the *pardon* you ask for; but will pray you to allow him to *add* "kindness" to his "grace," "whereas you sue for "grace"—pardon—only, he will grant that, and the "kindness," moreover, to grant you whatever *further* favours you may require of him."—This, I think, gets in the full force of the *legal term.* . . .

When Prof. Corson made his emendation on that *"busie lest"* crux in the *Tempest*, I sent a copy of it to Dr Ingleby,[6] together with a synopsis of my letter in reply to it to Corson. In a very pleasant letter, just recd from the Dr, he says:

> "I return herewith Corson's slip. I am sorry he should disseminate such conjectures, which have the double vice of throwing suspicion on the folio text, without elucidating the difficulties in it. If his note was only "half serious," there was the more reason why he should have kept it to himself. I particularly thank you for sending me a copy of your well-written and interesting reply to him. As you know my view of the passage already, I need not discuss it further. The only question worth considering is how far a dislocation in the text of an intelligible sentence should be allowed to open the door to emendation. Your letter is chiefly valuable to me as suggesting a new chapter for my book[7] in reply to Halliwell's tentative rule. The examples you cite in support of it do not alarm me in the least. One of these I have explained in the "Supplementary Notes" to *Shakespeare Hermeneutics.* You will find it at the bottom of p. 156. One of the others—"who cannot want the thought"—was fully explained & justified by Professor Spencer Baynes; and the others will all fall in so soon as we get them into position, or view them under the proper angle and in the right light. I have no faith whatever in Shakespeare having been either a muddle-brained thinker or a slip-shod writer. All that is wanted for understanding him is patience, faith, and perception. x x x Grant White has returned to New York. He was my guest for part of two days, and I found him a thorough gentleman and scholar. If you meet him, ask him how he liked his moonlight walk under our old trees. . . ."

I have not yet answered either of the Doctor's letters, but shall do so in a day or two. If he were not quite so conceited and positive about everything, I shd like him better. And he is so admirable an expounder of the text of Sh. himself, that I always write to him with fear & trembling, expecting every minute I may be "smashed"; as he says of himself speaking of Furnivall. But what must Furnivall's conceit be, when he talks of "smashing" a man of Ingleby's learning and abilities?—But laying aside all malice, don't you honestly think Furnivall does deserve a whole heap of credit, as a painstaking, indefatigable, *editor*? . . .

[1] The [Albany] "Sunday Press" conj.: *Cym.* 1.1.133.
[2] Do: Ditto.
[3] "teterrima *cunnus*": Horace, *Satires* I.iii.107 (slightly misquoted).
[4] Mercutio's banter with the Nurse: *Rom.* 2.4.112–13.
[5] *pray in aid* for kindness: *Ant.* 5.2.27.
[6] I sent a copy of it to Dr Ingleby . . . to Corson: These survive in Folger MS. C.a. 7, under date 14 December 1876; the crux is at *Tmp.* 3.1.15.
    [7] for my book: I.e., for vol. 2 of *Shakespeare: The Man and the Book* (1881); Halliwell's tentative rule is presumably the statement in "The Formation of the Text" in his Folio Sh Edn. (1851–65): ". . . no phraseology shall be altered, if it can be shown to be consonant to the grammatical usages of the time, unless it can be distinctly proved to be a mere vulgarism of language" (1: 266). Ingleby was no doubt determined on a straiter course for editorial emendation.

[a] (which . . .1627).] (which . . .1627. MS.
[b] Priapus] ↑Priapus↓ MS.
[c] Co-suitor] Co-| suitor MS.

162:   25 January 1877   Athens, Ohio

. . . I must, ere I forget it, try to explain the objection you state to my exposition of "prick of noon,"[1] in *R. & J.* You say—"If the hand of the god Priapus was on his penis, then the 'hand of the dial' was *not* 'on the prick of noon.' "[a]—Now, as Dr Ingleby would say, there are two or three items of wisdom to be remembered in the case. (1) That Priapus with his penis in hand, and the circular plate with its figures, are all necessary to constitute *one* figure or idea, viz. that of a *Sun-dial*. (2) That Sh. is punning or quibbling on *point* and "prick," which, as you & Dyce say, mean the same thing. Now let us look at the language, apart from the figure. "The bawdy hand of the dial is on the prick,"—not of *Priapus*, for had he said that merely, there would have been no quibble; it would have been a bare assertion of fact—but of *noon*: the bawdy hand is on the "prick" or *pointer*, which throws its shadow directly on the *point* of 12 o'clock: and all, remember, included in the *one* figure of a *Sun-dial*. Mercutio would have no *pun* at all to laugh at, unless he stated it just as he does. The image of the *dial* includes the whole, Priapus, penis, hand, plate, figures, pedestal, & sun. The "bawdy hand" of this "dial" is said to be on the "prick" of noon, because it is on the god's prick [*point*] which *points* to the *point* of "noon."—Do you see the "point"? It is as plain to me as the nose on a man's face; plainer than the nose on some men's,—brother Fish's, for instance.—Sh. would have appealed to the *poet's license*, a very limited—even infinitesimal—amount of which would make his figure & quibble perfect; and Mercutio himself would have pointed to the image of the garden-god before them, in confirmation, if any supersubtle hypercritic should doubt his joke and its apparent application. 'There,' he would say, 'stands Priapus, with prick in his bawdy hand, which *prick points* precisely to the *prick-point* of noon'; why, then should I not observe that "The bawdy hand of the dial is on the prick of noon"?—Mrs. Nurse, remembering her "maidenhead at twelve year old," and the happy times she had spent with her husband "a merry man, rest his soul,"—*she* appreciated Mercutio's allusion perfectly; and one can imagine the dignity of the old lady as she straightens up, and bridles, and simpers, "Out upon you! What a man are you!"—

You ask me how I "found out about Priapus in the gardens." I learnt most of what I know about *him* from Lemprière's *Classical Dictionary*, when I was a schoolboy; and from the Latin authors generally, all of whom mention him as the "god of gardens," who protected flowers and fruit from the depredations of the birds. Then I saw myself pictures of his Horticultural Godship in books, which generally did ample justice to his "particular vanity." Finally, I saw figures of the god himself in bronze or copper in the *British Museum*, though they generally present a *rear as*pect, standing with their—faces—to the wall. The *thing* that struck me—and *may* have *generated* the idea in my brain that the above was Sh.'s meaning in the passage in question—was, that these figures almost universally had their "bawdy" hands on their rigid and elongated p—ks. Whether Sh. ever saw any of these Priapuses or not, I could not say. But most likely he did. If not in the *British Museum*, as there was no *British Museum* I believe in his day, then he may, in some other places in England: or he may have seen them in Italy—in Verona, as some biographers think he had visited the Continent, both Germany and Italy. But there is no accounting for Sh.'s *omniscience.* When Cadwal and Polydore are burying Fidele, (in *Cymbeline*), one says, "We must lay him with his head to the east,[2] father has *a reason* for it," how did Sh. know that this is the common—almost universal—rule in the Northern Counties in England? . . . I have written so much on these bawdy[b] subjects in this & my last letter, that both you & I may say, "an ounce of civet, good apothecary, to *sweeten* my imagination withal." . . .

[1] "prick of noon": *Rom.* 2.4.113.
[2] with his head to the east: *Cym.* 4.2.255.

[a] 'on the prick of noon.' "] "on the prick of noon." MS.
[b] these bawdy] these MS.

163:   2 February 1877

. . . I thought you would agree with me in my expln. of "bawdy hand of the dial," &c. in *R. & J.*—It seems to me that it *must* have that allusion. I am very well aware that Sh. uses *prick, prick'd*, &c. frequently in other senses: it by no means *always* refers to the *membrum virile*. And it is as "distasteful" to me, as it is to you, to give this expln. to *any* passage of his. . . . Such allusions in his day, instead of insulting or offending the taste of his readers or hearers, were accepted as *witty* & *piquant*, even by refined women. I need not tell *you* how very much *less guilty* our dearly-beloved Sh. is, in this regard, than most of the poets and dramatists of the Elizabethan, Jacobian, & Carolian eras. Whenever he does introduce a pun or quibble of this character, it is generally done in a spirit of fun or frolic, & never purposely with any impure object.— . . .

—I have read Grant White's last art. on Sh. in the Febry "Galaxy."— There is not *much* to be learned from these articles. He is bound that we shall not forget that it is *he*—**Grant White**—the *great White* authority on every matter Shakespearian, is writing these papers for our benefit and instruction. His superciliousness and *patronage* are apt to *provoke*, rather than please & guide: as his *own* honour & praise are quite as much looked after, as the Poet's. I don't like, either, the way he speaks of æsthetic, or higher criticism, which he designates as "impertinence"; and he has no right to call Ulrici "a mad mystic," or Gervinus "a literary Dogberry." He takes care, however, to tell us that **he** *could* have written æsthetic criticism in *his edition*, as well as these men have done, if he had so desired.— . . .

I have just finished reading W. Aldis Wright's C. P. Ed. of *As You Like It*. I have gone through it with a good deal of care and interest. Taken altogether, it is, as Bottom would say, "A very *good piece of work*, I assure you." Wright has the same aversion to "æsthetic, or what is termed *higher*, criticism"—"*sign post* criticism," that Grant White has, and about which he speaks so dogmatically in the Feb. No. of the "Galaxy." I cannot agree entirely with these learned commentators; because I think that *some* æsthetic criticism is not only useful, but absolutely *essential* to the correct understanding of the play. . . . As you observe, we are all too apt to run too much after *philological* explns. only. These, of course, are also of absolute importance: The text *must* be understood *verbally* & *critically*; but commentators should not confine themselves *exclusively* to philological explanations. The "Rugby Series" run, I think, into the other extreme; their notes are almost entirely æsthetic, & some of them very fine indeed, especially in *Hamlet* & *Coriolanus*. A happy union of the two would make a perfect edition. Still, of the two, the "C. P. Edns" are by far the *best*, for the purpose of young scholars; inasmuch as a philological, & grammatical, & verbal knowledge of the *text* is of such *vital* consequence; and must come before any æsthetic criticism could be comprehended.— . . . Several of Mr. Wright's notes are new, original, and very interesting. . . . In one place he makes a *conjecture* that *I made some 3 years ago*, viz. in the line, "This is the right butterwomen's *rank* to market,"[1] where I have a note proposing to read "rack" for "rank." Did I ever communicate it to you? My only fear about it was, that it was an *Americanism*, as I thought; but it is *not*, as Mr.

Wright shows from Cotgrave's Dictionary. It is an old English word for "amble." I think there is no doubt that it is the right word here. Orlando's verses go "hobble-de-hobble-de," just like a *racking* horse over the pavement. I never heard the word "rack" applied in England to this pace of a horse; there they call it a *canter*: it is exactly what the clown afterwards designates as "the false gallop" of horses, or verses. Read Wright's note on p. 126.—Do you know I felt about half jealous when I saw my old conjecture in Mr. Wright's note, and sorry I had not communicated it to something,—the *"Bibliopolist,"* or *"N. & Q."*—I should have done so, had I been *sure* it was in use as a term for a pace in horses in Sh.'s day.— . . .

Ant. & Cleo: I, i, 40:—

> "*Cleo.*   Excellent falsehood!
> Why did he marry Fulvia and not love her?
> I'll seem the fool I am not; Antony
> Will be himself.
> *Ant.*   But stirr'd by Cleopatra."

The only way that I see to make these lines harmonize with the rest of this scene, and dovetail with the context, is by adopting the reading of Capell, "*I seem* the fool," instead of "*I'll seem* the fool," and by placing a dash—after "Will be himself," instead of a full stop, to indicate that Antony's speech is an interruption of Cleopatra's. The whole scene is one of exquisite banter and coquetry between the royal lovers. Cleopatra maintains her hold upon Antony, not so much by flattery and exhibitions of affection, as by *teasing*; and she plays her part splendidly. . . .

What a delightful scene of royal, exalted love-making! Caprice, taunts, teasing, on one side; forbearance on the other; and *love*, not platonic by any means, but animal, sensual, passionate, love, on both. It would require the talents of a magnificent actress to perform the character of Cleopatra, as designed by Shakespeare. . . .

> "The itch of his affection should not then
> Have *nick'd* his captainship."[2] . . .

In some of the provinces of England, and I don't know but in New England also, when an animal—a young horse, bull, boar, &c.,—has been *cut* or *altered*, it is said to have been[a] "nicked." I imagine that the rough-spoken soldier Enobarbus uses "nick'd" with that meaning here. "The itch of his affection should not then have gelt, or *emasculated*, his captainship; i.e. enfeebled, and destroyed it. . . .

---

[1] The right butterwomen's *rank* to market: *AYL* 3.2.98.
[2] *nick'd* his captainship: *Ant.* 3.13.8. Howard Staunton had proposed the gloss "emas-

culated" in his edn. of 1864, but without rationalizing it; C's interpretation (not in *OED*; not in Variorum *Ant.* 1907) fits the emasculation imagery associated with Antony at Actium, e.g., 3.7.69–70.

^ato have been] to ↑have↓ been MS.

165:   21 February 1877

. . . I have finished *A. & C.*, & am now on *"The Merry Wives"*—a much easier play—yet with much in it to study nevertheless. By the way, let me tell you a little matter that I came across the other day in reading Sir W. Scott's novel of *Kenilworth*, that illustrates a line in this play, & is probably new to you. You remember in the 1st Act, near the beginning, *Justice Shallow* accuses Sir John Falstaff of killing his dogs, stealing his deer, &c.; and Falstaff replies

"But not kissed your keeper's daughter."[1]

In *Kenilworth* there is this dialogue:—

> *"Sussex.* By my faith, I wish Will Shakespeare no harm. He is a stout man at quarterstaff, and single falchion, though, as I am told, a halting fellow; and he stood, they say, a tough fight with the rangers of old Sir Thomas Lucy, of Charlecot, when he broke his deer-park, and kissed his keeper's daughter.
> *Elizabeth.* That matter was heard in council, and we will not have this fellow's offence exaggerated—there was no kissing in the matter, and the defendant put the denial on record."—

Now isn't that good, and worth knowing? and a much better explanation than the ordinary one, which is a mere conjecture, that the line is the refrain of some old ballad. . . .

—In Hastie's Catalogue I saw 2 odd volumes advertised of *Rowe's edition*. I bid for them, hoping to *improve* my copy of Rowe, which is a wretched one. (By the way, if you ever see one advertised, please let me know.) When they came, they were not *Rowe's* at all, but 2 odd volumes of other editions; the 1st vol. of *Harding's*, and the 7th of *Dr Hugh Blair's*. As they did not cost much I did not return them. Harding's vol. has Rowe's Life, Johnson's Preface, Farmer's Essay, and 2 or 3 plays, with some pretty plates. Blair's is a vol. of a *good edn.*, with notes, and I would like to have the whole edition. Then I got 2 vols. of *Dodsley's Old Plays*; of the edition of 1744; and *6 vols.* of the 1825 or Collier's edition, of Dodsley. Each vol. contains about 5 old plays, and is complete in itself. This is a *capital* edition. I like it better than W. C. Hazlitt's new edition, as far as paper & printing are concerned. It is well printed, on good ribbed white paper, and contains excellent *Notes* & Introductions. The vols. are in cloth, *uncut,* and only cost about 90 cents a vol.—I am having them bound in Hf. mor., *uncut,* and they are a welcome & useful addition to my library. . . .

I was real sorry to learn of your disappointment in the copy of Ben Jonson's first folio. By the by, is not yours the same copy that I once sent on a bid for[2] at some Auction in New York, & missed because my bid was not received in time? You remember that you wrote the Auctioneers about it. It was sold very low—I think for only $10. for the 2 vols.—A 2d Fol. Shak. was sold at the same Sale for $75.., bought by some gentleman near New York. I remember your telling me that the Auctioneers said that the 2d vol. of *Jonson* was a "made-up" copy. I think it very wrong—*criminal*—for the compilers of "Catalogues" to *deceive* in this way. We *ought* always to make them take back books bought under such false pretences, & pay all expenses; *then* they would perhaps learn to be more *careful.* . . .

[1] "But not kissed your keeper's daughter": *Wiv.* 1.1.113.
[2] I once sent on a bid for: See letter 120.

166:   21 February 1877

. . . I have the work you speak of—Mrs. C. Clarke's "Girlhood of Sh: Heroines"; but I never read much of it. Its object seems to be to interest the young—especially young women—in these characters, by putting them in supposititious positions in their youth, so their future lives, as narrated by the Poet, may be studied & made more intelligible. My copy is a very beautiful one, cost a guinea in London, 3 vols. sq. 12mo; new, red vellum cloth, gilt edges, sides, & backs. Each vol. contains several Tales, & nearly (one, over) 500 pages each. It is published by Bickers & Co, Leicester Square. Is yours the same edition? What did it cost you?—. . .

I entirely agree with you about that long, dull, un-Shakespearian passage[1] in *Cymbeline.* Sh. no more *wrote it* than I did. It has not one of his earmarks—neither in style, versification, nor sense. Then, moreover, it does no good to the *action* of the play. Cut it out, & the connection is still perfect. From the time Posthumus falls asleep to speak with his dear Imogen "in silence," to the time he awakes, all that is down is absolutely *impertinent.* Then that "label" business! How utterly unlike anything we have in Shakespeare that is, and its absurd, riddling interpretation! Pope, you know, first put it in the margin, as not Shakespeare's; and Capell put his "asterisks" against the greater part of it. The common opinion is, that it was foisted in by the players, as you say, "for scenic effect." We know that there are other lines, and sentences, that are so foisted in, throughout these glorious works. R. G. White points out several, & I think rightly.

Hudson thinks that Sh. inserted it to gratify some friend, and that it is the work of some outside hand. Very possibly. Others, again, think that Sh. may have had it on hand, and worked it in here, although impertinent to the scene, and of no use—only to prolong it, and make a show, while Posthumus was asleep. This I do not believe: because I cannot suppose *Sh. ever wrote such poor stuff*—poor in language, & poor in thought and imagination. Sh.'s work speaks for itself. It is as easily recognizable as a genuine bank-note is from a counterfeit. But there it is in the old copies; and we must let it stand now. All we can do is to protest, in a note, against laying its authorship to our great Poet. Hudson's idea that he complaisantly permitted some one of his London friends or companions—or possibly some of the players—to write & insert it—as a sort of mythological or classical *show*, to fill in the time & give an "effect," while P. was asleep, is not an unlikely one.—. . .

[1] that long, dull, un-Shakespearian passage: In *Cym.* 5.4., the theophany of Jupiter.

167: 24 February 1877

. . . What you say about the dates &c. of White's edition is very interesting. When I bought my first copy of White—the best, thick-paper,[a] edition, I took it, as it came out, 3 or 4 vols. at a time. I paid $1..50 a volume for it, as I see by referring back, for all but the 1st (last pubd.) vol., which was $250, making the set cost me $19.00. I was aware that the price was advanced afterwards, tho' I never, I believe, saw it advertised by the publishers. I bought a new set of the *thin-paper* edn.—same typography—for $10.— which I afterwards sold. As you say, I think Mr. Francis will keep his copy *some time* ere he get $35.00 for it. I did not know it was "scarce," did you? It was stereotyped I believe; so the publishers can easily get out new copies to supply the demand. I noticed that a copy of the really scarce *large-paper* edition was sold at Hastie's Sale for $120.—$10. a vol.—a splendid copy in Hf. olive morocco, gilt tops, uncut, only 48 copies printed.—I should have said *Menzie's*, not *Hastie's* sale. At the same Sale a sumptuous copy of Knight's original edn. with 530 *inserted* portraits, views, &c. extended to 9 vols., in crushed levant morocco, gilt tops, uncut, sold for about $25.. a vol. As to the *dates* of Grant White's edition,[1] I think *he* is "wrong"—not *you*. I know that mine was one of the very *earliest*, as I only recd 3 or 4 vols, at a time, & had to wait—sometimes a year—for more. The dates in my vols. are: Vols. 2, 3, 4, 5, *entered* 1858—*published* (title pages) 1859 (probably early in the year): Vols. 6, 7, 8, *entered* 1859—*published* 1859 (close of the year); Vols. 9, 10, *entered* 1860, *published* 1861; Vols. 11, 12, *entered* 1861, *published* 1861; Vol. 1, *entered* 1865, *published* 1865. What I mean by '*published*' is the dates of the titlepages.—So he is entirely "wrong" about the date *1857*, and also that of *1862*. I presume, by what you say of the *N. A. Review*,[2] that the *first four* vols. (Comedies) came out in 1858 (close of the year), tho' the title-page dates on mine are 1859. I well remember waiting for the next three vols. *several months*, tho' they have the same year (1859) on their titlepages. Then there was a long interval—nearly 2 years before the 9th & 10th vols. came out, and nearly another year before the 11th & 12th did. The date *1862*—that White gives you—does not occur on any of my vols.—The 9th & 10th were entd at Sta. Hall *1860*, & the 11th & 12th in *1861*, and all the last four dated on titlepages *1861*.—The copy that you sent me is at the binder's; so I do not know what date it carries;—but I think the *publishing* dates are all later; the dates of *entering* of course must be the same.—. . . My copy of C. Knight's *Second Pictorial* I also took as it came out in London—generally receiving two parts at a time; but all the 8 vols. have *1867* on the titlepages. How is that? It was certainly two years, or probably longer, being issued. Were all the Titlepages printed together at the close of the work? They must have been, I suppose, to have a uniform date. I entirely approve of what you say about dating editions. Let each vol. have the year on its titlepage when it was *first* issued. If a work is several years in publishing, make the dates accordingly—as the *Cambridge Edition* has them. Then, if the work is stereotyped, & a 2d or 3d edn. issued, from precisely the same plates, keep the same old date; so there can be no mistake about when a vol. or work was first pubd. It is all right to change the date or year, if the edition or plates are changed in any way; as in Dyce's 3d edition, for instance. I am, like you, sorry to see different years of dates to Mr. Furness' volumes. Twenty years hence, how is anyone to know *when* it was published?—I am glad to learn that his *Hamlet* is so nearly ready. I wish it could be put on the booksellers' counters on the *23d April*, here, and in England too.—. . .

Notwithstanding Miss Neilson's divorce from her husband, or her husband's from her, or both, still, when on the stage, in the character of *Juliet*, I must claim that my quotation is apposite:—

> "Thou hast the sweetest face I ever look'd on:
> Sir, as I have a soul, she is an *angel*."[3]

In her *private rôle*, and considering as *true* the antics and adulteries she is charged with, perhaps it were just as apposite to say of her, as someone (I forget who) of the old Dramatists named his play:—"'Tis pity she's a whore!"—. . .

---

[1] As to the *dates* of Grant White's edition: See *Papers of the Bibliographical Society of America* 71 (1977): 279–94.

[2] *N. A. Review:* The *North American Review* notice by E. H. Abbott of the White Edn., January 1859, pp. 244–53.

[3] "Thou hast . . . an *angel*"; *H8* 4.1.43–44; C may be alluding to the fact that Anne Bullen was herself later accused of adultery.

[a] thick–paper] thick–I paper MS.

168: 26 February 1877

. . . "Then like *hedgehogs*"[1] &c. (*Temp.*) *Fairies* of one class,—the small or pigmy elves—were supposed to put on the form of *hedgehogs*, because the hedgehog is an animal that is nocturnal in its habits, weird in its movements, and has a ghostly reputation on account of its *whining*—("thrice and once the *hedgepig whined*,"[2] *Macb*), and because plants wither where it works, as it cuts off their roots.—In the North of England, *urchin* is the common term for the *hedgehog*, from, I suppose, its Latin name *echinus*.— And so, because *fairies* are small and mischievous, and *children* are small and mischievous, *a child* and an *urchin* are sometimes synonymous. "You little *urchin!*"—*That's* worth knowing, ain't it?

J. C.

[1] "Then like *hedgehogs*": *Tmp.* 2.2.10.
[2] the *hedgepig whined*": *Mac.* 4.1.2.

169: 26 February 1877

. . . Mr. Leighton's views on critical explanations &c., and mine, don't seem to *hitch* well together, on hardly anything. My note on "Affection," &c.,[1] which you adopted at first, which even Mr. "Dean" Fish said was *right*; and which Mr. Veteran Hudson was so delighted with, and in such a hurry to adopt, that he forgot (?) whether I or he himself was the father of it—this, Mr. Leighton does not agree with "entirely," yet he condescends to say it is "interesting." As for the other in this Month's Bibliopolist,[2] that on "*stricter* render," &c.,[3] which Mr. Hudson took to his bosom at once, and which Dr Ingleby, who (in the *Hermeneutics*) had written the only really good & exhaustive note on the difficult passage, even he paid it the delicate compliment of adopting as correct, *this* Mr. Leighton had found out long ago. "The meaning which he [I] educes is one which I had already adopted in my reading, but I had never so carefully analyzed the passage as he has done."—Well, I am glad to hear it.—It gives me renewed confidence in the explanation; and I am pleased to know that there is *one* point on which we can agree, although he *did* know it *before* he saw it in the pages of the *Bibliopolist*. It is undoubtedly a compliment to be even *second* best to a poet

and dramatist.—He has sent a copy of the "Sons of Godwin" to the Editor of the *Bibliopolist* to be reviewed. Isn't that a hint for *you*, my boy? Come, my dear fellow, buckle on your whole armour, and give us a first-rate critique & review of Bro. W. Leighton's New Drama. But you must not stint your encomiums on it: no half-way or half-hearted eulogy will be satisfactory. I am glad he has not "hinted" me; I fear I should have to act on Enobarbus' advice, "Would you praise Cæsar, say 'Cæsar': **go no further**": and that would not suit *him*, at all. You must make him "Ho! the *nonpareil*: the *Arabian bird.*"—I am ashamed of myself for writing this way of Leighton; I am really sorry for it; because he is a nice, good fellow, and *I hope* a *sound* scholar: but somehow I cannot—at least do not—*take to him* as I ought. I cannot eradicate the idea out of my head that he is *shallow*; like so many of the so-styled "self-made" men—spoiled in the making. He is certainly a *gentleman*, and, I think, free from that intolerable bane of genius, conceit; he writes fairly well, spite of his *orthography*, [in his last letter to me he spells "encourage" with an 'i']—yet there seems something *loose* about his style, or thoughts; I don't think he has had the solid rock of a *classical* education (I mean a *sound, radical* one) to rest his subsequent studies and attainments upon. He seems to me to be a man who could, offhand, make a pretty speech at a dinner party, or write up a "neat," little complimentary essay on almost any subject given him. I'll bet you that he would not hesitate, from any *suspicion* of his ability, to write you a Review of Mr. Furness' new *Hamlet* for the *Bibliopolist*, should you ask him. He will, *either*, "roar you, that it will do any man's heart good to hear him"; *or*, "he will aggravate his voice so that he will roar you as gently as any sucking dove"—ay, "an 'twere any nightingale."—But ask him suddenly for some ordinary verbal *derivation* or *definition*, and I question whether he could answer as well as some of the poor frightened girls[4] that I "examined" the other day. He would "bethump" you with no end of *words*, and wind you round & round in a labyrinthine maze of *talk*; but this would not make the certificate of scholarship forthcoming, from a sharp "board." As Holofernes says of the Don—"He draweth out the thread of his verbosity *finer* than the *staple* of his argument." But I had better cry a halt to my nonsense, or you may give me a hint to look out for my own "verbosity."—
. . .

    You refer to two expressions in *Hamlet* that have often & often worried my poor brains to know what they meant; "country matters,"[5] and "puppets dallying."[6] I cannot now pretend to give any satisfactory explanation. You know of course what all the commentators have guessed, so I need not repeat that. It is just as like as not that Hamlet *meant* to be as *broad & vulgar* as he could, to deceive Ophelia, & the rest, into the idea he was *mad*. Could "Country matters," then, be "*cunt*'ry matters"? This is a fearfully rough expression to attribute to the *prince* & the lady. Yet it *may* be the poet meant nothing else. As for "puppets dallying," I give it up. Some say it means if he could see the images of *babies* in her eyes—the diminutive figures one sees, when looking into another's eyes. Terribly far-fetched. Dr Schmidt thinks it refers to some "puppet show" (probably connected with the play), in which Hamlet & Ophelia were to take part.—"*Dallying*," and "*dalliance*," you know, in Sh. often mean the *act of coition*: the meaning then would be, he could tell how she was affected if he might hug or embrace her, as the puppets hugged & embraced in the show. I cannot believe that "puppets" meant her *breasts*. "Puppets" were *dolls*—images made up to represent men & women. How do you get *breasts* out of "puppets"? "*Mammets*" would come nearer to *breasts*; but I cannot find *any* connection between "puppets" & *breasts*.—. . . .

[1] "Affection," &c.: *WT* 1.2.138.
[2] this Month's Bibliopolist: It actually appeared in the December 1876 *Bibliopolist*.
[3] "*stricter* render," &c.: *Cym.* 5.4.17.
[4] the poor frightened girls: C was Examiner of Teachers for the Zanesville Public Schools in 1877.
[5] "country matters": *Ham.* 3.2.116.
[6] "puppets dallying": *Ham.* 3.2.247.

170:   1 March 1877

. . . I hate it that Englishmen should suppose that Wilkes is speaking for *many* Americans on "Shakespeare, from an *American* point of view." I am very sure that *few* cultivated readers of Shakespeare entertain any such "views" of the Poet—in America. Just think for a moment of the absurdity & untruth of one of his main arguments, against Americans—especially the young—reading Shakespeare—viz[a] the fear that he will inculcate in their minds a perverted regard for *aristocracy*! That Englishmen—nobility especially—have advocated & upheld Shakespeare, because he advocated & upheld their class, & favoured monarchy—as opposed to republicanism; and that Americans have blindly & foolishly permitted themselves to be "bull-dozed" into reading & admiring the Poet, from love of imitating the opinions of "foreigners." That, as Americans, we do not want any "Shakespeare" in ours; especially keep him out of the schools, & out of the hands of the young & susceptible. They might learn to like Queen Elizabeth, or Victoria, better than Tilden, or John Morrisey, and prefer *Hamlet*, & *Henry IV*, to Wilkes' "Spirit of The Times," which would be a lamentable thing, you know. This ass hopes, I suppose, to tickle the patriotic ears of the groundlings with such arguments, but it is "too late a week" for *him* to write down Shakespeare in America. He might take *The Bible*, and put it through the very same course of reasoning, and by picking out isolated passages, such e.g. as "Fear God, and *honour the King*," prove that its tendencies were aristocratic, and monarchical, & consequently "un-American," & so to be kept away from the young lest it might contaminate their innate principles of *freedom, equality, & fraternity.* But a truce to Wilkes & his book.—

I have read every word of Fleay's Marlowe's *Edw. II.*, Introductions, Text, Notes, & all. It is well worth it. . . . Marlowe's *Edward II* is a very good historical Play—*for Marlowe.* The text has few, if any, difficulties; and his lines run along with an easy flow. It is said to resemble *Richard II*; but except in the horrible death of the King, in the last Act, I cannot trace much likeness. It has none of those fine passages, & exquisite descriptions, that remain on the mind *forever*, that are in *Rich. II.* Nothing like that touching garden scene,[1] where the Queen overhears the gardeners discussing affairs of state, & the old gardener, "old Adam's likeness," plants a bank of rue where the queen dropped a tear; no such magnificent episode as that on *England*,[2] beginning "This royal throne of kings, this sceptred isle, This earth of majesty," &c.; no such discriminating characterization as that of the ambitious Bolingbroke,[3] giving the tribute of his supple knee to a brace of draymen, or vailing his bonnet to an oysterwench, in order to supplant his cousin in the love of the people, and get the sceptre into his own hand; no heart-stirring & affecting descriptions like that of Bolingbroke's & Richard's progress through London, where—

> "You would have thought the very windows spake,
> So many greedy looks of young and old
> Through casements darted their desiring eyes
> Upon his visage, and that all the walls
> With painted imagery had said at once
> 'Jesu, preserve thee! Welcome, Bolingbroke!' "

x x x

> "*Duch.* Alack, poor Richard! Where rode he the whilst?
> *York.* As in a theatre the eyes of men,
> After a well-graced actor leaves the stage,
> Are idly bent on him that enters next,
> Thinking his prattle to be tedious,
> Even so, or with much more contempt, men's eyes
> Did scowl on gentle Richard; no man cried 'God save him'!
> No joyful tongue gave him his welcome home;
> But dust was thrown upon his sacred head;
> Which with such gentle sorrow he shook off,
> His face still combating with tears and smiles,
> The badges of his grief and patience,
> That had not God, for some strong purpose, steel'd
> The hearts of men, they must perforce have melted
> And barbarism itself have pitied him."[4]

&c. &c. &c.

But how easy it becomes for the frequent & loving reader & student of *Shakespeare* to pick out his glorious work! I had almost said that I could have known *Edw. II* was *not* by *Shakespeare*, had I been blindfolded. Mr. Fleay has done very good work in the editing of the play. The Introductions contain, besides large extracts from the old chroniclers, where Marlowe got his materials, a great deal of useful matter not generally found in introductions, regarding the[b] æsthetic qualities of the play,[c] what the critics have said of it, its division among the actors, history of the Stage, and stage business, &c.—. . .

[1] that touching garden scene: 3.4.
[2] episode. . . . on *England*: 2.1.40–66.
[3] characterization . . . of the ambitious Bolingbroke: 1.4.23–36.
[4] "You would . . . pitied him": 5.2.12–36.

[a] viz] ↑viz↓ MS.
[b] regarding the] regarding its [*the* written over *its*] MS.
[c] of the play,] ↑of the play,↓ MS.

171:   9 March 1877

. . . I am glad you were pleased with my note on "one touch of nature"[1] &c. There cannot be a doubt that it is right; i.e. that the commonly assigned meaning of the line is entirely wrong. Yet how few *know it*. I sent it to Hudson a couple of years ago, but he thought it a "pity" to disturb the bit of sentimental twaddle, or jingle, generally attached to the words! I'll bet you a cake, however, that he *has it* in his new edition. He *may* acknowledge it; tho' I am inclined to think that all the acknowledgment that *I* shall get[2]— for *scores* of such explanations—(many thought out after much trouble & care)—will be a *general* one, in his "Preface": e.g.—"I also take this opportunity of thanking my Western friend, Mr. J. Crosby, of Zanesville, Ohio, for some suggestions received from time to time during the preparation of this edition."—That, you know, pays the obligation, as so many of my business debtors are now doing, at about 5 cents on the dollar, yet grants him a receipt in full of all demands legal & equitable. I don't grumble. Tho' I get *no* credit for my work, I shall recognize it again in print, myself; and shall have the satisfaction of knowing that it will do *somebody* good, all the same. I must say, candidly, that the good old gentleman—apart from his voracious appetite for "**adopting**"—has always treated me, and all my conjectures—readings, explanations, references, &c. &c. very courteously & kindly. He has appeared & acted more like a *father* towards a studious & forward son—than as a *master*. I should never have *dared* to write all these *hundreds* & *hundreds* of pages of MS. notes (many *crude* no doubt—how could it be otherwise where there were so many?) to Grant White, or Mr. Furnivall. . . .

I have been reading & *studying*—yes *studying*—Milton. He is harder often to accurately understand than Shakespeare. I presume because I am so unfamiliar as yet with the intricacies—the "tricks & flourishes" of his grand, involved, comprehensive, classical Style. Did *you* ever read much of his Poetry? If so, *which* Poems? It does one good to get, sometimes, out of the rut of Shakespeare, & take a "flying trip" on a new track. One decidedly helps the other. Milton was a close student of our dear Dramatist,—the earmarks of this study crop out frequently. Now that I have got a fair start on the great Epic poet, I intend to keep it up—not, you know, to *neglect Sh.*, but to *add a little Milton* to him. . . .

[1] "one touch of nature": *Tro.* 3.3.175. N pubd. the note in the April 1877 "Shakespearian Gossip": *touch* = defect, blemish (cf. Fr. *tache*). C sometimes uses the sentimental interpretation of the line, as in the alteration of it that provided the title of this book (see title-page epigraph).

[2] all the acknowledgment that *I* shall get: H was somewhat more generous than this in the statement that ends his "Preface": "I must not let this Preface go without expressing a very deep and lively sense of my obligations to Mr. Joseph Crosby. The work of preparing this edition was set about in good earnest on the 23d of April, 1873, and has been the main burden of my thought and care ever since. From that time to the present, a frequent and steady correspondence, of the greatest use and interest to me, has been passing between Mr. Crosby and myself. The results thereof are in some measure made apparent in my Critical Notes, and still more in the foot-notes; but after all, a very large, if not the larger, portion of the benefit I have received is not capable of being put in definite form, and having credit given for it in detail. Indeed, I owe him much,—much in the shape of distinctly–usable matter, but more in the way of judicious counsel, kindly encouragement, and friendship steadfast and true." A similar statement appears in H's edn. of *Ham.* (1879) in his school series. (W. J. Rolfe rptd. the latter with approval in *The Literary World* 1879, p. 142.) H's most generous tribute to C came after the appearance of the Harvard Edn. when he prevailed on Ingleby to secure for C the rarely accorded title of "Foreign Honorary Member" of the Royal Society of Literature (see Folger MS. C.a. 9, letter of C to Ingleby 29 June 1882, and cf. *Literary World* 21 October 1882, p. 356).

173:   13 March 1877

My dear Norris:

In a Catalogue just received from *John Pearson*, York Street, Covent Garden, London, I see advertised a *Second Folio Shakespeare*, in old calf, with *four leaves missing*, and the portrait cut out of the title page, for £5..10.— Isn't that remarkably cheap? I have serious thoughts of buying it. I have written the owner for a fuller description; & if it be, otherwise, sound, clean, and perfect, I shall order it. A facsimile portrait could easily be inserted; and when put into a nice new morocco binding, with gilt edges, it would do very well—for lack of a better. It will depend somewhat on *where* in the book the 4 missing leaves are. £5..10, as prices of the folios go, seems very low for a copy only wanting 4 leaves and the portrait. What do *you* think about it? What was it you paid for *your imperfect* copy? And what did your *perfect one* cost?—. . .

—A Methodist preacher was on one occasion expatiating very eloquently on the *wonders* of the Creation: and quoted the verse "And God made *man* in his own image"; adding . . . "and then He made *woman* in the likeness of man, *with a slight variation*"; whereupon one of the flock enthusiastically exclaimed, "Thank God for *the variation!*"—The old man evidently knew a thing or two; he had had some experience of the virtues of "the variation," and his feelings so far got the better of his manners in Church that he was compelled fervently to *thank God* for it. I wish some of our "chaste commentators" would occasionally be as *explicit* as this old Methodist, and express themselves *intelligibly* when they have anything to say, or otherwise keep still & say nothing.—. . .

174: 22 March 1877 Chillicothe, Ohio

. . . I amused myself, while compelled to spend a Sunday at this Hotel, by re-reading *three old pieces,*—Rowe's Life of Sh., Dr Johnson's Preface, and Dr Farmer's "Essay on the Learning of Sh."—Rowe's Life is interesting, as being the first we have; there is not much spirit in it, but the style is good and quaint, and the facts detailed generally trustworthy. Johnson's "Preface" is exceedingly well-written, and much of its criticism is judicious; but there is a great deal of it that is *provoking.* The learned Dr was too formal, & stiff, & *regular* in his own notions justly to *appreciate* Sh.'s great, free, natural genius. He tries to subject the Poet to his own contracted views of good writing, and finds all manner of fault with little matters that Sh., in the glow of composition, thought beneath regard. Sh. *follows* **Nature** throughout; but Johnson would bend and bind him down to forms of *Art.* He says: "he sacrifices virtue to convenience, and is so much more careful to please than to instruct, that he seems to write without any moral purpose." Now Sh. wrote as he felt; and saw, & as Nature dictated, perfectly indifferent about making his characters "examples" either of good or evil. He left the **moral lessons** to take care of themselves. Then he (Johnson)[a] has nothing but blame for the "indelicacy" of the language frequently put into the mouths, not only of his clowns, but of his ladies & gentlemen; and makes a terrible bugaboo of his propensity for "quibbles." Hear him: "A quibble is to Sh. what luminous vapours are to the traveller; he follows it at all adventures; it is sure to lead him out of his way, and sure to engulf him in the mire. It has some malignant power over his mind, and its fascinations are irresistible. Whatever be the dignity or profundity of his disquisitions, whatever be the enlarging knowledge, or the exalting affection, whether he be amusing attention with incidents, or enchaining it in suspense, let but a quibble spring up before him, and he leaves his work unfinished. A quibble is the golden apple for which he will always turn aside from his career, or stoop from his elevation. A quibble, poor and barren as it is, gave him such delight, that he was content to purchase it by the sacrifice of reason, propriety, and truth. A quibble was to him the fatal Cleopatra, for which he lost the world, and was content to lose it."—Now, isn't all this very much exaggerated? It seems to me to be written much more for the sake of showing off the Dr.'s facility of making nice pointed antitheses, than of speaking the *sober truth*.—

His argument about Sh.'s ignorance, or neglect, of the *Unities* of *time* & *place* is excellent, and modest, and convincing. So long as he (Shakespeare)[b] preserved the unity of *action* perfect, he was indifferent to the rest—This Preface is, however, justly celebrated for many *beautiful criticisms*, both on the Poet and his commentators. I think he does less than justice to Theobald, and he never mentions *Capell*. Capell's edn., however, & notes, were not pubd. when this Preface was written. It is well deserving of an attentive reading, as being long in advance of anything that had heretofore been written on Sh. in the shape of criticism. A great portion of it is *admirable*; and there is much that one *now* has to blame. He speaks entirely too favourably of Warburton, and is quite severe in his strictures on Warburton's two critics, *Edwards* and *Heath*, two authors, whose books did more (especially Heath's *Revisal*) to illustrate the Poet, than all that had been previously written.—The following sentence bears on the point that you, and I, and Mr. Leighton, were talking about when together in your library: "Our author's plots are generally borrowed from novels; and it is reasonable to suppose that he chose the most popular, such as were read by many, and related by more; for his audience could not have followed him through the intricacies of the drama, had they not held the thread of the story in their hands."—

Dr Johnson was a lazy and slovenly editor; and I suppose his failing eyesight also had something to do with his work. Had he **really collated** as faithfully as he says he did, his edition would have been[c] very different, better, more useful.—

Dr. Farmer's Essays, or Essay rather, is a really *interesting* & *convincing criticism*. He makes his points well, and without any great show of learning himself.—Apart from the general topic discussed, it contains a good deal of useful & valuable Shakespearian information. Every Sh: student should read it carefully. In dozens of places the text is incidentally illustrated & explained. See, e.g., where he shows that "affection," as used by Shylock,[1] was *technical* for "sympathy," in Sh.'s time: so used by Bacon, Sir Kenelm Digby, & other writers. See, too, his remarks on the character of Wolsey in *Henry VIII*; on "proface," "monarcho," "baccare," and numerous other words, phrases, & passages.—It is several years since I read it before, & I had forgotten how interesting & *capital* it is all through. . . . Had Dr Farmer edited Shakespeare, I have no doubt that we should have had full light on many and many an obscure passage that is now set down as *corrupt*, and made the test of each succeeding editor's & commentator's ingenuity & conjecture.—

Just as I was leaving home, I received the Feb. & Mch. Nos. of *The Western*, containing friend Snider's essays on *King John*. I have read them (one, really) with considerable pleasure. . . . He gives[d] a very good analysis of the drama; and he pleases me by doing full justice to one of my especial favourites, *Falconbridge*. He metes out their just deserts & motives to each of the leading characters, from the vacillating King, to the conscientious Philip, the conscienceless Dauphin, Hubert, and all the women, Elinor, Constance & Blanche. Poor distracted Blanche! I always feel sorry for her. She has a "hard row to hoe." She would have naturally been an affectionate & devoted wife, had she not been assigned to a hard, ambitious, & unprincipled husband. . . .

Mrs. Quickly, speaking of Mrs. Ford to Falstaff, says—"you have brought her into such a *canaries*,"[2] &c. Johnson says "This is the name of a brisk, light dance, and therefore is properly enough used for any hurry or perturbation." But I am almost *sure* the dame uses it for "quandary," with the accent on the 2d syllable—"quandā'ry—as it *ought* always to be placed, & generally *is in the best English dictionaries*, though not in Webster's. This word is derived from the French *qu'en dirai-je*? "what shall I say about it?," and this shows how the word the word should be accented. Otway uses it as a verb "quandary'd," (I have the quotation at home, but cannot quote it exactly now) and he uniformly accents it "quandā'ry'd." No doubt it is the word Mrs. Quickly *meant* to use here.—J. C.—. . .

Act II, Sc. i:—"*Mrs Page.*—What?—thou liest!—Sir Alice Ford! these knights will *hack*;[3] and so thou shouldst not alter the article of thy gentry."—

This work "hack" has bothered me fearfully. The usual interpretation is, 'these knights will be hackneyed, or become so *common*, that thou wouldst be no better off than one of the untitled people; and so thou shouldst not alter the article of thy gentry.' The allusion being to the *enormous number of knights* (some 200 or 300 in a few months), which James I created in the early part of his reign. Dr Johnson read—"these knights *we'll* hack," i.e. we will disgrace and unknight, by *hacking off their spurs*, as was done to cowardly or recreant knights. But I think there is a *licentious allusion* in the term. Hanmer says that *to hack* meant to turn hackney, or *prostitute*. Mrs. Page is enraged at the *knight*, Sir John Falstaff, for his attack on her virtue, and seems to insinuate that they are all a licentious, blackguard set, & for that reason Mrs. Ford should not wish to become *a knight*, as she had just said she might be, if she would but "go to hell for an eternal moment, or so."— Query, altho' perhaps Mrs. Ford would not use so broad an expression, does she not *mean*—"these knights *will* fuck; and so *thou* shouldst not change thy own title for one of theirs."[e] I am almost ashamed of myself for suggesting so coarse a word: but the context seems to me to show that "hack" has this meaning, if the word I wrote above was not originally the one used by Sh.—Probably he said *hack*, unwilling to put the other into the mouth of a *woman*.

[1] "affection," as used by Shylock: *MV* 4.1.50.
[2] such a *canaries*": *Wiv.* 2.2.60.
[3] these knights will *hack*: *Wiv.* 2.1.52. We think the context too subtle and playful for such a direct obscenity as C finds in the word. On the other hand, an allusion to James I's knights is precluded by the date of the play, now generally agreed to be well before James's accession.

[a] (Johnson)] ↑(Johnson)↓ MS.
[b] (Shakespeare)] ↑(Shakespeare)↓ MS.
[c] would have been] would have ↑been↓ MS.
[d] He gives] It gives MS.
[e] one of theirs."] one of theirs. MS.

176: 26 March 1877

. . . In the February *part* of "N. & Q.," there are several "Shakespeariana" articles, that you *ought not* to omit seeing. Some from "Jabez" (Dr Ingleby), and some from others. Snider has sent me his last article "on the Historical Plays," in the *Jour. Spec. Phil.*; but I have not read it yet. His "Western" articles I have. I have just received a quite good letter from him, which I enclose you, as it contains his *private* opinion of Grant White, and other matters, that will amuse you. I have also a very pleasant letter from Corson, on some Shakespearian explanations, that we have been corresponding about; and a lengthy & excellent letter from Dr. Ingleby, on several matters of Shak*n* readings & interpretations. I enclose you all these letters to read, as I know, if you will do so, you will get a good deal of useful Shakespearian information, that you ought to have, as a *student* of the Poet. Ingleby's letter is really valuable for that; and in it he also tells many things about *Dyce* that are interesting. His explanation of "*imperseverant*" (Dyce, & Globe, &c. "*imperceiverant*") is just *capital*, & undoubtedly correct. It is entirely *new* to me. Do you think it would be doing anything wrong to copy out this explanation, & print it in the *Bibliopolist*,[1] of course crediting it fully to the learned Dr? If so, I will fix it up; it will be only a *short* article, but the expln., I am convinced, would be very welcome to Shakespearians generally. If you approve of this, how much of what he says about *Dyce* would it be proper to insert? Or would it not be, perhaps, better first to write him, and ask his permission? Calling *Dyce* "a contemptible creature" is pretty strong language; and his *pun*, "*prejuDyced*," is I think not very gentlemanly. How does it strike you? Still all *that* might be left out, & the really valuable *etymology*, and *expln.*, of "imperseverant" could be given, (without his private "prejuDyces,") as they are too good to be lost, or buried in a private letter. You will observe that he pays me a splendid compliment for *two* of my interpretations. . . .

He does *not* accept my "Affection! Thy intention stabs the centre" explanation;[2] but gives it a fearfully hard, & I think far-fetched interpretation; illustrating it from Kant, and the German transcendentalists. All right; I still think I am right, for the reason that mine is so much easier to understand—*more simple*—more consistent (by a long way) with the context, about "dreams," &c. &c., which he never alludes to at all. Then I do not believe that our Great Poet of Nature meant to puzzle his audiences with sentiments & "philosophies," that no one but a German hypercritic could explain. What need for all this talk of "ethic sovereignty," &c, when so *much less* and *simpler*, gives a plain meaning.—. . . I was very glad to know that what I wrote in answer to Mr. Lamb's "article"[3] pleased you. I was afraid you would think it perhaps too fault-finding, or maybe too long. But since I have read Mr. Asa Lamb's letter (which I herewith re-enclose to you),—I have had no "compunctious visitings" for being too severe. I do not fancy he is "much." He does not speak of *Shakespeare* as a *genuine* lover & student does. He says he has gone through "the idolatrous period," and has now come to his senses, & has discovered that Shakespeare is not much elevated above "Pope and Byron, and Moore, and the great novelists."—Depend upon it, this man has never been infected with the right *virus*, or he would *never* have "recovered." Had his heart *ever once* been touched with a *live coal* from the true altar of Shakespeare, he would never have "*gone through* the idolatrous period"; he would have *remained* an idolater to the end of his days. He seems to be a gentleman, and something of a scholar; and doubtless a good citizen and neighbour; but a man to gain *my* heart must have no "ifs" or "buts," when speaking of the Great Bard. . . .

In 1872, the Lippencotts published a small 12mo volume, by a Dr Meredith, called "Every-day Errors of Speech." It is an admirable little manual, full of useful information, principally regarding mistakes commonly made in *pronunciation* and *spelling*. Last year, an Englishman, a Rev. Mr. F. Leary, took it in hand, and published in London a *revised* and corrected edition. His is certainly *somewhat* of an improvement on the American edition, but not much. So, do you know, during the last few weeks, I have employed *some* (only *some* of my leisure time [after writing, and collating the different dictionaries, until 4 o'clock in the morning,] in again *revising, correcting* and *enlarging* this book for another *new edition*, which will never be published. I have made it "as large again as it was," adding from *one to two thousand* more words; I have, in scores & scores of places, corrected *pronunciation* and *spelling*, and added numerous curious *derivations* of words, and many of the little *facetiæ* of language, not generally known. . . . **To-day I finished it**: writing the little vol. all over, wherever there was an atom of blank space. It has, of course, done *me* good, if no one else should ever see it; so I don't think it *time lost*, by any means. I shall read through the little book 4 or 5 times a year, to keep all fresh in my mind, and shall add new words & corrections as they turn up.—

In the quotation which I made from Ar: Brooke's old poem of "Romeus and Juliet," in my letter on Mercutio, perhaps it would *look better* to have the words in the *antique spelling*. May I trouble you to change them with your pen, i.e. if you have[a] the MS. yet by you.—You will find it on p. 86, Vol. I., of *Hazlitt's* "Shakespeare's Library," thus:—

> "At thone syde of her chayre her lover Romeo,
> And on the other syde there sat one cald Mercutio;
> A courtier that eche where was highly had in pryce,
> For he was coorteous of his speche, and pleasant of devise.
> Even as a Lyon would emong the lambes be bolde
> Such was emong the bashfull maydes, Mercutio to beholde."

———————

By the by, did you ever read the whole of this old poem? There are some rich descriptions in it. How is *this*, for instance, where the Nurse is telling Romeo about Juliet—trying to inflame his passion:—

> "A pretty babe (quod she) it was when it was yong;
> Lord how it could full pretely have prated with its tong!
> A thousand times and more I laid her on my lappe,
> And clapt her on the buttocke soft, and kist where I did clappe.
> And gladder then was I of such a kisse forsooth,
> Than I had been to have a kisse of some olde lecher's mouth."

His description of the wedding-night is very voluptuous:—

> "Thus passe they foorth the night in sport, in joly game;
> The hastines of Phoebus' steeds in great despyte they blame.
> And now the virgin's fort hath warlike Romeus got
> In which as yet no breache was made by force of canon shot.
> And now in ease he doth possesse the hoped place:
> How glad was he, speak you that may your lovers *parts* embrace."
> &c. &c

I want to ask another favour of you, namely, after the following words in my letter: "Why, that a gratuitous brawler and butcher hath provoked and received his just deserts," to insert the following:—"To adopt the quaint language of the old poem:—

> "So met these two, and while they chaunge a blowe or twayne,
> Our Romeus thrust him through the throte, and so is Tybalt slayne.
> *Loe here the ende of those that styrre a dedly stryfe:*
> *Who thyrsteth after others death, himselfe hath lost his life."*

Do you think you can manage[4] to put that in? It will have a good effect on the argument, as showing what *Brooke's* opinion was of *Tybalt*; and it exactly coincides with what I have been saying about him. . . .

———————

I see by the papers that our old Shakespearian friend, Charles Cowden Clarke, is *dead*! Died at Genoa, a few days ago. He has lived to a patriarchal age; and I fancy his widow, Mary Cowden Clarke, is also quite aged. She will not live long now.[5] It generally happens that when one of an old couple, that have lived happily together for many years, drops into the grave, the other soon follows. . . .

I suppose we shall have the "Leopold Shakespeare" here shortly. I see it is out. Furnivall has written an "Introduction" for it. The plays are arranged according to *his* chronological order, and the "doubtful plays" included. Furnivall sent Mr. Hudson the advance sheets of his "Introduction," but the latter spoke to me very slightingly of it, and especially of Furnivall's analysis & remarks on the "Sonnets." . . .

Living so far West, and distant from all literary centres, as I do, it is almost a wonder that I have got together so nice a library of "Shakespeariana" as I have. . . . My books are crammed away in some 5 large cases, the best way I can. Those I want *oftenest* are kept in the *handiest* places. Sometimes they are two rows deep; & that, you know, is a fearful bore. Then I have so many *other* than Shakespeare books, that are also good & useful; and they are all together. I cannot do, like you; keep a separate room for my "Shakespeariana," and another for my "miscellaneous" books.—I am great on **Dictionaries**, *Encyclopædias, Glossaries*, &c, and they take up a large amount of my small space. Then I have all of Dickens, Thackeray, Scott, Macaulay, Hume, several sets of Milton, Byron, Moore, Pope, Spenser, Dryden, Coleridge, and a thousand and one others, that a gentleman wants to have near him.—. . .

I think the plan you mention of the new way of describing books, by inches, instead of 8vo, 12mo, &c. a good one; especially that part of it about *numbering plates*. Many books are sold for "perfect," that have had some, more or less, of the plates rifled out by "illustrators." This plan will enable a purchaser to collate easily. It will take one *some time* to learn to form an eye, or rather a "mind's eye" measurement & size of a book by simply saying so many inches by so many. But it will be easily learnt; and by having a small rule in your pocket you can "lay off" the exact size on a piece of paper. If *all* 8vos, and *all* 4tos, &c. were the same size, it would not matter. As it is, there is no uniformity. Besides, the *English* & *American* sizes are not alike, I believe. An English 8vo is either larger or smaller, (I forget which) than its American brother 8vo.—Do you think the new plan will be generally adopted?—

Your list of "Bacon controversy," or "infidel corner," books is very complete indeed. I also possess almost all the same, except some of those you have got from newspapers. I never saw any of the "Newcastle Chronicle" articles. Are they *good*, or did you read them?—The *best*, most compendious, & at same time, most comprehensive, reply to this Baconian foolery, is Mr Spedding's letter to N. Holmes, pubd by the latter in the 3d edn. of his book. It is simply unanswerable; and I was astonished that Holmes should have published the "antidote" to his "poison," in the same volume. George Wilkes takes the ground that Bacon could *not* have been the author of Shakespeare, mainly for the reason that Bacon was a stiff *Protestant*, while Shakespeare's works show (as he attempts at great length to prove by quotation, misrepresentation &c., but as usual *fails* to prove, & fails signally) that their author was a *Roman Catholic*; and another of his beautiful arguments is, that Shakespeare's works show that their author was too **ignorant** (!) a man to have been Lord Bacon, who was highly educated, and a Lord Chancellor. . . .

Mr. Furness thought he had *somewhere* seen my explanation of "less than kind," &c.[6] It is very possible. I can only say, which I do truly, that it was new **to me**. But why should not someone else have before hit on the same thought? The idea with me was that of making the reflection intended by Hamlet for **both his Uncle & himself**. I don't exactly remember how I worded it; but, at the moment, I thought it made the passage easier to understand, as well as more general in its application; and I think so still. Some commentators naturally referred it to the prince; others to Claudius; but no one, *that I ever saw*, made its reference mutual to both uncle & nephew, which was my point. Probably Mr. Furness may have met with the same among some of the German commentators, or the French, and that was what he was thinking of.—There is nothing *new* in the explanation I gave of *kin* and *kind*; but there *is* in noting that those terms correspond exactly to the Scotch "kyth and kin," and to *our* every-day expression "friends and relations."—. . .

---

[1] Do you think . . . & print it in the *Bibliopolist*: *Cym.* 4.1.14; the question became academic when *The American Bibliopolist* ceased publication after the April 1877 issue.

[2] my . . . explanation: In the passage, *WT* 1.2.138, *affection* = lust.

[3] what I wrote in answer to Mr. Lamb's "article": N pubd. both Lamb's claim that Mercutio is not a gentleman and C's long refutation in the April 1877 "Shakespearian Gossip."

[4] Do you think you can manage: The copy apparently had gone to the printer, as N did not make the insertion.

[5] She will not live long now: Mary Cowden Clarke (1809–98) survived her husband by more than twenty years.

[6] "less than kind," &c.: *Ham.* 1.2.65.

[a] if you have] if you ~~intend to publish it,~~— have MS.

178: 27 March 1877

. . . My main[a] object in writing you was to send you the contents of a postal card from Furnivall, pitching into Dr Ingleby's note on "defect of judgment,"[1] pubd in the *Bib.* You will have[b] noted the harsh language Furnivall uses regarding Dr Ingleby: "it is just a mare's nest, (like so many other of his things)." This is a nice way for the Director of the N. S. Soc. to speak of one of his ablest & best coadjutors, and "workers." I expected as much. You will probably soon see the learned Dr withdrawing from the Committee in disgust, as so many other able scholars have done before. Furnivall will bankrupt & scatter the "N. S. Soc."[2] to the winds, I fear, before long.—. . .

[1] "defect of judgment": *Cym.* 4.2.111. N had pubd. Ingleby's interpretation (*defect* = defective use) in a letter from C in the October 1876 "Shakespearian Gossip."
[2] Furnivall will bankrupt & scatter the "N. S. Soc." . . . before long: Despite nearly constant controversy, which became even more inflammatory in the early 1880s, the Society did not disband until 1894.

[a] My main] my main Ms.
[b] you will have] you ↑will have↓ MS.

179: 29 March 1877

. . . I enclose herewith Sabin's card, Mr. Furnivall's article, and my reply to it,[1] for publication in the *Bib.*, so that the *bane* and the *antidote* may appear together. I put my remarks into as brief a compass as I well could; and I must ask you to **very carefully** read my paper. You will see that I have written quite hurriedly, in order to get it off in time; and you will quite likely find some errors both of language & sentiment. Please erase and add—"what you will"—to make it suitable. I have not spared him, as you will observe. His *argument* does not amount to "a row of pins," and his language, & the tone of the whole paper, are very conceited—almost *impertinent*,—I do not mean to *me* (that would be no consequence) but to so clever & able a scholar as Dr Ingleby. It is the boldest thing I have ventured to do for many years, to attempt to reply to him; but my "dander riz," and I could not help speaking out. I thought it best not to wait for the Dr himself to answer him. You know how it is: before his reply could get here and be printed, all the interest in Furnivall's saucy letter would have evaporated, and all the points been forgotten.[a] . . .

. . . P.S. If you think I have said anything too harsh of Mr. Furnivall's article, or that will *hurt* too badly, strike it out. I have not gone to the length (as you once did, in print too) of calling His Directorship "an ass"; although I have referred to his few—very few—*weeks'* study of the poet; and the amount of brains he carries needed to understand Dr Ingleby's explanation. . . .

[1] Mr. Furnivall's article, and my reply to it: They never appeared, as F withdew the attack on Ingleby (see letter 180).

[a] been forgotten] ↑been↓ forgotten MS.

180: 2 April 1877

My dear Norris:
Since I wrote you last, enclosing you my "reply" to Mr. F. J. Furnivall's attack on Dr Ingleby's expln. of "defect of judgment," and my "enthusiastic approval" of it, I have received one more English postal card from His Royal Highness, reading as follows:—

> "Feeling now that the difference between Ingleby and me had better be settled here—friends think so too—I write to the Editor of *The American Bibliopolist* to cancel my letter. Meanwhile I am clearing the ground by a preliminary skirmish with I., and unless we can come to a better understanding, by his modifying or re-stating his case with new limitations, we'll fight the question out at home in the *New Shak. Soc. Trans.*—This will be better than having a duel in the U. S. A.   F. J. F. 15/3/77."—

Well; I wish he had known his *own mind* sufficiently *before* he wrote his first *saucy, sneering,* & *imperious* letter; it would have saved us all the trouble & annoyance of replying to him, as I presume, now, all will be cancelled. Do you know, I was rather sorry than otherwise, when he withdrew it. I should have liked no better fun than a good regular stand-up and knockdown *tussle* with his haughty Directorship. . . .

181: 7 April 1877

. . . You ask me about the Collier's Quarto ed. of Shakespeare. He sent me some months ago "The Two Gentlemen," & "The Merry Wives," in sheets, but perfectly clean & correct; so I now only lack "*The Tempest*,"—to make my set complete. I write to him every time I remit my £1..—to try & procure this "Tempest" for me. He promises to get it if possible, & he thinks he *can* soon. I am afraid to bore him too much. He has been remarkably kind to me, in sending *reprints*, &c. of scarce old books: and he sent me his *Trilogy*, the three parts, long ago. I recd. his "Hamlet" yesterday. He will soon now be out of the woods, as far as the *genuine plays* are concerned. . . .

I have this moment received a lovely note from one of our best young ladies, stating that she and some others have organized a "Shakespeare Reading Club," and elected me a member, and "confidently expects to see me on Monday evening at her house"—"but I will be very glad if you can conveniently spend an evening with me before the meeting of the club, as there are several things I am anxious to talk with and consult you about. Yours, Very Truly, *Agnes Fillmore*." Miss Fillmore is a relative of the Ex President Fillmore, a lady of about 29 or 30,[1] of excellent judgment, and very intelligent & highly educated. I take it as a great compliment, and shall aid her all I can, and attend the meetings whenever I am at home.—
. . .

[1] a lady of about 29 or 30: Agnes Fillmore was a little older than this, born 25 January 1844.

182:   9 April 1877

My dear Norris:
   I am just getting ready to start out on a trip of 10 days, or maybe two weeks; and I shall not see your letters until I return, so you will know why they are not answered. I thought I would just drop you a line to let you know. I should have gone this morning, only for another note from the "Shakespeare Reading Club," that they have their "first meeting" to-night, and I *must* be on hand. "Dear" Miss Fillmore will not take any excuse—"it will be a particular favour to *her*"—"the ladies will all be *So* disappointed"—"no one knows anything about Shakespeare but *you*," &c. &c. [Pardon my *vanity* in copying all this.]. So I shall go. How it will "eventuate" I cannot tell; but I will write you, by & by, & let you know.—I think I shall arrange to invite the "Sh. Reading Club" to meet at my new rooms, when they wish to read Shakespeare. It will be greatly more convenient, as I would have all my working tools handy. Fancy a new edition of *A. I. Fish*, and his "young ladies"!—Sich is life. I would gladly have got rid of this *bore*; for such I sadly fear it will be. However, I must do the *best* I can, which will be as *little* as I can.—Now, don't laugh at me: for *you* may, someday, be in the same box, i.e. if your wife will let you off to instruct gay, pretty, "young ladies," in the art and mystery of understanding Shakespeare. In my last I spoke of Mr. Collier. I enclose you a letter which I have just received from the dear, kind, old scholar. I hope he will succeed in getting me the *"Tempest."* Why should he not *reprint* a dozen or two more copies of it, to replace the lost ones? Those having imperfect sets would gladly pay for it.—. . .
   Well, I have got all *moved* at last,[1] and well moved too. Last week at this time, I would gladly have offered anyone two hundred dollars who would have *insured* me everything should be as well done as it is, in a week. Aside

from my own time & work, it has not cost me over $25., as nothing was
lost, nothing broken. And I am now *so* much nicer *fixed* than I was. Besides, I have rubbed off, & replaced, every book & picture, on some of
which the dust had settled, although I am very careful about *dust*. Most of
my books are sheltered behind glass doors, tight. I am now satisfied all are
clean, & safe,—without a scratch or tear, and arranged as well as *I* have
room & time for at present. But not—oh! not—like your excellent arrangement, or even like Fish's. I have put, of course, each *set* by itself; & 4 of my
5 cases are *all* "Shakespeare": but I know where I can put my hands on any
vol. I want; and I have but few, now, in two tiers deep. I have one shelf of
Dickens, one of *Thakeray*, one of *Sir W. Scott*, &c. also. Then I have got my
pictures all hung, since I wrote you last. Poor little & old pictures! Not like
your beautiful pictures, & handsome frames: neither have I any handsome
(or ugly) *busts* to adorn my library. But when you come West, & call on me,
(which I pray God you soon may,) and come into my "den," you will see
many a memento of J Parker Norris' kindness to J. C.—Your own photograph (with your dog) is over the mantle on one side of an oil painting (a
large one) of myself taken many years ago; and Mr. Furness' is on the
other.—Over the other mantle is a large oil painting of my late dear wife,
with two pictures of Shakespeare (one the *Halliwell-Droeshout*, that you
gave me) one on each side. Then I have the three (handsomely framed)
"rubbings," that you also gave me, hanging one over the other; the "*Good
friend*," at the top; the "*Iudicio Pylium*"&c, next; & Mrs. Shakespeare's
epitaph, below. They look real well. Then I had a neat black walnut *shield*
made, and D. Garrick's *mask* (another present from you) hangs on it, and
has a good light, & looks well. These "rubbings," and "mask," are *unique*
ornaments in Zanesville. In another place I have a steel-plate "Shakespeare
and his Friends"; a fine plaster-of-Paris[a] moulding of the "Last Supper";
"Evangeline"; the "Ashbourne" Shakespeare; two large excellent photographs of the *Death-Mask* (likewise your bounty); an oil painting of Landseer's "Dignity & Impudence"[2]—copied by a son of *Douglas Jerrold's*,[3] for
me. He got stranded in Zanesville, for want of money, and stayed here
some months, teaching French and drawing; and painting in oils, & making pen & ink sketches, of which I have several. He was a handsome,
accomplished young fellow; he was travelling somewhere in New York,
was taken sick, & was waited on by a young woman of no education at all,
a very common person indeed, but kind to him; and he most foolishly
married her. It is several years—15 or more—since he was in Zanesville. He
went South before the war. I do not know where he is now; not heard of
him for years. I have also a valuable lithograph (coloured) of the "Death of
Nelson" at the *Battle of the Nile*, that belonged to my uncle. It was made at
the time (1805 I think), and every member of the *St. George's Club*, in New
York, had a copy. My dear old Uncle—James Crosby[4]—was a thorough
Englishman, & a noble specimen of the "old English Gentleman."—My

rooms are well lighted—5 large windows; and two gas chandeliers. You cannot imagine how *glad* I am that I have gotten all done! I am very much *Safer* now, too, against *fire*, than I was in the old Hotel. I keep a good insurance, of course, on my "stuff"; still *you* know how many books, pamphlets, pictures, &c. you & I both have, that we could not *replace*, perhaps for years. See how long we were getting a "Warburton's Sh." or a "Capell's Notes," or a score of other very rare things. Then, when we bought[b] these, they were much *cheaper* than now: and I question whether we could recover from the Insurance Companies any more than we *paid* for them. Indeed, on many books, it would be difficult to fix the value, or get an impartial set of assessors of *damage* & *loss*, to give us what would replace them, if destroyed. I have no rich, luxurious furniture, like yours; my stuff is all plain—very plain, & poor, & common;—still it is all I have; it is tolerably comfortable, & *decent*; and I should be sorry enough to have it burnt up. As the poor man said of his poor *bed*, "I can get lots of good sleep out of it," so I can get lots of good *reading*, and *study*, and a fair amount of *comfort*, out of my rooms & fixings, & especially my prized books.—

The Halliwell edition of *Marston*, and Jephson's book,[5] came Saturday. I am well pleased with both, and only sorry I missed the others, especially the *Shirley* & *Middleton*; but I live in hope of another chance. The *Marston*, 3 vols. cr. 8v., in Hf. maroon calf, extra, gilt backs, is a beautiful book, well printed on ribbed paper. It has *Wm. Ellery Sedgwick's* autograph, & underneath—"This is the only complete and correct edition." Jephson's is also a very pretty sm. 4to—entirely *new*—in green cloth, gilt edges. The 15 photos are pretty, and the letter-press, well printed in large type. Mr. Sedgwick has made several MS. notes in his neat hand; e.g., on p. 109, where Jephson (very foolishly) says, his readers will be obliged to him for giving them a few "extracts" from "Venus and Adonis," & "Lucrece," so they may not *have* to read the *whole* of these poems, which are so gross as to be driven from drawing room tables, &c.,—Mr. Sedgwick has written— "Bah! The best way in the world to make your readers search, beyond a drawing-room perhaps, for the whole thing." And in several other places, his little *mems.* show that he was a *sensible* & *tasteful* reader. The "Marston" cost me about $9..50, & the "Jephson" $2.50, here.

Did you notice that Henry Irving, (the popular Actor in London,) is about to contribute a series of *Sh: notes* to the New *Review* called "*The Nineteenth Century,*" (an offshoot of the old "*Contemporary Review,*")?—The April No. will commence with "The Third murderer in *Macbeth.*"—I see also advertised, "in the press," "The Sweet Silvery Sayings of Shakespeare on the Softer Sex; by an Old Soldier." Cr. 8vo.; and "New Readings and Renderings of Shakespeare's Tragedies," by H. H. Vaughan. Demy 8vo.— Both by Henry S. King & Co.—The latter will be (probably) an acceptable book; the former doubtful. I am tired of "Sayings" & "Proverbs," & "Aphorisms," &c. &c. from Shakespeare. "Dodd's Beauties"—one of the oldest—is probably one of the *best* of its *kind*; but they are all a *bad kind*, & always remind me of the man who carried round a *brick* to show people what kind of a *house* he had to sell.—But I must stop. Excuse this hasty letter, & believe me, (*ut semper*,) **tibi totum traditum**, (*t*wig *t*he *t*hree **t**'s).—

Joseph Crosby.—

[1] all *moved* at last: C had been living for years in the rooms in the Mills House Hotel which was to be demolished.

[2] Landseer's "Dignity & Impudence": Edwin Landseer's canine burlesque hangs in the National Gallery, London.

[3] *Douglas Jerrold*'s: British author, best known today for his nautical melodrama, *Black-eyed Susan*; it is not clear which of his sons C is referring to.

[4] My dear old Uncle—James Crosby: (1777–1858). He came to New York from London in 1808, representing an insurance company. During the War of 1812 he settled in Zanesville, where he was a glass manufacturer and insurance agent. His favorite song was "Admiral Nelson." (Zanesville *Sunday Times Signal*, 4 January 1959).

[5] Jephson's book: John M. Jephson, *Shakespere: His Birthplace, Home, and Grave. A Pilgrimage to Stratford-upon-Avon in the Autumn of 1863* (1864).

[a] plaster-of-Paris] plaster-of Paris MS.
[b] we bought] [word partly illegible] bought MS.

183:   13 April 1877   Bellefontaine, Ohio

. . . I think I wrote you on Monday, before our meeting of the "Shakespeare Reading Club." Well, on that evening, according to promise, **I went**. There were present about *twenty* ladies & gentlemen—all the *nicest*, and most intelligent, people of our city. Two or three clergymen—a Judge— several lawyers, and all their *wives*; & several *young ladies*, & *widows*. They began by making me "President"—**nolens volens**.—I tried every way to get out of the honour, but it was hopeless—I had to submit, with the best grace I could. Hon. M. M. Granger was elected for Vice Pres., and Miss Fillmore, Secretary. Then—in order to "evitate & shun" all the work & responsibility I could—I got a committee of three ladies appointed, to manage the *invitations*—to get up a set of by-laws or regulations, and to make selection of the play, and distribute the "characters" among the Members for reading, at the next meeting. After I got the ice broken, & fairly started, I really enjoyed the occasion. I gave them (and a more pleased & attentive *audience* no one could desire) a sort of extemporized lecture on Shakespeare,—some little of his Life—some facts about the Text—the Folios—the formation of the Text through the different editors, &c.—And, to try their voices, I commenced with a couple of scenes in *A. Y. Like It*—taking a part myself, and getting the rest to read other parts: I stopped the reading about every minute, or less, to explain some obsolete word, or expression, &c. They were all well pleased, & complimented their President, and I went home—feeling much better than when I went. I left a paper of directions for the Secretary to give each reading Member: to especially guard against letting in *too many* members—never to exceed 20; to admit none but such as were willing to *read & study,* and to *stick to it;* to expect to both *hear & make* **mistakes** of all sorts, & not to be ashamed of them; and to submit to have them **corrected,** without being mortified or chagrined, so it be done courteously & kindly. I shall endeavour to keep them from turning into a *mutual admiration* society, & to make a *mutual benefit* society. . . .

184:   24 April 1877

. . . Last night—the glorious natal day of Shakespeare—the "Zanesville Sh. Reading Club" held its *first* regular meeting at my rooms. By 8 o'clock P.M. they had all arrived—just 20—two-thirds ladies. I need not say that we had a very delightful evening. There was a good deal of "clack" & gossippy chatter for a few minutes; but I told them if they expected me to be their *President* I should rule with a rod of iron; so I got them to work. *As You Like It* had been assigned to the several members for reading, and they were all tolerably well prepared. I took Orlando, and we had a capital Rosalind, and a good Jaques. After each speech I explained each "tough place" that might occur in it—obsolete word or custom—the idioms of Sh. &c., putting in a little here and there about the *Text* & its corruptions, & formation,—the various editors & commentators, &c. In this way we got through 3 Acts very satisfactorily in about 3 hours, reserving the rest for next meeting in 2 weeks, at same place. They seemed all well pleased. . . . And here let me tell you (in answer to many a hard shot you have given *me,*) that I reaped the first fruits of my being the means of getting the folio or Imperial Edn. of Knight introduced into so many families, last night. Several of the members I discovered had read up the play in this edition, with all the Introductions, Notes, and Supplementary Notices, and this had given them a good preparation they would not otherwise have had. And, despite the wretched plates, the miserable paper, the poverty-stricken typography, &c. of the Imp. Ed., the *matter*—the Notes, & text, & Introductions—are excellent, well-written, accurate, interesting.—. . .

I will try & get a copy of last night's *Cincinnati Commercial* for you, as it contains an article on the *Death Mask;* also an account of my friend Enoch Carson's *Shakespearian Collection,* &c.—I cut out my copy to preserve. Our Daily paper here wanted to "interview" *me,* anent my Sh. library, &c., to write up an article for the 23d April, but I resolutely forbade it. I cannot *bear* this cheap kind of popularity. Some people like & encourage it; but it irks me to death; hence I fancy you need not fear I will ever become vain, or "too big for my boots." I am naturally of a retiring disposition. I cannot *show off,* as some can. I can laugh, & be egotistic enough with a close, intimate friend, but "Odi profanum vulgus, et arceo,"[1] as friend Horace did. . . .

[1] "Odi profanum vulgus, et arceo": Horace, *Odes* III.i.1.

186:   30 April 1877

. . . Yes! There you go! Just as I expected! I knew as soon as I told you of my "Shakespeare Reading Club" here, that you would be at your old tricks, and *making fun* of me. Well, I must take it, I suppose: but just wait until *you* get caught in a similar scrape (and you *will* be), and then won't I go for you? You need look for no pity. "They say Blood will have blood," and the measure you mete out to me, I will measure to you again. Suppose I did say, the young ladies read charmingly? So they did; & very much better than I could have anticipated, and they showed themselves (some of them at least) no novices in interpretation, although their preparation had mainly been derived from "Virtuous Yorston's Imp. Edn."—

This Club is of course only yet in embryo; yet from the *stability, culture,* & *intelligence,* of most of its members, I cannot but foresee both permanence, pleasure, & profit; and with these on the one side, like John Gilpin with his two jugs,[1] I will balance all your jokes at us on the other, & button them up carefully in my pocket, until I catch you, & then expect them home with interest. Our next meeting is one week from to-night, at my rooms; to read the rest of *As You Like It*; Mrs. Jameson's essay on *Rosalind*; an installment of Grant White's "Sh. Scholar," & perhaps a few pages of the *Prolegomena* to Craik's *Julius Cæsar*.[2] . . .

[1] John Gilpin with his two jugs: In William Cowper's "The Diverting History of John Gilpin" (a children's rhyme), the hero tries unsuccessfully to ride a horse to a picnic while carrying two jugs of homemade wine.
[2] Craik's *Julius Cæsar*: G. L. Craik, *The English of Shakespeare Illustrated from a Commentary on his "Julius Caesar"* (1857).

187:   1 May 1877

. . . You *will* persist in wanting *me* to explain all the defects, & smooth away all the complaints, your fastidious taste finds with Virtue & Yorston's Imp. Knight's Ed.; and when I get on the subject I almost invariably (without intention) write myself into a bad humour. I know you feel disappointed in the ed.; but *I* am not to blame; because I told you expressly *not* to buy it on my recommendation, which was not intended for scholars & Shakespearians, like yourself, but for persons, especially young persons, who not only had no ed. of *Knight*, but none of *Shakespeare* in any form. And of the 100 or 110 who take it, in this little town, I have never heard of one who was not pleased with it. . . .

I am glad to hear that Mr. Furness is copyrighting his *Hamlet* in England, though I don't understand how he does it. I was under the impression that an author had to *live* in a country, or at least that the book, or some portion of it, should be *written* & printed in a country, before he could get a copyright there. And *why* cannot Lippencotts sell the work now here? Must its appearance here & in England be simultaneous?—. . .

188: 3 May 1877

. . . I have . . . received the "Leopold" Shakespeare. A. R. S.[1] sent it by mail, in two parcels, & the book was nearly all to pieces when it arrived. I have taken it to my binder, to be clothed anew in Hf. brown morocco, red edges. Like yours, it is *cut*, & red edges is the only way I can think of to make it look nice at all. My binder has a *dark fluid red*—almost brown—that looks well, and does not rub off, when polished, as the usual red edges often will. I have not examined the book very much. It seems to be accurately printed from Delius' text, and the type & paper are very good for the price, & the size of the volume. Furnivall's Introduction is the very quintessence of the writer's "subjectivity," to give it a mild name; some would call it egotism or conceit. "F. J. F." is *prominent* throughout. Notice "my friend H. H. Furness, the Editor of the New Variorum"; "my friend the Poet Laureate"; "my friend Prof. Dowden"; "my friend H, R. H. The Prince Leopold," *etc.* As Macbeth said to the murderers "your spirits shine *through* you," so "F. J. F." is the prominent figure on each page. It seems to be a *reprint* of his "Introduction to Gervinus' Commentaries," with more of the same sort added. Mr. Hudson wrote me that he had sent him (Hudson) the proofsheets of this Introduction, and that he did not like it at all,[2] especially the dogmatic way in which he spoke of & handled the Sonnets & Poems. F. nettled the old gentleman right sharply by his *patronizing* airs, & Hudson told him "a piece of his mind" very plainly.—. . .

I think the new "Leopold Shakespeare" a cheap vol., don't you? Only 10/6 for cxxvi, and 1056 pp, quarto, fair paper & type. It will take some time to become accustomed to the *arrangement* of the plays, and to mixing up the *plays* and *poems* together; but we shall thus become better posted in their chronology. The woodcuts are of little merit or account. They give the book a cheap look, tho' perhaps they will make it sell better. Anything to get Shakespeare *introduced* & *read*. The "Droeshout" is tolerably well engraved, for a frontispiece. . . .

[1] A. R. S.: A. Russell Smith, the bookseller.

[2] he did not like it at all: It could be predicted that Hudson the aesthetic critic would object to Furnivall's scholarly methods. F and H eventually came to open enmity, F attacking H in print and H returning F's letters and telling him he was no gentleman. (Some details are to be found in letters from C to Ingleby, dated 14 September 1880 and 1 March 1881—Folger MS. C.a. 8.)

189:   5 May 1877

. . . With your satire and sidewipes at my unwished-for position (God knows!), as the President of the "Z. R. Club," and Goddard's slanderous *libel* on me, & the members of it, I shall be compelled either to shut my ears, or resign the place. I could not help laughing at Charlie's malignity in the description he gave you. There is considerable *malice* mixed up with it. *He* was left out in the organization & membership; and that accounts for the milk in the cocoa-nut all turning so suddenly *sour*. Those rascally grapes sticking up there would set his teeth on edge, even if he could *reach* them.—. . . Some months ago, perhaps a year, a "Murdoch Club" was formed in Z., for the purpose of *performing plays* on the regular stage. It was composed of many of our nicest young folks, and Goddard was one. It went on for some time, but much complaint began to spring up against Charlie for being tipsy at rehearsals, & sometimes at the performance. Finally one night he was absolutely so *drunk* that he could not perform his part—hardly could stand up—and when, in the play, he had to *pretend* to kiss a young lady, he insulted her by catching hold of her, & kissing her in reality. This and several other things, that I will not mention, so enraged the members, especially the young ladies, that they resolved never to perform again unless he were dismissed, and he has *never been on the stage since*! I tell you all this, my dear fellow, **in strict confidence** of course, as I sincerely like Charlie, & have always been, & now am, his friend, and would not say, or do, anything to injure him. I deeply regret to see that he is still drinking very hard. He seems to keep "full" all the time. At the dedication of the new Court House, he was *left out* of the programme, tho' his father was one of the finest lawyers Ohio ever produced, for no other reason than fear he would disgrace the occasion if he were allowed to make a speech. And, *entre nous*, I have no doubt *that* was the reason he was not invited to belong to the "Zanesv. Sh. Reading Club"; and *hinc illæ lach-rymæ*![1] Still, he might have spared *me* in his spite. He could not say '*I did it*.' Calling the ladies, who belong to the society, "old maids and widows" was a piece of virulence that is not *true*. Their ages run from 15 to maybe 30, and one or two married ladies perhaps 35. But *what of it*? Suppose they *had been* "old maids and widows," is *that a disgrace*? . . . As for *my* "hanker-ing after one of them, and that one neither a man nor a brother," that is another gratuitous slander. Not one word of truth in it; and Charlie knows it is *untrue*. I have lived "honestly" a widower nearly 13 years, and am just as far now from paying any *particular* attentions to any lady, young maid, old maid, or widow, as I was the first day I became a widower. . . .

Of the numerous books on Stratford, and Shakespeare's Home, that you and I have, I think a little one by *John R. Wise*, pubd by Smith and Elder, London, in 1861, is by all odds the *best*. It is not perhaps as beautiful and gay in photographs, &c., as some (Jephson's, for instance), but it is so sweetly and appreciatively written. One chapter alone, Chapter XII, p. 103, "On the provincialisms of Shakespeare," is worth many times the cost of the book, which was only $150. Do you know I never understood that expression of the old Nurse in *Rom. & Jul.*, "Shake, quoth the dove-house,"[2] until I found it explained in Mr. Wise's charming book. . . . This is only *one*, out of many of the same kind, of real *useful* illustrations of Shakespeare. I *love* this little book. . . .

Could I visit my native land once more, one of the first men I should call on would be J Payne Collier, Esq., of Maidenhead, Riverside, Berkshire: and what a *talk* I would have! A friend of mine in Zanesville (now dead) had a relative in England, who owned and lived in the house that Collier occupied when he first got his celebrated folio. There is a facsimile Note by Collier, written from this house, in Ingleby's "Complete View." This gentleman knew Collier well. In one of his letters, which I saw, he said that Collier had spent his whole life delving in the well-wrought mines of Shakespearian criticism. That he had a son,[3] who tried to be an engineer (civil), but was not successful at it; and many other matters he told about him.—. . .

[1] *hinc illæ lachrymæ*: Terence, *Andria* I.i.99. The allusion carries a possible sharp edge, as in the play ad loc. a young man is said to be weeping for the loss of a girl he lusted after.
[2] "Shake, quoth the dove-house": *Rom.* 1.3.33. *Quoth* = *went* or *did* when applied to inanimate objects. Wise shows that this was a Warwickshire idiom.
[3] he had a son: This was William, the second son; C's informant is probably thinking of the years around 1850, when William Collier was an impecunious clerk in the Stamp Office.

190: 7 May 1877

. . . Now—don't laugh, and call me (in derision) a "potent, grave, and reverend President," &c. &c. &c.—If you only saw what a pretty note— epistle rather—I received this A.M. from a lady—a member, who is neither "an old maid nor a widow"—nor yet "a man or a brother," you might *envy*, rather than laugh at me. It is full of *good sense, kindness*, and *gratitude*, and repays me a thousandfold for any trouble & pains I have been at to do them some little good in helping them to read and understand our beloved Poet.—. . .

191:   9 May 1877

. . . You say my letters are *shorter* since the Z. R. Club was organized: that is only your imagination,[1] my boy. If you look back, I think you will see I have written you every 3 or 4 days the last month, longer or shorter, besides 3 papers (short to be sure) for the *Bib.*—Anyway, I wrote you just as often, and as long, as I had time, you may be sure. I have (I may say) no other correspondent—none certainly to whom I so love to write. I tell *you* everything that happens—all my studies, & journeys, & troubles, & (very few) *happinesses.*—E. g. I spent a delightful evening, last evening, with an excellent & interesting young lady—no "old maid," or "widow" either: it has been so long since I have gone out much into ladies' society, that I feared to venture almost, lest I could not manage all the little nothings— the quick jest—the witty repartee, &c. that constitute the conversation of so many modern ladies & gentlemen. But this one is quite of a different style of belles. I was at home in 5 minutes, and got along splendidly, & passed as pleasant an evening as one could desire, with many (I think sincere) invitations to come *soon* again. There! I would not have told that to anybody but *you.*—. . .

I think with you, that Furnivall and Ingleby cannot long[a] keep from hostilities. Their friends may get up a 'protocol'; but the 'war' will commence, and be a bitter one too. Such sweetmeats as the Dr applies to F.'s "post cards"—"flippant"—"arrogant," &c. show how the wind blows.— The only thing I should regret would be to lose Ingleby's labours from the New Sh. Soc.—He is really one of the best critics in England to-day, spite of his little peccadillos of conceit & egotism.—. . .

[1] only your imagination: C wrote as often in April 1877 as in March, but more briefly: the average is 8½ pages in April, 11½ in March.

[a] cannot long] ↑cannot long↓ MS.

192:   12 May 1877 Wheeling West Va.

. . . Last evening (Friday) I spent very pleasantly indeed here, at Mr. Leighton's house. An intimate friend, a member of the 'W. Sh. Club' went with me; and Mr. Leighton was exceedingly agreeable. He lives, with his father, his wife (who is a remarkably clever lady), & children, in a comfortable home, nicely furnished. His library is *very* deficient in Shakespeare. An old copy of Reed's 12mo. edn. of 1809, the Clar. Press little vols., & your former *Cambridge*, are all the edns. he has; and no (or nearly no) "Shakespeariana" at all. . . .

193: 14 May 1877

. . . I have read R. G. White's essay on *Isabella*[1] several times. It is a bright, well-written paper, and (like you) it injured *my* rather favourable opinion of her character. But I think *now* it is somewhat overdrawn & exaggerated. The best way to arrive at her character is to entirely (if possible) divest your mind of anybody's estimate of it, and, with unbiased judgment, read it up for yourself *in the Poet*, and mark the *natural* impression it produces on your mind. Mrs. Jameson's is probably as much overdrawn[a] on the other side. The truth is most likely between the two. . . .

I have never been able to find out what the "grosser name"[2] in England was for "dead men's fingers," in *Hamlet*. The notes all leave us in the dark, saying it is sufficiently well known, particularly in Shakespeare's country. Its botanical name is *orchis morio mas*, anciently *testiculus morionis*. *Orchis*, you know, means a *testicle*; and I presume the 'grosser name' has some relation to the masculine (*mas*) testicle, probably on account of its oval shape. One of the notes says that its various names, too gross for repetition, are preserved in *Lyte's Herbal*, 1578; and another, that *one* of its "grosser names" was "*the rampant widow*," a name that *Gertrude* would not be very willing to recall.—

About that everlasting passage in *All's Well*,[3] I'll not bother you more than a word or two. It is the line, "while shameful hate sleeps out the afternoon," that "gets" you. Now had he said 'while shameful hate sleeps the sleep of death' you would see what he meant; & the other means I think just the same. It is the fact of the King's speech being a *general* observation that puzzles. But it is intended to apply strictly to Bertram. He entertained (as the King says) *two* distinct feelings or passions towards Helena, *love* which was her due from him for her own virtues, and for the King's request; *hate*, because he was *compelled* to marry her against his will. After he got rid of her, & ran off, *both* these passions lay dormant in his heart, because he had simply *forgotten* all about her. But, when he heard that she was *dead*, his better nature got the ascendancy; his *love*—his "own love"—*awoke*, and he lamented that he had been the cause of her death; while the other—the bad passion—*hate* ("shame*ful*," i.e. *full of shame*, or, of which he was now thoroughly ashamed,) did *not* awake anymore, but slept the sleep of endless death; in other words, was forever *extinguished* in his bosom. Doesn't this make it plain to you?—. . .

---

[1] R. G. White's essay on *Isabella*: In *Shakespeare's Scholar* (1854), 135–50; see esp. p. 135: "She is a pietist in her religion, a pedant in her talk, a prude in her notions, and a prig in her conduct."

[2] the "grosser name": *Ham.* 4.7.170. The "grosser name" may have been "cuckoo-pint" (*pint* = *pintle* = *penis*). The Wild Arum was so called; it has a long purple spadix of phallic shape. See Karl P. Wentersdorf, "*Hamlet*: Ophelia's Long Purples," *Shakespeare Quarterly* 29 (1978): 413–17.

[3] that everlasting passage in *All's Well*: 5.3.66.

[a] overdrawn] over-| drawn MS.

194:   23 May 1877

. . . I have received a very pleasant letter from Dr Ingleby, (which I enclose you to read, as it will interest you,) who is still suffering from his eyes. You will notice that he has, at last, come entirely over to my interpretation of "Affection" = *lust*, in the *W. T.* passage;[1] but he even goes farther than I dared, and interprets "centre" = *fem. pudendum*, very plainly. He has been having a "pow wow" with Prof. Leo of Berlin, who told him that he & his German confrères had long ago so explained the passage. "Stabs the centre" being a phrase of archery, the Dr asks me what is the "bull's eye" of *lust* ["Affection"], and the answer to that question solves the riddle of the passage. The *"intention"* means (I presume) that the "centre" need not necessarily be "*stabbed*" *in reality*. It can be done in *imagination*—thought—dreams, &c., as Ixion with the cloud. What are we coming to? I thought I was going a great length to explain this terrible *lust* as omnipotent, omnipresent, pervading the whole habitable *globe* ("centre"); but these German critics, & Ingleby fully accepts the idea as correct, go the **whole hog**. . . .

[1] the *W. T.* passage: 1.2.138.

196:   6 June 1877

. . . We had a delightful meeting of the "Reading Club," on Monday evening. All hands were promptly present by 8 o'clock; and we read the whole play—*Julius Cæsar*— by a little past 11. You know what a simple & easy play it is—no difficulties, & consequently few or no *interruptions* for explanations, &c. They read, generally, very well; *Brutus* (a Judge of our Common Pleas Court) reading his part about the worst. *Portia* was splendid, and *Cassius* (a merchant here, and an educated & genial gentleman,) being also capital. I had *Antony*, and I let myself loose, when I came "to bury Caesar, *not* to praise him," Oh, no! "*not* to praise him."—I had prevailed on several to buy Rolfe's edn. of Craik's book,[1] and they had studied it usefully. The main trouble I have is to get them, in reading, to give the prolonged '-ed', and -'tion' = ti-on, &c. &c., so as to make the proper poetical rythm of 10 syllables, or rather 5 feet. Too many want to read blank verse like *prose*; but a little more practice will regulate all this.

The Secretary of the Club, Miss Agnes Fillmore, (a dear friend of mine) and the originator and organizer of the Club, was compelled to be absent, owing to the recent decease of her mother; but she kindly sent me a whole basket full of bouquets, to adorn my rooms. (When I say 'dear'—I mean Platonically, of course; and *not* in the sense in which Charlie Goddard meant, when he said I "hanker'd" after "an old maid"; but I need not tell *you* that: *she* is to me a dear, kind, friend, as *you* are to me a dear, kind, friend; and having but *precious few* such, I do indeed appreciate them. Pardon this personal digression)—I have consequently made an engagement with her to go over & read the plays with her, until she shall feel like again coming to the Society. Now please don't laugh, or tell Goddard all I tell you.—. . .

[1] Rolfe's edn. of Craik's book: W. J. Rolfe revised G. L. Craik's *English of Shakespeare* (see note 2 to letter 186) in 1867. Rolfe's Craik went through several edns.

198:   29 June 1877

. . . I received the "Bibliopolist" (April), and was highly pleased with both your articles and mine. So well & *accurately* printed. But I was sorry on account of poor Leighton's article. It *is* a bore to have his comment, prepared no doubt all carefully, thus spoiled and made nonsense of. Of course it is no fault of yours. The Sabins alone are to blame. They seem to be utterly *careless* about the "Bibliopolist" in every way.—. . .

I have received a delightful letter from Mr. Furness, in reply to one I wrote him, congratulating him on finishing his *Hamlet*. I enclose it to you to read, & you will please return it to me, as I value so very kind and complimentary a letter from him very highly indeed. In addition to this, he has sent me, by express, a copy of the "Hamlet," as a *present*; with the words by his own hand written on fly leaf of 1st vol.—"Mr. Joseph Crosby, with the Sincere Regards of Horace Howard Furness. Philadelphia, June, 1877." The gift was as *unexpected* as it is *welcome*. I had already bought a copy: now I have *two*. Except the Preface, abt. 25 pp. of text, and 2 or 3 articles in the 2d vol., I have not, as yet, had time to read it. But these are enough to show me what a treat I have in store. The careful study of such a condensation of the wealth of Shakespearian research & wisdom is not the work of a week, or a month. It cannot be *hurried* over: I shall take it leisurely; & I intend to keep up my correspondence with the learned editor from time to time as I advance in it. It asks *time* to study it thoroughly as it did to prepare it. I am glad to see that *you* also are adopting this course, & taking it leisurely & carefully. It is the only way to get all the good from it one ought to.—But wasn't it *kind* of Mr. Furness? I never once thought he would send *me* a "presentation" copy. I shall value it, among my jewels, as long as I live.— . . .

Where you[a] think the Folio text right in "An anthonie it was,"[1] &c. I am almost positive that if *ever* a correction were required, it is here. The way it came to be misprinted is this: *Anthonie's* name has been frequently used in the context, with a capital A of course; and "Automne" being so spelt, & with a capital 'A,' the error was easy. But I think the *sense* absolutely requires Theobald's (wasn't it Theobald, or was it Rowe?) correction. Look at the whole metaphor: "As for his bounty There was no **Winter** in't: An **Autumn** 'twas, that grew the more by reaping." I can perceive no sense in "An Antony it was"; because it was *not* "Antony," but his "bounty," that grew the more by reaping. *Antony* didn't grow, but his *bounty* did; it was "cut & come again" with *it*: and instead of making a *simile*, and saying 'his bounty was *like* an Autumn,' &c, he uses a *metaphor* (the same one as he had been using), and says 'his bounty *was* an Autumn, and grew the more by reaping,' i.e. like a *rich field, or harvest in autumn*, the more it was cut & reaped, the faster it grew, & was again ready for the sickle. The whole of this beautiful image of a rich cropping autumn is spoiled, unless we adopt the emendation. Corson, you know, wanted to retain the Folio text, but he would explain it, not as you do, but by deriving *Anthonie* from the Greek ἄνθος, a flower, and making "Anthony" = a *flower garden*. But this is fearfully forced, and, besides, it is not *true in fact. Flowers* when *reaped* or cut, never grow again; that is the end of *them;* whereas a rich autumnal harvest-field, or (as Longfellow uses the term)[2] *aftermath, does* grow again after it is reaped. And the Poet wished to make Antony's bounty of this rich *exhaustless* character—there was no end to it—the more he gave, the more he was ready to give; his bounty, in a word, was "an *Autumn*, that *grew* the more by *reaping*.". . .

[1] "An anthonie it was": *Ant.* 5.2.87.
[2] (as Longfellow uses the term): C is remembering "Aftermath" in the book of that title (1873):

> When the summer fields are mown,
> When the birds are fledged and flown,
> And the dry leaves strew the path;
>
> . . . .
> Once again the fields we mow
> And gather in the aftermath.

[a] Where you] where you MS.

199:   7 July 1877

. . . I wrote to Mr. Hudson to review the *Hamlet* Variorum[a] for the *North American Review*. To-day I have received a long, and very kind letter from the old gentleman, full of all sorts of good things. He is off duty now with his "classes," and has more time to write. He says he wrote to the Editor of the *N. A. Rev.* about a notice of Mr. F.'s *Hamlet*; but the Ed. told him he could only spare him *a page*; and that he (Hudson) thought that was not enough in which to do anything like justice to so important a work, and so he gave it up. . . .

I have been hoping & hoping the everlasting "panic" would be over long ere this. If it continue much longer, I see nothing but a general bankruptcy in store for little fellows like me. Old Mr. Hudson says it is the "hard times" that have prevented his publishers—Ginn & Heath—from undertaking his new "Shakespeare." It would take over $12.000, stereotyping and all, to bring it out. Lockwood & Co., who own the copyright of his old edition, wanted the new one; and so did Hurd & Houghton; but they would not interfere until Ginn & Heath should give it up. He thinks, however, this latter firm (G. & H.) will be able to begin with it[1] about the beginning of next year: at least so they have promised.—. . .

[1] able to begin with it: The edn. did not appear until 1881.

[a] the *Hamlet* Variorum] it MS.

201:   19 July 1877

. . . I have received nothing new in the way of books since I wrote you last, except the new *Globe* edn. of *Milton*, edited with Introductions, &c. by Prof. Masson, (a nice new book in Hf. calf); the Collins' Series *Julius Cæsar*; and Fleay's "Introduction to Shak. Study." The last I have read carefully, and have written Mr. Fleay a long letter about it. I have also written a note of thanks to Dr. Ingleby for his presentation copy[1] of "Sh. The Man, and the Book." . . .

I was sorry to see you sneering and laughing at me in your letter, because my name was conspicuously printed by Dr Ingleby, and Mr. Fleay;[2] and I did not think it at all kind. I would not have done so to you. "You look up to me with wonder and astonishment"! &c. &c. You know that I had nothing whatever to do with this prominence. Anything of the kind is the farthest thing from my thoughts or wishes: and I would have prevented it, if I could have known it. It is unfair I think to ridicule & make fun of *me* for what I am not to blame. God knows I have never sought the distinction of having my humble name in print; it has, on the contrary, always pained me to see it. Dr Ingleby's is nothing but a notice of a conjectural reading that I sent him; and, as for Fleay's, I had no more to do with his coupling my name to Mr. Furness', as "American Shakespearians," than I had with that "absurd notice" of myself in the little Zanesville paper. . . .

I was simply amazed at the prices you got only for your books at Leavitt's.—$2. for Capell, and $*250* for Warburton! and $*200* for J & S. 1785 edn.! You say "J. & S. 1785 in *8 vols*"; don't you mean *10 vols*?—J. W. Bouton charged me $15..00 in New York for my copy. $200 for the "Hermeneutics" was not so bad; but $150 for Boaden's very scarce book, with the 5 portraits, is simply ridiculous. What a fearful pity such good books shd be so wasted! I am real sorry you parted with them, & lost so much money. Is the scarcity of money the reason of such unheard-of low prices? Second-hand booksellers, who can afford to buy now, and store up such good & rare books, will make a fortune. I was very, very sorry to read that part of your letter. . . .

I have received Mr. Collier's *Antony & Cleopatra*, and quite a long & pleasant note from the old gentleman. He writes in the best of spirits. He has not yet heard of any extra No. of *The Tempest* for me, but thinks he will, ere long. He says he issued 65 copies, being 15 extra, of that play, & that 15 were lost or stolen in the P. office. I'll bet that he will find one for me yet, to complete my set. He likes to keep me in suspense as long as possible, and then have a copy "turn up," *providentially* you know. He says he intends to publish all the doubtful Plays, and all the Poems. Do you ever look over his *Annotations* in his 4to edition? They are very few, as you know; and those few are very thin and useless. He sticks in the main to his Corr. Fo. 1632, but not always. He retains considerable of the abuse of other editors in his notes, that was so offensive in his 1858 edition. Altogether the edition, except for its lovely form, typography, paper, &c., does him no credit. He does not appear to have read, or if he has read, to[a] have cared for, any of the modern critics on the text. And he is so *inconsistent* in the use of his "Corr. Fo. 1632"—sometimes making it an authority equal to the Poet's own autograph, "settling" a disputed point at once; & then again he will retain a Fol., or textus receptus, reading, discarding the "Corr. Fo." emendation,—"*No change is necessary here.*" But if this authority is paramount in one case—if, as he claims, the Old Corrector made his changes of the text from Sh.'s own copies, &c., surely it must be *paramount in all.*—. . .

[1]his presentation copy: This would be vol. 1; vol. 2 appeared in 1881.
[2]conspicuously printed by Dr Ingleby, and Mr. Fleay: In *Shakespeare: The Man and the Book* (1, 1877), Ingleby comments (p. 150) on a conjecture C once made on "defect of judgment" (*Cym.* 4.2.111); Fleay mentions C in the Preface to his *Introduction to Shakespearian Study* (1877) as an American friend who has encouraged his further work.

[a]read, to] read, ~~not~~ to MS.

203:   26 July 1877

My dear Norris:

Your kind and most welcome letter written on the 21st inst. I did not receive until this morning, owing I suppose to the delay in the mails, caused by the terrible state of affairs at Pittsburgh & elsewhere.[1] I was very glad indeed to get it, and to read your most kind and acceptable words. My dear fellow there is no need of apology. . . .I *always was*—most foolishly—very sensitive to *ridicule*. I can stand and parry off anything better than ridicule; the fact is I cannot ward it off at all. I do not like to have my own feelings hurt, & consequently I try, at least, to be careful not to hurt those of others. I have heard of men who would sooner lose their friend than their joke; but I am not one of them. Perhaps it is unfortunate for me. However this has nothing to do with *us*. During the 6 or 7 years of our acquaintance & correspondence, I have first learned to like, then to admire, then to *love you*—truly, loyally, & sincerely. Excepting my own little boy, and one other *person* ("neither a man nor a brother"), *you* are the dearest friend I have in America. . . .

But I will. . .show you I *meant* no malice, by telling you that, notwithstanding the excitement, my Sh. class met on Monday evening at my rooms—all hands present—and we had one of our very pleasantest meetings. We finished *The Merchant of Venice*; and I read them a little essay I had written on the play, & esp. on the character of *Portia*. A lady-friend (and a dear one) of mine, who is a member, resembles Portia in so many points of character, that I wrote this essay *con amore*. The lady herself was not present, has not been for 6 weeks or more, owing to the death of her mother. She is the Secretary; and will resume her place again after about a month's longer absence. . . .

I have received nothing new since I wrote you, except the Macmillan, with Fleay's article on R. & J.—Like you, I was surprised that he made no reference to Mr. Furness' edition in it: otherwise it is a good paper: tho' I am not yet prepared to adopt his views. You know he propagated the same, about *Macbeth* & *Julius Cæsar*, and afterwards (measurably) retracted the heresy.[2] I have not read very much yet of Furness' *Hamlet*—i.e. I mean carefully & consecutively, tho' I take it up more or less every day. I have been living amid too much excitement lately, and my old, useful, valuable (to me at least) course of study is terribly interrupted. . . .

[1] The terrible state of affairs at Pittsburgh & elsewhere: The great Railway Strike of 1877; C describes its course in Zanesville in great detail later in this letter and in letters 205 and 206.
[2] afterwards (measurably) retracted the heresy: Furnivall made such an uproar about Fleay's attempt to take the Porter scene in *Mac.* away from Sh that Fleay recanted his theories about *JC* and *Mac*.

205: 31 July 1877

. . . Many thanks for referring me to the Augt *Galaxy*, and for your extracts from it. I will certainly get it. I fancy, however, that Mr. G. White exaggerates somewhat for the sake of writing a taking magazine article[1] to please the *people*. Tho' only a boy[2] when I was at Stratford, I certainly made no such observations as he does. I think his bump of *reverence* for things of the past is pretty small. He forgets that over 300 years—years wherein civilization has made its greatest advances—have transpired since Shakespeare lived at Stratford. What he now calls a *hovel* was then thought a comfortable dwelling; & all things must be judged by their contemporaneous surroundings. As Portia says:[3]

"Nothing is good, I see, without *respect*,"

i.e. nothing is *absolutely* good—but *relatively* so, as its surroundings are *respected* or *considered*; for Sh. often uses "*respect*" = *consideration*. . . .

[1] a taking magazine article: "A Visit to Stratford-on-Avon"; W liked nearly nothing, even spat out the water they gave him to drink at Anne Hathaway's cottage.
[2] only a boy: C was nineteen in the fall of 1840, on his way to matriculate at Oxford.
[3] As Portia says: *MV* 5.1.99.

206:   8 August 1877

. . . I was deeply interested in your criticism of my article on Dr Ingleby's new book. It is very evident that you and I do not agree—to any great extent—on the abilities of the learned Dr as a critic of Sh:, or on his merits as an Author. I am *exactly* of the same opinion *after* reading carefully your remarks that I was *before*; and it would take arguments very much stronger than anything you have advanced to induce me to hold any other. What I stated in my review I *meant*—every word of it. It is *not* "fulsome flattery" in my mind—but genuine conviction. "Put me to the test, and I the matter will re-word," which fulsome flattery would gambol from. No: for ten years—ever since I read his earliest productions, e.g., the "Fabrications" & "Sh: Controversy," I have never wavered in my high estimation of Dr Ingleby as a Shakespearian; and to-day, to quote Professor Corson's language to me in a letter—"I have the highest regard for Ingleby's learning, abilities, judgment, and sagacity: in matters pertaining to Shakespeare, and Shakespearian literature, I almost uniformly have adopted his views, and I regard him as the *soundest critic in England.*" This, you would say, is strong language; but it is "my sentiments"—tho' expressed in Prof: Corson's words. . . .

Your tastes & mine differ widely, in some things; *not in many*; and we can well afford to "agree to disagree" in some few matters, where we harmonize so well & truly in the great majority of cases. You admired highly, & wrote rapturously about, Sabin's book on Stratford, a book that, you know, seemed to me a very poor specimen of the thinnest patchwork and "bookmaking"; and you recollect how "wide as the poles asunder" we disagreed on your *scheme* of "resurrecting" Shakespeare's dust.—But this is all no reason why we should not be *good friends*; & where we do agree, admire our points of agreement more ardently, for disagreeing on some few others. Did we agree on *everything*, in as long & extensive a correspondence as we have maintained, it would imply great weakness, I think, on one side or the other—fear to express a candid opinion, lest offence might be taken,—or a very poor judgment, that had no candid opinions of its own.—. . .

In the case of *my* ailing pup, I must ask you to send him home,[1] where he belongs, so his owners can put him in hospital, and excise him scientifically; and then his friends can look after him, and sit up with him, if necessary, after the excision; as you know he is but a young pup, and his health is weakly at best; and he is rather a bad-tempered pup too, & might bite the doctor, who only wanted to perform a neat job on the close of his exordium.—Terence, I think, says:[2] "Redentem dicere verum, quid vetat?", which means in plain English,—**please return the Ms. notice of mine on Ingleby's book**, and I'll "fix" it: it's too long anyway, and needs to be *razeed*; and then I can doctor it up to suit your views better. But, I forgot; probably you would be adverse to having *any* notice at all of "The Man and The Book"—in the *Bibliopolist*. If so, just say so, plainly, and we will send this one to the "tomb of all the Capulets"—or farther—"down, down to Hell!"—There; don't say, hereafter, that I am not an obliging fellow. . . .

[1] *my* ailing pup . . . send him home: C has quoted the joke about the Irishman who cured his sick dog by amputating its tail just behind the ears. (*Tail = exordium*, N's word for the somewhat full conclusion of C's review.) It is odd that C should have written fulsomely about vol. 1 of *Shakespeare: The Man and the Book*, since he was harshly critical of the ch. on the portraits a few weeks earlier (see letter 153). N did not send the MS. "home," but without telling C, later submitted it to *Robinson's Epitome of Literature* (see letter 249).

[2] Terence, I think, says: The expression is from Horace, *Satires* I.i.24–25.

207:   13 August 1877

. . . Respecting myself, what I have said, or may say, to *you*, of course *you will hold sacred*. It is a sacred matter for *me*. This lady I do truly esteem & love; and I know too that she esteems & loves *me*. She has told me so—over & over. Besides, she has discarded a wealthy & importunate lover, in Washington City, on my account. I have her father's "hearty consent and approval" (his own written words) to my addresses. Yet the disparity of our ages (she is 17 or 18 years younger than I am),[1] and my humble circumstances, (for she is the daughter (only daughter) of one of our *wealthiest* merchants), are barriers that *I* cannot get over. I love her so dearly—so tenderly—so unselfishly—I cannot bear to ask her—*willing as she may be*— to unite her lot to mine.—However, I shall continue to visit her, for the happiness & attraction are too great to permit anything else yet,—and leave the rest to God or Providence. She has refused several eligible offers, & is now only about 30 years old. She is highly accomplished, and *loves* "*Shakespeare.*" . . .

[1] (she is 17 or 18 years younger than I am): C was 56 at this time, Agnes 33.

208:　18 August 1877

My dear Norris:

I am in receipt of your most kind & pleasant & welcome letter of the 15th., which reached me yesterday. I thought I had better answer it to-day, as I shall be quite busy next week. On Monday my "Shakespeare Club"— which takes *some*, tho' but little, preparation. Tuesday, I am invited to Mr. Fillmore's to dine with Dr and Mrs. Theo Cuyler.[1] On Wednesday I have to prepare the questions for an "Examination" of our High School Teachers. They have assigned me "Latin & Greek" for my share of this examination. Now I *used* to be thoroughly well able to undertake such an examination; but *now*—only think—almost 30 years since I have looked into a Greek author—that is, to read critically. No wonder I am *rusty*. But then I am just about these days so *happy*—owing to various causes "too tedious to mention"—that I am perfectly *reckless* what I undertake. I believe I should not hesitate to examine a *bishop* in theology, or Tyndall and Huxley in science and chemistry. This examination occurs next Thursday & Friday; after which I am booked for Cleveland and Detroit for a few days' visit.

I enclose you, to read, a letter that I have just received from Mr. F. G. Fleay,[2] every word of which is very *interesting*, & I think will please you. I wrote to him some time ago, giving him a little criticism on his "Collins' Series" book—"Shakespearian Study," and asked him for his "picture." This is his reply, & his "photo" enclosed. . . . I know of no publishers in this country, who would be willing to undertake such an edition of Shakespeare, as Fleay speaks of. The "lines" I gave him[3] resembled somewhat those I indicated in my article on Dr. Ingleby's book. I feel the want of such an edition for my Club; and no doubt it would be acceptable to *many such* in both this country & England. Do you know of any publishing House, such as he names, in the U. S.? I fear he will have to abandon it, or print at his own expense.—. . .

Did I ever tell you that some time ago I noticed an article in "N. & Q.," signed "M. P.," particularly referring to the verb *fen* or *fend*, & rather pluming itself on the discovery (!) that the poet Wordsworth, who uses the word "*weather-fend*," was the *inventor* of the word? I wrote a little "Note" to "N. & Q.," which was published on p. 495 of the June 23d, 1877, number, stating that "M. P." must have been very forgetful of his "Shakespeare," or he would never have given Wordsworth the credit of *forming* this compound;

reminding him[a] of Ariel's using it to Prospero, in *The Tempest*:—"All prisoners, Sir. In the line-grove which *weather-fends*[4] your cell." On p. 19, of the July 7th, 1877, No. of "N. & Q.," "M. P." writes a very gentlemanly note about it, saying

> x x "When I at that time sought for it in glossaries without success, [what kind of "glossaries" could they have been?] and remembered never having heard that compound, I attributed to Wordsworth its formation or introduction; and, finding it in his works, might have claimed it as a *Cumberland word*, but for J. C.'s timely reminder from the New World, for which I am particularly obliged and delighted," &c. &c.—

It is singular how anyone who had ever once read the passage in Shakespeare, & seen how *appropriate* it is— —the *right* word in the *right* place— could have ever forgot it, or attributed it to Wordsworth!—. . .

I told you that she—**Miss Agnes Fillmore**—was an only daughter of one of our best citizens—a wealthy merchant here. Owing to her mother's delicate health, for years she has been her father's companion—very dearly beloved—and I knew the trial it would be for him to give her up. He is withal a most sensible man—a Christian & a gentleman. She is to-day wearing a diamond ring that I gave her, the *first present* she ever accepted from any gentleman. And, by the by, one of the first presents I ever made her, was a set of Mr. Furness' New Variorum Shakespeare—the five vols,[5] including Mrs. F.'s Concordance, having heard her speak admiringly of that work. She has read nearly all through the *Hamlet*. Last evening I asked her opinion of the Prince's *insanity*, and she very modestly said that while she could not presume to advance it as against Mr. Furness', yet "upon a simple reading of the play, in her judgment it was *feigned*"—an opinion that of course I subscribe to *now*.—. . .

Her qualities & accomplishments are of the sterling kind—the accompaniments of a *golden* disposition & heart. Yet she plays well & sings— draws—& paints in oils—knows French, & a little Latin, and is perfectly well read in not only the Poets, but in *general literature*; a noble companion for any gentleman, & *much—much too good for poor me*! *How* this has all come to pass, I'll be hanged if I can tell you. Though I always admired her character and her manners—was always pleased & happy to be in her society—and bowed, talked to her, and walked with her, whenever luck threw us together; yet four months ago I had no more conception that to-day *we should be engaged, lovers* than I had of taking an aerial flight to the moon. . . . It all seems *too much* happiness—so unexpected after 13 years of lonely widowerhood—*too good* to last—a blessing of which I am too–too unworthy! I am so *much* older than she is, it looks like a sacrifice on her part. And I am such a *poor* devil!—It is all very nice to say, had I been master of an income of twentyfive thousand a year, with a gorgeous mansion—elegant carriage & equipage, &c., it would have made no difference; I should have laid them all at her feet, & loved her just the same. I *have no* such attractions. What is it that Othello says? "Poor and content is rich, and rich enough." All very nice. "Something declined in the vale of years: yet that's not much."—The best thing he says is—"Yet She had *eyes*, and chose *me*.". . .

⸻

[1] Dr . . . Theo. Cuyler: (1822–1909), the evangelical clergyman whose fiery sermons, conservative theology, and temperance activity made him well known beyond his Brooklyn congregation.

[2] a letter . . . from Mr. F. G. Fleay: It is not known to survive, but the reply C wrote to Fleay is #2 in MS. Y.c. 1372; C's letter about the Collins book is #1 in Y.c. 1372.

[3] The "lines" I gave him: I.e., the desiderata for an edn.

[4] *weather-fends*: *Tmp.* 5.1.10.

[5] the five vols: *Rom.* (1871), *Mac.* (1873), *Ham.* (2 vols., 1877), and Helen Kate Rogers Furness's *Concordance to Shakespeare's Poems* (1875).

[a] reminding him] reminding ↑him↓ MS.

⸻

209:   22 August 1877

. . . Monday evening we had a delightful meeting of our "Club." All hands there *before* time, & every moment was interesting. We finished *Rich. II*—having given it 2 evenings of abt 3 hours each. What with the careful reading *aloud*—the explanations & criticisms, verbal and æsthetic, &c., I felt as if *I knew* more about the play, after we had finished, than I did before we took it up. And so with all of the plays. I am getting benefit from the exercise—*discere docendo*—as well as the "club." They all appeared to enjoy the meeting hugely. So far we have not had a "rub," but everything pleasant, harmonious, instructive. Next play is "Twelfth Night"; and my friend—Miss Agnes, is to be there—for the first time in 3 months nearly. I shall escort her home, which will be the first public recognition of our engagement. She sent me several beautiful bouquets of choice flowers, to adorn my poor apartments for the last meeting; and they are still "stealing & giving odor" around me. So far, "the course of true love" &c. has been, I fear, *too "smooth"* to last. It *may*—and Pray God it *always may*: yet Sh. says it "never does," and he certainly knew. A feeling somewhat resembling that which the Queen spoke of so mournfully in *Rich. II*, before her troubles commenced, sometimes possesses me; a feeling that the present happiness is too great to endure, & that some unexpected cloud will ere long darken my horizon. But it is *folly* to anticipate evil. It may exist only in my jealous imagination; and "Sufficient unto the day is the evil thereof." Good bye, my dear fellow! God bless you, and us all!

Ever your friend,
J. C.

211: 7 September 1877

. . . It is so strange I did not find this out ten years ago. Here have I been
living within a few squares of this same young lady for years, & never once
thought of her as anything more than a very desirable *friend*. I *always*
admired her noble & solid character, & especially her freedom from that
everlasting taint of young ladyhood—*gossip*. *Her* name was never mixed up
with the fashionable talk of beaux & belles, thanks, I think very much, to
one of the best of *mothers*, who was one of our most refined & elegant
ladies. One Sunday night, when I was feeling especially blue, & *lonesome*,
and just thinking of moving my boarding place, (it was the last week in
March), her pew in Church being *full*, she took a seat in mine, where for 13
years I have been sitting "alone in my glory." I fancied she felt, & appreciated, & perhaps *pitied* with those kind loving eyes of hers, my lonely
condition: instead of duly listening to the sermon I could not *help* thinking
of her; and so I ventured, after service, to escort her home. We walked
much farther than there was really any need for, our talk was so thoroughly
& mutually agreeable. As I was parting from her, she told me she had
something on her mind to say to me. She wanted my *help* with a "Shakespeare Reading Club"; but as she knew I had so positively declined, &
refused some two or three other ladies, she feared it was hopeless to ask
me. Something in her manner, &, besides, something in my own heart, so
attracted me, I gave a sort of hesitating consent. . . .

212: 27 September 1877

. . . I have just received another very kind note from Mr. Fleay. He says
he has ordered the publishers to send me a copy of his little book "Chaucer
and Spenser"—published I think in the "Collins' Series." I put out his pipe
about getting a "Shakespeare" published in the U. S., and advised him to
publish his Notes & Commentaries in a volume by themselves.[1]. . .

I cannot tell you how delighted, as well as edified, I am with Mr. Furness'
Hamlet. What a laborious condensation, yet how very copious & exhaustive! To read this play in this edition, with all the notes & criticisms, is a
liberal education of itself. What a debt of gratitude the world of Sh. owes
Mr. F.! . . .

[1] in a volume by themselves: The materials for the intended edn. were probably subsumed
in F's *Chronicle History of the Life and Work of William Shakespeare* (1886).

213: 14 October 1877

. . . I am exceedingly pleased with Dowden's new "Primer." It is really an
admirable compendium of accurate & valuable Shakespearian information,

knowledge, & criticism, well-written,[a] & brought down to date. I have read it through three times—some of it oftener. Every student of the Poet should have it *by heart*. It has none of the *grandiloquence* of Dowden's other book: and I like it better. I think it very superior—every way superior—to Mr. Fleay's "Shakespearian Study." It has none of those vexatious "theories" that Fleay is so ripe in. . . .

The publishers of Virtue's Knight's "Imperial Shakspere" took from 70 to 75 copies of the work from Subscribers in Zanesville, and I presume in proportion[b] from other places all over the country, and got them all bound in New York, at prices ranging from $8.00 to $25.00 for the 2 volumes. Mine is *sumptuously* bound in Half Levant morocco, bright brown, gilt edges, and heavy gilt mouldings, and beautifully tooled & gilt in Shakespearian & emblematic designs. It cost $16..00 for the 2 vols. folio. It is a magnificent specimen of binding. The sides are leatherette I think. It looks as if *full bound*. It is very strong & substantial, as well as beautiful & rich. One could not well imagine a more *superb binding*, in every particular, except being *full bound*, & that would have cost, in the same style, $25.00.—I entirely concur in every word you say about *binding*. As a general thing, all my books are well bound—many very elegantly. But before I knew much about such things, I had one lot of some 60 volumes almost spoiled, by letting a new binder do them, *cheap*. They are strong enough, but clumsy, and look common. As you observe, one never has any pleasure or comfort taking down a book poorly bound. Like you, I am a real *dandy* about my books. I cannot *bear* dirty or imperfect copies; and I don't like to see anyone's *writing* in books, except *my own*. Occasionally I get hold of an *old* annotated book that is additionally valuable on that account, e.g. my copy of Capell's Notes; but mostly the "pencillings by the way" are very shallow; I always expunge them when I can. My taste in binding has improved, I think, vastly since I knew *you*. Yours is so exquisite, & correct, & fastidious, that you have done *me* good.—I am taking my copy of The *Encyclopædia Britannica* in Hf. russia, extra, gilt, and it is well & strongly and very neatly bound; much better than I could get it done here, for the extra cost.—. . .

[a] well-written] well- | written MS.
[b] in proportion] ↑in proportion↓ MS.

214:   27 October 1877

. . . Travelling suits me very well, barring the absence from home and my library. I always have *some* books with me of course. But one cannot *study*, you know, when racing from town to town, & hotel to hotel. I regret it most on account of the break up of my regular, exhaustive, study of *Shakespeare*. I went through *Twelfth Night* lately, very thoroughly, but it took twice as long as it ought. What a blessing it must be to the Shakespearian student of the future, when he can have *All* he can want in one volume, or two at most, for each play: i.e. when Furness' "New Variorum" is completed. At present we have to read such a fearful amount maybe a dozen times over, in order to *miss* nothing. . . .

What G. White says on Grammar, philology, &c., is always readable & instructive. A New York correspondent of the *Springfield Republican* says of him:—

"Richard Grant White, who is safely back from Europe, and has got the salt out of his clothes, has been offered the chair of English Literature[1] in our city college. He has held an office in the custom house, which enabled him to *live*, while doing excellent literary work which hasn't paid, and the appointment to a field of congenial labour will doubtless be as acceptable to him as it is creditable to the college. Mr. White is *not* a very popular man. His pen has a very sharp point, and his ink is apt to be vitriolic. His teaching capacity is as yet an unknown quantity, and perhaps he would make a much better Librarian than Professor. But he is a man of ideas, a studious, acute, suggestive, provocative, combustible person; and it is hardly a credit to American institutions that such a man has been obliged to get his living by purely secular labour so long. Mr. R. H. Stoddart is another instance in which a man of real culture and literary creativeness has been sacrificed to bread and butter necessities. After working hard in the Custom House for years, often too weary to write a word after his work for the day has been done, he has been appointed City Librarian at a salary of $1.000 a year. This is the way New York rewards her sons, and shows her appreciation of literary effort. Mr. E. H. Stedman,[2] one of the finest of American poets after Longfellow and Emerson and Lowell, and one of the most appreciative of our critics, too, is obliged to support his family by exacting Banking operations, giving to literature only the crumbs of time that fall from the brokers' board. But then we have erected an elegant statue to the dead poet Halleck,[3] which many people seem to think atones for any amount of injustice to living writers."—. . .

Do you know what Watt's *Bibliotheca Britannica* is? It is an elaborate work, something like Lowndes "Biblio: Manual," or Allibone's "Dictionary of Authors." It is in 4 vols., quarto—the 4 generally bound in two; & was published in 1824. Allibone copied extensively from this comprehensive & most valuable Work, & is still everlastingly referring to it for more. The first 2 vols. contain the Lives, &c. &c. of all the *Authors*, the last 2 accounts of their *Works*—the different editions, &c.—I have long desired to own a copy; but it is scarce & high; generally brings from £6 to £10—according to condition & binding. I saw one advertised by Bangs, at Auction, the latter part of this month, & sent an open bid, i.e. to buy it for me, providing it did not go beyond its jobbing value, & *not* to give any *fancy* price for it, or bid for me at all if there was *much* competition for it. I am anxiously waiting to hear from it. I should dearly love to have it, if it sold at a *fair bargain*. . . .

Did I tell you that *Snider* has arranged to publish his book[4] in St. Louis, in 2 vols. of about 450 pp. each, sm. 8vo, good paper, wide margins, & good typography? I have been ding-donging for a long time into him to be very careful to have a nice-*looking* book; as the matter itself being so *dry*, unless *invitingly* published, it would fall "flatlong" from the press. He has revised & rewritten most of the essays, & adds about 100 pp. of new matter never before printed, and an "Introduction," &c. He has to *advance a portion* of the expense of printing &c., and will have an edition of 1,000 copies. The contract is that it shall be a superior piece of typography; and altogether I give him great credit for his enterprise in bringing to light his firstborn in *sightly* form. He sent me a couple of signatures of the proofs of his "Introduction," and really it is *very beautifully* printed in clear good size type, on good white paper, and has fine *wide margins*. It speaks very well for his printers.—. . .

Like yourself, I have been "watching & waiting" to see a good long "Review" of Furness' *Hamlet* in the *Athenæum* or *Academy*, or both; and I am truly surprised it is not forthcoming. Now *here* is something that richly merits a review by a Shakespearian critic & scholar, able to do the work justice, & give it an introduction to English & German students. And yet *non est inventus*; while they have reviews of books that have but little or no interest to the mass of readers. . . .

[1] "offered the chair of English Literature": *DAB* does not mention it, but does say that W left the Custom House in 1878.

[2] E. H. Stedman: Edmund Clarence Stedman. By the 1870s, S owned his own brokerage firm; he is said (*DAB*) to have enjoyed the work, but to have written creatively late at night after long days in the office.

[3] dead poet Halleck: Fitz-Greene Halleck; the statue was unveiled in 1877.

[4] his book: *System of Shakespeare's Dramas* (St. Louis: G. T. Jones, 1877).

215:   30 October 1877

. . . Old Mr. Collier has sent me "Two Noble Kinsmen," & "A Yorkshire Tragedy," and says, one more—"Mucedorus"—will complete his undertaking. I have remitted to him my last *Pound*, and once again urgently coaxed him to "beg, buy, borrow, or steal" a copy of *The Tempest*, to complete my copy. In his last, he said he *thought he might* find, or pick up, a copy. And, as Timmins says, he always has *one copy* hid away, to be miraculously forthcoming on an emergency. I often have fancied that that weakness of his— to *find* something no one expected, & so to show his research—was the source of much of his trouble with the "Corr. Fo. 1632." If he had not made such a fuss about procuring it so cheap & so unexpectedly, or made so much *mystery* about its age & authority, &c, but had taken the *find* as an ordinary occurrence, & used the "emendations" for what they were worth, he would have acquired *honour*, instead of envy, & odium, & *suspicion*. . . .

216:   10 November 1877 Wheeling, West Va.

. . . I have not yet called on our friend *Leighton*, and I fear I shall not have time at present. I would like to do so, as he has just got out his new "Dramatic Poem"—*At the Court of King Edwin*—pubd by the Lippencotts of Philadelphia; so I presume *you* have seen it ere this. I expect to find a "presentation copy" from the author, when I reach home. I have just read a notice, or review, of it, in a Wheeling paper, (which Leighton will of course send you); and it speaks in very glowing terms of it indeed; quoting passages that "the great Shakespeare himself rarely equalled, & never excelled"! Mr. Leighton read to me a large portion of this "drama," when I was here in June last. I thought it was more spirited, possessed more poetic *imagery*, than "The Sons of Godwin." Still, *entre nous*, it is *rather* **dry** *reading* to me. . . .

You are perfectly right about Āvon, not Ăvon. I have always so called it, & that is its pronunciation on the ground. Nothing *sickens* me more than to hear some *prig* of a bumpkin quote a line or two of Shakespeare, with—"As we have it in the bard of Ăvon";—bah!—. . .

I have ordered the No. of the *Nation* you refer to, containing Review of F.'s *Hamlet*. How you must prize that scrap of Mr. F.'s *Preface*![1] Some future day, it will be invaluable. Why *did* he destroy all the rest? How "some dozen or sixteen" of his intimate friends would have *rejoiced* to have preserved it among their archives! . . .

[1] that scrap of Mr. F's *Preface*: Presumably proof sheets.

217:   22 November 1877 Coshocton, Ohio

. . . Thanks for calling my attention particularly to B. & F.'s "Bonduca." I shall read it carefully the first opportunity. I read *all through* B. & F.'s Works, several years ago; but not critically. I remember being pleased with *Bonduca*, and I remember the character of *Caratach*. I think with you that *Fletcher* is a far superior dramatist & writer to Beaumont. In those plays— *Henry VIII*, & *Two Noble Kinsmen*, e.g., where he worked with Shakespeare, it is *no easy* matter to me to distinguish their scenes. Fletcher draws *men* with a masterly hand: he is a thorough observer of human nature, & probes its motives to the core, and *describes* all so beautifully. In his *women* he is not fortunate—not like Shakespeare. He yields too much to the custom of his time, & makes them too coarse & licentious.—. . .

I was surprised to learn that Mr. Fish does not study & read the "Old Dramatists." I think, with you, that no one can be[a] a through student of Shakespeare, without being thoroughly posted in these writers. Not alone for the sake of noting the vast *superiority* of our beloved Shakespeare over *them*, but also for the sake of learning numberless words & phrases of the time, customs, habits, manners, &c. &c. needful to illustrate *allusions* in the text of *our* Poet. I have received Wagner's edn. of *Dr Faustus*, & am reading it. It is *very ably* edited indeed. The whole of the Series of "London English Classics" is ably edited. I have ordered several of their books, & will report. . . .

[a]no one can be] ↑no↓ one can be MS.

218:   22 November 1877 Newcomerstown, Ohio

. . . I forgot to tell you that I sent for the No. of the "Nation," containing the review of Mr. F.'s *Hamlet*. I do not think much of it. Mr Furness' epithet "childish" fits it very well. By the way, *when* (if ever) are we to have *your* "*Bibliopolist*" *review*? Is the "Bibliopolist" a *defunct* institution? It might as well be—the year nearly up, and, I believe, only 2 numbers issued! Do you ever write to the Sabins about it? Their subscription list, for *next year*, will be slight I fancy.—As for the *Nation* review, without conceit I think I could have done one as well as that *myself*, on very little provocation. . . .Have you seen Longfellow's recent tributory sonnet to Tennyson? I think it is capital & clever. . . .

220:   26 November 1877

. . . Sometime ago I bought at Auction (New York) a whole year, 12 parts, with the Indexes—2 vols—for 1866—of "*Notes & Queries*" (London) for $1..80, & thought it **very cheap** (as it truly was): but last week I bought at another auction a similar whole year, 1868, 12 parts, 2 vols, for *63 cents*! Can anything beat that, unless they *give* them away? They cost *a guinea* a year in London; and *less than a dollar* delivered in Zanesville! I am gradually picking up the back years, which are hardest to get, being mostly out of print. I commenced to subscribe to it in 1872, & am sorry I did not begin sooner. I like this periodical—particularly for its "Shakespeariana," of which there is more or less in nearly every *week's* No.; and there are lots of other entertaining & interesting articles on literary topics in it. . . .

I saw a *Halliwell Folio* advertised, in an English Catalogue, for £70..; as there is no duty now on it, that would be about $420; or $466 ⅔ counting 3 shillings to the dollar. The price keeps up well; had it not been such "hard times," it would no doubt have been a great deal more. However, had it been £50, or even £40, I don't believe I could have bought it *now*. But I still live in hope. Whenever I go to Cincinnati, O., I always take "a good read" in the copy in their Public Library. . . .

My dear *fiancée* is well, and as *lovely* & *loving* as ever. I want (if possible) to get back home to dine with her on "Thanksgiving Day," tho' I fear it will be hard to make it. I gave her a beautiful copy of the "Characteristics of Women," when I found that she was a great admirer of *Mrs. Jameson*. Who can help loving that charming book? I should think all *women*, of taste & education, would especially like it. I also presented her my handsomely bound Knight's *Imperial*.[1] It looks more *comme il faut* on her table, than on mine. In fact I had no *room* for it on mine, so the gift was, as Ingleby says, κἀν σμικρῷ χαρις,[2] and did not deserve thanks. . . .

I have been urging Snider[a] to employ his pen in translating some of the best papers[3] in the 9 years of the German *Shakespeare Year Books*. I think a *rich volume*, useful to English Shakespearians who cannot read *German*, might be made from selecting the most interesting Sh. articles in those valuable volumes, and translating them *well*. It was a *selfish* request, or *desire*, on my part. I am always mortified when I see the *titles* of these articles, and cannot read them. Snider is a splendid *German* scholar, and his knowledge of Shakespeare, & experience in writing, would make him *more* than a mere *translator*. But he says he is *tired* at present—written out—& can not bear[b] the drudgery of translating. I often wish too that someone would translate Delius' *notes* on his edition of Shakespeare. I have the edn. & read the *Text*, occasionally, which, as well as long extracts in the Preface & Introductions, is in English; but the greatest portion of the Notes is in German, and might as well be Hindoostanee for me. . . .

[1] my handsomely bound Knight's *Imperial*: I.e., his complimentary copy of Virtue & Yorston's Edition.
[2] κἀν σμικρω χαρις: *And if so, with small generosity.*
[3] to employ his pen in translating some of the best papers: Such a translation from *Shakespeare-Jahrbuch* has never been made.

[a] urging Snider] urging him MS.
[b] can not bear] can ↑not↓ bear MS.

221:   28 November 1877 Mt. Vernon, Ohio

. . . I got a sheet of paper, and have just written a letter to *Sabin & Sons*, asking them about the "Bibliopolist," and urging them as politely, but earnestly, as I could, not to suffer it to become defunct. The fact is *I miss it greatly*. It is the only substitute we have in America for the London "Notes

& Queries," & you know what a valuable & entertaining little periodical *that* is: and every year becoming more so. I ventured to tell them that they could not expect it to pay *financially*, unless it were issued *regularly*, & *some* care & attention devoted to it. Every good thing requires care & attention. I urged them, if necessary to make it successful, to enlarge it, publish it monthly, and charge more for it. I should think that as a "Catalogue" of their Stock of Secondhand Books alone, it would be indispensable & profitable to them. The fact is, they have simply let it go by default through sheer neglect & carelessness. I *miss* the "Shakespearian Gossip" *most*, and it was beginning to attract notice, & would have increased in interest and value.—Well, I have done all I could; and if it die out, I cannot help it. . . .

223:   3 December 1877

. . . Thanks. . .for telling me what Bro. Hudson says and thinks of me.[1] I am sure I am grateful to him for his kind opinion. When I was trying to help him in his work, I can truly say I had no thought of any acknowledgment: I did it quite as much for my own improvement as for anything, and I found it *did* do me good. The numberless passages I worked over, collating & **thinking**, became thus impressed on my mind. He kept me up to the work—giving me no rest, but when I had finished & sent in one batch of *notes*, down would come another list of obscurities, or *cruces*, to try to solve in some better way than they had been heretofore. I find all this useful to me *now*, in reading the Poet with the "Club." Tho', of course, we do not attempt to enter upon very intricate points of textual criticism, yet I can often, in plain language, make a difficult spot clear to them, from myself understanding everything about it, & the context.—And speaking of the "Club" reminds me of your kind offer to send us some copies of Mr. Brae's books. If not too great trouble to you, I can assure you they will be gratefully received. I will most gladly pay the express charges. If you do not think it would be too many, I could nicely, and to good advantage, distribute say 15 or 16 copies of each. I would not give them to *all* the members of the Club; but would send a copy here & there among appreciative Shakespearians in the *West*. I would send 2 or 3 to Cincinnati, & one or two to Wheeling, &c. and help you, in so doing, to carry out Mr. Brae's intention. I *bought* 2 copies myself (one when I was at the Centennial.) The "C. C. & S." is one of my especial favourites. The criticisms on *Love's Labour's Lost*, in that tract, are very excellent. It was thro' that book I first became acquainted (by correspondence) with Mr. Brae. In the copy I received from A. R. Smith was a MS. letter from Mr. Brae to *John* Russell Smith, regarding its publication, or that of some other of Brae's books—perhaps the *Astrolabe*. I returned it to Mr. Brae, and so commenced our correspondence. . . .

What is Mr. Rolfe's address? I should sometime like to drop a line to him, & make his epistolary acquaintance. I like his editions, and (as you say) they seem to be very successful. At 60¢ apiece they are cheap books, & well worth the price. . . .

I was very glad to hear that you were able to disabuse Mr. Furness' mind regarding Mr. Hudson's being the author of the Hf-page notice of his *Hamlet*. Mr. Hudson wrote me to the same effect, of the *N. A. Review* being only willing to give him a Hf-page, & his refusing to accept it for *such a book*.—I entirely agree with you, that it cannot be from any *jealousy*, that the *Academy* & *Athenæum* have not pubd reviews of Mr. F.'s *Hamlet*. The *Athenæum* pubd a very fair one of his *R. & J.*; *why* any has not appeared of *Hamlet* I cannot conceive. There is no *reason* for jealousy. Surely Clark & Wright could have no cause. Their Cam. Edn. is out of print; & Mr. F. has ever written in the highest terms of that edn. Perhaps one or both may yet issue one. They are fearfully *slow* in old England. . . .

I told you, I think, how puzzled I had the members of our Club over the expression "Than if you[a] had at *leisure* known of this," (*vide K. John*, Act V. Sc. vi. line 27,)—some contending it was perfectly correct, & others that it expressed the very opposite to what it meant. I have since noted down some other passages, where the Poet uses *leisure* peculiarly. In *Rich. II*: I, i, 5—"the boisterous late appeal, Which then our *leisure* would not let us hear." Here it evidently means—not what *we* mean by 'leisure,'—but—*want of leisure*; "which then we *had not time* to hear."—Cf., too, *Rich. III*: V, iii, 97: "the *leisure* and the fearful time cuts off the ceremonious vows of love"; & (line 238): "The *leisure*[b] and enforcement of the time forbids to dwell upon," and *Hen. VIII*: III, ii, 140: "you have scarce time to steal from spiritual *leisure* a brief span to keep your earthly audit." . . .

"Miss Agnes" is also well. I spent last evening there, and we read Dickens' "Christmas Carol" together. What a "pretty & pathetical" little story. To-night another engagement prevents my going there again; but she writes me so that I receive letters from her at nearly every town I go to. How much happier I am *now*, than I *used to be*! As Malvolio says: "Well, Jove, not I, is the doer of this, and he is to be thanked."—. . .

---

[1] telling me what Bro. Hudson says and thinks of me: As early as 12 December 1873, H was telling N of the "highly valuable aid" he was getting from C. There are references to C in the highest terms of praise in several letters written to N by H in the late 1870s. The letter alluded to here may be the one H wrote to N 27 November 1877, which praises C's work, expresses anxiety that impending marriage may distract C from Sh, and promises "if the edition should ever come out, the result of his help will be fully set forth. That is all I can do to repay his very able service . . ." (Hudson Letters, Uncatalogued Autograph MS Collection, Folger Shakespeare Library). For H's statement about C in the Harvard Edn., and for his further effort to repay C, see note 2 to letter 171.

[a] "Than if you] "Than if ┼ you MS.
[b] "The *leisure*] the *leisure* MS.

224: 7 December 1877 Morrow, Ohio

. . . What you say of Mr. Simpson's[1] "School of Shakespeare" is *every word true*. It is a fearful price (abt. $6..25) for such a book. I often think if I were to begin again collecting a "Shakespeare Library," I would not be so careful about getting *all the modern trash* that is printed; but make such a selection of new & modern Sh. literature as was really *good*; & spend more money on the old & rare Folios & Quartos, which are always increasing in value & rarity, & would be a good[a] investment *financially*. My collection contains almost everything printed, with the Poet's name to it, since 1709; but it is very deficient in the old & scarce 17th century rarities: and yet in a Shakespeare library Catalogue, these are what are most noted & quoted. If you and I, when we first began collecting, had put our money into the Folios & Quartos, which were *then* so very much cheaper, & more easily obtainable, than they now are, we should have done a wiser thing, than to expend the hundreds of dollars we have expended on such a lot of modern books, that have really no value either intrinsically, or financially. However, it is now too late; and "crying over spilt milk" was never a wise thing.—. . .

[1]Mr. Simpson's: Richard Simpson was an enthusiastic believer in Sh's putative role as "Johannes factotum" in a number of plays from the 1580s and early 1590s. It was he who first proposed (4 *Notes & Queries* 8 [1871]: 1–3) that Sh had a hand in *The Play of Sir Thomas More*. Seven apocryphal plays are rptd. in the two vols. (1878) of *The School of Shakespeare*.

[a]would be a good] would ~~have bee~~ ↑be↓ a good MS.

225: 19 December 1877

. . . You really are a charming letter writer. I also found the package by express, containing 15 copies each of Mr. A. E. Brae's "C. C. & S.," and "Astrolabe." Your suggestion that I *write him*, I had before thought of; and shall certainly do so, very soon. Thanks for his address—He was my *first* English correspondent—I mean anent Shakespeare. And it was he, living *then* at Leeds, England, who kindly introduced me to Dr. Ingleby. . . . . I shall carefully distribute these copies, as gifts from *him*; I do not intend, by any means, to give copies to *all* the Members of our "Club." Some would hardly appreciate them duly. But some 8 or 9 *would*, I think, do so. I will give one to Capt. Goddard, the first opportunity, with your best regards. I shall place a copy of each in our "*Athenæum*," a quite large Public Library here; and one of each in the "Buckingham Library," another public subscription library in Putnam. I also intend to send copies to the Cincinnati Public Library. I shall be in no *hurry* about distributing them; but try in each case to place them where they will be likely "to do the most good." Poor old Mr. Brae! I am sorry he is so poor. For he is an excellent, acute, Shakespearian scholar. His only fault to my mind is, he is too hasty—too hot-tempered. How he hates old Collier! It will give me great pleasure to renew my correspondence with him. Do you recollect a most *incisive*, yet witty & scholarly, letter he wrote you, reviewing Prof. Corson's note on Hamlet's "good kissing carrion"? I copied it into my "Collectanea," with your permission. It is *capital*. Do you know what he is doing? How he lives? Or anything about his habits, age? &c.—He & Ingleby, I once understood from the latter, had simply *stopped* corresponding; no good reason for it, only *just stopped*. His p.p.[1] tract "Prospero's Clothesline,"[a] &c. has some admirable criticism in it. It is such a man as Brae, who ought write reviews of new Sh. books. One would think *that* would *pay* him too, as the edd. of English periodicals generally, I understand, *pay* their contributors well for acceptable articles. What an admirable "review" *he* could write, if he would, of Mr. Furness' *new Variorum Shakespeare*. Poor old gentleman! Perhaps he has not *had a copy*; too poor to buy one, & none given him, & he living at some out of the way spot at Guernsey!—

It was real kind of you to undertake to try to get some of his books sold in America. Such a treatise as that of Chaucer's on the "Astrolabe," must naturally be a hard book to *sell*, in any country. I wonder that he should go to the trouble and expense of editing it. Did you ever *try to read* it? Possibly it might interest a natural-born astronomer: but then I am *not* one of that species of *genius*; & I found it Dutch, or Hebrew, or Bengalee, to me. . . .

Do you ever read any of Joseph Cook's lectures?[2] They are very able; and many of them very interesting. I wish you could get hold of a "Boston Advertiser," containing his lecture delivered on Monday evening, the 3d inst.—I suppose that dated the 4th Decr. would be the one. I got it in a Cincinnati paper. It contains the lecture entitled *"Conscience in Shakespeare"*; and it well deserves both reading & preservation. He pits Shakespeare against Tyndall, the celebrated scientist, who, it seems, recently said in a lecture at Birmingham, Eng., that whenever a man offended, he could not help but offend; that there was no such thing as freedom of will. His delineation of the *life* and *philosophy* of our Shakespeare is grand; and his array of well selected quotations from the poet on *conscience* is splendid. If I can get another copy I will send it you.—By the by, speaking of Boston, did you see the account of a Boston business man, a gentleman of considerable wealth & culture & social distinction, who had lived to a good old age without ever having read *Shakespeare*. At length he was persuaded by his friend one winter to take up the poet, and read him through. Several months afterwards his friend met him & asked what[b] he thought of these productions, and if they were not very fine? *"Fine,"* said he, in a glow of enthusiasm, "that does not begin to express it; they are *glorious,* Sir; I was delighted with them, Sir; why, there are not twenty men in Boston could have written these Plays, Sir."—

Mr. Collier's 4to edn. of *Venus & Adonis,* and *Lucrece* is to hand. I suppose 2 more Nos., containing the Sonnets & Poems, will close the set. I am sorry

he pub*d Yorkshire Tragedy*, and *Mucedorus*, in this lovely edn. They are no
addition to it. It was right enough to include *Edward III* and *Two N. Kinsmen*,[3] because I think there is no doubt of Sh.'s hand in these, more or less,
especially in the latter; but I see nothing of Sh. in the two other plays. Do
you? . . .

The boys & young men of the present day have a great advantage over
those in my youth. *We* had no annotated, handy little edns. of Shakespeare, Milton, *et alii*,[c] and so we either did not read them at all, or in the
unweildy, inaccurate, collected edns. in our fathers' libraries. . . .

Many thanks, my dear fellow, for *post*ing me respecting the new regulations of our *Post* office in sending dutiable books by *post*. It is a regular *bore*.
The whole thing of collecting *duty* on books, or literature of any kind, is
absurd in a "free and enlightened" country—the *"only* free country in the
world." Science & knowledge should be as *free as air* to all; nursed, &
circulated among our citizens, no matter where it comes from. If from
England, or France, or Germany, so much the more should it be encouraged & disseminated *here*; it is so much *clear profit* to our country.
Suppose a scientific man,[d] or a literary man, see a work advertised[e] on
some special subject, connected with his business, or manufacture, that he
wants to aid him in that business. How is he to get it? Probably so few
would be required, it would not pay to *reprint* here; so it's no use waiting
for *that*. If he order it, it must come through the Custom House, with a long
bill of items (*crede experto*) tacked to it, amounting to 10 times the price of
the book, duty included. It is simple robbery at the N. Y. Custom House. I
got a small box that way, not long ago; & tho' there was *not one* dutiable
book in it, the "charges" were over $1300! I wrote for the "items," and you
never saw such a string of swindling charges. Postage $100! Insurance
$150! Storage 75¢! Cartage $125! Fees $4..50! &c. &c. *ad nauseam*. The ex-
pense of *collecting* the duty on books comes to more than the government
realizes from any duty. It is all wrong, & should be abandoned, *tout de suite*.
I fancy this pushing the books from the mails is the work of the Democratic
majority now in the house. I don't know what we can do about it. . . . A
Congressman who would originate, & carry through, a bill, making all
books & literature, newspapers, &c. &c. *duty-free*, first; then, making the
postage *the same* on books as it is on newspapers, viz. 1¢ for every 2 oz., or
fraction of 2 oz.; & finally allowing a parcel to come, or go, of say *10 lbs.*[f] wt.
(the old maximum used to be 5 lbs)—would deserve well at the hands &
hearts of his countrymen. It should be *done*, & done *immediately*. Circulate
& encourage *knowledge*, of all kinds, *free* to everyone, instead of shutting it
out. What blind policy to "protect" knowledge! Let us have the *freest* trade
in it. If we cannot *make it here*, as fast, or as good, as they do in Germany or
England, so much the worse for *us*; but dont force our citizens to live on a
poor article, or worse, *to do without*, by making a good one "prohibitory,"
on account of *duty*, & custom house "fees." . . .

Of course you have read Mr. J. W. Hales' *notice* of Mr. Furness' *Hamlet*, in the *Academy* (Dec. 1). . . . This notice is, merely, a few additional illustrations of passages in *Hamlet*, (overlooked by Mr. F.) from some of the *Old Dramatists*. He gives no *account of the Work*; what all it contains; its priceless *worth* to all students; the immense labour spent on it; its beauty as a specimen of American book-manufacture; its accuracy of typography; its copiousness, yet conciseness; the "scholarly aroma," that someone speaks of, as pervading the whole work; Mr. F. 's individual preferences of text; his views on the insanity question; or 1001 other matters, deserving notice, & pointing out. No one could tell, from *this* brief article, what kind of an edn. it is. It seems merely an exhibition of the *writer's* knowledge of old dramatic literature. And his introduction, respecting the vast mass of Sh. writing & illustration now being published, is poor—poor—*a poor attempt at wit*, I think.

Since I began this letter, Mr. Snider's package has come to hand, containing his 2 vols. "System of Shakespeare's Dramas." Of course he has sent *you* the same. How do you like *the looks* of the book? For as to *its inside*, I doubt if you will summon up courage to read very much of it. For myself, when looking through the numerous (nearly 1000) closely-printed pages, and calling to my mind his "hard" style, his peculiar fancy of diagramming & analysing the plays; his "threads," & "motives," &c., with the too sparse introduction of quotable passages from the poet's works to enliven & beautify his arid desert, then I was glad that I had already done my duty by him, and *already read* so much, that I should not *have* to go over again. I think it is rather a well-gotten-up[8] book, for St. Louis. The paper & type are good; & he has given good fair margins. I wish he had taken your & my advice about *gilt tops*, & made his fore edges *rougher*. And I do not admire the binding. The boards are *too heavy* I think—too thick & clumsy. But it is, withal, better than I expected. And, no question, if (that *"if"*!) anyone would only pin himself down to a close, attentive reading of Bro. Snider's book, excluding everything else, "giving his whole mind" to it, he would carry away a good deal of Sh. wisdom, and a better knowledge of the *analysis of the poet's work*, than can be got from any other one book I know. Snider has worked faithfully—thought deeply—& planned and "schemed" laboriously, throughout. But it will *not* make him *immortal*; it is too dry—& not popular enough. I doubt if he will *sell* (he may give away) the edn. of 1000 copies. I hope he don't expect *me* to review it, by sending me a "presentation" copy. All this I say to you is, of course, *sub rosâ*. I would not, for the heavens, discourage him a particle. I truly wish him success, & thank him cordially for his book, & hope, with all my heart, he make make it a successful pecuniary venture. . . .

---

[1] p.p.: Privately printed.

[2] Joseph Cook's lectures: Flavius Joseph Cook's "Monday lectures" on science and philosophy from a religious viewpoint were an ornament of Boston in the 1870s. His vol. of lectures, *Conscience*, was pubd. in 1878.

[3] It was right enough to include *Edward III* and *Two N. Kinsmen*: C's view of the apocrypha is

close to twentieth-century thinking. In 1930, E. K. Chambers recognized only *TNK, E3, STM,* and *Cardenio* as having serious canonical claims.

[a] Clothesline,"] Clothes-| line," MS.
[b] & asked what] ↑& asked↓ what MS.
[c] Shakespeare, Milton, *et alii*] these works MS.
[d] scientific man,] [punctuation uncertain] MS.
[e] advertised] ↑advertised↓ MS.
[f] *lbs.*] *lbs.* MS. [not a deletion, but the British abbreviation]
[g] well-gotten-up] well-gotten-| up MS.

226:   21 December 1877

. . . I have insured several libraries, but never yet paid any losses on *them.* I always direct the insured to keep a careful catalogue in some safe place. I know it would be difficult for you and me to get the *value* of our books, if destroyed by fire. All we could do would be to give a list of them, with *our* figures, sworn to, to the adjuster; & if he would not allow our *prices,* to have them referred to "expert" booksellers, the Co. choosing one, you one, & they two a third, should they not be able to agree between themselves. These booksellers would "appraise" the books, & place the prices at what they could be replaced for. There are not very many books that could not be thus valued by such appraisers as Bouton, Sabin, Luyster, Ashworth, or the great book houses, such as Lippencotts, Appletons, &c. I know no fairer way to do.—. . .

Speaking of the *character of Desdemona,* I have frequently thought it over, and it is difficult to make up one's mind about it. Some critics have gone so far as to say that the poor woman's dreadful & cruel death was designed by the poet as a retributive punishment for her *sensuality,* on one hand, and her *disobedience* to her father, on the other hand; and read a great moral lesson to women on the subject. **This I do not believe.** Desdemona was a young girl of strong, warm, Southern blood & passions. But I think Sh. intended her to be drawn strictly pure & chaste. She had probably never had[1] the guiding care of a *mother,* at least we never hear of her mother. After her marriage, she was as *passive,* and obedient to her husband, as she had been devotedly & passionately in love with him. Had she been more *self-assertive* & independent, shown a little will of her own, it would have been better for her. Most wives, now-a-days, would call her "a little goose," for *minding* her husband's caprices & jealousy. But I really must not begin to write about her character. It is so full of distinctive peculiarities,— such a mixture of warm passionate feeling, purity of thought, submission to her lord, *womanly* sweetness, guileless *un-suspicion* of anything wrong, unreservedly-devoted *love* for her husband, that absorbed her whole soul, so that she reverenced and regarded *him as the* **only man** to be thought of in the world, & that his word was her law & gospel; to delineate the outlines only of such a woman from the traits given us by the Poet, would fill a moderately large volume. The three *best* analyses of her character, that I remember, are Mrs. Jameson's, R. Grant White's, in his "Shakespeare's Scholar," and Lloyd's, in the 2d edn of Singer's Shakespeare, Vol x, p. 175.—I have always *felt* in her character a want of *intellectual power*, and of *energy of will*. She is too innocent, too artless. When Othello first attacks her, and outrages her fine womanly sensibility, she is stupefied. She cannot tell what to make of it. She is so good, & pure, & innocent, & *unsuspecting* herself, she thinks others must be so too. And she tries to excuse him for his brutality; lays the blame on affairs of state, business, &c. Poor girl and poor wife! For such a woman is *not* all a wife should be. I want some self-reliance in a wife, and I could put up with considerable independence in one, so she would have some *backbone* when I needed support or consolation myself. Desdemona is *not* a good "help mate"; she is more of a parasite. If you were in trouble, she would hang around your neck, & kiss you tenderly, and lovingly watch every movement of feature, & listen for every word; and if you attempted to tell her your annoyances & failures, she would open her eyes wide in astonishment, and fancy that her "splendid" husband, with his superior intellect, judgment & *will*, would soon put all this to rights. But, as I said, hugging & kissing, and coddling, and getting out nice things to tempt your appetite, and bathing your head with cologne and bay-rum, and your feet in hot water, all these, tho' mighty "nice," do not make a wife a good "helpmate." You need, many times in life, a woman's quick *discernment*, that comes by *instinct*, & not by reasoning, & which often hits on the right course out of a trouble so much easier than a man can do, with all his wit & intellect. I suspect that from what you and I know of good women, & good wives, we would, each of us, be very loath to say Desdemona was a sensual, impure woman. My dear deceased wife had very many of the characteristic traits of Desdemona; yet a purer-minded woman God never made. Such women, I feel inclined to think, "go to it" (as Sh., or Lear, says)—more *to gratify their husbands* than for any great selfish enjoyment. God said to Eve, "thy *desire* shall be to thy husband." If ever they go astray, it is when their husbands prove unkind to them; they become reckless; their first heart's love, & genuine, true gratification, is blighted, cast away; and they seek in another that satisfaction of heart & love, which they do not get at home. And how many poor things are obliged and willing, *knowingly too*, to put up with the refuse leavings of some other woman, to unmurmuringly take the husks that the swine would not eat; and still live on, doing their duty, and putting on a fair face to their neighbours & the world. Society, I often think, does wrong in this, that a known libertine man—married or single—is received, with but little if any disdain, into its fold; indeed often his character as "gay," "fast," or "a roué," is about all he has to recommend him; while let a woman, no matter if seduced under the most heaven-bound oaths of matrimony, vary from the strict, narrow path of virtue, and all she can do is to die of a broken heart, if she cannot, through her purer nature, descend into the lower depths of infamy.—However, this letter is not intended to be a sermon; & I must beg pardon for "preaching.". . .

[1] She had probably never had . . .: Here C adopts the perspective of Mary Cowden Clarke's *The Girlhood of Shakespeare's Heroines*, a book he had just given to Agnes at N's suggestion.

228:   27 December 1877

. . . Instead of being "offended," I am obliged to you for calling my attention to such an inelegant, improper, & ungrammatical expression as "real kind." . . . The only apology I have in the present case is the *license* of letter-writing, where, from custom, colloquialisms, grammatical inaccuracies, phrases of common conversation, abrupt and elliptical expressions, even sometimes a mild decoction of what is termed "slang," are semi-pardonable,[a] from the *freedom from rule* in rapid letter writing. . . . Cicero, you know, was one of the most elegant of the classical authors, writers, & speakers. Yet his "Epistolæ" *abound* with just such errors, and grammatical faults. I remember when at College[1] I once attempted to excuse a fault in my Latin composition by quoting a similar expression exactly in Cicero's Letters. I shall never forget the Professor's telling me that neither Cicero's, nor any man's "letters" could be quoted as *authority*; that he, tho' so lovely, elegant and correct a writer, introduced, purposely or not, many strictly inaccurate expressions, when they were the ordinary conversation of the time. "Real kind" is one of these; it is wrong, yet one is so apt to get into the habit of using it from *hearing* it in daily conversation. . . . As a proof that *"humanum est errare,"* in the very same sentence, in which you criticize my "real kind," you say, "don't retaliate upon me by telling me to take the beam out of my own eye, in order that I may the better see the **moat** in my brother's.". . .—Had you written it *moth*, I should have shaken your hand, in congratulation of your scholarly emendation; as *moth* in Elizabethan literature was pronounced *mote*, and what we mean by *mote* was spelled *moth*. In M. N. Dream, the fairy *Moth*, I have no doubt, should be called *Mote*, as all the rest of the fairies have the most diminutive names the poet could imagine, e.g. *Cobweb, Mustard seed* ("one of the very least of all seeds," *Bible*),[2] *Moth*, &c. . . .

I expect when you see Mr. Eugene Robinson's Cat. of books, for sale by Bouton, you will be sorely tempted. Some lots are quite reasonable in price—away below their cost to him no doubt. Others, again, seem to me high. $4.000 for the 4 Folios is a huge price. They are, no doubt, in very fine, elegant *bindings*, & good, perfect copies. It must be a fearful trial to a literary gentleman, who has at great care, pains, & money, collected *such* a library, to have to part with it in this way. . . .

A perpetual caution I nightly receive from Miss Agnes is—'Now mind & *do* go to bed early.' The fact is, I have hardly ever gone to bed, lately, before 2 or 3 o'clock, A.M.; and getting up at 7, leaves too little time for "Nature's sweet restorer, balmy sleep." Do you know, I am ashamed to confess I have not yet finished—as thoroughly as I want, Mr. Furness' *Hamlet?*—Of course, I have *read* it all; but not carefully, and with the study, & collations, & references, I ought to do. But *Deo volente,* I will begin the whole work *de novo,* and not stop, until I can conscientiously say—"It is finished!"—It is simply impossible for me to *read,* in my careful way, when *travelling.* Newspapers, & novels, & light literature, are all I can manage on the cars or at the Hotels.—

Rev. Mr. Hudson kindly sent me a copy of his new book, "The Classical Reader." It is a very admirable Selection of Poetic & Prose pieces, with footnotes. It is far in advance of any of the "Readers" I ever saw,[3] for College or School use. The pieces are, some of them, perhaps a trifle *severe;* but they are none the less to be read & studied on that account; and when *Mastered,* what a treasure the mind acquires! The food—mental food—is as *nutritious* as it is *tasteful;* dishes that will make backbone, & sinew, and good healthy blood. There are several articles both *from,* and *on,* Shakespeare. . . .

He wrote me a very kind letter too; said that in sending Mr. Furness a copy of the "Reader," he took occasion to speak of the paltry, pitiful review (!) of his *Hamlet,* in the "N. A. Review," & to disclaim the authorship. He says "I should like to write a strong, severe, elaborate notice of this work [Hamlet]; and if I knew of a suitable place where such a notice would be acceptable, I should not be slow to go about it; as I am not likely to be much crowded with other labour for the present."—I recommended him to try *Scribner's Magazine,* or, still better, *The Atlantic Monthly.* The bulk of his interesting letter relates to his new ed. of Shakespeare. He is getting ready the "Life," "Introductions," &c.—I urged him, by all means to make the latter short, and interesting: to intersperse the most of his æsthetic criticisms & comments throughout the Notes, & not have a long, closely printed essay, at the beginning of each Play, which is hardly ever read. Further on he says: "I have prepared the copy on the plan of printing the plays in the old order. Furnivall writes me strongly against doing so. Perhaps he would like to have me adopt *his* order. But that I shall hardly do." [I have written him a long letter on this subject, and urged him, for God's sake, *not* to take Furnivall's order. The "Leopold Shakespeare," with a comedy here, a History there, then a Poem or two, then a tragedy, then a few Sonnets, then another History, is most unattractive—even repulsive to *me.*] He continues: "I have pretty much concluded, however, to give the

Comedies and Tragedies, as nearly as may be, in the order of their writing. As for the Histories, I think I must set them in the historical order of the subjects. The changing from the order in which the copy has been prepared will give me a good deal of rather troublesome work in overhauling the Notes, and rectifying the references, which are rather numerous. But the old order of the plays is very objectionable,[4] in fact almost insufferable. I rather think I must face the labour of the alteration. If the Shakespearians had been at one, or nearly so, as to the chronological order of the writing, I should have adopted that from the first. But indeed a good deal of progress in that matter has been made since I began the work;—one good result, perhaps, of the unexpected[b] delay in getting the work to the press. However, I do not yet feel certain that the publishers will go about it the coming year, and am not a little anxious on that point, as I am getting old. Should the "Reader" make a good hit, it will much strengthen the publishers for the Shakespeare. They have been confident that it would, and therefore I was the more willing to put the "Reader" through. So, if you can do anything towards starting the "Reader" in the Schools thereabout [what a funny expression! "thereabout," I suppose, means about where I live], that will, in its measure, further the cause."—

I don't know how *you* feel about it; but I fear that *I* am a fearful "old fogy." Were I editing a Shakespeare, I believe I shd be very apt to print the plays according to the old Folio 1623 arrangement. It may be the result of habit, or prejudice, because I first learned my Shakespeare in that order: but to me it is still the most attractive order; especially as, if you go outside of it, no two editions agree in their chronological order of writing. . . .

I suppose you read, in the *Academy* for Decr. 8th, the long and *slashing* review of Mr F. G. Fleay's little shilling, "Collins Series," "*Guide to Chaucer and Spenser*," by H. R. H. Furnivall. It is rough and heavy on brother Fleay. But when Furnivall pitches into Fleay, for setting up for a critic & authority on Chaucerian matters, when he is only & professedly a novice in the study of Chaucer, and has not given six years of hard study, & close examination of MSS., as he (Furnivall) has, will not the argument rebound on himself, like the Australian *boomerang*, when he claims to be allmighty & all supreme on Shakespeare? Mr. Fleay never exposed his ignorance anent Chaucerian matters so much as Mr. Furnivall did *his* anent Shakespearian matters, about the time of the organization of the "New Shakspere Society." . . .

---

[1] when at College: In the early 1840s C was at the Queen's College, Oxford.

[2] Bible: I.e., Matthew 13:31–32; Mark 4:31.

[3] far in advance of any of the "Readers" I ever saw: *The Classical English Reader* became a standard text in the 1880s.

[4] the old order of the plays is very objectionable: It was borrowed for HUD1 from Singer's Chiswick Edn. (1826), and was a whimsical variation on the order of plays in F1. HUD2 is arranged as proposed here, chronologically within genres, except for the histories.

[a] semi-pardonable] semi-|pardonable MS.

[b] the unexpected] its the unexpected MS.

229:   2 January 1878

. . . Alger's "Forrest"[1] must be a beautiful book, and I should like to own it. But cash is too scanty to spend $10. for it now. I will watch for some chance at Auction, or otherwise, to pick it up some day for say abt. $5.— Forrest, as a man, or even as an Actor, was never an excruciatingly great favourite of mine. I have seen & heard him in most of his best characters; & I generally thought him too *boisterous*, as well as "Forresty,"[2] i.e. *self-conceited*. But he was a good Shakespearian, & loved our Poet, & had a fine Sh. library, &c., and so one must respect him, and his memory. . . .

I have recd. another letter from our friend Mr. Asa Lamb, thanking & flattering me. It is a very stiff & formal letter—"*palabras*, neighbour Verges." A gentleman that boards at our house knows him well: says he is quite a learned man, a good deal of an antiquarian, & very eccentric. He has a pretty, but somewhat *fast* wife. (That is *entre nous*.) He is Clerk of the Court of Ashtabula County, Ohio. He [Lamb][a] says that the Sabins[b] have sent him a new "circular" regarding the "Bibliopolist,"—that it will be resurrected, & more care given to it, *if it is patronized*. If not, it must die.

I have sent out 9 of the copies each of Mr. Brae's books.[3] I sent 3 to Cincinnati; one to Mr. M. F. Wilson, a Sh. friend, & member of the "N. S. Soc."; I think the *only* member in Cincinnati. He is a lawyer, & a very nice fellow; one, to Mr. Enoch T. Carson, another Shak. friend, and collector of Sh. books, portraits &c. . . .He has recently been collecting "Secret Societies" literature, & all appertaining thereto; much of it perfectly useless, tho' highly *entertaining*. The other copies (1 of each) I sent to the "Cincinnati Public Library"; all in Mr. Brae's name. I shall send a copy each to Mr. Lamb, and to Dr Reuben Vance, of Gallipolis; and the *rest* I will distribute *at home*. I sent notes with each, explaining the circumstances of the present.—. . .

[1] Alger's "Forrest": William Rounseville Alger, *Life of Edwin Forrest, the American Tragedian* (1877).
[2] I have seen . . . "Forresty": F's chief Shn roles were Lear, Coriolanus, and Richard III; "his weakness lay in his egocentric passions, his vanity and arrogance" (*Concise DAB*).
[3] Mr. Brae's books: See letter 223.

[a] He [Lamb]] He ↑[Lamb]↓ MS.
[b] the Sabins] ↑the↓ Sabins MS.

230:   8 January 1878

. . . Last night was our regular meeting of the "Reading Club"; and it was one of the most pleasant, profitable, & really enjoyable meetings we have had. I was in splendid trim for *talking*; I had looked over and prepared what I had to *say*; made several interesting selections from the æsthetic critics to *read*; and besides I was inspired by the presence of Miss Agnes, who every once in a while *would* smile at me (unseen by anyone else). She read her part of *Beatrice* well; as cunningly, and archly, & smartly as one could desire; & she had a capital Benedick (*not me*) to support her. When time came to adjourn, I found all reluctant to *leave*; a good sign. In fact, our "Club" has been a splendid *success*; (I *hate* that expression; but, as you say, one gets to using slang, & unauthorized words & phrases, from others; & *you*, careful as you are, say "it was *a success*";)—last night, the thermometer was *at zero*—(this morning 13 *below!*—) yet *all* the members (who were at home) were *punctually* present. It has taken the place of a "Whist Club," which we have had every winter for several years heretofore. Our next play is "Macbeth." I have not seen the "cast" yet.—Sometimes a funny circumstance occurs. Not long ago, while reading *Rich. II.* (II, i, 237), an unmarried lady, of some 30 or 32 summers, and one of the keenest, *knowingest*, sharpest, of the "Club," was reading the line—"Bereft and *gelded* of his patrimony." She read it, & then looking me right in the eye, asked, "Mr. Crosby, what is "gelded"?—Fortunately I never smiled or showed any embarrassment, but I just quietly said "O, it is an old Saxon word, meaning *deprived*." Now, I am well convinced that *she*, of all others (her name is Miss Emma Allen) *knew* just as well as I did what *gelded* meant; for she prides herself on her fine education, and powers of sarcasm & satire in conversation.—Last night, a married lady was reading the line in *Much Ado* (III, iii, 146), "like the shaven Hercules in the smirched, worm-eaten tapestry, where his *codpiece* seems as massy as his club."[1] She read it, & looked up with—"Mr. Crosby, what *is* "his *codpiece*"? Is it his *head*?"—But I was so busy, explaining by a drawing I was trying to make of the watchmen's *bills* of old times, that I did not hear her, i.e. she thought I did not, and I went on with my picture of the "bill," talking fast of the poet's quibbles on these *bills* and the *promissory notes* that "commodities" were "taken up" on; & she sensibly *forgot to repeat* her question.—But we have never had any annoyance or trouble with these things. I told the members at the beginning, that I had not enough of expurgated editions to go round; & if I had, they were not expurgated alike; so we use the regular *full, best* editions; and whenever a reader comes across a word or passage that she or he thinks too *broad* to be read out aloud, they just quietly pass over it. I would not allow any *substitution* of more modern or presentable words to be made at all. *Aut Shakespeare, aut nullus.* . . .

[1] his *codpiece* seems as massy as his club: *Ado* 3.3.137–38.

231:   11 January 1878

. . . The . . . emendation,[a] "not neat, *but* cleanly, Captain,"[1] where Mr. B[2] proposes to read, "not neat, *not* cleanly, Captain"—is not only superfluous, but *erroneous* in my judgment, and it destroys Leontes' meaning altogether. His boy has "smutch'd his nose"; and Pa, with one eye on his wife, struggling with that infernal fit of jealousy that is killing his peace & comfort, and at the same time trying to distract his thoughts by talking to his boy, & calling him all manner of pet names, takes out his handkerchief, and wipes clean the little smutch'd proboscis. As he does this, he says, "We must be neat, Captain"; then his mind running off with the quibble on *neat*— (anything for talk, & to occupy his distracted mind—) he adds—"not *neat*, in the sense in which the steer, the heifer, and the calf are called 'neat,' "[b]— that's not what I mean,—"**but cleanly**, Captain"; continuing, "for the steer, the heifer, and the calf are" termed "*neat*," "and yet *they* are anything "*but* cleanly." . . .

While on Shakespeare, I want to tell you of a little conjecture that has occurred to me. It is only a *stage-direction*, but one which I think necessary to explain the context. In *Much Ado*, IV, i,—

> "*Beatrice.*—Kill Claudio.
> *Benedick.*—Ha! Not for the wide world.
> *Beat.*—You kill me to deny it. Farewell.
> *Bene.*—Tarry, sweet Beatrice.
> *Beat.*—I am gone, though I am here:—there is no love
>   in you:—nay, I pray you, let me go.
> *Bene.*—We'll be friends first."[3]—

What I would introduce is a Stage direction—"Seizes her hand," or still better,—"puts his arm around Beatrice," *after* Beatrice says "Farewell," and *before* Benedick says "Tarry, sweet Beatrice." This would then account for her saying "I am gone, though I am here," i.e., plainly 'I am gone in heart, though you *do detain* me.' He probably then attempts to kiss her, which explains her adding "There is no *love* in you"—it is all *affectation*—"Nay, I pray you, *let me go*."—A good actor would do all this on the stage; but I think it would help the reader to introduce it into the copy. . . .

"Nay, but his jesting spirit, which is now crept into a lute-string, and now govern'd by stops,"[4]—I fancy that you, along with every commentator that I have seen, have missed the sense of the passage. Will you pardon my egotism if I copy for you my original note on this passage, from my *Collectanea Shakespeariana*, (Vol. II, p. 103). It is from one of my letters to Mr. Hudson, some time ago:—

> "In this passage, I have been puzzled to find much, if any, point to the joke. The first part is explained (correctly), that as the *lute* is peculiarly the *lover's* instrument, his jesting spirit has taken a fancy for it. "Govern'd by stops" is explained as the *stopping* of his lover's mouth by *kisses*—(vide "stop her mouth," &c *passim ap. Sh.*)—But this is surely much too far-fetched to be right. The other part of the quibble on *stops*

is generally said to refer to the *stopping* of the strings with the fingers on the upper part or handle of the lute, to produce the different notes. But this explanation gives no force to the second "now," which might as well have been omitted, and the line read "is now crept into a lute-string, and govern'd by stops." Besides, in a lute these stoppages of the strings are called "frets," not "stops."

I fancy that the words "now ———— and now" mean, as they often do, 'at *one* time ———— at *another* time,' and that the "stops" are the stops of a flute or recorder, (also a lover's instrument,)—what Hamlet calls "ventages"; "*govern* [note the word] these ventages with your finger and thumb": and the holes of a flute, pipe, flageolet, or recorder, are called the "stops" to this day. So that the sense is, 'his jesting spirit takes refuge at *one* time in the *strings of a lute*, at *another* in the *stops of a recorder*.' And the quibble on "stops" may also refer to the *checks* or *pauses* in his jesting spirit, occasioned by his melancholy.—

P. S. Since writing the above, I observe that in the "School Shakespeare" you adopt Walker's conjecture,[5] and read (as Dyce II. also does) "*new*-govern'd by stops." But the explanation here given obviates any necessity for change. His friends are enumerating the love-signs about him, and, among many others, they say that instead of jesting and joking as he was wont to do, he has betaken himself to love-songs, sometimes accompanying himself on the *lute*, at others on the *pipe*.—You also explain "stops" = the ridges on the sounding-board of the lute. But I can nowhere find that *these* were called "stops"; they were "frets." Shakespeare in several places speaks of the "stops" of the pipe or recorder, E.g. in *Hamlet*, speaking of a recorder: "Govern the ventages with your finger and thumb; x x x look you these are the *stops*";[6] and again, "that are not *a pipe* for fortune's finger to sound what *stop* she pleases."[7 c]—

[So far my *Collectanea* on the passage; and I have nothing to add to it now.]—

I am glad you are reading Snider's book, because you will give me your opinion occasionally on some of these essays. I read them all once; but have not yet attacked the book, tho' I fully intend to do so. Like you, I thought *Othello* and *Julius Cæsar* his 2 best; and that he was entirely wrong in adopting the notion that *Macbeth*'s witches were "creations of the brain" only. Had only Macbeth seen them, there might have been a more plausible argument for the notion; as they might have been supposed to represent *his* ambitious imagination, & the *temptations* to which he somewhat willingly yielded. But Banquo was neither ambitious, nor tempted to be so. All his *imaginations* were *clean* and pure; and yet *he* too saw them. No; the poet unquestionably designed these witches should be existent, talking, visible creatures. They corresponded with the *traditions* of the rude time when Macbeth lived; could make themselves air & disappear; but always were *weyward, weyard, weird* (from A. S. *wyrd*, fate), i.e. **fatally prophetic;** all that ever listened to their words & obeyed them were *sure* to be led to destruction, & **thus** they represent the inner mind of man, which first broods over, & then yields to the *temptations* of the evil one.

I am a thousand times obliged to you for the splendid extract on German criticism from the "Standard." It expresses my own opinion exactly, only in infinitely superior form & language than I could give it. I have copied it into my *Collectanea*. It is the truth, & nothing but the truth, & shd be written in letters of gold. What an amount of precious time and eyesight would be saved, if the conscientious student of our great Poet, who thinks it his duty to read and possess everything in the shape of criticism that is in the slightest degree connected with the name & works of Shakespeare, had digested and believed in these sensible remarks; & resolutely ignored all the insane, improbable, useless speculations; plans, schemes, diagrams, and philosophies; that compose nine-tenths of what is called "æsthetic criticism," written by our German co-students. Tho' the sentiments of the "Standard" have always virtually been the same as my own, unfortunately I have not possessed the will or courage to live up to them, in my studies of Sh:, and his immortal dramas. . . .

A. R. Smith sent me a package containing Stopford Brooke's Primer of "English Literature," which I have not yet read, but it looks very enticing. . . . Also a book that I have "longed long" to possess, viz. Dryden's "Essay on Dramatic Poetry." Did you ever see this work? It is intensely interesting, and contains a great deal about Shakespeare. . . . I sat up 3 hours last night reading it, so very interesting did I find it. I often have seen it highly recommended; & I am greatly pleased to get a copy, without having to buy the whole of Dryden's Works for this work alone. . . . In the package from Smith I found the "Prospectus," and *sample sheets* of the large & small paper editions of Prof. Leo's new "Extracts from North's Plutarch." How *well* it is photolithographed! I shd greatly like to have a copy of *either,* the large or small paper. Both are very beautiful. But *why* did he take the 1595 edition to photolith., when I suppose he *must have had the first,* or 1579, edn. by him, as he says the "Notes compare the edns. of 1579, 1595, 1603 & 1612"?[8]—How could he compare all these edns, unless he had them by him?—I see the price is £1..11..6 for the *Library* edn., & £3..3..0 for the *Amateur* Edn.—I notice Sotheran has a copy of Halliwell's Grand Folio Shakespeare, the plates on *India paper;* for which he wants £84.. . . . .

[1] "not neat, *but* cleanly, Captain": *WT* 1.2.123.
[2] Mr. B.: A. E. Brae.
[3] Kill Claudio . . . friends first": *Ado* 4.1.289–97.
[4] "Nay, but his . . . stops": *Ado* 3.2.59–60.
[5] you adopt Walker's conjecture: Despite C's arguments, H adopted it in the Harvard Edition as well.
[6] "Govern the ventages . . . these are the *stops*": *Ham.* 3.2.357–60.
[7] *a pipe* for fortune's finger to sound what *stop* she pleases: *Ham.* 3.2.70–71.
[8] "Notes compare the edns. of 1579, 1595, 1603 & 1612": See R[obert] A. Law, "The Text of 'Shakespeare's Plutarch'," *Huntington Library Quarterly* 6 (1943): 197–203, for the minimal differences among the four edns. and the probability that Sh used 1579.

^a The . . . emendation] the other emendation MS.
^b calf are called 'neat,' "] calf are ~~neat~~ called 'neat,' MS.
^c she pleases."—] she ~~will~~ ↑pleases↓.—MS.

232:   16 January 1878

. . . Speaking of Leopold (H. R. H. *the Prince*),[1] I only stated what I saw in the review I sent you, and what I have read frequently in English & American papers. Mr. Moncure D. Conway, an American gentleman, who lives in London, & is a fine scholar, & writes occasionally for the "Cincinnati Commercial," several times has made reference to the Prince's very *studious* disposition, and especially to his *love* & *study* of **Shakespeare**, & his Collection of Shakespearian books. He has, it seems, rooms at Christ Church College, Oxford, where he resides a great deal of his time, & reads. But others too have spoken of his penchant for *Shakespearian* study. I fancy that *A. R. Smith* would hardly be very likely to know much of him. It is probable that he procures his books through the *Parkers*, the large Oxford Booksellers. They had (& still have) an immense collection, something like Bouton's, & only second to Quaritch's I believe. Besides Parker, there are several other second-hand very immense bookstores. When at college, we used to select some one bookseller, give him all orders, & he *got for us* what he did not already have in stock. So A. R. Smith, in *London*, would not be likely to know much of Prince Leopold, tho' he might fill some orders for him through another bookseller. But *is* A. R. Smith "headquarters" for Shak: books in London? His *stock*, judging from his Catalogues, is only a small one: not a drop in the bucket to *Quaritch's*; & will hardy compare with H. Sotheran's, & 20 others. . . .

You did perfectly right in writing to *Prof. Leo*, and offering him the use of your *North*. I should have done so gladly, had I fortunately owned a copy of the 1579 edn.—He must have contemplated getting, or seeing, one *somewhere*, as in his Address, accompanying the two "specimens" of the large & small paper photolithographs, he expressly says—with Introduction, Notes, &c, in which the edns. of *1579*, 1603, 1612, are textually collated with that of 1595, the one he prints from, I hope he will take *good care* of your book, & return it in as good condition as it now is. But some of these Professors, esp. German, are so terribly slovenly with books. We had one at Oxford, I remember, and his rooms were like a pig-pen, littered up, & all smelling of *rascally tobacco-smoke*.—

I really envy you the pleasure of seeing *Ant. & Cleo*. performed. It is one of my **especial favourites.** I may almost be said to have *edited* this play, so copious are my notes on it, both in my books & *Collectanea*. I read it again, not very long since, with most *exhaustive* care; & *Hudson* & I have had *long discussions* on its textual difficulties. Respecting the 3 passages you refer to,

I will tell you my opinion about them as briefly as I can; and I am sorry I cannot sit down by you, & *talk*, instead of *write* about them. One cannot say half what is needed in a short letter; and I have several notes I would like to read to you on these and a hundred other places, that would, I believe, much *interest* you. . . .—"Let him marry a woman that cannot *go*,"[2] &c. Now, altho' this *may* mean, 'Let him marry some old woman, so crippled up she cannot *walk*,'—yet I fancy the wild, gay, Charmian's prayer for Alexas' future wife was by no means so immaculate in imagination. She more likely meant, let him be tied to a wife who is too old to enjoy, or care for, the pleasures of the marriage bed; in a word, who is too much of a *smoothbore* to be a good "diddler"; who cannot "*go*"[a]—i.e. "diddle," in American slang phrase. And *one* reason, why I think so, is that this word "go" is to-day (or was when I was a boy) the **very word** used in London by the *nymphs du pave* for *fornicate*. I myself have heard (I recollect it was in London close by Exeter Hall,[b] or Exchange, in one of those streets that run into the Strand, in 1851, when I was at the first "World's Fair,") I heard a *whore* say to her "fellow,"—"now surely you'll treat to a bottle of wine after the two good *goes* I gave you."—"Come with me upstairs and we'll have a *go*," is the *ordinary invitation*. You will notice, of course, that nearly all of both Charmian's & Iras' talk with the Soothsayer, & Alexas, "werges on the wulgar," as Sam. Weller says. Shakespeare knew this use of the word "go," I think, from *Lear* IV, vi, 114, "The wren *goes* to't, and the small gilded fly Does lecher in my sight"; and (l. 126)—"The fitchew [polecat, a most sala-cious animal], nor the soiled horse [the horse that had been kept up in stable all winter, & fed on dry food, with no chance to see a mare in the fields, & consequently fearfully "horny"] *goes* to'it With a more riotous appetite."—It is barely possible that Charmian included in this meaning, that the wife of Alexas should be *too old* to bear children—become preg-nant: cf. *2 Henry IV*: V, iv—"*Doll Tearsheet*—x an the child I now *go* with[3] do miscarry"; & *Henry VIII*: IV, i, 77: "Great-bellied women, that had not half a week to *go*," &c., and V, 1, 20—"The fruit she *goes* with I pray for heartily"; & *Timon* IV, iii, 188, "*Go* great with tigers, dragons, wolves, & bears."—For its ordinary meaning of *fornicate*, we could not have a plainer example than that in *Pericles* (IV, vi, 80,)[4] where *Lysimachus* says to *Marina*, "Did you *go* to't so young? Were you a *gamester* at five or at seven?"—Of course I never suggested to Hudson that I thought *this* was the Poet's meaning; but isn't it very likely?—Charmian ["like mistress, like maid"] was no doubt a trifle "fast"—at least in her tongue; her companion, Iras, calls her "you wild bedfellow"; and to *her* notion, nothing worse could befal Alexas than to get a wife who was of no account between the sheets—an old "played-out" bedfellow. Don't you think so too? i.e. I mean, don't you agree with my explanation,—not with Charmian's notion?—The last thing she says shows what her head was running on—"may the last & worst of all follow him laughing to his grave, *fifty-fold* a *cuckold*."—

All this—I need not tell you—is *between ourselves.*—You can burn it up when you have read it. . . .

[1] Leopold (H. R. H. *the Prince*): George Duncan Albert Leopold (1853–84), Duke of Albany, etc., fourth son of Queen Victoria. He was resident in Oxford (a student at Christ Church) in the mid-1870s. Sh and Scott were his favorite authors; the *Leopold Shakespeare* (1877—see letter 176) was dedicated to him.
[2] "Let him marry a woman that cannot *go*": *Ant.* 1.2.63–64.
[3] an the child I now *go* with: *2H4* 5.4.8–9.
[4] *Pericles* (IV, vi, 80,): I.e., *Per.* 4.6.74.

[a] who cannot "*go*"] who cannot *go*" MS.
[b] by Exeter Hall] by ~~the~~ Exeter Hall MS.

233:   22 January 1878

. . . Last night we had a very pleasant meeting of our "Reading Club": it rained hard, & was a terribly disagreeable night out of doors, but all hands were promptly present. We read *Macbeth*; but only got through 2 Acts in the 3 hours. You would be really astonished to observe the Very Great improvement in *reading* & *comprehending* Shakespeare these folks have made in the nine months we have been reading together. All that diffidence & shyness either in reading, or expressing an opinion of the meaning or criticism of what was read, that existed at the beginning, has entirely vanished; and we have the pleasantest times talking & maintaining each his or her views of the different matters of æsthetic or verbal criticism that you can imagine. I have encouraged this freedom of opinion & conversation; and it has removed anything like the stiffness of a "Professor" lecturing to his class, from my part of the work. Instead of that, I aim to be rather *primus inter pares* only. I often, to stop discussion, "move the previous question," & settle a point by a *vote.* E.g., you recollect in *Macbeth*, where *he* says,—"If we should fail," & Lady Macbeth replies, "We fail But screw your courage to the sticking place," &c., the point is which is best— to place a full stop, an exclamation point, or a note of interrogation, after the Lady's "We fail."[1]—Strange to say, and contrary to my judgment, the ladies almost "to a man," voted for a *full stop*; i.e. 'Well, *we fail*; and that's the end of it; **but** screw your courage, &c., and we'll *not* fail.' This, you remember, is Mrs. Jameson's idea,[2] which she advocates very well. My own opinion is that the exclamation point is the correct reading, for the reason that the other allows a *chance* of failure, which the Lady was seeking to dispel from her husband's thoughts altogether. It should be read with a strong contemptuous, incredulous, accent—"*We* fail!" There is really little (or no) difference between the *exclamation* & *interrogation* points in this case: either will do very well. Mrs. Siddons used all three at different times,[a] but settled down on the *full stop*, (so says Mrs. Jameson,)—owing to a strong favourable note of Steevens'. . . .

The weather in Ohio has made another *summer*sault; from intense cold, frost, & snow, it has changed—& suddenly again, to very warm, close, wet, murky weather. What they call in the North of England *roaky*, from *reek*, i.e. smoke. *Roaky* is damp, dark, moist, murky; and is, no doubt, the *very word* Sh. uses where in *Macbeth* (III, ii, 51)[b] he says: "Light thickens; and the crow makes wing to the rooky wood." It was just getting dark; and the thick pine woods in Scotland, where the crow builds her nests, & rears her young, are always dank, damp, misty, "*roaky.*" I have heard the word so often, when a boy, & know its application so well personally, that nothing to me could be plainer than that this is the very epithet the poet uses for such woods, at twilight. A "*roaky* day" (i.e. reeky, smoky), *there*, is like *our* "Indian Summer" with this important difference, that the former is *wet, moist*, the latter *dry* & warm. Of course a good sense may be made out of "rooky," viz. woods where the *crow* or *rook* builds her nest. The crow & rook are very nearly synonymous: the difference is the *crow* is larger, more ravenous, more a *bird of prey* than the *rook*. But the other word is so much more picturesque, & lifelike,[c] and *expressive* of night coming on in a thick piece of woods, that I am nearly certain it is the poet's word.—

Did you ever hear Forrest play *Macbeth*? If so, do you remember whether he placed a full stop at the end of the line,—"If it were done, when 'tis done, then 'twere well,"[3] or carried it on, as in the common editions? The reason I ask is, one of my class said that he *did*. You know what a flourish of trumpets R. Grant White gives over *his* so reading the line. Yet long before Grant White pubd his "Shakespeare" it was suggested by a Mr. G. Blink, in "N. & Q." for *1850*. And C. Knight, in his 2d.. Pictorial Edition, (Vol. II, *Tragedies*, p. 16), says: "Without venturing to alter the common punctuation, we would recommend an attentive consideration of the reading of the first line as given by *Mr. Macready*;[4] and then carry on the soliloquy, as suggested by that alteration:—

> "If it were done when 'tis done, then 'twere well.
> It were done quickly, if the assassination
> Could trammel up," &c.—. . .

I suppose, ere this, you have heard Rose Eytinge in *Cleopatra*.[5] You must not forget to give me your impressions of her acting the character. It is no *easy* one to perform well. I should dearly love to see it well done.—. . .

---

[1] "We fail": *Mac.* 1.7.59.

[2] Mrs. Jameson's idea: See Anna B. Jameson, *Characteristics of Women, Moral, Political, Historical* (1832 etc.): a flat period is "consistent with the dark fatalism of the character . . ." (p. 326, 1847 edn.).

[3] then 'twere well": *Mac.* 1.7.1.

[4] the reading . . . as given by *Mr. Macready*: It would be odd if Forrest imitated Macready—they were deadly enemies.

[5] Rose Eytinge in *Cleopatra*: This production (opened N.Y. 1877) was her "principal success" (*Concise DAB*); she produced as well as starred in it.

[a] at different times] ↑at different times↓ MS.

[b] (III, ii, 51)] (III, iii, 51) MS.

[c] lifelike] life-| like MS.

234:   25 January 1878

. . . You are, and have been, exceedingly kind in . . . giving me the benefit of your noble Halliwell edition. It has almost been to me the same as if I owned a copy: as I have never hesitated to ask you for the light of the learned editor's notes, where I got stuck for want of help. The only copy, I believe, West of the Alleghanies, is in the Public Library, at Cincinnati; and I never go there, and have an hour or two of leisure, that I do not go & *revel* in these grand volumes. Mr. Vickers, the librarian, seems always to know what I want when I go in, and gives me the key to that case where they, and the "Boydell" copy, are placed. . . .

It has often struck me, in reading *Macbeth*, that there is a typographical error in one line, viz. where Rosse, speaking of the prodigies that occurred at the murder of Duncan, says:

> "And Duncan's horses (a thing most strange and certain!)
> Beauteous and swift, the minions of their race,
> Turn'd wild in nature,"[1] &c.

In the first place, I would print in the first line "horse' " [one syllable, with an apostrophe, to denote the abbreviation] instead of "horses." You know Walker speaks of this abbreviation of similar words; and it helps the metre, which otherwise would have an extra syllable. At least *in reading* I think the word should always be pron. in one syllable. There could be no misunderstanding of the singular for the plural in this instance, as we very commonly hear people to this day speaking of *horse* for several horses. But the other change is more important, viz., to read "the" for "their," and print "Race" with a Capital 'R.';—

> "Beauteous and swift, the minions of *the Race.*"

"Minions," you know, is *favourites*; and Rosse simply means that Duncan's stud were the *favourites* on the Scottish *Epsom*. Don't you think this a much more vivid picture and description of these noble, high-bred animals; they were not merely the favourites of their *race* generally, but ran highest in the betting pools of the *Race-track*? Tell me how this strikes you. I mentioned it to Goddard several years ago, & he, being what is called a "horse man," said it seemed "mighty sensible" & likely.—. . .

Thanks for telling me all about your attending "A. & C.," & hearing Eytinge as the "Sorceress of the Nile," the "star-eyed Egyptian." I was much interested, & I would dearly have liked to be with you at the theatre. I love this play so much.—

Respecting the two readings that you speak of,—"termagant" [Steevens 1793, Mason's conj.] for "arm-gaunt,"[2] and "cloth of gold *and* tissue" for "*of* tissue," I fully agree with you that the old readings are *right*— unquestionably right. For the first, all sorts of words & phrases have been conjd & adopted,—"arrogant," "arm-girt," and (by Lettsom & Grant White) "rampaunt" or "rampant." Mason first conjd "termagant." But to my mind no term could be better than the original "arme-gaunt," or better convey the idea of a large, raw-boned, mettlesome, spirited, war-horse, *thin in flesh*, but full of fire. It includes the *two* meanings of gaunt as to its arms, i.e. *thin-shouldered*, as high-bred horses always are, (and they are the best travellers;) and *thin in flesh*, from carrying its own *armour* as well as its *heavy-armed* rider.—As for the other phrase, the words "cloth of gold of tissue"[3] simply mean 'cloth of *tissued* gold,' i.e. clóth made of threads of gold so fine as to look like tissue. In Shakespeare we not unfrequently find, (and this is a little point well worth your remembering) two Nouns, or two phrases, or two clauses of a sentence, connected together by the copulative conjunction 'and,' or the preposition 'of,' where the latter is merely a *qualifying addition* of the former; acts as an adjective. . . . So, then, in the passage in *A. & C.*, "cloth of gold of tissue" is *cloth* [made] of gold of tissue, i.e. *tissued* gold threads. It seems nothing could be plainer than this; whereas the generally adopted reading "cloth of gold *and* tissue" is to me obscure and ambiguous; implying *either* that the "cloth" was made of gold *and* some other (thin) substance called tissue, *or*, that Cleopatra's dress was composed of *two* distinct substances, viz. partly of "cloth of gold" & partly of "tissue"; and surely neither of these is right.—So much for that. And it reminds me of those delightful hours when you and I promenaded the avenues of the "Main building" in the *Centennial*, and saw a web of this gorgeous yellow-looking silk in the Egyptian department; evidently the same thing that formed the material—"cloth of gold of tissue"—that adorned voluptuous "Egypt."—I never can bear to look at the portrait of *Cleopatra* as taken from the Ashmolean medal.[4] It is most *disenchanting*; the nose, mouth, chin, give me the impression of one of the "strong-minded" *bas-bleux* of a "Woman's rights" meeting. There is nothing soft, or feminine, or fascinating, or "luxurious," in any feature. But Plutarch says her great charm was in her *conversation* & *manners*. Then Antony's portrait is not much better. Our young ladies would say he was anything but a "handsome" or "proper" man.—

Miss Fillmore told me she had seen in some N. Y. paper an account of a slander-suit, or some scandal, connected with the name of *Richard Grant White*. Have you seen anything of it? I fancy it is something regarding his intimacy with Lydia Thompson[5] (wasn't it Lydia?), and her troupe of *blondes*. I have heard before of his getting himself into a fearful scrape by his becoming fascinated by the charms of some stage leg-woman; and that he spent so much money on her, he became so terribly in debt, he had to sell his *library*. I think Miss Agnes said the article stated that he and his wife had not spoken to each other for over two years, although they still lived together. Another thing was, that he was a *very homely* man personally. I have never seen a picture of him. I think you have one; & once I believe you described him to me; but I do not remember that you thought him *homely*. What a shame it is for a man of his ability & talents to be such a *roué*. I should have supposed his pride, & self-conceit, would (if nothing else would) have kept him from such *disgraceful conduct*. . . .

[1] "And Duncan's horses . . . nature": *Mac.* 2.4.14–16.

[2] "arm-gaunt": *Ant.* 1.5.48.

[3] "cloth of gold of tissue": *Ant.* 2.2.199. Support for C's interpretation of the phrase can be found in the learned note in the Arden Edn. ad loc.; "cloth of gold and tissue" is a Perkins Folio emendation.

[4] the portrait of Cleopatra as taken from the Ashmolean medal: The medal is reproduced in Knight's Pictorial Edition (1838–43) and several edns. based on it. The medal was one of the original bequests of Elias Ashmole to Oxford University (1677). The portrait of Cleopatra (from a coin) reproduced in J. Dover Wilson's New Cambridge Edn. is also sharp featured.

[5] Lydia Thompson: (1836–1908). C might first have connected White with Lydia Thompson from reading his spirited defense of her and of the burlesque, *Ixion*, she starred in (*The Galaxy*, August 1869). The appellation "stage leg-woman" in the next sentence alludes to the fact that Miss T was one of the first women to appear on stage in America wearing tights without a skirt.

235:   8 February 1878

. . . I have recd. from Mr. Collier his final part of his "Qto Shakespeare," containing "Sonnets & Miscellaneous Poems." He gives 8 new titlepages, and a brief but *nice* "Preface," a little conceited, & egotistical, & Collier-y, but not more than one might look for. Poor old gentleman; I hope he is *happy*. He has done great things for Shakespeare, from his 19th to his 90th year; & had luck so willed it that he had never found that ill-omened[a] Folio, or rather had he, when he did find it, used it as Singer did *his* 2d folio MSS.[1]—viz. taken the emendations for what they were worth, & not claimed entire & universal authenticity for them, he would today have ranked very high—perhaps at the top—as an *authority* to be consulted on all points of Sh. reading, interpretation, and criticism. His closing of his "Preface" is melancholy, "The work that I was born to do is done!"—I am still *minus* "*The Tempest*." I can but *hope* he will unearth me an odd copy somewhere. I have so often written him on the subject—offered everything I could for a copy—that I am ashamed to write again. He has so frequently *promised* to do all he can to get one to complete my set, I think *he will*. You have observed that he made his 50 subscribers into 58, to cover the *actual cost* of the paper & printing. He could just as well have had 100, and the work would have been nearly, if not quite, as rare & valuable. I have not had a letter from him for some time. He sometimes acknowledged my remittances, sometimes not; but I have preserved all his letters, except one or two that I gave away to collectors of autographs. Someone will be glad to get them in the future.[2] It is a good plan to *bind up* one or two with the books of an author. You observe how it adds to the interest & value of a book to say, "with autograph letter of the Author inserted.". . .

Like you, I never saw *Forrest* in any Shakesp: character except *King Lear*; & then he played old Tate's version; & I did not like him at all. . . .

The scandal that is going the round of the newspapers, respecting Grant White, seems to be of quite recent occurrence. I have seen it in several papers. It appears that he introduced himself to a pretty, & young, & accomplished New England girl, in New York, by a fictitious name, and as an unmarried man. He gained her confidence and affections, & probably seduced her, tho' that is not expressly stated. Anyway, it came to the ears of his wife. And it seems, too, that he and his wife, tho' not formally separated, but still living under one roof, have not spoken to each other for two years. Mrs. White went to this young lady, and told her that the man who was visiting her was Mr. Grant White—a married man, & her husband,—all news to the young lady. The consequence was G. W. stopped his visits, & the girl has commenced a suit against him for *damages,*— maybe for *seduction*. Anyway it is a first class *scandalum magnatum* in New York. Now I give you the tale as given in the papers, but *please do not breathe a word of it as coming to you from* **me**. It *may* all be false; and I should hate G. W. to hear I had propagated it. You & I can talk of these matters *entre nous*, but further, well *cave canem*. I had heard an inkling of what you told me about him & Pauline Markham[3] before, but no particulars.—

The other evening, I enjoyed a long & very pleasant conversation with Mr. Murdoch, the late Actor—now Elocutionist & Reader. He was in Zanesville, giving "Shakespearian readings," and they were very *fine* indeed. He was the guest of Goddard. He reads about as well as ever—some places I think better. He is a scholar, & a Christian gentleman—no less than a fine Shakespearian. He gave several of the best portions of *Hamlet*, with a well-thought-out running commentary. Many of his points were excellent. He had a very fine audience (probably 500) of our most cultivated people, & was well received. I never—on or off the stage—heard Hamlet's soliloquies better rendered. After the reading, I spent a long evening with him. He *hates* Grant White cordially. It seems after Murdoch returned from England, because he refused to pay & truckle to the so-called "theatrical critics of the press," of whom G. White was then a leading representative, they tried to run him down, & eventually succeeded in driving him out of

New York. White was especially active & bitter at Murdoch's independence. An especial friend of Murdoch's was greatly incensed at this conduct. He called on Murdoch, & said to him "Here, I have in my possession
$1000 worth of Notes given me by Grant White for Cash borrowed of me. I
have dunned & dunned him, and cannot collect one cent. He is an unprincipled rascal, & wants to be blackmailed. Now I will make you a present of
these 1000$ of notes, and you take them to White, & demand payment,
and tell him that unless he stop his d——d abuse of you, you will expose
him in the papers. White cannot pay, & you will have him fast." But Mr.
Murdoch was too honourable to condescend to even that, and left N. Y.—

I had several pleasant discussions with the old gentleman on Sh. points.
He persisted that—"*Macb.* If we should fail—*Lady M.*—We fail."[4]—was
right. "We fail; and that's the end of it." His main argument was from the
succeeding "*But*"—"But screw your courage" &c.—I contended that this
'But' was not used in its *exceptional* sense, but meant only the same as
'**only**'—"*only* you screw your courage," &c. It is often so used—derived
from "*Be out*"—as Abbott, Horne Tooke,[5] & many others prove. I argued
for "We fail!" as best expressing the Lady's temper at the time. It was her
object not to allow *any chance* of failure to her husband; which the other
reading would do. "We fail." admits a *possibility* of failure, which "*We* fail!",
uttered in a tone of surprise, indignation, & incredulity, forbids. With *her*,
as Cardinal Richelieu says, "there's no such word as *fail*."—I should not
particularly object to a (?) after "fail," which is the punctuation of the *folio*.
But I think the (!) *better*; & you know in the Folio these two, (!) & (?), are
used interchangeably.

Again, Murdoch contended for the reading (adopted as *original* by Grant
White, but first given years before in "Notes & Queries" by a G. Blink):—

> "If it were done, when 'tis done, then 'twere well.
> It were done quickly, if the assassination,"[6] &c.

He argued that the common punctuation made it only *a matter of time*, &c. I
convinced him, however, that the old reading was *right*—& no mistake.
The first proposition of Macbeth ends with "quickly." Then he commences
another hypothesis—which is only an *extension* of the first in other words. If
this assassination of Duncan could *prevent* ("trammel up," *trammail*, a net
to catch birds or fish; generally a net placed across a river to *prevent* fish
from going up stream,) could prevent the consequence following it [in this
life], and by the *arrest* ["*surcease*," a legal term, *sursis*, Fr. from *surseoir*, to
stop, arrest), and by the *arrest* of this consequence obtain success, *then*
"we'd jump the life to come." In the clause, "And catch with his surcease,
success"—"his surcease" is gen. interpreted = *his*, viz. Duncan's, *death*.
But "his" is the old neuter, always (nearly) used by Sh. & the Bible for *its*,
and applies to "*consequence*," *its* consequence; and catch success "by his

surcease," i.e. by its (consequence's) arrest. These *consequences*, viz. the consequences of the murder **NOW**—in this life—are what Macbeth mostly dreads; were it not for *these*, he'd "jump the life to come" & future punishment. . . .

> "**But**, in these cases, we still have judgment **here**,"
> &c. &c.—

Again, Murdoch contended for the reading,

> "Hang out our banners! On the outward walls
> The cry is, "Still they come!"[7]—

His argument was, that the "outward walls" were not the places where the "banners" were generally hung out; but on the donjon, or keep, of the castle. The "they," in "Still *they* come!," he contended were the surrounding inhabitants who were on Macbeth's side, and who were coming into Macbeth's castle, to help defend it, and for their own protection. My argument was; (1) that these "banners," which Macbeth wanted hung out, were *not* the general castle-*colours*, which of course were hung from the tower, or *keep*, but the banners of the "thanes," who were in Macbeth's army in the field, & now brought into the castle; hanging out these, was to show the enemy the force & nobility of his adherents. (2) "They," in "Still they come!" referred to the army of Macduff & Malcolm, who were *undoubtedly, continuously* ["still"] discovered coming on to the assault. (3) and best of all, we have the very same expression in *1 Henry VI*: I, vi, 1, "Advance [wave, hang out] our waving colours **on the walls**."—

In reading *Hamlet*, he said "And with th' *incorporeal* air dost hold discourse," where the Poet says (and the rythm demands it)—"th' *incorporal* air."[8] His argument from the meaning of the word, that air is not *incorporal* but *incorporeal*, is all right enough. But in Shakespeare's day these words were not differentiated as they now are. *Corporal* means *now* something attached-to,[b] belonging to, dependent-upon, put-upon, the body; while *corporeal* means *having a body*, as distinguished from *spiritual*. Thus it is right to say *corporal*, & not *corporeal*, punishment. And air, of course, is *incorporeal*. But neither the words *corporeal*, nor *incorporeal*, ever once occur in Shakespeare; he **always** uses *corporal* and *incorporal*. Milton uses both words; but even in his time they were not strictly differentiated, and he often uses them interchangeably.—

Mr. Murdoch told me of several original "readings" he had heard Actors use—just for the sake of being original or bizarre. E.g. He told of an actor who always said—"Hўpĕrīon's curls,"[9] pronouncing the first 2 syllables *rapidly*, & accenting the word on 'i.' Now we all know that Hyperīon is the *correct classical* pronunciation; *but* both *here*, and in "Hypērīon to a satyr"[10];

and in *Henry V*: iv, 1, 292, "Doth rise and help Hypĕrīon to his horse"; in *Tro. & Cr.*, II, iii, 207,[11] "With entertaining great Hypĕrīon"; in *Tit. Andro.* V, ii, 56, "Even from Hypĕrīon's rising in the east"; and, finally, (the only other place where the Poet uses the word), in *Tim. of Ath.* IV, iii, 184, "Whereon Hypĕrīon's quickening fire doth shine"; in all these six passages the Poet plainly makes the 'i' short; and to change it to a long 'i,' because the classical authors so accent it, is *affectation* or ignorance.—

Another very silly affectation was the following reading in *Hamlet*; (new to me; did you ever hear or see it?)—

> "*Rosencrantz.* My lord, you once did love me.
> *Hamlet.*   So I do still, by——; *Aside*] these pickers and steal-
>   ers!,"[12]

i.e. Hamlet stops his speech, turns his back, & mutters aside, calling Ros. & Guil. "pickers & stealers"!! Did you ever hear such absurd nonsense?— But I have given you *quantum suff* of Murdoch, and my very agreeable evening with him.—. . .

So far, *Neil* is the *best* of the "Collins Series" editors. He is the same Samuel Neil, who wrote "Shakspere, a *Critical* Biography," the *best* short life of the Poet that, I think, we have. Glancing over this *Hamlet*, it seems to be very scholarly, terse, & ably done. What an advantage the boys of this day have over those in my boyhood!—The *only* Shakespeare I had, was a thick, roy. 8vo, 1 volume copy of Stockdale's edn., by *Saml. Ayscough*,[13] with *glossarial Notes*, at the foot of each page. But I loved it, and read it much & often. It was a fairly *correct* edn., and well bound in light calf, & I had the "Concordance," that goes with the edition, by Ayscough. (Do you know this editor's name is pron. in England *As'kew*?)—There is no excuse *now* for young people not knowing all about Shakespeare. The only fear I have is this, that having used the plays as *schoolbooks*, they will not love them, & study them, as they ought to do, when they grow up. . . .

I did not mean to insist very pertinaciously that "sleeve," & not "sleave,"[14] was the correct text in *Macbeth*, altho' I still think the word will sustain a fair argument in its favour. For one thing, it is the *original folio word*; and it is always a good thing to retain *that*, when it is capable of bearing an easy interpretation, as I do think "sleeve" does. That knitted garments were used in the Poet's day may, I think, be fairly presumed from his very frequent use (both literally & metaphorically) of the words 'knit,' 'knitters,' 'knitting,' &c. Even poor Launce enumerates it in the "cate–log of the conditions" of his sweetheart, that "*Item*, she can *knit*"[15]: and the Duke, in *Twelfth Night*, speaks of "The *spin*sters and the *knit*ters in the sun,[16] and the free maids that weave their thread with bones," i.e., I suppose, the pure-hearted girls, *free* from all taint or knowledge of vice, who weave their thread with *bone* knitting-pins, like the crochet-needles our "free maids" now use. But my main argument for "sleeve" is, that of the enlightened thousands who fill our theatres to-day, how many, when they hear the expression "ravelled sleeve of care," *know* that "sleave" is a term for knotted or twisted *floss-silk*? Do not their minds, (and how much more the minds of those who filled the *Globe* and *Blackfriars* Theatres?) naturally think of the *sleeve of a garment*, that has got untwisted & *ravelled* by care, or labour, or accident? Have you never worn an undershirt made of wool, cotton, or silk, of which a sleeve had got unravelled, and known how nice and comfortable &^{c} agreeable it was to have it "knit up" again? Surely it would be as *easy* to knit up a ravelled garment-sleeve, as to knit up, "by some marvellous agency," the knotty, coarse, floss, the refuse of the weaver. And may not the metaphor be as aptly applied to the one as the other; I mean, the soothing, softening, & erasing, by sleep, all the cares & worries of the day; so that we rise, after our anxieties, from sleep, refreshed like new men? I have often thought the Poet could have found a more appropriate metaphor to represent this refreshment, than either "sleeve," or "sleave" affords. Still I do not see much to choose between them. You have very beautifully paraphrased all this sentence in your letter. It is a grand apostrophe to *sleep*; particularly grand in Macbeth's mouth, under his present awful situation, and, as you say, every word teeming with meaning, & emotion.

By the way, speaking of the "second course" of Nature; to this day in the North of England, & in Scotland, the second course *is* the *main course*. I have seen it over & over again "with these eyes." First come on the puddings, dumplings, &c; afterwards, the great joints of roast & boiled; & closed up with bread & cheese and ale. This is on the *farmer's tables*, and ordinary classes of society, not, of course, on those of the wealthy or fashionable. I have been present at several great dinners, given by a lord of the manor, Lord Lowther,[17] e.g., to the farmers of his lands, who came in to his Castle twice a year to pay their rents. I was only a boy, & "looker-on in Vienna," but I well remember the *Second* course was the *main* part of the dinner; after that, strong ale, sometimes over 20 years old, was put into small kegs or barrels, holding perhaps 15 gallons; these ran *on wheels*, up and down the whole length of the tables, between the rows of men at dinner, with a fasset on each side, from which they filled their glasses as the barrel or keg was wheeled in front of them, to respond to the *toasts*, given by the "stewards" at the head of each table. I remember the *mottoes* on some of these ale-tanks. One, e.g., was—"Plenty, but none to waste"; another, "Waste not, want not"; &c. &c. This was just on the borders of Scotland; and Sh. *may* have seen this arrangement of the "courses." I have never seen this mentioned in print; but when you alluded to the custom, I at once recognized it as the *only* way of serving the "courses" on these festival occasions. . . .

We had a very pleasant & profitable meeting of our "Reading Club" this week. We finished *Macbeth*, & next take up *1 Henry IV.* I anticipate some fun in the "Falstaff," who is a lady, and the best "Comedian" in the party.—. . .

[1] *his* 2d folio MSS.: I.e., his copy of F2 containing MS notes. S owned a copy of F2 bought in 1852 which contained extensive emendations in the manner of the Perkins Folio. Hudson's view of the difference between S and Collier was like C's (see Harvard Edn. Preface, I, xx), but in his *Trilogy* (1874) Collier accused S of a fraudulent attempt to rival the Perkins Folio. Singer discussed his F2 (and a copy of F3 marked as a promptbook which he also owned) in the Preface to *The Text of Shakespeare Vindicated* (1853), an attack on the Perkins Folio. A letter from C to C. M. Ingleby dated 30 August 1881 (Folger MS. C.a. 9) indicates that Ingleby was trying at that time to acquire the Singer F2; its present whereabouts is unknown to us.

[2] Someone will be glad to get them in the future: C apparently saved all such letters; Agnes Fillmore Crosby mentioned them in her will: "Some . . . are valuable as the autographs of prominent persons" (Probated Muskingum County, Ohio, 10 October 1887). Local legend says that the letters were casually sold by a member of the Fillmore family many years later. We have not been able to trace them.

[3] Pauline Markham: A burlesque actress who starred with Lydia Thompson in N.Y. in 1869. W gave her charms, physical and vocal, the highest praise in *The Galaxy*, August 1869. According to P. K. Foley's *American Authors 1795–1895* (p. 306), *The Life of Pauline Markham Written by Herself* (N.Y., 1871, 31 pp.) has been "credited to Mr. White—but without absolute certainty." It is a self-congratulatory and sensational account of her adventures among male admirers, who always love her madly, and sometimes propose marriage (which she always declines, leaving them desolate). The book was obviously written to polish a tarnished reputation. One of the few favored friends among her many admirers is "one of the most eminent critics and Shakespearean scholars in the world" (29).

[4] We fail": *Mac.* 1.7.59.

[5] Horne Tooke: John Horne Tooke,   Επεα πτερόεντα, *Or The Diversions of Purley* (1786, 1798/ 1805, 1:190–215.

[6] "If it were done . . . assassination": *Mac.* 1.7.1–2.

[7] "Hang out . . . come!": *Mac.* 5.5.1–2.

[8] "th' *incorporal* air": *Ham.* 3.4.118.

[9] "Hӯpērīon's curls": *Ham.* 3.4.56.

[10] "Hyperion to a satyr": *Ham.* 1.2.140.

[11] iv, 1, 292 . . . II, iii, 207: I.e., 4.1.275 . . . 2.3.197.

[12] So I do still, by . . . these pickers and stealers: *Ham.* 3.2.336.

[13] a thick, roy. 8vo. 1 volume copy of Stockdale's edn., by *Saml. Ayscough*: It survives, in the possession of Anne Crosby Lane of Preston, Lancs. In addition to C's bookplate ("Joseph Crosby Powis House") the volume carries the signature of his brother John who after Joseph's emigration supplanted him as heir to Powis House. It seems extraordinary that Joseph did not take this treasured book with him to America.

[14] "sleave": *Mac.* 2.2.34.

[15] "*Item*, she can *knit*": *TGV* 3.1.308.

[16] "The *spin*sters and the *knit*ters in the sun: *TN* 2.4.44.

[17] Lord Lowther: The Earl of Lonsdale; the castle is now a ruin. C's father was his tenant; rents would be due on Lady Day and Michaelmas.

[a] ill-omened] ill-l omened MS.

[b] attached-to] attached-l to MS.

[c] comfortable &] ↑comfortable &↓ MS.

238:   6 March 1878

. . . —I do hope that Wood's Tariff will be *returned* to the "tomb of all the Capulets," where it belongs. The idea of putting a duty on old books is supremely absurd! It costs the government more to *collect* it than it comes to, and is a wretched burlesque on making "revenue."[1] All kinds of *literature*, new or old, books, pamphlets, magazines, reviews, & newspapers, should all be admitted & exported, to & fro', between enlightened countries, *free as the air.* Taxing intelligence! A nation that will do it deserves to remain in Cimmerian darkness. . . . Why don't some ass get up a bill to put a duty on the air we breathe, or the water God has given us to drink; books & literature are just as essential to our *mental* health & growth, as these products of nature to our *bodily* existence. And yet our d——d Congress throws every obstacle it possibly can—short of entire prohibition—in our way of acquiring all the knowledge we can. I believe in an "International Copyright." I think an Author is just as much entitled to the pay for the results of his brain work, as a mechanic, inventor, or speculator, to his. But this *duty* business is quite another affair. Protection! Whom does it *protect?* And then the Government *makes* nothing by it. The little bit of money got by this obnoxious tax is all absorbed by the Custom House & other sharks. . . .

In Leighton's criticism of Snider's Book, there are some points wherein he and I agree, but several wherein I must beg to differ with him. As he says, his judgment of the work is, I think, *hastily* formed, and he will change it on some material points on a second & more thorough reading. He is much *too severe* on our young friend, when he says—"The Author seems to me to seek originality at the expence of good judgment." Then just afterwards he affirms that "his theory is *not* new." Now I do think it *is.* At least, in my reading I have never come across any theory of the classification & analysis of Shakespeare's Plays at all resembling Snider's. I think myself that much of it—this classification, and arrangement of each play in its different "movements" and "threads," &c., is *fanciful.* Such analyses never occurred to the Poet's mind when composing his imperishable Works. But, still, if such classification can be made plainly out by such an analysis of each play as is not[a] *forced on it,* but *drawn naturally from it,* then surely it is all right enough to seek for it—to **discover** it. And Snider's work cannot but have this excellent effect, viz. to *impress* more clearly, vividly, graphically, *on the mind* the plots, with their varied movements, & threads, now joining in one grand movement, now intermingling, and now again separating & diverging, to be at last gathered together into a harmonious, satisfactory whole. Snider is not only *original,* I think, in this work, but very modest withal in presenting it. But from the structure of his mind, I should say he is not the best man in the world to write on & about such a poet as Shakespeare. Snider is essentially a *mathematician*: he loves *diagramming* (excuse the term), and working out a problem from given data. Now Shakespeare is one of the most "free and easy" of poets. He will be hampered with no laws, no theories, no unities, except those of *Nature,* "pure of itself." I believe he wrote, primarily, to please his audiences, & make money, by his attractive, *drawing,* plays. And he wrote harmoniously, because it was natural for him to so write. He could write no other way. It was not that he tried & planned to make his works *ethically just*. He made no systematic arrangement of his characters, further than by a pleasing & natural intermingling of the tragic & comic, the practical & sentimental, just as he saw them exist all around him, in London or Stratford, he sought to render the whole thing *attractive* and *natural*. He made no *diagrams* of his plots. By a most wonderful *insight into human nature*, he was enabled to tell exactly each man's or woman's **motives** of action, & he makes them act accordingly; he knew also what each man or woman would naturally *say* under certain circumstances and he makes them say it accordingly. It is this *unique* faculty (at least unique in its extent), that makes his works so powerful, as well as pleasing, and above all *so immortal*; for Human Nature is the same thing *now* that it was in his day; that it was *before* his day; & that it will be,[b] as long as the world endures, & men & women live. Now Snider, altho' he does not altogether ignore this grand characteristic of our dear Poet, yet he has read so much of the German critics & their Works on Shakespeare, that, like them generally, he has caught the trick of *imagining* a certain ethical or philosophical theory for each play, & goes to work to make his essay conform to his *ideal model plan* thereof. He arranges, and analyzes, & twists the action & characters until, like old Procrustes, by lopping off a few inches from one man's legs, & stretching out another's a few inches longer, he makes them all fit, & harmonize with his preconceived & prettily delineated diagram. There is this great difference, however, between our friend & the Dutchmen. The latter have no mercy on their victims. They absolutely force the compound mass into their models; it *must* take shape only by their standard; whereas Snider, (e.g. in *Troilus & Cressida*), when he finds he Cannot, with any reasonable ease, thrust his design (or *any* design) on Shakespeare, is content to say the play is an *anomaly*; that here the Poet worked without his plumb, level, & square, & let the job turn out as it might. Again; what Leighton says about Snider's *poetic* temperament is *exactly true*, I think. "It is evident the *poetry* of Shakespeare is a *sealed* book to Snider." Just so, Mr. Leighton; I fully agree with you; and more than once, more than a dozen times, I have insinuated the same thing to Snider himself. I have tried, & tried, & *begged* him to make his essays more interesting, more readable, by introducing more of those glorious gems of poetic thought, fancy, philosophy & language, that are so richly scattered throughout the plays; diamonds, of the first water, sometimes sparkling in clusters, sometimes in a grand, immense solitaire. But it was not *in him*. I never knew a man, who was so clever, & such a true admirer withal of Shakespeare, as far as his natural temperament permitted, who had so little & poor appreciation of sublime, or sweet, or beautiful *Poetry*. How different from dear, old "good Knight"! I over & over asked Snider to read those simple, lovely "Supplementary Notices," by Charles Knight, after each play, & make them his *exemplar*, in his essays. These of Knight breathe the very spirit, & exhale the very essence, of Shakespeare himself. These are so imbued and saturated with the Poet, that their language, their phraseology even, altho' simple *prose*, is but a repetition of the very words, & figures, & idioms of the *Poetry* of Shakespeare. And how beautiful and attractive they are to read; while Snider's, tho' very clever, and top-full of thought, will always be *hard reading*. I know that, for one, I take up & *study*—not hardly *enjoy*— but *study* his essays, because I think it a *duty*—rarely a *pleasure*. I am sorry to say even this harsh thing of friend Snider's work. But it hath, to me, this extent of *repellent attraction*—"no more." I am done fault-finding.ᶜ—All that Mr. Leighton says of the Poet narrating his story without much regard to "ethical excellence or fault"² is exactly true—the whole truth & nothing but the truth; and it is well expressed. It corresponds with what I have just stated, viz. that the Poet wrote simply from *nature*, and from his supereminent *insight* into the motives of the actions of men. He *knew*, for he saw it within the scope of his large daily observation, that "in the development of the lives of men a perfect ethical harmony is not always apparent"; and he made his men and women accordingly. Virtue is by no means always rewarded, any more than is vice always punished, apparently, in this world.—

Now, just look for a moment as Snider's & Leighton's two "declarations" of the *wherein* consists Sh.'s "supreme excellence." The former says it "lies in the poet's comprehension of the *ethical order of the world*." The latter, that it is in his "*exhibition of the psychological condition of his characters*." There is no question that Leighton is right. For his proposition simply amountsᵈ to this, that Sh. makes his characters act and talk from **natural motives,** & just as he & we see the men & women of the world act and talk when their *motives* are laid bare (as they always were to the *unique insight* of this grand Master of Nature & Poetry). It has been somewhere stated that, to our poet's vision, men's actions & conversations resembled the figures on the dial of a timepiece with a *crystal face*, so he could look *through* & *behind* the mere figures, & see the *machinery* that moved & actuated the hands on the dial. This, all will allow, is Sh's grand excellence. But, with a proper understanding of Snider's proposition, is *he* not right too? What does Snider mean by "the *ethical order* of the world"? If he mean its *natural* & *every-day* order, as regulated by the Creator, wherein we see often "the righteous forsaken," and the wicked "flourishing like a green bay-tree," utterly unable to account for many facts of life that daily come before us, because our vision is simply *finite* whereas the Almighty's is *infinite*; in other words, if he mean the World *as it is*, then he is certainly right also; and the propositions of the two critics really amount to the same thing, or at least that one is merely the *general result* of the other. For surely this is the light in which Sh., & every true poet, regards the "ethical order of the world." It may do for theorists, or philosophers, or novelists, to make *Utopian* ethical worlds,

& people them with impossible men & women; but *they* are not *natural*; and Sh's grand excellence is in making *his* world, & *his* characters, truly, simply, perfectly *natural*. **But**, if by "ethical order" Snider means making every-thing and every person conform to some preconceived standard, no matter how perfect, according to *our* finite views, such standard may be, then he is as surely wrong. For this is what Shakespeare, despite of all the beautiful imaginings & theories of the German critics, *does not do*. And this is my cheif objection to Snider; tho' he by no means follows this idea up as far as the Germans do. *They* make a *round* hole, & try to force—*do force* in a measure—Shakespeare's *square* characters & plots into it. Snider en-deavours to *elicit from* the plays a "System," &, having got it, to apportion such & such characters to it, as will fit it: of course, he often finds such as will *not* fit, by any fair means; *then* he says that here the poet has taken his own way, & the work is *anomalous*, without rule or harmony; ascribing the anomaly to the poet's being confined to the *old story*, or *history* that he worked from, which did not suit his idea of correct ethics. The very fact, that in Snider's analysis, hardly any two plays are regulated by exactly the same "System," shows this; & shows too, I think, Snider's good sense in not attempting to make every square stick fit into every round hole, that he supposes it *ought naturally* to fit.

I am terribly afraid all this is *boring* you. So I will stop; although when I get mounted on my Shakespeare *Pegasus*, Bellerophon was nowhere to me. I keep on *flying* & *flying*, and slaying all manner of imaginary Chimæras.—I was, altogether, interested & pleased with Mr. Leighton's letter on Snider, tho' I repeat I think him too severe on the young author. I only wish I were capable of writing as *good* and *thoughtful* a Book, on "The System of Shake-speare's Dramas," as Mr. D. J. Snider has done. And I hope enough copies of it may be sold to pay him well for his time, money, & brains, put into it; and gratify his proudest ambition. . . .

—I have never read Dryden's "All for Love," I don't think I ever saw it. I should much like to read it; & am watching for a good chance to buy or borrow a copy. . . .

If you will look into your copy of Mr. A. E. Brae's "Prospero's Clothes-line," &c, on page 31 you will find a capital note on that much be-commentated passage in *1 Henry IV*: IV, i;—

> "All plum'd like estridges that with the winde
> Bayted, like eagles having lately bath'd."[3]

In it, he speaks of Mr. C. Knight having decided for a certain punctuation, "in which he had been anticipated by the unknown editor of Scott and Webster's edition of 1833, printing thus"—&c. "In this punctuation Mr. Knight was, in my opinion, decidedly right; but in his interpretation—especially in understanding estridges to be falcons, and not ostriches—as decidedly wrong. The **Unknown** editor, above mentioned, whose edition anticipated Knight's by nine or ten years, was right as to the first branch of the simile, but wrong as to the second. His note is:—

> 'The meaning is that they were plumed like ostriches, which bated with (or shook their wings against) the wind, like eagles that have lately bathed.'

Very nearly right; but mistaken in supposing that it is the ostriches that are compared with the eagles, and not the Prince and his comrades."—Now whenever I have read the above passage in Mr Brae's excellent pamphlet, I have always felt bored that I did not possess a copy of this edition of Scott & Webster, 1833, by the "unknown editor."—An editor clever enough to make so good a note, I thought, could hardly have been anonymous. So I looked through all of my annotated editions of the Poet to find it, or something like it, and I was rewarded, today, by finding it *verbatim* in **Harness' edition of 1825.** And this "unknown editor," so be-praised (and justly so) by Mr. Brae, was no other than *Mr Harness*, tho' Mr. Brae did not know it; and the annotation instead of anticipating Mr. Knight's "by nine or ten years," anticipated it by 18 years.—I intend to inform old Mr. Brae of this, the next time I write him. Do you think the irascible old critic will get mad at me, if I do?—And, moreover, I discovered that Scott and Webster's edition of 1833, with the "unknown editor," is neither more nor less than a *Reprint, verbatim,* of Rev. Mr. Harness' edition of 1825, with the addition of about 40 steel plates, engraved by Heath, from paintings by Smirke, and other artists. It is in 8 vols. 8vo. *Vide Bohn's Lowndes.*—The passage and note are on p. 398, note "c," Vol. IV, of Harness' edition, in 8 vols. 8vo, printed by J. F. Dove, and published by Saunders and Otley, London, 1825.— . . .

[1] a wretched burlesque on making "revenue": Fernando Wood, Democratic Congressman from New York, was the spokesman for a tariff policy based solely on production of revenue. His Tariff Bill was being debated in the House early in 1878.
[2] without much regard to "ethical excellence or fault": The doctrine is in a descent from Keats's concept of "negative capability": an artist accepts beauty without rationalizing it.
[3] "All plum'd . . . bath'd": *1H4* 4.1.98–99.

[a] is not] its not MS.
[b] that it will be] that ↑it↓ will be MS.
[c] fault-finding] fault-| finding MS.
[d] amounts] amoutnts MS.

239: 15 March 1878

. . . Your remarks on the numerous smutty allusions in the *M. of Venice*, although I knew them all, & have always interpreted them just as you do, yet they were so *plainly* written down & brought out to the light, that I laughed, do you know, all by myself in my rooms, until the tears ran down my face. When you have a mind to be *plain* you can with a vengeance. All you say is capital. No question it is true too. In nearly every case where your modesty has permitted you to give me your explanation of a passage in Sh. you have done it *well* & correctly. Keep on, do; you will become as good a commentator as the best of them soon. I always love dearly to have your good, common-sense, explanations. My dear boy, you do flatter my vanity hugely by saying that I have been a father to you in your Sh. studies, as Brae was to Ingleby.[1] I cannot, of course, admit *all* you are good enough to say: but I do *some*; & I thank you, *toto corde*, for the pleasant compliment. I always *wished* to help you, as you know. . . . I often think that Shakespeare has been unusually kind to me, and far more than repaid my devotion to him by giving me the best *gentleman*, & the best *lady* friend I have today. It was through *Shakespeare* that you & I began to correspond; & it was owing to *Shakespeare* that I became intimately attached to Miss Fill-more. I often fancied that she was the main means of organizing the "Sh: Reading Club" in order to have more of *my* society—& to bring us, who had long admired & respected each other, into closer intimacy; partly too, I fancy, to get even with a certain "Whist Club," of which I was a member, but from which *she* was debarred by *its* organizer being *also* a friend of mine. "Thereby hangs a tale" too long to tell now. The other lady is a *Miss Lily Convers*, (never breathe her name to Goddard, as she is his own cousin.) Her manœuvers were, however, too thin. Miss Agnes carried off the honours from her at her own game. *She* was the "Secretary" of the *Reading Club*; and when her mother died, and she could not attend, I had to go over to "read up" with her what was done at the meetings, and so—and so—and so!—The same old story: But *Shakespeare*, God rest his *bones* in peace, as he desired!—Shakespeare was the *primum mobile* of my acquaint-ance with *you*, and my acquaintance with *her*.— . . .

Dyce's second edition of Shakespeare[a] is certainly the best *reading* edn. we have; the type is excellent, and altogether a better book than the 3d edn., with the exception of the *very few* additional *annotations* in the latter. The *only* objection I have to Dyce's latest text is, that he has admitted many Collierisms, and other conjectural emendations, which, while certainly improving the rythm of the lines often, and often the construction, and often too the *easy intelligibility* of the text for popular readers, yet I fancy they were[b] unneeded, where the Folio text was *explainable*. Like Hanmer's edition, in the last century, Dyce's, in this, will always be the most popular edn. for readers who care nothing about the *original*, only wanting an easy edition to understand. But . . . Dyce was far too good an antiquarian, and too conservative a scholar, to allow any *random* emendations to deform his text. His alterations are all scholarly, & well digested, & he has plausible reasons for them. The Sh. world, and literary world generally, owes Mr.

Dyce a long account of gratitude. He did good work that will last forever.
Requiescat in pace! . . .
You ask my expln. of the lines in *A. Y. L.* IV, 1:—

"*Orl.*—Who could be out, being before his beloved mistress?
Ros.—Marry, that should you, if I were your mistress;
or I should think my honesty ranker than my wit."—[2]

The quibble, or *double entendre*, is, of course, on the word "out"; and it is
certainly somewhat broad for the tongue of a young lady talking to her
lover. But then people were not so fastidious, in *talk*, in those days, as they
now are; tho' I believe every whit as virtuous *in reality*. They called things
by their right names. Fancy a gentleman now-a-days telling his wife,[3] when
she *swore*, to use a "good mouth-filling oath," and leave "*protest* of pepper
gingerbread"—i.e., little, dainty, *spicy* oaths, to "velvet guards," i.e. city
fashionable dames.—In the above case, too, Orlando did not know but
Rosalind was a *man*, a *fellow* like himself; & perhaps she went further in her
quibbling than she otherwise would have done in order to blind him to her
sex. When he says, "Who could be out [of matter for talk, conversation],
being *before* his beloved mistress?" She replies,—You should be out [*side of
my "ring"*], if I were a girl and your mistress, or I should think my honesty
ranker, i.e. grosser, *hotter*, than my "wit," i.e. than my ability to keep you at
your distance. In other words if I were your mistress, and you, being *before*
me, were not *out*, but *in*, my "sanctum sanctorum," I should think my
virtue ["honesty"] of that *easy* character as not to be affected by any of my
"wit," or arguments of a prudent nature.

The sentence is somewhat crooked, & hard to catch; and it is singular
that both Dr Schmidt (s. v. *rank*), & Collier's MS. Corrector, should entirely
miss the sense. Schmidt defines "ranker" = *greater*; but surely it is the *very
reverse*. "Rank" often means "gross," & is applied to bad smells, &c. Here it
means "grosser," "hotter"; and so much so as to be **dull**, *blind* to the
dictates of her "wit" or prudence. In the supposition that Orl. *were in*, it
would be because her "honesty," or *virtue*, were so *rank*, gross, licentious,
hot, passionate, as to be oblivious, blind, to anything her wit, or prudence,
or common sense, might urge against the thing.—Again; Collier's MS.
corrector reads "Marry, that should you, or I should *thank* my honesty
rather than my wit," What absurdity! Take her supposition to be accomplished; let Orlando be "in," and where would her "*honesty*" *be*? Gone after
Jim Fisk's "grapevine."[4] She would have *no honesty* to *thank*! Isn't it strange
a man like Collier should not have seen so plain a fact?—Now, tell me if
you think I am right or not? . . .

Excursus on Shakespeare's use of the word "though" in his
Plays.—Written for the amusement and help of my dear Co-

student of the Poet, Mr. J. Parker Norris, of Phila., by his obliged
& grateful friend, J. Crosby, Zanesville, O. March 15th, 1878.—

In the course of many years reading and somewhat careful study of the
works of our Great Poet Shakespeare, I frequently came across passages in
which occurred the common conjunction 'though,' and which, when construed with this conjunction's ordinary interpretation, were so entirely
inconsequential & often inexplicable, that it struck me the Poet must have
used this conjunction in a sense of his own, and different from its usual
Conditional acceptation of 'notwithstanding.' As I could obtain no light or
help from the commentators, some of whom, for instance Johnson and
Dyce, confessed their inability to understand these difficult passages, and
consequently resorted to the usual mode in such cases, of altering and
amending the words, I determined to get together some of these passages,
and by collating, & trying to discover what the Poet was endeavouring to
say and mean, to find some clue, or key that would open the door, and
solve the mystery. In this I fancy I have succeeded, at least to my own
satisfaction, even better than I could have anticipated. And although this is
but a small matter, yet as it is a key that has often helped me to unlock and
bring forth sense out of passages heretofore dark and unintelligible, I propose here, in a plain, hasty way, to show how I think Shakespeare used
and understood this common conjunction. Of course in a large majority of
places where he uses the word, he uses it conditionally, as commonly
used. But I will enumerate a few of the instances of this anomalous construction of it by the poet: and others will occur in the course of any
student's reading.

Instead, then, of giving to this conjunction its ordinary conditional construction of 'notwithstanding that,' 'granting,' 'admitting,' &c., our Poet,
in several passages gives to it the positive sense[5] of 'inasmuch as it is,'
'since it is,'[c] 'being as it is,' 'seeing that it is,' or in a single word *'because.'*
This construction will be most readily understood by two or three examples. In *Much Ado about Nothing*, Act II, Sc. 1, Benedick, smarting under the
masked conversation he had just had with Beatrice, soliloquizes as follows:—"But that my Lady Beatrice should know me, and not know me!
The prince's fool!—Ha! it may be I go under that title, because I am
merry.—Yea, but so I am apt to do myself wrong; I am not so reputed: it is
the base, *though* bitter, disposition[6] of Beatrice, that puts the world into her
person, and so gives me out." What first attracted my attention to the word
'though' in this passage was that in the Folio the words "though bitter" are
in a parenthesis. Dr Johnson's note is, "I do not understand how *base* and
bitter are inconsistent, or why what is bitter should not be *base*. I believe we
may safely read,—'It is the base, *the* bitter disposition'." Steevens says, "I
have adopted Dr Johnson's emendation, though I once thought it unnecessary." And this reading—"the base, *the* bitter"—is the text of Boswell-

Malone's Variorum of 1821. Mr. Dyce, even in his 3d, and last, edition, retaining 'though,' says, "I do not understand this; but I believe it was not questioned by any editor till the time of Johnson, who conjectured "the base, *the* bitter disposition," &c. And Sidney Walker, quoting the text as "the base, *the* bitter," remarks, "I doubt." (*Crit. Exam.* Vol. III, p. 30.) Now let us apply our key to it. Benedick says, "It is the base, *because* bitter disposition of Beatrice, that so gives me out"; base, *being as it is* bitter, or base, *inasmuch as it is* bitter. His self-love is terribly wounded by a lady he has a hankering love for. She has spoken of him basely, meanly, shamefully; still he wants to find some apology for her conduct, as well as some salve for his own sore. Why should she treat me so basely? It is **because** her disposition is *bitter*; ay, that's it. She is base to me *because* her natural disposition is to be *satirical*—"bitter." Being masked, she had taken the opportunity of wreaking her powers of satire on him; and it is, to Benedick's mind, this disposition of hers to be satirical or "bitter," that makes her "base," that is cowardly, mean, and lying. "It is the base, *because* bitter, disposition of Beatrice that so proclaims me the prince's fool." Is not this sufficiently plain? "Though," in this passage, to afford any good sense, must mean 'inasmuch as," or '*because.*'

Again, in *Timon of Athens*, Act IV, Sc. iii, after Timon had run away from his house and "friends" in the city, & taken refuge in the woods, he is visited by the meddlesome cynic Apemantus, among others, who offers him food:

"*Apem.*—There's a medlar for thee, eat it.
Tim.—On what I hate I feed not.
Apem.—Dost hate a medlar?
Tim.—Ay, *though* it look like thee.[7]
Apem.—An thou hadst hated meddlers sooner, thou should'st have loved thyself better now."

Here, what possible sense can we give to Timon's reply that he hated a medlar though it looked like Apemantus, if we give to 'though' its ordinary conditional meaning of 'notwithstanding'? But applying our key, and construing 'though' as meaning "inasmuch as," or 'since,' or '*because,*' we obtain a perfectly plain & intelligible meaning. Timon, quibbling on the *name of the fruit* offered him, & the *meddling*, busy, cynical disposition of his visitor, refuses the offer, and tells Apemantus that he hated the fruit *because* it looked like him. What need of more words to prove that here this is the meaning of 'though'?—

Again, in *All's Well*, Act IV, Sc. iii, where Bertram and his friends have got Parolles into their trap, blindfolded him, and are making him unravel his opinion of their several characters, very much to their amusement and sometimes to their intense disgust; he having[d] said something more than usually biting and severe of "Captain Dumain," probably because it was true, the stage direction is, "First Lord lifts up his hand in anger"; this "First Lord" or "Captain Dumain" intending to take immediate and summary personal revenge on the poor blindfolded braggart. Here Bertram says, "Nay, by your leave, hold your hands; *though* I know his brains are forfeit[8] to the next tile that falls." Construing "though" in its common acceptation of 'notwithstanding that," Bertram's reason why they should hold their hands would be absurdly inconsequential and silly. But construing it 'inasmuch as,' 'since,' 'for the reason that,' we obtain a sensible reason; there is no need that they should lose their temper, or dirty their hands, in his punishment; the next tile that falls will do the business. Don't *you* bother touching him, *because* the brains of such a scoundrel, as he is, are doomed to be knocked out by the first tile that drops from a housetop.

Once more, in *Twelfth Night*, Act II, Sc. v, where Malvolio has just picked up & is reading Maria's decoy letter, and comes across the letters *M, O, A, I.*, and seems to stumble over making them fit his views of the case, he says:—

> "What should that alphabetical position portend?
> if I could make that resemble anything in me,—
> Softly!—**M, O, A, I,**—
> *Sir Toby.*—Oh, ay, make up that:—he is now at a cold scent.
> *Fabian.*—Sowter will cry upon't, for all this, *though* it be as rank as a
> fox."[9]—

Here, again, we must give to "though it be" the sense of "being as it is," or "because it is," in order to gain any consistent sense. We can imagine the merry conspirators watching the pompous, conceited Ass, Malvolio, puzzling over the letter, & trying to make the mysterious letters adapt themselves to his name. He is almost in despair over it, and when Sir Toby says—"Oh, ay, make up that:—he is now at a cold scent," they begin to fear the riddle is above him—too much for him. But Fabian knows better; he knows what the fellow's conceit can accomplish; and he sings out, "Sowter [probably the name of some hound about the lady Olivia's household] will cry upon't, for all this"; the scoundrel will strike the scent of it again in a minute or two, and give mouth again; for why, the thing's as plain as day, the scent is as rank as a fox; Maria has made it all so palpable he cannot miss the catch if he wanted to, and he does not want to; hold on a minute, "Sowter will cry upon't, for all this" apparent[e] blundering of his over it; he *cannot* miss it, **because** "it is as rank as a fox." And, sure enough, when Malvolio begins to smell it out & give tongue again: "*Mal.*—M,— Malvolio; M,—Why that begins my name"; Fabian exultingly says, "*Fab.*— Did not I say he would work it out? The cur is excellent at faults."—

I will just mention one more instance of the poet's use of "though," because it differs slightly, from those just enumerated, in its construction. In *Troi. & Cres.*, Act II, Sc. ii, where Troilus and his brother Helenus, & old Priam, & his other sons, are disputing over giving Helen back to Menelaus:

> "*Troi.*—Fie, fie, my brother!
> Weigh you the worth and honour of a King,
> So great as our dread father, in a scale
> Of common ounces? Will you with counters sum
> The past-proportion of his infinite?
> And buckle in a waist most fathomless
> With spans and inches so diminutive
> As fears and reasons? fie, for godly shame!
> *Helenus.*—No marvel, *though* you bite so sharp at reasons,[10]
> You are so empty of them. Should not our father
> Bear the great sway of his affairs with reasons,
> Because your speech hath none that tells him so?"

Here, the quibble between "reasons" and *raisins* will be noticed, (a quibble quite common in Shakespeare,) and the *biting* at them because so *empty* of them. But in this instance, the reason, or the "*because*" implied in "*though*," agreeable to the examples before mentioned, is thrown forward to the next line. "No marvel, *though* you bite so sharp at reasons, You are so empty of them," means, therefore, "No wonder, then, that you should bite so sharply at reasons, *because* you are so empty of them." For similar examples of *inversion*, or[f] *transposition* in the construction, see Abbott's Grammar, sections 406 to 427, where they are quoted by the score; but the conjunction 'though' retains its meaning of 'because,' or 'inasmuch as,' all the same. "Inasmuch as you are so empty of reasons, it is no marvel that you bite so sharply at them."

One more illustration or two, and I have done. In *As You Like It*, Act III, Sc. v., Rosalind, chiding Phebe for her scornful treatment of Silvius, says,

> "Who might be your mother,
> That you insult, exult, and all at once,
> Over the wretched? What *though* you have no beauty[11]
> (As, by my faith, I see no more in you
> Than without candle may go dark to bed),
> Must you be therefore proud and pitiless?"

Here, the "no" before "beauty" has been omitted by some editors, and by others changed into *mo*, and *more*, and *some*; but the old text[g] is right, and the seeming want of connection in Rosalind's argument arises entirely from misunderstanding the word "though." Rosalind intimates that it would be *too much* to expect that Phebe should be *beautiful*, and at the same time free from pride, and abounding with[h] pity; but, she argues, *inasmuch as* ["though"] you possess *no beauty*, "must you be *therefore* proud and pitiless?" Plain and homely as you are, one might surely look to find you clear of pride, and possessed of some decent share of kindness and pity. Does not this explanation of "though" render all change of the Folio text not only needless, but erroneous & nonsensical? I think so.

My last instance is from the same play, *As You Like It*, Act V, Sc. iii, where the two "pages" having sung their song to the clown, "It was a lover and his lass," &c., Touchstone says:—

> "*Touch.*—Truly, young gentlemen, *though* there was no great matter in the ditty, yet the note was very untuneable."[12]

Here, on account of the "First Page" replying, "You are deceived, Sir: we kept time, we lost not our time," it has been proposed to change *untuneable* to *untimeable*. Either word, however, will do; for they were almost, if not quite, synonymous in our Poet's day; and in writing could easily be mistaken, one for the other.—In this sentence of Touchstone's, he uses the same construction of *though* exactly, as that noticed in my last example. He says in effect, that it would be quite too much for one to expect "great matter" or *sense*, in the ditty, and at the same time good *time*, or tune, in the music; but *inasmuch as*, ["though"], *because*, there was no great matter in the ditty, surely a fellow had a right to look for a note that was reasonably tuneable. Hence we see the sense and drift of his argument, "Truly, young gentlemen, *though* there was no great matter in the ditty, yet the note was very untuneable."—

I shall never forget how these last two passages used to annoy me, fixing an intelligible construction & meaning for them, before I understood how our Poet so frequently used this common conjunction "though."—

J. C.—

---

[1] as Brae was to Ingleby: Ingleby acknowledged his indebtedness to Brae in textual study by dedicating his *Shakespeare Fabrications* (1859) to him.

[2] Who could be out . . . my wit.": *AYL* 4.1.81–85.

[3] a gentleman . . . telling his wife: *1H4* 3.1.253–56.

[4] Jim Fisk's "grapevine": During and after the Civil War, the term *grapevine* (for an unsubstantiated or false rumor) was widely current. "Jubilee Jim" Fisk was notorious for his stock swindles in the years just after the War; presumably his chicanery included false information derived from "the grapevine."

[5] our Poet . . . gives to it the positive sense: This causative sense is not to be found in E. A. Abbott, *A Shakespearian Grammar* (1869 etc.) or in Wilhelm Franz, *Shakespeare-Grammatik* (1898–99—cf. his *Die Sprache Shakespeares*, 1939), or in K. Deutschbein, *Shakespeare-Grammatik für Deutsche* (2d edn. 1897). Modern editors do not interpret *though* as C does in the passages he explicates here.

[6] it is the base, *though* bitter, disposition: *Ado* 2.1.207–08.

[7] Ay, *though* it look like thee: *Tim.* 4.3.307–08.

[8] *though* I know his brains are forfeit: *AWW* 4.3.189–90.

[9] *though* it be as rank as a fox.": *TN* 2.5.123–24.

[10] *though* you bite so sharp at reasons: *Tro.* 2.2.33–34.

[11] What *though* you have no beauty: *AYL* 3.5.37.

[12] *though* there was no great matter in the ditty, yet the note was very untuneable: *AYL* 5.3.34–36. Here we may differ with C, as Touchstone may be seen to intend a *non sequitur.*

[a] Dyce's second edition of Shakespeare] It MS.

[b] they were] ↑they were↓ MS.

[c] 'since it is,'] ↑'since it is,'↓ MS.

[d] he having] ↑he↓ having MS.

[e] this" apparent] this apparent MS.

[f] *inversion,* or] ↑*inversion,* or↓ MS.

[g] but the old text] ~~yet~~ ↑but↓ the old text MS.

[h] abounding with] ↑abounding with↓ MS.

240: 3 April 1878

. . . I am glad you liked my "Excursus" on Sh.'s use of the word "though." I believe it is right, and it has certainly been a help to me; and it pleased old Mr. Hudson "muchly." He had never thought of it; and he has since sent me several instances of places where he adopted my "key," and where it fitted the grooves & opened the mystery. I never *thought* of "publishing" it[1]: unless perhaps in the "Bibliopolist," should it ever be revivified. But it would need re-writing first. I put it together for *you* alone, to be of service perhaps in your study;—without due care of *composition.* . . .

I entirely agree with you, on the character of Cassio, as given by Mr Hudson and Mr. Snider; only I think the latter just a trifle too severe on the "lieutenant." No doubt he was what the world generally would pronounce a good-natured, rather weak, good-hearted man. His liaison with Bianca, of course, is immoral and wrong; but there must have been some good, affectionate, honourable points in the man, albeit he had "poor brains for drinking," or such a woman would not have so devotedly *loved* him. How naturally our Great Poet has drawn him! what a vivid picture! One has just seen such men, strangely compounded of truth and frankness, guilelessness and weakness, *loveableness* and immorality, all springing from a warm heart. You like them, yet you cannot exactly *trust* them. Pleasant company, (because there is[a] nothing about them to excite envy or jealousy,) for an evening, or a stroll; but would not do for partners in *business,* or even to tie to for a trip across the Atlantic. Cowden Clarke's last sentence, "from geniality of disposition easily swayed from his better reason," well describes Cassio. Isn't it truly astonishing, in comparing Sh.'s characters, one with another, (Cassio with Mercutio, for instance,) how nicely the lines are drawn, how true to *nature,* and at the same time how perfectly sustained? Even in two such contemptible characters as Pistol and Nym, there is no mistaking one for the other. . . .

Mr. Spence, in this paper,[2] seems to have picked out the *very hardest knots* in "Hamlet" he could find. . . .

> "The dram of eale
> Doth all the noble substance of a doubt
> To his own scandal."[3]

He says: "The conjecture is surely reasonable that 'eale' is a misprint for 'evil'." [He might have adduced in aid of this supposition one fact that I have noticed, viz., that in the 1604 Qto of *Hamlet* (see p. 42 of Timmins' Reprint) the word 'devil' is spelt *deale*;—

> "The spirit that I have seene
> May be a *deale*, and the *deale* hath power"[4] &c.

Argal, if 'devil' be spelt *'deale,'* why may not 'eale' be the old spelling of 'evil'?] He continues: "That granted, the 2d line may be restored without adding to, or taking from it a single letter:—

> "The dram of evil
> Doth o' the noble substance fall a doubt
> To his own scandal";

Giving to "fall" its active sense of "let fall," as it often has in Sh., e.g. in *A. & C.* III, ii, *"Fall* not a tear."—This is very ingenious, but I think it hardly makes the sense complete. What does it mean to say—the dram of evil lets fall a doubt "o' the noble substance"? Is the "o'" for "of"—lets fall a doubt *of* the noble substance? That is scarcely right, I think. *But*, by going a very trifle farther, and reading "on" instead of "o'," it seems to me it would be good sense:—

> "The dram of Evil
> Doth *on* the noble substance fall a doubt
> To his own scandal."

i.e. the least dram of evil *lets fall a doubt upon* the noble substance, to his [= its, i.e. the noble substance's] own scandal.—How does this strike you? . . .

In the same number of "N. & Q." (p. 104), a correspondent, "Pelagius," asks: "What is the meaning of the word *peereth* in

> "As the sun breaks through the darkest clouds,
> So honour peereth[5] in the meanest habit"?
>
> *Tam. of Shr.* IV, iii.

Does it mean simply (as its etymology from *paroir* might show) "appeareth," or is it from *par*, a peer? And has it then the signification of excelleth?"—

In reply to "Pelagius," I would say, that it is certainly *not* from *par*, but from *paroir*,[b] to appear. But that this form of the word, in Shakespeare, means considerably *more* than simply "appear." It has the additional force and sense of shy, modest, shrinking *unobtrusion*; something like our word *peep*. In the sentence above, the meaning is, that the poorest clothes *cannot hide* "honour"; it will "peer," or *peep out*, somewhere. It not simply appeareth, but "peereth," quietly and unobtrusively. You cannot conceal it—nothing can eclipse "honour"; it will peep out somewhere. You remember in *M. W.*, where Ford, thinking his wife unfaithful, hits his forehead, and says "peer out! peer out!"[6]—meaning the *incipient horns*; i.e. I know you are beginning to grow; you cannot be concealed; so *peep out* at once, and show your little knobs. In *W. T.*—"When daffodils begin *to peer*,"[7] you can *feel*, better far than I can express, *the propriety* of the word, & how superior it is to "appear";—you can fancy the sweet little buds & flowers just *peering out*, making their first shy, retiring, début on the earth. Again, in *Venus & Adonis*, we find another good instance of its most appropriate use, "like a dive-dapper *peering* through a wave" (l. 86). Is not this *a picture*? You have seen the little flitting birds skimming over and through the water. "Peering" is the very word to express it—now in sight—now out of sight: while "appearing" affords no picture at all, hardly good sense. In *W. T.*—"Flora *peering* in April's front";[8] & *R. & J.*, "an hour before the Sun *peered forth*[9] the golden window of the East"; are two more examples of our Poet's beautiful & proper use of this verb. . . .

Henry IV Part II II.ii.[c] "From a god to a bull? a heavy declension! it was Jove's case. From a prince to a prentice? a low transformation![10] that shall be mine." I have always thought that here the words "declension" and "transformation" have been *transposed*. Isn't "transformation" the *word* "from a god to a bull," as in Jove's case? and "declension" the word "from a prince to a prentice," as in prince Hal's? It seems so to me.—Also in V. ii, the C. Justice speaking to the Prince:—

> "I then did use the *person* of your father;
> The image of his *power* lay then in me,"[11] &c.

"person" and "power" seem to have become *transposed*: read them **vice versâ**, & see how much more fitting & apt is his argument & phraseology. . . . Did you ever notice particularly the number of quibbles, puns, & *double-entendres* in the conversation between the Prince & Poins,[12] (II, ii.)? The Prince says it is a disgrace to him to bear the inventory of Poins' shirts; "but that the tennis-keeper knows better than I; for it is a low ebb of linen with thee when thou keep'st not racket there." There is, I think, a pun on *racket*, noise, bluster, and the *bat* used in the game; and as men commonly played tennis in their *shirt-sleeves*, so when Poins was not on hand, the tennis-keeper justly supposed it was because his linen was at a low ebb, or his other shirt in the wash. Hal goes on to tell him that he (Poins) had not been at the tennis court for a great while "because the rest of thy low countries have made a shift to eat up thy holland." Note first the quibble on "*Holland*" and "*Low Countries*"; then between "low *cunt*ries," "*shift*" and "*holland.*" He is intimating that his *whores* get his *shirts* to make themselves *shifts* (chemises) of; and to make use of for wrapping up his bastard children in. He adds: "God knows whether those that *bawl* out of the ruins of thy linen shall inherit His Kingdom"; referring of course to the Bible passage "Suffer little children to come unto me; for of such is the Kingdom of Heaven." But he has his doubts about Poins' children, (being illegitimate, & probably not christened,) inheriting His Kingdom. They, however, keep Poins low in shirts, by needing them to make *diapers* of: and how natural the expression,—"The midwives say the children are not in fault; whereupon the world increases, and kindreds are mightily strengthened." One would think the Prince had had some bastards of his own. . . .

In *2 Henry IV*: V, iii, Shallow, speaking of Davy to Bardolph, says"—the knave will stick by thee, I can assure thee of that: *he will not out*; he is true bred."[13] And also in *1 Henry IV*: II, i, Gadshill, referring to those engaged with him in his robberies, calls them "burgomasters, and great oneyers, such as *can hold in.*"[14] Both of these expressions, as we learn from Turbervile's "Booke of Huntynge," are taken from hunting, and apply to hounds. The "true-bred" will *hold in* together merrily," meaning keep *in the cry*— won't straggle; while the base bred, and untrained, would get *out*—leave the cry—and so offend the huntsman.

The legal meaning of the term "purchase" is, anything acquired by any means[d] whatever, *except by inheritance*. Property bought, stolen, or acquired by gift, was all *purchase*, provided it was not acquired by inheritance. It is from the Latin *perquisitio*. But in Shakespeare, nine times out of ten it means *property acquired dishonestly* or *dishonourably*: so that Nares describes[15] *purchase* as "a cant term among thieves for the produce of their robberies." In Hen. V; III, ii, we have—"They will steal anything and call it *purchase.*"[16] In 1 Hen. IV: II, i, Gadshill says to the Chamberlain, "Give me thy hand: thou shalt have a share in our *purchase*,[17] as I am a true man." The word "convey" had also the same sense in rogues' cant; Pistol says—"Steal! a fico for the phrase. *Convey*, the wise it call."[18] This particularly explains the term "purchased" in 2 Hen. IV: IV, v,[e] where King Henry is speaking to the Prince; "for what in me was *purchased*, Falls upon thee in a more fairer sort,"[19] i.e., the crown that I obtained by base treachery, hypocrisy, and every other dishonourable means, now descends to thee fairly & honourably: meaning by rightful succession. . . .

---

[1]I never *thought* of "publishing" it: C did publish it six years later in the September 1884 issue of *Shakespeariana* (pp. 285–87), writing under the pseudonym "Senior." There the essay is in part verbatim as here, showing that C took some of his papers with him when he fled to

Canada in July 1884. The pubd. version mentions or discusses six further Shn passages, some of them borrowed from the supplement (letter 247) to the "Excursus." The *Shakespeariana* article also makes the acknowledgment that the accompanying subjunctive verbs are a difficulty to be explained: "But it is possible the printer made the mistake; if he supposed 'though' always had its common hypothetical or concessive meaning he would naturally print the verb in the subjunctive."

[2] this paper: *Notes & Queries,* 9 February 1878, pp. 103–4.

[3] "The dram of eale . . . scandal.": *Ham.* 1.4.36–38.

[4] "The spirit . . . the *deale* hath power": *Ham.* 2.2.598–99; C later made use of *deale* to explicate *eale* in an article in *Shakespeariana,* December 1883, pp. 55–56.

[5] So honour peereth: *Shr.* 4.3.173–74.

[6] "peer out! peer out!": *Wiv.* 4.2.26.

[7] "When daffodils begin *to peer*": *WT* 4.3.1.

[8] "Flora *peering* in April's front": *WT* 4.4.2–3.

[9] "an hour before the Sun *peered forth*: *Rom.* 1.1.118–19.

[10] "From a god to a bull . . . transformation!: *2H4* 2.2.173–75; Upton proposed the transposition in 1746.

[11] "I then did use the *person* of your father; / The image of his *power* lay then in me": *2H4* 5.2.73–74; George Daniel (alias John O'Keeffe) had proposed this transposition in 1831. We may object that the meter is disturbed by the emendation.

[12] the conversation between the Prince & Poins: *2H4* 2.2.18–27.

[13] *he will not out*; he is true bred": *2H4* 5.3.66–67 (slightly misquoted); the hunting metaphor goes unnoticed in modern edns. except Arden.

[14] such as *can hold in*: *1H4* 2.1.77; the interpretation does not appear in modern edns. except Arden.

[15] Nares describes: Robert Nares, *A Glossary . . . of Words, Phrases, Names, and Allusions . . . in the works of English Authors, Particularly Shakespeare and his Contemporaries* (1825), s.v.

[16] "They will steal anything and call it *purchase*.": *H5* 3.2.41–42.

[17] thou shalt have a share in our *purchase*: *1H4* 2.1.91–92.

[18] *Convey*, the wise it call.": *Wiv.* 1.3.29.

[19] "for what in me was *purchased*, Falls upon thee in a more fairer sort": *2H4* 4.5.199–200; of modern edns. we have checked, only Arden glosses the word correctly.

[a] (because there is] (because ↑there is↓ MS.

[b] from *paroir*] ↑from↓ *paroir* MS.

[c] *Henry IV Part II* II.ii.] II.ii. MS.

[d] any means] any ~~other~~ means MS.

[e] IV, v,] IV, iv, MS.

241: 16 April 1878

. . . A. R. Smith sent me the "Clarendon Press" Series "Midsummer Night's Dream," edited by W. Aldis Wright. It *looks* as interesting, and ably done, as the other 7 plays of this Series. I have not dipped into it yet; but shall go through it carefully soon. I have all these little, but excellent, editions *almost by heart.* By the by, I recently read very carefully all through Mr. Rolfe's *Henry V;* and I took the liberty of writing to him,[1] and introducing myself; & telling him what I thought of his little books. Of course I did not tell him that I like the "C. P. Series" better than his; *but I do.* I told him it was hard for me to decide *which* was the best; that, too, is no fib, because *it is,* tho' I *did* decide in favour of the "C.P." The latter is more *scholarly,* & more *original* by far: Rolfe's is a *variorum* in a small way, with rarely *anything original*. Rolfe's & Hudson's "School Shakespeare" are both good, tho' very different in design. Rolfe's is confined almost entirely to verbal & textual explanations, & grammatical (Abbot's Grammatical) points. Hudson's is more æsthetic, and his "Introductions" are especially useful and valuable. Next to these comes the "Rugby Series" (almost entirely *æsthetic*), then the "Collins" for beginners, tho' that series has lately very much improved, and Neil's *Hamlet* is really a fairly good piece of work; and finally Mr. Jno. Hunter's last; tho' even in that series I have been able to pick up many grains of good wheat.—. . .

I forgot to tell you that Mr. Hudson thinks his publishers (Ginn & Heath, Boston) will get at his "Shakespeare" sometime during this year. *Stereotyping* is very much reduced in cost the last 2 or 3 years; & they think it is now about as low as it can well be. . . .

Did you ever notice that in some of his plays Sh. uses a peculiar word, or expression, several times over, and perhaps never uses it again, or in any other play? It seems as if some word or expression had gotten into his head, & taken possession of his fancy, for the time being, and he cannot help using it over and over in some one particular play that he is engaged on, and then never uses it again elsewhere. The expression, "to bear one hard," meaning "to bear or owe[a] one a grudge," he uses three times, at least, in *Julius Cæsar*. "Cæsar doth *bear me hard*, but he loves Brutus," I, ii, 317; "Ligarius *doth bear Cæsar hard*," II, i, 215; "if you *bear me hard*," III, i, 157. And **he never uses it in any other play**. Some time ago there was a long, learned discussion, in N. & Q, among the literati, regarding the origin of this expression. They derived it from the Latin, and Greek, and other languages, that had something like a similar idiomatic phrase. But they never once gave what has always seemed to me (with all due deference to their learned opinions), the easy, simple origin of the expression. I believe it is a metaphor from *riding horseback*. A horse that you *know* and *love*, and that knows and loves *you* in return, you ride with an easy, loose, and gentle rein; while, *au contraire*, one you don't know or understand, one that has sometime played you a jade's trick, & which consequently you *suspect* all the time, & watch le'st he do it again; and one which is a *stranger* to his rider, and in which his rider, consequently, places no confidence; *this* horse you "bear hard," keeping a tight rein, never relaxing your steady pull on the snaffle. This, I think, gives the poet's exact idea in each of the above passages. "Cæsar bears me hard," *suspects* me, keeps a tight, *jealous* rein over me, & treats me as a *stranger*. And so with the other passages. *In the same play* occurs a similar expression, and evidently *from the same metaphor*, showing that the poet had it in his mind throughout. Act I, Sc. ii, l. 34, Cassius says to Brutus:—

> "I have not from your eyes that gentleness
> And show of love as I was wont to have:

> *You bear too stubborn and too strange a hand*
> Over your friend that loves you."—

What do *you* think of this idea? It seems strange commentators shd. have missed it,[2] as it is so plain. This is the case in several other plays that I have noticed. Each one will have some chartered, copyrighted, word or phrase several times over in it, while it never occurs in any other play. I will name these to you, *seriatim*, some day. At present, in the play I have been recently most closely reading, *King Henry Fifth*, the word is *"Memorable."* This word occurs *four times* in this play,[3] and **never again throughout the whole works of the Poet.** . . .

In that "memorable" passage in *Henry V* (Act II, Sc. iii), where the Hostess so graphically, yet touchingly, describes the last moments of poor, old, discarded "Sir John," she says, you remember, " 'A made a finer end, and went away, an it had been any christom child.'"[4] Here Capell, I believe, first read "made a *fine* end," for "finer," thinking the *comparative* wrong, because there was nothing to compare it with. W. S. Walker advocates the same reading, which is adopted by Dyce II & III, by Hudson's "Sch. Shakespeare," and by other editors. Here, in the face of so many learned men, it behoves one, especially a little humble fellow like me, to be "awfully" careful of disputing their judgment. But it has always struck me that *finer* was the correct reading, and a much *finer* one too than simply *fine*, in the garrulous old hostess' mouth. She *started out* to say—" 'A made a *finer end than any christom child.*" But I need not recal to your recollection her propensity to *branch off* in her talk. Witness her celebrated description[5] of Sir John's proposal of marriage to her, in her Dolphin chamber, by the parcel-gilt goblet, on her round table, by the sea-coal fire, while she was washing his wound; and Goodwife Keech coming in at the time, coming in to borrow a mess of vinegar, saying she had a good dish of prawns, whereby Falstaff did *desire to eat some* (the old glutton), *whereby* she told him they were ill for a green wound, *whereby* he told her to be no more so familiarity with such poor people, *whereby* he did kiss her, and bade her *lend him thirty shillings,* &c. &c. And that other scarcely less amusing & characteristic scene,[6] where she has the old selfish, cowardly, yet beloved, *loafer* arrested, before the Chief Justice. This characteristic of her talk—this running off at a tangent— is just what she exhibits in the speech I allude to. When she had started out to say—" 'A made a finer end than any christom child," she bethinks herself to add "and went away"; and this latter clause requiring a different construction of the sentence to end it, viz., "an it had been" instead of "than"; in her slip-shod way she mixed the two together, and said, " 'A made a *finer* end, and went away, an it had been any christom child." Now this seems so natural & lifelike to *her*, I cannot but believe it was exactly what she did say. And moreover, "a *finer* end" is to my mind much more forcible and pathetic than merely "a *fine* end."—By the by, did you ever attend a Catholic christening or baptism? The priest rubs some "chrism," or *holy oil* on the child; then puts a white cloth on its head; and from that time the child is called a *chrisom* child, (corrupted by Hostess to *"christom"*). This white cloth the child has to wear seven days; and should it die within one month of the time of its baptism, or being made a chrisom child, it is buried with this white cloth for its shroud.—"So much for dat.". . .

Where Lord[b] High Constable, speaking to the Dauphin of Prince Henry, now King Henry V, says:—

> "And you shall find, his vanities forespent
>   [i.e. heretofore enacted]
> Were but the outside of the Roman Brutus,
> Covering discretion with a coat of folly,"[7] &c.

The allusion is to Lucius Junius Brutus, whose father & brother were murdered by Tarquinius Superbus, and who, to save his own life, and obtain revenge, **feigned idiocy**. When Lucretia was killed, after being debauched by Sextus Tarquinius, Lucius Junius Brutus no longer concealed his purpose of vengeance under this disguise of insanity and imbecility, but threw it off, & roused the citizens so that the Tarquins were expelled. The comparison[c] between him and the new King, throwing off all the errors & companions of his past riotous life, is very *à propos*. I have often thought, tho' I never saw it noticed,[8] that *Hamlet* may have had Lucius Junius Brutus in his mind, when he determined to "put an antic disposition on," the better to conceal his purposes of vengeance on his Uncle; & to give him time to lay his plans & measures accordingly. . . .

There is a word in *Henry V*[d] that has long been lost in Old England, but which survives in full vigour in New England. Did you ever hear of "emptins"? The correct word is *emptyings*, and is the Yankee housekeeper's name for *Yeast*. When making bread, they scrape the bread bowl, where the dough was made, and save every scrap of it carefully, rolling it up into a ball, & keeping it until it becomes *sour*. This is called "emptins," i.e. lees, dregs, refuse, and when it is *sour* and *old* and *stale*, they crumble it up, & mix it with the new fresh flour, for another batch of bread, and this sour refuse of the *old* baking of dough is the "emptins" that makes the *new* batch of dough "rise"—the *yeast* of the new bread. In Henry V: III, v, 6, the Dauphin, speaking in scorn and contempt of the English, says,—

> "O dieu vivant! Shall a few sprays of us,
> The *emptying* of our fathers' luxury," &c.

i.e. the refuse, dregs, lees, of the *lust* of *our* fathers, do so and so? This is the very Yankee term, in its exact modern Yankee meaning, ain't it?—. . .

Last night I tried to *disband* my "Sh. Reading Club"; but it was *impossible*. They simply would not be disbanded. The best I could do was to get an *indefinite furlough.* And so they elected another gentleman *Vice President,* to hold the Club together, until such time as I feel willing to resume my work. I prophesy it will die a natural death, if I do not attend. They will meet a few times, and read Shakespeare as well as they can; but "under charge of bragging be it spoken," they will *miss me,* my explanations, talk, & Selections, so much, they will get tired. However, as Nym says, "things must be as they are." I have done them good, honest, faithful service for *a year* and I feel entitled now to a rest, or rather a freedom from responsibility. We finished *Henry Vth,* making 13 plays read, very carefully in the 12 months. The Class have acquired an interest in the Poet they never anticipated; one that will stick to them. They can now better read & understand Sh. than before; & can pursue the study, with help of some good annotated editions, at home. . . .

[1] I took the liberty of writing to him: C's correspondence with Rolfe is not known to survive, except for one letter in Folger MS. W.a. 301. Letters in the Folger (MS. C.a. 10) written by C to C. M. Ingleby in the early 1880s indicate that C sent Rolfe textual interpretations of the kind he had sent to Hudson in the 1870s, but that R treated him shabbily, appropriating his work without acknowledgment; C spoke of R then as "a very selfish, overbearing, *school-masterly* nervous man."

[2] It seems strange commentators shd. have missed it: The interpretation was exactly anticipated by Howard Staunton in his 1858–60 Shakespeare edition. It is not noted in the Variorum of 1913 nor in most modern edns., though the Arden and Pelican and Bevington recognize horsemanship in 1.2.35.

[3] This word occurs *four times* in this play: 2.4.53, 2.4.88, 4.7.104, 5.1.72.

[4] "'A made a finer end . . . christom child": *H5* 2.3.10–12.

[5] her celebrated description: *2H4* 2.1.85–103.

[6] that other scarcely less amusing & characteristic scene: *2H4* 2.1.23–53; the two scenes are really one.

[7] his vanities forespent . . . coat of folly": *H5* 2.4.36–38.

[8] I never saw it noticed: It seems not to have been, before Sir Israel Gollancz's *The Sources of Hamlet* (1926).

[a] or owe] ↑or owe↓ MS.
[b] Where Lord] where Lord MS.
[c] comparison] ~~allusion~~ ↑comparison↓ MS.
[d] *Henry V*] this play MS.

242:   25 April 1878

. . . I enclose you, to read, another very characteristic letter from old Mr. Brae. He is fearfully *down* on Dr Ingleby, Mr. Furnivall, and the "New Shakspere Society." What a crabbed old fellow he has become! And how terribly *touchy* lest anyone appropriate any of his conjectural emendations, without due credit to him. I fancy Dr Ingleby has been too much guilty of this offence to Mr. Brae. That has been apparent to me ever since Ingleby's p.p. tract on "The Soule arayed"; and I think I spoke of it to you at the time. The only *good thing* in that tract was the discovery of Mr. Brae. He is very savage with all the English literary publications; and I am sorry for it; as it debars us from getting any more of his always judicious, & sound, & generally admissible, emendations. I fancy he is a disappointed, old, crusty John Bull,[1] who has had his hair rubbed the wrong way, and refuses to be comforted by any charmer, "charm he never so wisely."[2] I always, however, respected and liked him; he uniformly has treated my crude conjectures and letters with more respect than they deserved; and I have gained much information from him anent Shakespearian matters. . . .

The text[a] of the Poet is an *everlasting study.*—There were 2 or 3 of the Notes I sent you that (I think) are original and right; . . .—"he breeds no bate with telling of discreet stories."[3] This is so *easy,* one wonders that no one before saw it, and yet I don't believe anyone ever did. The point that they missed was, that Poins 'bred no bate by *telling* discreet stories,' instead of, he 'bred no bate by telling *discreet* stories'; i.e. he kept on the right side of the Prince by always keeping a *discreet* tongue in his head. Falstaff meant to say that he was a trimming, cold-blooded, *toady.* I think it is in Mr. Maurice Morgann's book on Falstaff (but I am not sure) that it is stated that there is a considerable spice of *malice* in Poins' composition, arising perhaps from his jealousy of the Prince being "so engraffed to Falstaff"; and this accounts for his being so anxious to plan & execute the Gadshill robbery, to get Falstaff to show his white feather & cowardice, and make him tell such "incomprehensible lies," & so try to discredit him with Prince Henry. But he failed, thank God. Tho' Poins was a fairly respectable fellow, and Falstaff a cowardly, sensuous, lying, selfish, old Sinner; *who does not like the fat old rogue better than the rascally Poins?* . . .

You ask me why I gave up my Sh. class. Partly, because I was tired, & wanted a rest; & partly because (*entre nous*) one or two of the ladies were not exactly *delighted* at my engagement to Miss Fillmore, and consequently not quite agreeable to her to meet. We may probably resuscitate it "in the sweet by & by," with some little changes. It had lasted just a year, and had been, in every respect, what is vulgarly termed (tho' I hate the phrase—"a vile phrase") *a success.* They, (the remaining 18 members, I mean), were very loath to give up, and will try & hold together under a Vice President— still retaining me as President. But I fear it will be very short-lived now. Strange to say, they have selected for their next reading the play of *King Lear,* one of the *very hardest* of all the Poet's dramas; packed full, as you know, of the toughest cruxes in Shakespeare. I avoided it on that account, until the class had become more familiar with the Poet's idiomatic style, obsolete phrases, words, and grammar, &c. I fear they will find "a heavy miss" of me, i.e. if they attempt to do anything in the way of explaining & paraphrasing hard places.—Then I managed to hold them well under rein; now they will *all* be explainers—with each his or her opinion; some will get offended, and the "Club" will shortly expire a good, fair, natural death. But the good they have acquired, the impetus to the study of our great poet, and the interest in his glorious works, will live, I believe, in the minds of the class for a long time.

Respecting my marriage, I thought I had told you that we contemplate the happy event to take place in *June* sometime. I spend all my leisure evenings, when at home, in the Society of my beloved fiancée, and I need not reiterate to you how happy we are in each other's company. I see daily new beauties of character & disposition; no matter how blue or depressed I am feeling over the dullness of trade & the hard times, I always find my melancholy vanishes in the sunlight of her kindness. Her qualities are of the sterling not the showy order; her *goodness*, I can give it no better name, increases on acquaintance; like Antony's bounty, there is no Winter in't: "An *Autumn*[b] 'tis, that grows the more by *reaping*." We never *tire* of each other; on the contrary, parting is always a regret: and that I take to be a capital sign. But I must keep off this topic, or I shall spin out an unending letter.—Believe me, my dear fellow, I do truly congratulate you, and your beloved wife, on the happy event of the birth of a desired daughter. May God bless you all! Amen.— . . .

[1] I fancy he is a disappointed, old, crusty John Bull: Brae had been that way for many years. His attack on Collier in *Literary Cookery* (1855) was so intemperate that J. Russell Smith, the publisher, suppressed the pamphlet, and Lord Campbell ruled that "Mr. Collier needed no justification from such a brochure."
[2] "charm he never so wisely": Psalms 58:5.
[3] "he breeds no bate with telling of discreet stories": 2H4 2.4.249–50.

[a] The text] the text MS.
[b] "An *Autumn*] An *Autumn* MS.

244: 3 May 1878

. . . I was sorry enough to hear of our dear friend Mr. Furness' troubles: you need have no fears that I will ever abuse your confidence in telling them to me. Isn't it too bad that, in a *year*, not enough copies of the *Hamlet* should have been sold to pay expenses! I did hope that at $4. a vol. the venture might financially have not been a loss. But so heavy a dead loss as $3.000! It is almost sufficient to deter him from going on with any more plays. He was kind enough to send me a presentation copy; but I *bought* one too, and paid my bookseller here $8. for it. It ought to have been more thoroughly & extensively advertised; also more reviewed in the great literary Reviews & papers. Your excellent review would have done good; but it never appeared. And only think of the *N. A. Rev.* trying to limit Mr. Hudson to a column or so! And I can never forgive the *Athenæum* & the *Academy* for their meagre notices. Indeed I believe the latter had no notice whatever!

I thought, at first, I might perhaps do something to help it, by writing a notice or brief review of it: but I did not suppose any paper or review

would publish anything from one so "unknown to literary fame" as I am.—
I presume, after this, that all the sales will be **profit** to Mr. Furness, having
settled for the *cost* of the production. It is a lucky thing for the Shakespearian world, & literature generally, that he is so well off. Few men would
have sacrificed so much *time, labour, genius, & taste,* in addition to so much
hard cash, purely for the sake of the honour, and of doing an everlasting
benefit to the readers and lovers of our Great Bard. But then *au contraire,*
Mr. *H. H. Furness* has made his name *immortal* as the Poet's itself is. Every
play he accomplishes is perfect in itself. No Library, no student, no reader,
of Shakespeare, can in future afford to do without his noble editions. God
grant him health, strength, courage, & long life, to persevere! . . .
P.S. I don't quite agree with you about the study of Shakespeare in Colleges. As a text book merely of Elizabethan literature, I think Sh. should *not*
be used. But all must admit that it is important that the Poet be studied by
the young people of both sexes, as a *polite accomplishment*. And if this study
is to be *taught,* some people must be qualified to teach it; and how are
Colleges, or High Schools, to know *who* are competent & qualified to teach
this study, unless by some such examination as that indicated by the examination paper on *As You Like It*[a] I sent you. Now don't you think it would
be a pleasing as well as profitable exercise for you, & me, or anyone who
loves the poet, to take these questions (so well prepared to draw out the
most information in the least room), and, using every help in our means, to
write out full, copious replies to these several questions? To do this *well*
would take some time, & study, & research among the commentators, &c.;
But after doing it thoroughly, one would have a better knowledge of the
play than we had before.— . . .

[a] examination paper on *As You Like It*] examination paper MS.

246:   14 May 1878

. . . Respecting correcting the dates, quotations, &c. of Prof. Hart's MS.
Life of Sh.[1] (I mean the Proofs)—I can only say, that I have, and will do all I
can spare the time for. I have gone over the whole of it once, very carefully,
& corrected many scores of typographical errors—punctuation, &c, putting
in, & crossing out, where I *dared* to do so. Now, to please you, I am going
over it all again, to correct dates, &c. It is considerable of a job, hunting up
every date; tho' I find them generally *correct*; still, should I *miss* any, *that*
might be the *very one* that was *wrong*. In quoting, I observe that he sometimes quotes in modern spelling, & sometimes in the old spelling, & very
often *half and half*; & this last is the greatest *bore*. I have in such cases
corrected it to *all* one way, or *all* another; where he pretends to give the

original spelling, I have had to alter scores & scores of words, and collate the originals. I will try & get it done this week, & return it to you by express. You *must* then go over it again yourself; as I do not want to be considered responsible for errors; tho' I have done what I could spare the time for to avoid *any* errors. I have mostly made the corrections with a hard pencil; I presume that will do for the printer, as I have made them as *plain* as possible: but I am not a professed "proofreader," & never studied the hieroglyphics of the business. . . .

You must have been *delighted* to receive from Prof. Leo the handsome & valuable Bronze statuette of the Stratford Bust & Entablature. It was kind & thoughtful in him; & your kindness to him in loaning him your "North" *deserved* it, as a recognition. Still, you know, it is not everyone who would have been so thoughtful. I shall think more of the German Shakespearian for this mark of his gentlemanly generosity to my friend; and you may well be proud of the ornament. Where do you intend to place it? You have so many beautiful, & valuable, and characteristic, Sh. ornaments in your library, I fear they will attract you from your books & studies. . . .

Thanks for the quotation from *The Pilgrim*,[2] anent the old use of "for." It is a very uncommon usage, & might lead one astray if not carefully watched. Shakespeare uses it in 4 or 5 places; the most noted one I now remember is in *Two Gent. of Ver.* "here they shall not lie *for* catching cold";[3] where the meaning is "for fear of," just similar to "face patch'd over *for* discovery." In addition to the references you give, Prof. Marsh,[4] I recollect, has a notice of the idiom in his "Lectures," but exactly where I forget. In 2 *Henry VI*, also, there is this usage very plainly: "Now will I dam up this thy yawning mouth *for* swallowing the treasure of the realm,"[5] i.e. to *prevent* thee.—

In Marsh's **valuable**[6] book, too, you will find an excellent history of Sh.'s use of *his* for the *its* that only was coming into vogue, and the possessive *it*—"lifted up *it* head,"[7] &c. &c. Marsh places 1600 as the date (about) of the change of *his* to *its*. It does not occur at all in the *Bible*,—I mean *its* does not.—In *Leviticus* XXV, 5: "That which groweth of *its* own accord" is the only place, and *that is a modern alteration*, as in the original King James Bible (*our* Bible) of 1611, it is printed "of *it* own accord"—the change to "its" is made by the printers.

Marsh also speaks of, and dilates upon, that idiom of Shakespeare, that I call the *subjective genitive*, very well. That is a usage that requires to be carefully watched, or one may be led astray. E. g. in *Lear*, where Cordelia, hanging over her father, says (as usually printed):—

"Restoration, hang thy medicine on my lips."[8] Here, *thy medicine* is the *subjective genitive*; and the comma after "restoration" should be deleted; as the passage means 'Let restoration hang on my lips *the medicine to cure thee*';[a] "*thy* medicine" is not restoration's medicine, but Lear's, or rather

Cordelia's; she wished *her lips* to be her *father's medicine*; quasi dicat, 'May the kisses which I now give thee *restore* to thee thy former health and soundness.' . . .

I told you that I had sent 3 or 4 little notes, *more meo*, to the "Lit: World"; they were not of any importance; little matters such as I send to you, here & there. I have heard nothing from them; & do not know whether they will be accepted or not. I do think, however, that you, and I, and Rolfe, & others, could, without much effort, manage to supply a couple, or *two couple*, of columns, monthly, with Shak. gossip, readings, explanations, notices of new books, &c. Don't you think so? With all the irregularity of the *Bibliopolist*, yet *I miss it* much; & I cannot doubt that other Shakespearians, over the country, miss it as much as, or more than, I do. . . .

Since I began this letter, I have received two very pleasant and agreeable letters from England, which I enclose you to read, as I am sure they will interest you. One is from old Mr. Collier, who, at 90 years old, says he is about undertaking a new edition of his "Annals of the Stage," to be as complete as he can make it, & which will probably occupy *600 pages each* of *two Qto vols*, the size of his "Shakespeare." Is not the old gentleman's *pluck* wonderful? He writes a very kind letter, and assures me he is doing *all he can* to get me a copy of *The Tempest*, the only play that is wanting to complete my set. I have faith to believe *it will come*. He has good luck in *finding* things; and I have urged him, all I know how, not to fail me, if possible. Do you think that at 90 years of age either you or I will be able to undertake to edit—(*re-write*, for it amounts to that)—a laborious work of 1.200 quarto pages; or even to write as plain and good a letter as he here does? Methinks it very doubtful. God spare him to accomplish it, is my sincere prayer for him. Probably it is better for him *to be employed* on his lifelong work. Were he to *stop* writing, and working, and proof-reading, &c., he would probably *die*!—The other is from our old friend, Mr. Timmins. I had not heard from him for a long time before. You remember I told you I only had a very poor, dilapidated copy of *Rowe*, 1709; & *that* I have since sold. It must be 2 years since I asked Timmins to look out for another, & better, copy for me; and now, at last, *he has found one*,[9]—"a good respectable copy," for 15/- —dirt cheap, truly. I lost no time asking him to save it for me. He says he will probably, ere long, be making up a package for either you, or Mr. Furness, & he can then enclose the "Rowe," for me. I think that a good plan; then I can reimburse you, or Mr. F., for the expenses of freight to Phila., & you can forward it, when it comes, to me here, by express.—I am glad enough to get it; & it is kind of Timmins to remember me so long, & to secure so good a copy for a mere song. I now have *all* the modern editions, except *Rowe II*;[10] & that I hardly hope ever to see. No; I want a *Hanmer*, 1744, 6 vols. 4to, 1st edition. I sold my copy, as it was not an extra good one, & to rebind it would have cost too much. So I will look out for another—a well bound copy, to replace it. I have a splendid copy of Hanmer's *2d edn.*, 1771,[11] 6 vols. *very large quarto,*—large paper, I think, tho' I am not sure. It is marked "Large paper copy" on fly leaf, and is very, *very much larger*, every way, than the 1st edition. It is a lovely copy, in *full, polished*, light calf; contents lettered; and is marked $60.—I paid $45. for it, a big price; but *it is a fine set.*—Since I wrote Timmins, I have got a "Warburton," & a "J. & S.," 1773, both *excellent* copies; only the "Warburton" has *no* portrait. I have had it very handsomely bound, in Hf. dark mor., red polished edges,[b] and contents lettered. . . .

"This bonny[c] priser."[12] "Bonny" was changed to "bony" by Warburton, & this is now the text of nearly every edition; but I prefer the old word. The term "bonny" is still even in our day, applied to such characters as "prisers," or prizefighters, meaning *"favourite."* It is, & was, a regular "P. R"[13] term; a "bonnie" or "bonny" boy, being the common designation of some "pet of the fancy"—or Morrissey bruiser, & I believe it is the very epithet the poet used, in the P. Ring slang of his day.—

"*Ducdame.*"[14] The farfetched explanations given to this word of Jaques' are "wonderful to see."—Amiens, at the cynic's "desire," had just sang a song, of which the burden was "come hither." Then Jaques burlesques and parodies it, and sings *his* song, making his burden "ducdame"; his object is to *mystify* his hearers, which he does by transposing the regular Latin version of "come hither," viz *huc ad me,* into "ducdame," making one word of it, and pronouncing it *duc-dā'-me:* and he follows up this object by further calling it "a *Greek* invocation——to call *fools* into a circle." These last words are simply a sly hit at his friends all *gathering around him,* wanting to know what this "ducdame" invocation means. That is all there is of *duc da me.* . . .

[1] Prof. Hart's MS. Life of Sh.: His biography included in the Avon Edn. 1879; H died in 1877.
[2] the quotation from *The Pilgrim*: Beaumont and Fletcher, *The Pilgrim* 3.4.
[3] *for* catching cold": *TGV* 1.2.133.
[4] Prof. Marsh: George P. Marsh, *Lectures on the English Language* (1860).
[5] *for* swallowing the treasure of the realm": *2H6* 4.1.74.
[6] **valuable**: The book was highly respected—ten edns. by 1890.
[7] "lifted up *it* head": *Ham.* 1.2.216.
[8] "Restoration, hang thy medicine on my lips": *Lr.* 4.7.25–26.
[9] *he has found one*: This copy is now in the University of Wisconsin Library.
[10] *Rowe II*: I.e., Rowe III, 1714; see note 1 to letter 101.
[11] Hanmer's *2d edn.*, 1771: The 1771 edn. is now recognized as the third edn. of Hanmer's text.
[12] "This bonny priser": *AYL* 2.3.8 (slightly misquoted).
[13] "P.R": Prize ring.
[14] "*Ducdame*": *AYL* 2.5.54; *huc ad me* was first proposed by an anonymous correspondent in Steevens's edn. 1778. Brae advocated it in *Collier, Coleridge, and Shakespeare* (1860).

[a] *cure thee';*] *cure thee;* MS.
[b] edges] egdges MS.
[c] "This bonny] "this bonny MS.

247:   18 May 1878

. . . My dear fellow, you give me the *"blues"* when you say it is your conviction "that the days of our pleasant correspondence are numbered."! *Why* should they be? It is *my* "conviction," *au contraire*, that the *only thing* that can, or will, number them, is the shuffling off the mortal coil, by one or the other of us, most likely first by me.—"Death, as the Psalmist saith, is certain to all; all shall die"; but until *Atropos* does come, to shear our thread in twain, why should we not take life as comfortably as old Justice Shallow?—"How a good yoke of bullocks at Stamford fair?"[a] "How a score of ewes now?"—**"Thereafter as may be**."—As for my getting married, I can conceive, really, of no good reason why *that* should intercept our pleasant, sociable talks by letters. They *may*, for a time, be fewer and further between than now; but that will pass away; & the old source of gratification (to me, at least) will naturally reassert its claim. Never fear for *my* share of the intercourse. *You* are "a married man," yet that, so far as I can see, does not prevent, in the least, your enjoyment or exercise of friendly, chit-chat, correspondence, does it?

I received another pleasant note from Rolfe, which I answered right away; and urged him *to continue* sending notes, readings, conjectures, reviews, gossip, & "what not" of "Shakespeariana," to the Boston "Literary World," which seems to me to be the only substitute likely to fill the place of the defunct *Bibliopolist*. . . . One thing a good clever editor *ought to do*, is, to give his contributors some compensation for their articles; not much, only small, as circumstances might dictate; but, as a *matter of business*, it would pay him to do this. A man is entitled to *pay* for his time, research, & brains, as much as for anything else he disposes of to another. And this would give a deeper interest in the writers; it would *bind them* to his interests & his paper; & they would naturally seek to increase its circulation. In England, I have been informed, all **accepted** articles are paid for as a matter of course; and this it is that makes their "Reviews" and "Journals" so stable, & sound, & long lived. . . .

In my reading & studies, I always had the habit of scratching down notes in pencil on the margins; and my Shakespeares, and Commentaries, &c. are literally written over with these notes and memoranda. You would be astonished what a *real comfort* they are to *me*, when I come to read the places a second or third time. I save lots of time, by the mere *references* alone; and often I find I had forgotten some valuable bit of information, or conjectural reading, or elucidation; and I get to look at, and criticize, my own notes, as I would those of any other person. I began *wrong*, in writing them *in pencil only*, and in *the margins only* of my books. I *ought* to have kept a "Collectanea," & indexed it carefully; then it would have been greatly more useful. *Now* I often do copy into my "Collectanea" more important criticisms & notes; and that is how I come to frequently use these scraps; in my haste I jot down on a scrap a note to be elaborated subsequently; and sometimes I have *hundreds* of these, on one play, written in the lonely hours of the night, when you & everybody else are in the arms of Morpheus. . . . Like Timon's wealth in the woods, what I send you are only "some poor fragments, some slender *orts* of his remainder." They cannot hurt you, more than to take up a little of your time to read them; they do *me* a pleasure to send them to you; and I only regret I have, truly, not the *time* to copy & send you *more*, out of the many hundreds that accumulate on my hands; the result of reading, collation, thought, & study. . . .

Shakespeare's use of "though."

In addition to the examples of the Poet's use of "though" in the sense of "being as it is," "seeing that, or inasmuch as, it is," or often (in one word) "because," which I adduced in the "Excursus" I sent you on the word, I have found the following which are important as further proving my construction: *Othello* III, iii, "*though* I perchance am vicious in my guess";[1] Iago slyly insinuates to Othello not to base any final judgment on what he says of Desdemona's infidelity, *because* [forsooth] he *may* be vicious in his guess." (He certainly was "vicious," guess or no guess.)—Again, *L. L. L.* II, i. 224: "My lips are no common, *though* several they be"; where "though" means exactly *because*. But you must read the notes on this passage, explanatory of the peculiar & specific meanings of the terms "common" & "several"; & Cf. what Boyet asks afterwards, "Belonging to whom?"—(It is all **very interesting**.)—

Also in *A. Y. L.* V, ii, "by my life, I do; which I tender dearly, *though* I say I am a magician,"[2] i.e. **because**, as I say, I am a "magician," [a penal profession; a magician could be *put to death*, summarily,] therefore it stands me in hand to tender dearly my life, or to be especially careful what I do. . . .

"Full of wise saws and modern instances."[3]—I do not think that here the word "modern" is used in its Shakespearian sense of *trite, common, ordinary*; but that it has its *present* meaning. The Justice is "full of *old* lawmaxims and *recent decisions*": the antithesis of the passage requires this meaning. The "*modern* instances" are those that had come under the old 'Squire's' *own observation*; and are apposed to the "wise saws" which he bored his court with repeating, out of the "books."—J. C. . . .

---

[1] "*though* I perchance am vicious in my guess": *Oth.* 3.3.145.
[2] *though* I say I am a magician": *AYL* 5.2.71. Another interpretation is possible: "though I endanger my life by saying openly that I practice magic" (Riverside).
[3] "Full of wise saws and modern instances": *AYL* 2.7.156.

[a] fair?"] fair? MS.

248:   24 May 1878

. . . What little leisure I have had lately, I have been reading very critically, & writing notes on, *A. Y. L.*—I should like much to send you some more of these; but I cannot. I simply have not time to copy them. I find I am hurting my eyes, by late reading by gas light. I have worked[a] hard lately, with one thing & another: but I must *stop* now: my eyes pain me terribly every morning, after writing & reading late at night.

I have just rec*d* a very long, *scholarly*, letter from Snider, dated "Rome, May 9*th*." I will not trouble you with it, as it is almost all devoted to Art, Sculpture, Shakespeare, Homer, Ruins, picture galleries, *Form*, Structure, &c. He is a queer fellow. He says he has not heard a word about his book, its success, or want of it, &c. He flatters me up a great deal, and insinuates that I should "publish something" about his "System" &c. He calls me the "godfather" of his Work, a relation I am not so almightily thankful for, *entre nous*. In fact, I have read but very little of it, in the book form. I did read the essays, as they came out, pretty carefully, & wrote him long letters about them. But I fear it would take an Act of Parliament to get me to go over the Book, & write it up, as he would like. He seems to be studying history, ancient, mediæval or papal, & modern, Rome; *reposing*, & having a very fair good time, I should say. . . .

[a]I have worked] I ↑have↓ worked MS.

249:   3 June 1878

. . . I want to tell you particularly about some of the plays, that are just being pub*d* in New York, by Francis Hart & Co, for William Winter. I have received *five* of these plays, viz. *Rich. III, Hamlet, Rich. II, Richelieu,* & *King Lear.* They are published in square 12mo (I think), gray paper covers, running from 75 pages to 135 pages each; and printed only on *one side* of the paper. They are well printed on good paper; and are really very beautifully gotten up. They are called "Edwin Booth's Prompt Books; edited by William Winter." The first was issued at Christmas last; two in February, & two in March. They only cost 50¢ each. They are by far the *best* "Acting Editions" I ever saw. The text is close to the Standard. The "Rich. III," e.g., is Shakespeare, & not Colley Cibber. Of course, they are abbreviated for the Stage, but nothing is *added* except what is Shakespeare's. The "stage business" is very good; & it is a great aid sometimes to the understanding of the text. The *Hamlet,* e.g. has 3 pages of preface, 123 pages of text, & 10 pages of "Appendix," on "The Character of Hamlet"; "Facts about Hamlet"; "The Keynote of Hamlet"; "time, age, & persons of Hamlet," &c. &c. These plays are set forth precisely as Edwin Booth presents them on the Stage; and so far as I have yet examined them, I am well pleased with them. . . .

Again let me thank you for giving that MS. of mine[1] to the "Epitome." You cannot imagine how surprised I was to see it in print. It was real kind of you, considering that you disagreed with me in the matter of the very high praise I gave the Doctor. I can see, now, that perhaps it is *too great*. Still I cannot say I regret it. I fancy it will gratify our genial & kind friend to see it: and truly his books are all capital, scholarly, & original criticisms. . . .

[1] that MS. of mine: C's review of Ingleby's *Shakespeare: The Man and the Book*, written about a year earlier for the *Bibliopolist*, when there was still hope it might be resuscitated (see letter 206). The very positive review occupies 3½ columns in the June 1878 issue of the *Epitome*; oddly enough, C had been extremely harsh with one chapter of the book in a letter to N—see letter 153.

250: 19 June 1878

. . . Many thanks for the copies of the June "Epitome." I am ever so glad that you have again assumed the role of Editor.[1] I only regret it was not done sooner, as I fear that anything I have to contribute now must go to the "Literary World." I told you the Editor wrote me, offering to pay me for my articles, if I would agree to furnish him some monthly. And do you know, I received, in a very polite note, the Publisher's *check* on a Boston Bank for more than the little items were worth, in the June number. I would not like to do anything dishonourable; and I shall feel bound to give them all that their space allows, before giving any matter elsewhere. I have already sent them, for the July number, three Notes, something like those in the June no., on readings & interpretations; and, before you wrote me, I had sent them a quite long "Review" of Allan Park Paton's *Macbeth*; though I am not sure whether *it* will be in the July, or August, number. I am preparing (as I can get time) a notice of old Mr. Collier's new Qto Shakespeare, including criticisms on *two* readings, *one* of the "Corr. Fo. 1632," & *one* of Mr. Collier's own. I shall not permit a word to escape me derogatory to the dear old gentleman, but on the contrary; still I will have to combat a reading or two, by way only of example, that not only he adopts & sticks to, but abuses Mr Singer for adopting, without credit, when they *both* are undeniably— unquestionably *wrong*; & what is more, the slashing writer (W. N. Lettsom?) in the Edin: Rev:[2] (1853), while adhering to the old text, palpably misinterprets. I believe I can make a *useful* (& maybe at same time a readable) little article on this subject. I have plenty of Notes & matter in my head; and I would be pleased to send you some too—*provided* it would not be dishonourable. They (I mean the Edd. of the Lit World) seem to have given me what you lawyers call a retainer for my little services. Now I have stated the case to you; do you think I may, without censure, after sending them *all* they have space for (and which they *pay* me for) send any *other* articles to the "Epitome"?

I fear, my dear Norris, I am writing very egotistically. But you must not think so. I don't feel so. I was always glad, indeed, to help you out, (as you so modestly termed it,) in the old Bibliopolist, and so I shall be again, if I can in honour. However, as neither paper can have but about 3 columns, or a page, each month, for "Shakespeariana," there is no fear that you will not be able yourself to occupy your space; and then, too, Mr. Leighton & others will come in for a share. So you very probably will not want anything from your humble Servant. One thing struck me at once; Won't you publish right away your excellent Review[3] of Mr. Furness' "New Var: Hamlet"? It has never yet appeared. It is due to Mr. Furness, & it is exceedingly well done, & would, no doubt, please him, & do good. You ought to have had *that* in the July No., but "better late than never." Have it, sure, in the August No., and it will be *all* you need for August. By the by, I would suggest, if you have not already thought of it, that in printing Leighton's *Macbeth* article, you should *reprint* that portion of it that has already been printed in the *Bibliopolist*,[4] as you remember, *there* it ended so abruptly that it made nonsense of it. . . .

---

[1] you have again assumed the role of Editor: This editorship lasted only a year, through July 1879, when the *Epitome* was subsumed by *The Literary World*.

[2] Edin: Rev:: The long review appeared in *Blackwood's Edinburgh Magazine*, August, September, and October 1853; the author was not Lettsom, but James F. Ferrier. C's annotated copy of the review is in his Sh Collectanea, McMillan Sh Collection, University of Michigan Library.

[3] your excellent Review: N did not publish it in the *Epitome*; the matter is not mentioned again in the letters.

[4] Leighton's *Macbeth* article . . . in the *Bibliopolist*: "Shakespearian Gossip" April 1877; N printed it in two parts in the *Epitome*, July and August 1878. In the next year Leighton contributed five further articles on *Mac.* to the *Epitome*.

251:   26 June 1878

. . . I read with the *greatest interest* what you said about my accepting pay for the little notes in the "Literary World." For a day or two[a] I felt very badly and annoyed; as I thought, from the tone of your remarks, that I had been guilty of doing something very improper or unkind. But after coolly reviewing the circumstances, I must plead "not guilty," at least to any *intentional* crime. You know, after the *Bibliopolist* became defunct, for over a year I wrote nothing or very little, & that little I sent to the London N. & Q.—But I missed the *Bibliop.* very much; I wanted some place where I could send a note or two[a] *regularly*. There were some articles on "The choice of Sh." pubd in the *Lit. World*, & Mr Hudson sent me the Nos., & that was the first time I knew there was such a paper. I suppose that he gave the Editors my name; as I soon afterwards recd a Note from them asking me to send them contributions, and they would "compensate" me. I replied telling them that I was out of the way of "gossip," and that my notes could only be textual or critical readings & explanations &c. &c. of the Poet. I enclosed them the four notes, that appeared in the June number, as *samples* of what I liked to do; and for them, without any bargain, or a word about compensation from me, they sent me their check for a sum that I thought really liberal: and asked me to continue to send whenever I felt like it. They were very polite, & wrote like men of business. Now that was all long—or several days anyway—before I had the remotest idea that you were contemplating assuming the Editorship of a Sh. Dept. in the Epitome. I did not know of the existence of such a periodical, until you, or the Editor, sent me a copy, containing my notice of Ingleby's book. You had not intimated in any way or form that you intended doing so. Had I supposed that such was your intention, you may be very sure I should not have promised to contribute to any other journal. But it was not until after all this had transpired with the 'Lit World' that I first knew of your assuming your old place. When I recd the No. of the Epitome, that had my notice of Dr I's book, I was glad to see it, but I had no idea that you were even thinking of editing a Dept. in that paper. You speak of my writing "from a sense of gain"; that "had you known it, you would not have asked me to contribute," &c.; and apologize for printing that paper of mine in the "Epitome," "as it would have brought me in a nice little sum"! &c, all which was very painful to me to read. I never wrote a line "from a sense of gain" in my life. The only money I ever in my life received for writing anything was that check, and God knows I did not ask for it, or expect it. They sent it to me, in a polite letter; could I insult them by returning it? You know I could not *anticipate* that you were going to connect yourself with another paper, and that I could have a place[b] for my notes, as before in the old Bibliopolist.—I simply thanked them (the "Lit. World" men, I mean), and promised that I would try, when at home, to give them something readable & interesting to Sh. students, monthly. They only contemplate devoting 1½ or 2 col. each month to this dept., and I could easily furnish matter for 3 times that space, without any trouble. And I don't know any good reason why I cannot write for "N. & Q.," or the "Epitome," or any other paper I think proper. I have made no promise to write *only* for theirs. . . . The little bit of "proof" they sent me to correct for the July No. does not seem as if it would take over 1½ col.; and I have sent them (not yet set up) matter enough for 10 columns. So you see, whenever you want me to help fill any spare space in the "Epitome," I shall gladly & cheerfully be on hand. . . . What hurt me most in your letter were such expressions as taunting me for "writing from a sense of gain"; that had you known *such* were my motives you would never have asked me; that *"money* will tell, but there is something better than money," &c. Wherein have I *deserved* all that? Such thoughts are *unlike* you, my dear old fellow; and you ought to have known me better. It has always been my greatest pleasure to do what little I could to help you in your studies. Many an hour I have sat up to write out some little thing anent our dear Poet & his works or editors, that I hoped or thought would either please, or instruct you, at some time. I have done so ever since I knew you, partly from a sense of duty & *gratitude* for thousands of kindnesses to me, & partly, & much more perhaps, because I thought my letters & notes might sometimes *incite* you to deeper & closer study, to make yourself the Shakespearian Scholar & Critic that both your abilities & magnificent opportunities adapted you to be.—I did not think you would ever charge me with mercenary motives in my long & charming study of the Master Poet of the World, even tho' I *did* accept a gratuity from a stranger, for doing something he asked me to do. If that is mercenary, I shall quite likely do it again, & accept the imputation and its consequences. . . .

[a] or two] or two ~~to~~ MS.
[b] could have a place[cou[illegible] have a place MS.

254:   20 July 1878 Cresson Springs, Pennsylvania

. . . I was much obliged for the "Epitome." You open **real nicely**; & your review of Rolfe's "As Y. L. It" is *just right*—neither too much nor too little. I liked Mr. Leighton's article too. The "L. W." folks *did* hardly do me justice in the last No, only giving me abt ¾ of a Col. . . .

257:   4 August 1878

. . . I presume you have received the Aug. "Lit. World," ere this. I see they have given me quite a good bit of space, & put in my notice of Paton's *Macbeth*, and an article of textual criticism. I also recd. yesterday a very polite note from the Edd., covering their c'k for a nice little sum, really *far more* than the "contribution" was worth; but withal very acceptable these times, when *spending* money, & *not* receiving it, seems to be alone fashionable.—I am real glad you have enlisted Mr. Hudson in your corps of contributors.[1] In addition to the intrinsic merit & value of his textual criticisms, his *Name*, being a veteran in the army, makes his articles sought for, read, & adopted.

I was real sorry that circumstances were such my "answer dashed cold water" on your hopes; but you know *now* I could not help it; and perhaps it is all for the best. You will, beyond question, have not only all the matter you have space for; but infinitely better matter than poor I could have sent you under the most favourable circumstances. . . .

[1] your corps of contributors: During his twelve-month tenure as Editor, N successfully recruited a number of prominent Shakespearians, among them Fleay, Rolfe, Ingleby, Elze, Furness, and Brae.

258: 14 August 1878

. . . Since my last, I have received the "Epitome" for August; and I need not tell you how deeply I was interested in Mr. Furness' delightful and instructive article.[1] Mr. Leighton's "Macbeth" article was also very interesting to me, and he makes out a very plausible case. But Mr. Furness' is the attraction of the number. How nice it must be to *know* as much as he does; and to be able to write so easily, and with such pleasure and profit to all who are lucky enough to see & read his articles. I hope he will often favour us with an article from his well-stored repertoire.

You ask me what the Edd. "Lit World" send me for my little articles. I have been aching to tell you: and should have done so at first, had I not promised them not to mention it to anyone. They also wrote *me*, that they rarely, if ever, paid for contributions; and that must be their apology for asking me not to mention the fact of their sending me any pay. No one knows it, not even my wife, except yourself; & I know you will not breathe it. The amt. I will not mention; but leave you to guess at it, by only saying that during the 3 months it has *averaged less* than $10. a month. Now *that* is not telling, is it? Anyway, don't say anything; as it would be an unpardonable breach of faith in me. I have regretted that I was drawn into it, much more than you do: but it cannot be helped now. It would (as you may well suppose) have been infinitely more pleasant & satisfactory to *me* to have sent to you anything I had, that would help you. But, as I before explained, at the time I had not the remotest idea that you contemplated reviving your old Editorship of a "Sh: Gossip."—I was surprised at what you said of the cool way in which the Edd. "L. W." wrote you; as their correspondence with me *hitherto* has been very polite & gentlemanly. Their letters are always *breif*, but quite kind & pleasant. There is no fear that you won't always be able to fill all[a] the space at your command. With such men to draw on as Furness & Hudson, the "Gossip" *must* be a most attractive feature of "The Epitome." Should you really need any of my assistance "to fill in," let me know, and I will send you a pseudonymous or anonymous article anyway. There could be no harm in *that*.[2] . . .

---

[1] Mr. Furness' delightful and instructive article: F's sensible note is on the Fool's *non sequiturs* in *Lr.* and the misguided attempt of a German translator to make sense of one of them.

[2] There could be no harm in *that*: N did not ask C for anonymous contributions; C sent him a signed note on a crux in *AWW* for the 15 January 1879 issue and later that spring he published three signed notes on textual problems in *Lr.* in the *Epitome*. C was publishing prolifically in

The Literary World at the time; his notes and reviews appeared there regularly through mid-1880.

ᵃ fill all] fille all MS.

259:   28 August 1878

. . . I am quite anxious to see Mr. Hudson's new "notes," in the *Epitome.* Hadn't I better *subscribe* for the *Epitome*? I don't want to put *you* to the monthly inconvenience of sending me a copy. I know and appreciate your goodness, which is endless: but there is such a thing as running a free horse *too hard.* I was sorry that you countermanded your nicely bound copy of Professor Hart's book, in order to have 2 cloth bound copies, one for *me.* I intended to buy one; and if not too late, don't mind sending me one, but take the nice one that is your due. What little I did, I did it freely for *you,* not for reward. Pardon my mentioning this, but when I think of all your great kindness & generosity to me, I often fear I am terribly selfish; as I have no way to reciprocate it. I can well understand how anxious you are to get back to your books, and library comforts, at home. A "Boarding House"[1] is a poor place to study in at best.—

What a charming time you must have had with Mr. R. Grant White, and his Son! I envied you that call immensely. I was glad to learn that Mr. W. is so free from *conceit.* I have fancied from his books, that it was a considerable item in his mental composition. What is he now engaged in, besides writing? Is he *au fait* with Shakespeare matters & criticism, or has he let it drop of late years? Beyond all question his "Shakespeare" is the *best* American edition we have, always save & except Mr. Furness'. . . . This morning I received a nice copy of the new "American Edn." of the *Globe* Shakespeare, by T. Y. Crowell of New York. I don't mean I received it as a *present;* I bought it. I am quite well pleased with it; & wrote a notice, or brief review of it, which I have just sent to the "World"; but of course it will not come out until the Octo. No.—I notice that most of the few typographical errors detected in the Globe, so far, have been corrected in Crowell's edn. It seems to be very carefully printed & accurate: tho', as you say, the type being more *solid* than the Globe type detracts from its clearness. The 2 additional "Indexes" will be useful and acceptable. It is a marvel of cheapness; &, all things considered, the *best one vol. Shakespeare* in America. I have received nothing new in the book line, since I wrote you last: and except the papers & reviews &c., I have not had time to read much. But now that I am settled again,[2] I hope to re-commence my regular study of the plays, in my exhaustive routine fashion. I left off at *L. L. Lost;* & shall have to begin it again, in order to get a good start. I am looking anxiously for something from the N. S. Soc:, but nothing has come yet for 1878. Timmins sends me an occasional paper very kindly; but I have not written to, or heard from, either him, or Dr Ingleby, for a long time. I fear the Doctor's eyes are again troubling him. I have not heard a word either from Asa Lamb, or Prof. Corson, for a long time. . . .

My dear wife sends her best regards to you. If *only* business were better, & *cash* plentier, I should indeed be very happy. But every cup of joy & pleasure must have some dash of *bitters* in it, in this world.—

Good Bye, my dear Norris. With love & thanks, I am ever your friend,

Jos: Crosby.—

[1] A "Boarding House": N and his family regularly spent the hot months in Germantown, Pa.
[2] settled again: C and Agnes had been honeymooning in Cresson Springs, Pennsylvania.

INDEX

Crosby's correspondence in either direction appears under the name of the correspondent, indexed as a subentry under Crosby, Joseph. (Naturally Norris is included among Crosby's correspondents only by universal implication.) Correspondence of other persons (when not with Crosby) is entered under their names. Reprints of Shakespeare editions and other books are not distinguished unless Crosby attaches special importance to them; so the 1866 and 1873 reprints of the Globe Edition are subsumed under "Globe," and American reprints (legitimate or pirated) of English books are not normally indexed separately. Anonymous works appear under their titles. Shakespeare's characters will be found under "Shakespeare, William: Works." They are not indexed merely as speakers of lines Crosby is discussing; thus if an ·article or book dealing with Falstaff is mentioned (not discussed or quoted at length) in a letter, "Falstaff" will not appear in this Index. Applied to a person, *"quoted"* normally means that a private communication not otherwise available is quoted or paraphrased. *"Discussed" (disc.)* signifies that Crosby makes a definite value judgment, however briefly. We have reserved the term *"explicated" (expl.)* for explications of Sh. passages not involving proposed emendations, which are designated *"conjecture" (conj.).* Titles of books, periodicals, plays, and long poems, and references to passages in works by Shakespeare, appear in boldface.